Languages of Community

Languages of Community

*The Jewish Experience
in the Czech Lands*

Hillel J. Kieval

UNIVERSITY OF CALIFORNIA PRESS

Berkeley / Los Angeles / London

University of California Press
Berkeley and Los Angeles, California

University of California Press, Ltd.
London, England

Library of Congress Cataloging-in-Publication Data

Kieval, Hillel J.
    Languages of community : the Jewish experience in the Czech lands /
Hillel J. Kieval.
        p.   cm.
    Includes bibliographical references (p.) and index.
    ISBN 0-520-21410-2 (cloth : alk. paper)
        1. Jews—Czech Republic—Intellectual life—18th century.
    2. Jews—Czech Republic—Intellectual life—19th century.
    3. Jews—Identity.   4. Czech Republic—Ethnic relations.
    DS135.C95 K54 2000
    943.71′004924—dc21

                                                          99-053814

Printed in the United States of America
08 07 06 05 04 03 02 01 00
10 9 8 7 6 5 4 3 2 1

The paper used in this publication is both acid-free and totally chlorine free (TCF). It
meets the minimum requirements of ANSI/NISO Z39.48-1992 (R 1997) (*Permanence of
Paper*).

For my parents

Make your ear attentive to wisdom
And incline your heart to understanding.

Proverbs 2:2

Contents

Acknowledgments

Languages of Community is the product of a rather long journey, a project that has commanded much of my time and energy for more than a decade. This study of the Jewish experience in the Czech lands over the last two and a half centuries is built upon essays that were produced at different points in time, all of which have been significantly revised and reshaped to provide if not a unified *narrative* of Czech Jewish life and expression, at least a sustained and cumulative engagement with what I understand to be its central themes. In a project of such duration one accumulates many debts, intellectual and otherwise, which I am happy to acknowledge. I would like to begin by thanking the libraries and archives in Europe, Israel, and the United States that made available to me their valuable collections. In Prague: the National Library (Národní knihovna v Praze), the library of the National Museum (Knihovna národního muzea), the Jewish Museum (Židosvské muzeum v Praze), the Central State Archive (Státní ústřední archiv), and the State Regional Archive (Státní oblastní archiv). In Jerusalem: the Jewish National and University Library, the Central Zionist Archives, and the Central Archive for the History of the Jewish People. In the United States: the libraries of the University of Washington, Harvard University, the Jewish Theological Seminary of America, Columbia University, Brandeis University, Stanford University, and Washington University in St. Louis.

Periods of sabbatical study and travel to research collections were made possible by grants and research fellowships from the American

Council of Learned Societies (1988–89), the International Research and Exchanges Board (IREX, 1990), the ACLS/SSRC Joint Committee on Eastern Europe (1992–93), the Graduate School of the University of Washington, and the Keller Fund of the University of Washington Department of History.

Many individuals along the way have shared with me their knowledge of Central European Jewish history as well as other fields, read parts of my work, listened to my ideas, and offered sound advice (not always taken). Thanks go out to Alexandr Putík, Arno Pařík, Jiřina Šedinová, Bedřich Nosek, Jan Havránek, Jiří Kořalka, Michael K. Silber, Viktor Karády, Jonathan Frankel, Ezra Mendelsohn, Kenneth Stow, Richard I. Cohen, the late Jacob Katz z"l, Hadassah Assouline, Todd M. Endelman, Anna Foa, Sander Gilman, Steven J. Zipperstein, Aron Rodrigue, Pierre Birnbaum, Gary B. Cohen, Marsha L. Rozenblit, Stanley B. Winters, Yosef Hayim Yerushalmi, Michael Stanislawski, Franklin Ford, Israel Bartal, Zeev Gries, Shaul Stampfer, Kathryn Brown, Lois Dubin, David Biale, Daniel Chirot, Joel Migdal, Robert Stacey, Robert Wistrich, and Bernard Wasserstein.

Early versions of, or sections from, the chapters before you have appeared previously in the following sources: Chapter 1 in *Where Cultures Meet: The Story of the Jews of Czechoslovakia,* ed. Natalia Berger (Tel Aviv: Beth Hatefutsoth/Ministry of Defence, 1990), pp. 23–51; Chapter 2 in *Toward Modernity: The European Jewish Model,* ed. Jacob Katz (New Brunswick, N.J.: Transaction Books, 1987), pp. 71–105; Chapter 3 in *Assimilation and Community: The Jews in Nineteenth-Century Europe,* ed. Jonathan Frankel and Steven J. Zipperstein (Cambridge: Cambridge University Press, 1992), pp. 246–283; Chapter 4 in *Modern Judaism* 17 (1997): 1–23; Chapter 5 in *History and Memory: Essays in Honor of Yosef Hayim Yerushalmi,* ed. Elisheva Carlebach, John Efron, and David Myers (Hanover and London: University Press of New England, 1998), pp. 348–68; Chapter 6 in *Studies in Contemporary Jewry,* vol. 3, ed. Ezra Mendelsohn (New York: Oxford University Press, 1987), pp. 49–71; Chapter 7 in *Modern Judaism* 5 (1985): 141–157; Chapter 8 in *Jewish History* 10, no. 1 (Spring 1996): 75–91; Chapter 9 in *T.G. Masaryk (1850–1937): Thinker and Politician,* ed. Stanley B. Winters (London: Macmillan; New York: St. Martin's, 1990), pp. 302–27; Epilogue in *Les Cahiers du Judaisme* 1, no. 1 (Spring 1998): 4–13. I gratefully acknowledge the permission of the editors and publishers to use these materials in this new work.

All translations in this volume, unless otherwise indicated, are my own.

In closing I would like to single out a number of people for special thanks. Martin S. Jaffee has filled many roles over the past twelve years: next-door office neighbor, study partner and guide in rabbinic texts, mentor, critic, consoler, and dear friend. He has listened to more talk, read more drafts, and offered more criticism than anyone else. Thank you, Marty; *kaniti li ḥaver.* My children, Michael and Shira, who were a good deal younger when they saw my first book, have grown up with me and my preoccupations with Central Europe, Czech Jewry, and modern ritual murder trials. They have been patient and loving, ironic and supportive throughout. To my wife, Deborah, who approves of most of what I write and who understands the need for all of it: thanks, love. *Aḥaron aḥaron ḥaviv,* I dedicate this book to my dear parents, whose approaches to life—and impact on my own—are embedded in the verse from Proverbs. They will know how to read it.

The Czech Republic (Bohemia and Moravia)

Language, Community, and Experience

In a famous essay written in 1984, Milan Kundera (living at the time in exile in France) attempts to locate and define the elusive entity known as "Central Europe."[1] He attacks the subject from a number of angles, searching, in the process, not only the political map of Europe, but the record of modern Western creativity as well. One approach is to define Central Europe in opposition to what it is not: not Russia and not Germany. Kundera also entertains the notion that Central Europe epitomizes the continent as a whole, a kind of "condensed version of Europe ... in all its cultural variety: a small arch-European Europe." On the one hand, he intuitively understands Central Europe to be bound up with the historic Habsburg monarchy, the multinational empire at the heart of the continent, which managed to maintain some degree of political unity and geographic congruence from 1526 to 1918. Just as forcefully, however, Kundera insists that this "uncertain zone of small nations" is best understood as a culture or a "fate" whose boundaries exist more in the imagination than on land. It is not political frontiers that determine the scope of Central Europe but "the great common situations that reassemble peoples, regroup them in ever new ways along the imaginary and ever-changing boundaries that mark a realm inhabited by the same memories, the same problems and conflicts, the same common tradition."[2]

In what may be a final effort to arrive at some common denominator of Central European culture, Kundera appeals to the Jews, who were ubiquitous to the region in the past and ominously absent in its present.

He understands the Jews to be the one constant feature of the human landscape of Central Europe, at once its most distinctive and most integrative element. "They were," he wrote, "its intellectual cement, a condensed version of its spirit, creators of its spiritual unity." On the one hand, the family origins of so many of the artists, writers, and scientists of the early twentieth century—Freud, Kafka, Mahler, Roth, Husserl, Kiš—testifies to the quintessentially multiethnic, multilingual, and cosmopolitan quality of this piece of the human experience, as understood by Kundera. Beyond this, the Jews were the paradigmatic "small nation" to which so many Central European leaders likened their own communities, and it has been in the modern destiny of the Jews that Central Europe has seen its own fate "concentrated" and "reflected."[3]

The work before you makes no such claims. I do not wish to mystify the Jews of Central Europe or to lift their experience beyond the ordinary texture of life. To say that the Jews "epitomized" or "symbolized" an existential predicament, or that in the modern destiny of the Jews Central Europeans have come to see their own reflection, is to fail to take Jewish identity and experience on their own terms. In essence, statements of this kind rob the Jews of the reality of their particular existence as well as the individuality of their fate in Europe. I would, however, accept the observation that the Jews have constituted one of the most visible, and constant, minorities in Central Europe and even would argue—along with Kundera—that the history of the latter cannot fully be comprehended without reference to Jewish experience. *Languages of Community* focuses specifically on Jewish life in the Czech lands—the regions of Bohemia and Moravia, which today are synonomous with the Czech Republic—from the late eighteenth century to the twentieth century. My principal concerns in the pages that follow are with the changing nature of collective and individual identities, the shifting attachments to "community" and to "place," the breakdown and reconstruction of cultural and political alliances, and, above all, with the structural elements—as well as the connections across time— that make it possible to speak of a complex, yet coherent, "Jewish" experience in this part of the world.

In selecting the term *experience* to identify this book's main concern—as opposed to the *history* of the Jews, for example—I am revealing an intellectual indebtedness to a school of thought within cultural anthropology. Inspired by the social philosophy of John Dewey and Wilhelm Dilthey, anthropologists in recent decades have employed the concept of experience to underline three sets of distinctions in the study of collective behavior and consciousness: the differences between an event and its interpretation, between behavior and experience, and between individual experience and the interpretive categories placed on that experience by the cultural norms and collective memories of social groups.[4] The concept of experience emphasizes not *events* as such, but rather how reality presents itself to human consciousness and is, in turn, structured by received cultural categories and social memories. Experience, Dewey wrote, "includes what men do and suffer, what they strive for, love, believe and endure, and also how men act and are acted upon, the ways in which they do and suffer, desire and enjoy, see, believe, imagine."[5]

Those who study experience are aware of the problematic nature of the enterprise. One can never, for example, directly apprehend another individual's experience of his or her reality; one can only know the expressions of that experience (literary, artistic, ritualized, or dramatic). Moreover, the relationship between experience and its expressions has an intractable quality: cultural expressions do refer ultimately to the experiences that underlie them, but social norms and cultural expectations also structure the ways in which we experience the world. In the words of Roger D. Abrahams, "experience is, at one and the same time, illustrative of what individuals do and of the conventional patterns of culturally learned and interpreted behavior that makes them understandable to others."[6]

Finally, the notion of experience highlights my earlier concern with the problem of typicality versus uniqueness—the universality of a set of experiences versus their contingency. Experience comprises both ordinary and extraordinary occurrences, both individual emotion and socially constructed meaning. "The flowering of individual response," writes Abrahams, "continually gravitates toward typicality, so that afterward we can find words to talk about what happened." At the same time, this "gravitation" toward the universal makes us uneasy.

Because our individual experiences are so central to the ways in which we put together a sense of our own identity, to underscore the typicality is to confront one of our dearest held beliefs: that having been made individuals, we should do everything we can to hold on to our sense of uniqueness. Yet experience tells us that what happens to us is never so original, especially as we recognize ourselves as members of a generation, a network, a community.[7]

To write about experience, then, means to put the claims of the individual and the claims of the community—those of uniqueness and those of typicality—into a constant state of movement. As Abrahams would have it, "when an experience can be designated as typical, then the doings of the individual and the community become shared." And what is "shared" is not just the experiences themselves but also the sentiments arising from them: "the doings and the feelings reinforce each other." Finally, this linkage of individual and collectivity, of event and sentiment, points to a deeper connection between past and future, between collective memory and collective hope.[8]

As will become clear, I pay particular attention to the role that language has to play in this story. The choice, deployment, and even the abandonment of specific vernaculars helped to shape the collective identity of Jews in the Czech lands and also determined the ways in which they were perceived by the larger society around them. The book's title calls to mind the predicament of a Jewish community that "came of age" in a multiethnic Central Europe that possessed an ostensibly unifying high culture and language, whose doors were open to assimilating minorities, but whose hegemony was under attack from a variety of quarters. In such a situation, the very embrace of this high culture—and of the liberal political values associated with it—introduced new elements of vulnerability and instability to the social lives of Jews even as it provided what appeared to be a sure avenue of integration and mobility.

As in most parts of Central and Eastern Europe, to be identified as *Jewish* in the Czech lands has meant historically either to proclaim or be ascribed a status apart. Yet the nature and quality of this distinctiveness have varied over time. Faced with frequent challenges to cultural authority and power in their immediate environment, Jews in the Czech lands have felt the need to define over and again the nature of group identity, cultural loyalty, memory, and social cohesiveness, and periodically to relocate the points of intersection with surrounding cultures and groups. In preemancipatory times (discussed in chapter 1 ["Czech Landscape, Habsburg Crown"], which also serves as a broad overview of the subject), knowledge of Jewish "distinctiveness" derived from two "observations": that Jews deployed a private, communal language—Western Yiddish, or *Judendeutsch*—and that they lived their lives within the structures of a "foreign" religious discourse—rabbinic Judaism. These, together with subsidiary markers, such as dress, residential and occupational patterns, and accented speech, set the Jews apart not only as *different* from other inhabitants of the Czech lands but as members of a distinctive *community,* bound together by complex and exclusive social relationships and possessing and transmitting a coherent set of historical memories. With the rise of the absolutist "modernizing" state in the late eighteenth century (the focus of chapter 2 ["Caution's Progress"]), the possibilities of collective and individual action on the part of Jews were restructured in significant ways, while the traditional contours of community and individual identity lost their former coherence. Government policies initiated by Joseph II (and both extended and reduced by subsequent monarchs) clearly fell short of political enfranchisement or real social integration, but they did succeed in reshaping and redirecting preexisting understandings of Jewish distinctiveness and social cohesion. The absolutist experiments at reform helped to bring about a *partial* integration with Gentile society, on the one hand, and a closer alignment with the culture of the state, on the other. Within the Jewish communities of Bohemia and Moravia, social and cultural elites promoted a new ideology of "Europeanness" tied to a program of German linguistic acculturation and middle-class social aspirations.

During this period of gradual liberalization and Jewish adjustment—roughly 1780 to 1867—new assumptions about linguistic and political identity were ascribed to Jews living in the Czech lands, based in part on the collective Jewish responses to state initiative (i.e., their willingness to take advantage of new avenues for educational advancement and social mobility) and in part on the hardening of attitudes brought about by the emerging Czech and German ethnic struggle. Chapter 3 ("The Social Vision of Bohemian Jews") describes the predicament of secular Jewish intellectuals—graduates for the most part of German-Jewish *Normalschulen*—who in the 1830s and 1840s imagined themselves to be participating in what they presumed to be a shared project in the construction of a "Bohemian" identity, which united German speakers and Czech speakers, Jews and Gentiles. Their confrontation with anti-Jewish popular unrest in the 1840s, as well as with the unwillingness of a segment of the new Czech intelligentsia to entertain an alliance with Jews, led the bulk of upwardly mobile Bohemian Jews to "narrow" their vision of community by tying their fortunes to German liberalism—in effect crystalizing what had been a by-product of absolutist reform into both a political commitment and a cultural identity that would last well into the 1860s and beyond.

Chapter 4 ("Pursuing the Golem of Prague") traces the career of a well-known folkloristic and literary motif that purports to speak to the cultural life of Jewish Prague during the northern European Renaissance and locates its "modern" origins within elite Jewish circles in the city during the first half of the eighteenth century. The "recovery" of this tradition as an element of the modern folk identity of both Jewish and non-Jewish Bohemians dates, once again, to the 1830s and 1840s—thanks to the efforts of ethnographers and folklorists to capture a modern "Bohemian" identity. From this point forward, the sixteenth-century rabbi and communal leader Judah Löw ben Bezalel (known by the acronym *Maharal*) and the creature that he was credited—posthumously—with making entered the pantheon of Czech folk tradition as markers of local identity and historical memory. Finally, the version of the Golem legend that is most familiar to Western readers, which ascribes to the artificial being a redemptive role in saving the Jewish community of Prague from Gentile accusations of ritual murder, is in fact the most recent creation of all. It stems from a literary invention—or forgery—published by a Polish rabbi of Hasidic background, Yudel Rosenberg, in 1907, and owes its inspiration to a flurry of state-sponsored "ritual murder" trials in East Central Europe that had taken place over the preceding two decades. The Maharal would not have understood the need for such a Golem.

Chapter 5 ("On Myth, History, and National Belonging in the Nineteenth Century") explores the connections among myth, history, and national identity, especially as they relate to the growing self-confidence of the Czech national movement and the increasingly uncomfortable position of "German" Jews in nineteenth-century Bohemia and Moravia. Jewish writers in the Czech lands began to make their own contributions to a growing public contest over local history and memory following the political liberalizations of 1860–61. A minor pamphlet war, which appeared to pit one interpretation of Czech-Jewish history against another, wholly incompatible vision of the past, erupted shortly thereafter. One of the contributions to this debate, I suggest, ought to be seen as a "forgery"—not unlike earlier documentary forgeries in Czech historiography—an intervention, in fact, by a non-Jewish writer, which nevertheless influenced the developing reorientation in Czech-Jewish culture.

The mid-century retreat to an *Austrian* political, *German* cultural, and bourgeois economic identity would prove to be a highly unstable feature of the Jewish experience in the Czech lands. On the one hand, the demography of the Jewish communities changed. By the 1870s and 1880s, tens of thousands of provincial Jews, immersed in Czech language and culture, were flocking to Prague and other large cities in Bohemia and Moravia, providing the human material for yet another re-orientation in Czech-Jewish culture and politics. Moreover, the political and linguistic conflicts of the last three decades of the nineteenth century revealed just how fragile and tenuous the earlier acculturation had been. Linguistic and political choices that had been viewed—however briefly—as transforming boundaries of distinctiveness into lines of integration were now held up as yet another sign of Jewish "abnormality" and marginality. Largely urban German-speaking Jews were accused of denying the possibilities of place, local culture, and community by urbanizing Czech-speaking Gentiles (and Jews). Chapters 6 through 9, then, examine different aspects of the late-nineteenth- and early-twentieth-century Czech-Jewish relationship: the struggle over schools and language choice (chapter 6, "Education and National Conflict"); the movement among Czech-Jewish intellectuals to effect a religious reform that was inspired, to a large extent, by Czech philosophical currents (chapter 7, "Jan Hus and the Prophets"); the radicalization of political discourse in the 1890s and its obsession with the metaphor of ritual murder (chapter 8, "Death and the Nation"); and the relations between the social philosopher and nationalist politician T. G. Masaryk and the Czech-Jewish community before and after the First World War (chapter 9, "Masaryk and Czech Jewry").

I argue in chapter 8 that the rhetoric of ritual murder not only echoed widely diffused refrains of Jewish "danger"—which could be heard around the same time in other parts of Central and Eastern Europe—but also functioned as an indirect commentary on the national conflict between Czechs and Germans. In other words, a preexisting discourse on Jews as Germanizing elements in the Czech countryside led some activists (from Czech national liberals to the more radical national socialists) to take a particular interest in the growing, European-wide discussions on Jewish "ritual murder." While the national ambiguity of the Jews may have led to the suspicion that they were unreliable partners in ethnic conflict, this judgment now merged with other "information" concerning Jews and ritual killings to produce a volatile type of social knowledge, in which one set of symbolic associations tended to confirm the truth of the other.

A more hopeful side of the relationship is offered in chapter 9. Here I trace the efforts of both the Czech-Jewish movement and Prague Jewish nationalists (Zionists) to maneuver into position with the leader of the Realist wing of the Czech national movement, while I foreground Masaryk's own problematic attitudes toward Jews. Because of Masaryk's philosophical disapproval of assimilationist movements generally, and despite declamations of loyalty to the Czech cause, the Czech-Jewish movement found itself—curiously—to be out of favor at court, never able to fully escape a certain air of disrepute. Masaryk turned out to be more attuned temperamentally to both the project and the principles of cultural Zionism. After the war, the Beneš government made wide-ranging concessions to the Zionists on issues relating to Jewish nationality and cultural autonomy, while according Jews full status as Czechoslovak citizens. Czech-nationalist Jews appeared, then, to have lost the ideological battle with the Zionists; the long-term social and cultural trends, on the other hand, favored the former. All indicators pointed to unabated Jewish integration into mainstream Czech society and, had the German invasion not intervened in 1939, very likely a further, progressive erosion of the liberal German synthesis of the previous century.

I have chosen deliberately not to write about the destruction of Jewish life in the Czech lands during the Nazi occupation. I did not make this choice out of a conviction that the Shoah does not merit close study, nor that it does not—in some way—form a crucial element of the modern Jewish experience in this part of Europe. The reason is twofold. First, the destruction of Czech and Slovak Jewry during the Second World War has been the subject of a number of first-rate studies, to which the curious reader is hereby directed.[9] Second, it is the Czech-Jewish experience over the long term that has not received adequate attention from historians of culture and society, and it is to the issue of the structures of this experience, particularly from the eighteenth century through the twentieth century, that I wish to devote my energies. Just as important, Holocaust narratives have a way of introducing so much disruption to long-term patterns of experience as to blur them altogether, rendering them somehow trivial in light of the "inevitable" end of the story.

In fact, the surviving remnants of Czech Jewry discovered and resumed the thread of their collective narrative in the war's aftermath. On some levels, of course, nothing could be as it was before. Of the 88,000 Jews who lived in the so-called Protectorate of Bohemia-Moravia in October 1941, fewer than 8,000 remained in April 1945.[10] In the following years, a large part of the Czech-Jewish community would be made up of families and individuals who had migrated from Slovakia or Carpathian Rus. The political constellation of the Cold War and the rise to power of the Czechoslovak Communist Party in 1948 contributed to creating a "present" that seemed hardly recognizable to those who had known the past. Yet the Czech-Jewish past *was* recognizable in the postwar structures of experience. This is one of the points that I try to make in the epilogue, in which I seek to connect the post–Second World War complex of Czech-Jewish identities—characterized now by the shattering reality of the Holocaust, Communist rule in Czechoslovakia, and various forms of exile—to its roots in the modern Jewish experience.

The point of departure for the epilogue is an anecdote concerning the return to Prague in 1964 of the writer Max Brod, following an absence of twenty-five years, and the informal gathering of four Jewish figures that took place in the sitting room of another Czech-Jewish writer, František Langer. The purpose of the anecdote, as originally recounted to me, had been to characterize certain Jewish "types" as emblematic of fateful historical choices made by Jews in the Czech lands: the Zionist (now living in Israel), the German-speaking Jew (now enjoying a renaissance of sorts under a liberalized Communist regime), the Czech-Jewish patriot (whose lot was thrown in with the fate of the Czech people in their struggle against external oppression), and the Communist (who recognized that the last, best path to Jewish integration, mobility, and collective security lay in social revolution). The story looks fair enough on the surface; it appears to work on its own terms, but closer examination reveals the hopelessness of assigning fixed categories to individual (or even collective) experience. As I take apart and retell the story, I try not only to demonstrate the fluidity and unfixedness of ethnic, political, and cultural identities, but also to point out the deep connections that existed among, and linked, the so-called types, how the lives of the individuals in question intertwined precisely because they partook of a *shared* structure of experience. This experience comprised a rich but finite set of cultural, social, and political options— an intricate but distinctive path to modernity that stretched from Joseph II to the era of Rudolf Slánský, Eduard Goldstücker, and beyond.

CHAPTER I

Czech Landscape, Habsburg Crown

The Jews of Bohemia and Moravia to 1918

Settlement and Early History

The origins of the Jewish communities of Bohemia and Moravia lie in a distant and ultimately irretrievable past. Traditions in each of these lands attest to the existence of Jewish colonies attached to camps of Roman soldiers, but no written records of such early settlement have survived. If Jews *had* entered these regions with or shortly after the Roman advance, they could, perhaps, lay claim to a longer continuous residence in the Czech lands than either Czechs or Germans, but claims to Jewish antiquity in the region will always be unprovable. Properly speaking, such concerns occupy the realms of apologetics and myth, and appear to have had little impact on the development of Jewish life and institutions before the nineteenth century. It was only in the context of the changing relationship between Jews and Gentiles in the modern state that the question of Jewish "origins" in the Czech lands acquired importance.[1]

Hence, there is not a great deal that one can say with confidence about the earliest Jewish settlement in "the lands of the Crown of St. Wenceslaus." With regard to Prague, for example—by far the largest Jewish community of Central Europe before 1800—Alexandr Putík has concluded that reports on Jewish life before the thirteenth century are remarkably unreliable.[2] The best guess is that the oldest Jewish settlements were to be found in the Malá Strana (Lesser Town), on the left bank of the Vltava (Moldau) beneath the Hradčany Castle, and in the vicinity of the Vyšehrad Castle on the right bank of the river, south of what later became the center of town.[3] It appears that Jews did not establish themselves in what later would become known as the Jewish Town, or ghetto—the area of the city north of the Old Town Square (Staroměstské náměstí)—until after 1142, following the destruction, by fire or riot, of the Malá Strana community. A new Jewish community took root in the vicinity of the so-called Old Synagogue, to the east of the main Jewish Town (near today's Dušní Street), and a second, larger settlement grew up around Široká Street (Breitegasse), whose centerpiece was a proud Gothic synagogue constructed in the 1270s, known for a while as the New and later as the Old-New (Altneu or Staronová) Synagogue.[4] Remnants of Jewish tombstones from a cemetery in Prague's Nové Město (New Town), founded in the thirteenth century by members of the burgher estate, hint that Jews may have lived for a while in this district as well.

One can nevertheless surmise that Jewish communities of some sort existed in Bohemia and Moravia by the tenth or eleventh century C.E. The Spanish Jewish traveler Ibrahim ibn Yakub makes note of Jewish slave traders in Bohemia in the second half of the tenth century. The Raffelstätten toll regulations of 906 mention much the same thing with regard to Moravia, although they do not indicate where these Jews made their actual residence. Strong indirect evidence also attests to the presence of Jewish communities in Bohemia and Moravia by the eleventh century at the latest. These include the writings of the Bohemian chronicler Cosmas of Prague (1039?–1125), who knew about established Jewish communities in Bohemia in 1090 and in Brno (Moravia) in 1091 and who wrote about the disastrous effects of the First Crusade on Bohemian Jewry; and Isaac Dorbello, a student of R. Jacob ben Meir Tam, who described the Olomouc Jewish community around 1146. As for Hungary, Central European Jews probably began to migrate there during the reign of Andrew I (1047–1060), who pursued policies that encouraged the economic development of towns.[5]

In all likelihood, it was not until the thirteenth century that Jewish life truly began to flourish in the Czech lands. At this time references to Jewish communities in official documents begin to abound. Přemysl Ottokar II (margrave of Moravia, duke of Austria, and king of Bohemia) issued a charter to the Jews in 1254 that was more liberal than earlier proclamations. It granted wide latitude on the adjustment of rates of interest on loans, sought to protect Jewish moneylenders from having to redeem pledges on the Sabbath and holidays, and publicized recent papal bulls that condemned the ritual murder accusation. The

Jews of Hungary had received a similar charter from King Adalbert IV in 1251 as a reward for their services toward the reconstruction of the kingdom in the wake of the Mongol invasion. When challenged by the Church in Vienna to justify his favorable treatment of Jews, Přemysl Ottokar reaffirmed what was to become a principle of medieval royal politics, namely, that the Jews fell under the jurisdiction of the royal treasury (they were, according to the Latin phrase, *servi camerae*), and that the Crown—not local authority—had the right to collect Jewish taxes, regulate Jewish affairs, and offer protection.[6]

A sure sign of the vitality of Jewish life in Bohemia in the thirteenth century was the plethora of Jewish scholars who lived there, the most famous being Abraham ben Azriel, author of *Arugat ha-bosem,* and Isaac ben Moses of Vienna (ca. 1180–ca. 1250), author of the important *halakhic* work *Or zaru'a.* The Or Zaru'a, as he became known, was native to Bohemia; in his writings he referred to his country as "the land of Canaan" and frequently employed "the language of the land of Canaan," that is, Czech, to gloss difficult passages in rabbinic literature.[7] It is reasonable to conclude, then, that during the High Middle Ages the Jews of Bohemia and Moravia spoke the language of their surroundings. Their association with imperial culture and the German language would begin much later.

Within the hierarchical social fabric of medieval Central Europe, the Jewish community formed a distinct corporate entity. Organized politically at the local level—and supported by legal instruments issuing from either local or central authorities—the autonomous Jewish community provided for the education and welfare of its members, assessed and collected taxes, adjudicated legal disputes in its own courts of law according to the *halakhah* (rabbinic law), cared for the sick, and buried the dead. In economic and social terms it most closely resembled—but did not overlap with—the urban burgher estate. Community leaders often preferred to look beyond the town council to the territorial prince or to the Crown to establish their legitimacy and cultivate lines of protection. As a rule, Jewish life was most secure when royal or princely jurisdiction was firmly established. In those situations in which the lines of political power were vague or in which local authority competed openly against royal prerogative, Jewish fortunes suffered.

One such downturn occurred in the second half of the fourteenth century, when the cities of Bohemia and Moravia began to challenge Charles IV over the control of Jewish taxes. Both Charles and his successor Wenceslaus (Václav) occasionally allowed jurisdiction over Jewish affairs to slip from their hands in return for cash indemnities. At times they bowed to public pressure and canceled the debts owed by one or another estate to the Jews, again in return for a lump sum of money. As the towns grew in power and the religious ferment of the Hussite revolt became more pronounced, life for the Jews of Bohemia and Moravia became increasingly insecure. In 1389 members of the Prague clergy spread allegations of Jewish blasphemy and desecration of the host (the eucharistic wafer). Under their encouragement angry mobs looted and burned the Jewish quarter, killing scores of Jews and baptizing numerous women and children by force. One witness to the massacre was Rabbi Avigdor Kara, who died in 1439 and whose tombstone is the oldest to be found in the old Jewish cemetery. Kara mourned the tragedy of his community in a well-known elegy, "Et kol ha-tela'ah asher meza'atnu" (All of the hardships that befell us), which found a permanent place in standard editions of the Selihot, or penitential prayers, of Central Europe.[8]

The Hussite wars of the 1420s had the effect of further weakening the central authority of the Holy Roman Emperor in the political affairs of the Czech lands and, accordingly, increasing Jewish vulnerability to ad hoc local control. A number of the Jews who had been expelled from Vienna in 1421 had sought refuge in Moravia, for example, but dozens of them were accused of supporting the Hussites in their struggle against the Church and the emperor. Forced to respond to such charges, Albert V, duke of Austria and margrave of Moravia, called for the expulsion of the Jews from the royal town of Jihlava (Iglau) in 1426. At mid-century the Franciscan friar and preacher John of Capistrano (1386–1456) traveled widely in Central Europe, conducting an unremitting campaign against heretics—particularly Hussites—and Jews. In conjunction with the fiery rhetoric of Capistrano and partly as a consequence of the growing economic independence of the towns, five of the six royal cities in Moravia (Jihlava, Brno, Olomouc, Znojmo, and Neustadt) succeeded in expelling their Jewish populations in 1454. The sixth, Uherské Hradiště, followed suit in 1514.[9]

Consequently, from the middle of the fifteenth century until the middle of the nineteenth century, the cities of Moravia were closed to Jewish settlement. During this time the Jewish population in Moravia acquired a pattern that was quite distinct from that of neighboring Bohemia—much closer, in fact, to what could be found in Central and Eastern Poland in the seventeenth and eighteenth centuries. Moravian Jews lived by and large in small-to-medium-sized towns under the patronage of the nobility. They were able to preserve many of the features of urban culture and occupational life, but fell outside the purview of burgher control and competition, as the towns that they now inhabited were the private domains of magnate families. Mikulov (Nikolsburg), which was to become the seat of the organized Jewish community in Moravia, provides a case in point. The magnate owners of the town, the Dietrichštejns, received Jewish refugees from Vienna in 1421 and from the Moravian cities of Brno and Znojmo in 1454. Mikulov was a fairly large market town, which provided Jews with economic opportunities tied to agricultural production, trade, and commerce. The Dietrichštejns placed few restrictions on the Jewish population, and the community (nestled beneath the castle on a street named, appropriately, Za hradem) grew steadily throughout the early modern period.[10]

Autonomy, Traditional Culture, and the Royal Alliance

The permanent affiliation of the kingdoms of Bohemia and Hungary with the Habsburg dynasty in 1526 coincided with the flowering of Renaissance culture north of the Alps. For Prague Jewry, the sixteenth century augured growth and expansion as well as danger. New construction projects, which were begun between the 1480s and the 1520s in order to accommodate a rapid growth in the Jewish population, soon used up all of the open spaces in the Jewish quarter. New Jewish colonies sprang up in other areas of the city, and the Jewish quarter itself was enlarged through the purchase of Christian-owned houses. Between 1522 and 1541 the Jewish population of Prague is thought to have doubled; thereafter any additional population could be accommodated only by increasing the human density within the Jewish town.[11]

The Bohemian Diet (*Landtag*), an institution dominated by the nobility, renewed Jewish privileges in 1501, thereby laying the economic foundations for Jewish expansion. In the cultural sphere, the introduction of mechanized printing engendered a minor publishing revolution. The first Hebrew press in Prague began to produce books in 1512 and soon gained a reputation for quality and artistic innovation unmatched in the Jewish world. The printing establishment of Gershom ben Solomon Ha-Cohen produced Haggadot, Pentateuchs, and prayer books, many of them lavishly illustrated with woodcuts, that set both artistic and thematic standards for Hebrew publishing throughout northern Europe.

Under Ferdinand I (1526–64) royal policy toward the Jews oscillated between reaffirmation of ancient privileges and extension of royal protection in some areas and accommodation of anti-Jewish agitation in others. In one case in point, a wave of urban-based anti-Jewish riots broke out in 1541 in Raudnice, Saaz, and elsewhere. In the course of the now familiar struggle for power between the Crown and the burgher estate, Ferdinand acceded to the demands of the burghers that the Jews be expelled from all Crown cities in Bohemia. He belatedly excluded Prague from this category, only to bow to pressure from the urban estates once more, this time in 1557 at the behest of the Prague town council. By this time Ferdinand was prepared to order the expulsion of all of the Jews from Bohemia, though—characteristically—not Moravia, where the pressure from the nobility urging retention of the Jews carried more weight than the agitation of the towns. The 1557 decree was never fully enforced, however, and a remnant of the Jewish community managed to stay in place until the new emperor, Maximilian II, inherited the kingdoms of Bohemia and Hungary in 1564.[12]

If Czech Jewry can be said to have enjoyed a "golden age," this surely occurred during the reigns of Maximilian II (1564–76) and Rudolph II (1576–1612). Maximilian was rumored to have harbored Protestant sympathies during his youth. Upon his accession to the throne he cancelled the expulsion order for Bohemia and granted permission for the Jews of Prague to remain indefinitely. In 1571 he honored the Jewish Town of Prague with a ceremonial visit that included himself, the empress, and the entire court. But it was Rudolph's policies that made possible the most rapid expansion of Jewish life in Bohemia. His Charter of 1577 assigned the Jews major new privileges and promised that they would never again be expelled from Prague or the realm as a whole, though they remained excluded from the Crown cities. The Prague Jewish community grew from a few dozen in 1564 to over three thousand by 1600, representing the first important buildup of Jewish population west of Poland since the thirteenth century.

The tolerant and culturally iconoclastic atmosphere of Rudolph's court in Prague may have arisen from the need to transcend the Catholic-Protestant conflict that had been raging in Central Europe for half a century. Whatever the motives, Rudolph appears to have created favorable political, economic, and cultural conditions for Jewish life in Bohemia and Moravia. During his reign a segment of Prague's Jewish intellectual elite, though careful not to allow the erosion of Jewish belief and practice, nevertheless communicated extensively with the scientific and scholarly centers of non-Jewish society. David Gans (1541–1613), the German-born astronomer and historical chronicler, certainly embodied the most thorough appropriation of late Renaissance science and cultural concerns, subordinated, to be sure, to the parameters of traditional Jewish culture. Gans had studied with prominent rabbinic personalities of his day, including Moses Isserles in Cracow and Judah Löw ben Bezalel in Prague. But he then took the step, unusual for a Jew of his era, of devoting himself entirely to the study of the secular sciences, namely, mathematics, astronomy, geography, and history.

Gans collaborated with two of Europe's major astronomers, Tycho Brahe and Johannes Kepler, who were living in Prague at the time under the patronage of the imperial court. He recounted his visits to Tycho Brahe's observatory at the Benatek castle in his own astronomical work *Nehmad ve-na'im,* remarking that he visited the Danish astronomer three times, always for five days at a stretch:

And I ... was sitting with them in the observational rooms, and saw the wonderful things not only with the planets but also with the fixed stars.... In truth, I must say that in all my life-time I have not seen, nor heard of, such great effort and investigations: neither our forefathers told us nor did we see in any book, be it from the children of Israel ... or from the nations of the world.[13]

Though Gans acknowledged the work of Copernicus, calling him "a great scholar and excellent astronomer, greater than all the scholars of his epoch," he seems never to have felt the need to reconcile Copernicus's heliocentric view of the universe with traditional Jewish and Christian conceptions concerning the earth's place at the center of the cosmos. For today's reader, Gans's efforts in astronomy appear antiquated and unsatisfying. His historical writing, however, has had a more lasting impact. The chronicle *Zemah David,* published in Prague in 1592, concentrates on general history, selecting events that appeared to Gans to be particularly meaningful from a Jewish point of view. Gans was fascinated with the rising tide of theological strife and political turmoil within the Christian world and read these developments as signs of the easing of the oppressive conditions of exile for the Jews.

The most dominant figure in Jewish cultural life at the end of the sixteenth century, however, was Rabbi Judah Löw ben Bezalel (the Maharal, ca. 1520–1609). Born in the Polish province of Poznań, the Maharal served for two decades as *Landesrabbiner* of Moravia (1553 to 1573) before moving to the Bohemian capital to become head of the rabbinical academy. He left Prague on at least two occasions, once in 1584—returning four years later—and again in 1592, both times to assume rabbinical posts in Poznań following political disappointments in Prague. The chief rabbinate eluded him until 1597, when at the advanced age of seventy-seven he assumed the position that he had coveted for many years and occupied it until his death in 1609. Judah Löw's career combined political ambition, organizational talent, and creative genius in a way that left an indelible mark on both the structure and the content of Jewish life in the Czech lands. Recent scholarship has shown that while residing in Mikulov in Moravia, the Maharal had read Calvinist writings in Hebrew translation and had had contact with circles of Czech humanists, including the Bohemian Brethren.[14] This cultural exchange appears to have influenced the Maharal's own educational and national theories, which have long stood out as among the most original of the early modern era. His books *Tiferet Yisrael* (The glory of Israel), *Be'er ha-golah* (The well of exile), and *Nezaḥ Yisrael* (The eternity of Israel)—as well as his major commentary on the Book of Exodus, *Gevurot ha-Shem* (The might of the Lord)—contain remarkable contemplations of Israel's place among the nations of the world, the nature of nationality and national distinctiveness, the dilemma of exile, and the promise of redemption. In his *Netivot 'olam* (Paths of the world) one finds not only a treatise on ethics but also an elaborate statement of pedagogical theory, which rejects conventional methods of Talmudic study in favor of a graduated approach emphasizing the "plain" meaning of text and according separate and distinct status to the three pillars of Jewish learning: Bible, Mishnah, and Talmud.[15]

One of the most significant concessions made by Rudolph II to the Jews concerned their right to engage in a wide range of crafts and occupations. Rudolph purposefully curtailed the monopoly of the Christian guilds and granted the Jews—at least the Jews of Prague—what amounted to a partial economic emancipation. In addition to the old-style occupations of money lending, pawnbroking, and peddling, Jews also became active as artisans, shopkeepers, and merchants. The Jews of Prague plied their trades and sold their products not only within the Jewish quarter but also in the markets and squares of the city's Staré Město (Altstadt or Old Town). This expansion of Jewish economic life also paved the way for the emergence of the early-modern phenomenon of the Court Jew, the royal contractor and investor who was to play so important a role in the mercantilist programs of the seventeenth and eighteenth centuries.

The original Court Jew, in fact, may have been Mordechai Maisel (1528–1601), the Prague communal leader who also financed large-scale projects for Rudolph II. In 1598, in recognition of his services to the Crown, Maisel received unprecedented privileges from Rudolph in the area of finance (including the right to bequeath his property). The emperor authorized Maisel to display the "banner of King David" in his private synagogue, though the notion that he also achieved the title of nobility is unfounded.[16] During his lifetime Maisel supported numerous scholars and educational institutions, constructed synagogues, and reportedly paved the Jewish quarter at his own expense. Upon his death he left an estate worth more than 500,000 florins, which immediately became the object of a fierce contest pitting the Crown against the Jewish community and leaving the unfortunate heirs to fend for themselves.[17]

Whereas the "humanist" emperors, Maximilian II and Rudolph II, helped to reestablish Jewish life in the Czech lands during the last decades of an unfriendly sixteenth century, it was war prosecuted by a staunchly Catholic monarch that solidified the Jewish stronghold. The Thirty Years' War (1618–48) ravaged the countryside of Central Europe, destroyed the urban economies, and decimated the population, yet curiously did not undermine the conditions of Jewish life in the region. In fact, quite the opposite was true. Faced with the daunting prospect of mobilizing, provisioning, and sustaining an army to put down the rebellion of the Protestant Czech nobility (and soon thereafter to combat the armies of various invading countries), Emperor Ferdinand II (1619–37) took great care not to jeopardize the well-being of one of his most important human assets. He raised funds from Bohemian and Moravian Jews to help put down the original rebellion during the years 1618 to 1620. Ferdinand cultivated Jewish financiers such as Jacob Bassevi of Prague, who specialized in handling the output of Bohemia's silver mines. He protected those Jews who might be of benefit to the state and rewarded with special concessions those who had offered aid.

Hence, when the emperor's soldiers pillaged Prague following the Battle of White Mountain, they were under special instructions not to disturb the Jewish quarter. The quarter itself grew during the 1620s, when the government made available for purchase the adjoining houses of several Protestant families. In 1623 Ferdinand issued a new Privilegium to the Jews of Prague and Bohemia, reaffirming all traditional rights while guaranteeing to the Jews freedom of residence, protection from expulsion, and virtually unhampered trade and commercial activity throughout the kingdom, including the royal cities and the domains of the nobility. He reaffirmed the charter for the Jews of Bohemia and Silesia in 1627 and applied it to Moravia two years later.

When Moravia's Crown cities appealed to the emperor in 1636 to withhold Jewish privileges in their domains, Ferdinand II—joined by the governor of Moravia, Cardinal Dietrichštejn—refused.[18] Jewish policy continued along this pattern under Ferdinand III, who became emperor in 1637. With the steady growth of the Jewish population of Bohemia and Moravia in the 1630s, surplus numbers of Jews spilled over not only into the countryside but also to towns and cities that previously had excluded them. The first official census of Jews in Prague, taken in 1638, counted a population of 7,815; by the first decades of the eighteenth century, the Jewish community would make up approximately half of the total population of the Staré Město and about 28 percent of Prague's five districts combined.[19]

Toward the close of the war, the Jews of Prague participated in the defense of the city against the besieging Swedish forces. Jews not only financed and supplied the defense, but also manned a section of the walls and lost twenty-two men in the process. Historians and tour guides alike have been known to claim that Ferdinand III acknowledged the Jewish contribution to the Habsburg war effort by granting the community the right to adopt an emblem—the Star of David encircling a Swedish helmet—and to display it on public buildings in the Jewish Town.[20] The historicity of this bit of collective memory, however, has been effectively demolished in a recent study by Alexandr Putík, who points out the many ways in which it violates recorded Jewish experience, not to mention common sense. The Jewish community had displayed its own banner since at least 1490, in the absence of any specific royal authorization; the confirmation of Jewish privileges under Ferdinand III was issued on 8 April 1648, more than three months *before* the start of the Swedish siege of Prague; moreover, the emblem of the Prague Jewish community depicted a Star of David surrounding a medieval Jewish hat, not a Swedish cap or helmet.[21] What rewards the Jews did receive from the emperor for participating in the defense of Prague took the form of temporary tax relief and belated payments for a variety of war supplies, including meat and scrap metal.[22] The story of the "Swedish hat," while reinscribing an old emblem with new meaning, served the added, integrative function of linking the identity of the

Prague Jewish community to local patriotism and loyalty to the imperial house.

Since the Jewish policies of the two Ferdinands had from the start
been based on expediency, it was perhaps inevitable that once the war
was over, the position of the Jews in Bohemia and Moravia would decline once again. The *Judenpatent* of 1648 did in fact narrow the scope
of previous rights and privileges. The right of sojourn and freedom
from expulsion were now said to apply to royal cities and domains
alone. Interest rates on loans were limited to 6 percent, and restrictions
were set on the types of collateral that could be accepted. Jews continued to enjoy the long-standing right to practice the crafts but could no
longer employ Christian journeymen; Jewish artisans could sell their
wares only in the Jewish Town or in the flea market of the Christian
quarters. On the other hand, Ferdinand III was determined that Jewish
merchants and peddlers should have the right to trade in all of the market fairs in his kingdom. He specifically prevented Christian merchants
from restricting Jewish access to Moravia in 1657.[23]

Insisting on Jewish prerogatives with regard to regional trade served
the interests of the Crown in its perennial competition with the urban
estate. At the same time Ferdinand was prepared to punish the Jews in
order to promote the power of the monarchy vis-à-vis the landed nobility. Thus, in 1650 he sought to expel Jews from all localities in which
they had not legally resided on 1 January 1618 (most of these localities
were controlled by the nobility). Jews were to be disqualified from the
leasing of toll and monopoly rights and from the management of rural
estates. Rising to the challenge, the Moravian *Landtag* managed to de-
lay implementation of the royal edict. Eventually it forced Ferdinand's
successor, Leopold I, to change the cut-off date from 1618 to 1657, a
move that granted de facto recognition of the expansion of Jewish settlement during the Thirty Years' War.

Despite the reprieve provided by the Moravian noblemen, Habsburg
Jewry would not be able to avoid the long-term effects of a backlash in
popular sentiment. The close association of Jews and the Crown, born
of necessity and reason of state during an era of civil war, appeared to
be coming to a close. Leopold I, Joseph I, and Charles VI had other
worries, including the Turkish threat to Vienna. As had been the case
with their predecessors, their attitudes toward the Jewish community
were complex and not altogether consistent; increasingly they came to
view Jews more as a liability than as an asset. When both city magistrates and royal officials began to urge the placing of strict limits on

Jewish activity—particularly after the fire that destroyed the Jewish quarter in 1689—the monarchs were prepared to listen.

Curiously, the growing prestige of mercantilist theory—and the rush to "catch up" economically to the states of Western Europe—did not necessarily aid the Jewish cause. Rulers and advisors alike tended to regard the traditional forms of Jewish economic behavior as standing in the way of the creation of a strong and self-sufficient economy. Officials in Vienna also encouraged the emperor to take seriously the frequently raised complaints from the Bohemian crown lands concerning uncontrolled growth in the Jewish communities. In 1714 Charles VI created a commission to consider a number of proposals, among them the reduction of the Jewish population of Prague, the limitation of Jewish economic influence, and the effective separation of the Jewish quarter from the Old Town. The commission came back with drastic recommendations to reduce the number of Jews in the city, and these were passed on to the emperor by the governor's office in 1719.[24]

By this point the court in Vienna was acting in concert with the governor's office and the magistrates in Prague. But the emperor's advisors had difficulty convincing the Treasury to go along because of its fear of losing Jewish tax revenues. The *Landtag*, too, balked in 1724 when the regime placed before it the same anti-Jewish ordinance of 1650, which would have restricted Jewish settlement to pre-1618 localities. Not wishing to jeopardize the incomes derived from the leasing of rural property, the Czech nobility warned the emperor that any attempt to reduce the number of Jews living in the country would harm the overall economy.

In the face of opposition from the estates, Charles VI changed tactics. Rather than attempt to roll back Jewish settlement to pre-1618 levels and localities, he moved to "cap" the current demographic situation. In 1726 and 1727 he issued the infamous Familiants Laws (*Familiantengesetze*), which limited the number of Jewish families that might legally reside in Bohemia to 8,541 and in Moravia to 5,106. To keep these numbers constant, he also decreed that only one son from any household could obtain the right to marry and establish a family of his own.[25] More than any other single piece of legislation, the Familiants Laws came to symbolize the repressive stance that the Habsburg state had decided to take on Jewish policy. The intent of the laws was to block Jewish mobility, stifle economic development, and discourage the creation of new life, while maintaining a minimum level of tax contribution. The laws stayed in effect until the Revolution of 1848, playing havoc with Jewish family life, significantly delaying the age of marriage for most, and forcing the younger members of Jewish households to emigrate or, at best, settle in the towns and villages of the nobility, where they might be protected from the watchful eye of the state.

Although thousands of Jewish males from Bohemia are presumed to have migrated to Poland and Jews from Moravia to have settled in Hungary, the Familiants Laws did not fully succeed in preventing the growth of the Jewish population in the Czech lands. The eighteenth-century state remained relatively weak; its coercive powers were limited. One of the ways in which Jews circumvented the regulations—in Bohemia, at least—was to disperse throughout the countryside in a centrifugal pattern extending to isolated villages. The original government census of 1724 had indicated that the Jews of Bohemia were scattered among 800 localities, as many as 600 of which comprised small villages in which only a handful of Jews lived. Over the course of the next 125 years (i.e., while the Familiants Laws were still in effect) this dispersed pattern of settlement actually became more pronounced. When a new census was taken in 1849, it was learned that there were now 1,921 localities in which Jews lived: only 207 of these had formed actual communities of more than ten families and a formal synagogue; 148 managed to assemble a quorum (*minyan*) for prayer on Sabbaths and holidays; the rest were too small even for that. Meanwhile the Jewish population had grown. Instead of the 42,000 Jews that the government had counted in the 1720s, there were between 75,000 and 76,000 in Bohemia! Moravian Jewry had also expanded during this time, from some 25,000 to 38,000 or 39,000.[26]

At the same time, tens of thousands of Bohemian and Moravian Jews were forced to leave the kingdom. As noted above, the lion's share of the Moravian emigrants settled in Hungary. These refugees helped to create the first significant Jewish presence there since the Ottoman conquests. These same Familiants Laws, then, forged the historic connection between the Jewries of Hungary and the Czech lands. Between 1700 and 1800, upwards of 30,000 Moravian Jews settled in Hungary, mostly in the western districts. For many years they maintained close cultural and economic ties to Moravia, building synagogues along Moravian models, even paying taxes to their former communities. Slovakian children were known to attend Jewish schools in Mikulov, Prostějov (Prossnitz), and Bokovice, while youths from Moravia frequented the *yeshivot* of Bratislava (Pressburg, Pozsony) and Vrbové (Verbo). During this time the Jewish population of Hungary began to soar: it grew from about 15,000 in 1750, to 83,000 in 1787, and to 245,000 in 1830.[27]

During the War of the Austrian Succession (1741–48), Jewish life in the Czech lands was plunged for a time into genuine chaos and despair. Maria Theresa, the daughter of Charles VI, had ascended the Habsburg throne in 1740 in a climate of uncertainty about the legitimacy of a female succession (despite her father's efforts to win recognition of the so-called Pragmatic Sanction before his death), and the monarchy quickly became embroiled in an international war in which it lost control of Silesia to an opportunistic Prussia. Maria Theresa, an intensely devout Catholic who evinced a healthy dislike for both Jews and Protestants, reacted to the brief occupation of Prague in 1744 by Prussian forces by punishing the Jews of Bohemia, whom she believed had behaved traitorously with the enemy. (Punishment was not meted out to the Bohemian nobility, nearly half of whom had acknowledged Charles Albert of Bavaria as their king in 1741.)

On 18 December 1744, Maria Theresa ordered the immediate expulsion of the Jews from Prague and their eventual removal from the rest of Bohemia; an edict issued the following month extended the expulsion order to Moravia and Silesia as well. The Jews of Prague were allowed to tarry for some months in the Bohemian countryside to tidy up their business affairs. Following much diplomatic intervention from England and elsewhere—as well as direct appeals from the Prague magistrates, the governor's office, and the Bohemian Treasury—Maria Theresa finally rescinded the expulsion decree in 1748. The international community had been shocked at the brutality of the expulsion, which had taken place during an unusually harsh winter, and at the implausibility of the queen's accusations against the Jews. Moreover, state officials, recruited from the nobility and influenced increasingly by Enlightenment ideals, no longer voiced the hostility toward Jews that had characterized Court opinion during the reign of Maria Theresa's father. Jewish life in Prague had been dealt a severe blow, which had had the overall effect of intensifying the process of Jewish dispersion in the Czech countryside, but the worst appeared to be over, and a time of rebuilding was about to begin.[28]

During the period of "old" Habsburg rule, from 1526 to 1780, the institutions of Jewish self-government in both Bohemia and Moravia expanded and became more highly structured and diversified. At the same time, the patterns of Jewish autonomy in the two provinces diverged significantly. In Bohemia, the Jewish community of Prague acted as the dominant force in communal affairs, at times representing all of Bohemian Jewry and at times competing with the rest of the province, which was organized as a single unit to serve as a counterweight to the dominant center. The power struggle between Prague and the Bohemian periphery stemmed in large part from distinctive, demographic effects of Habsburg Jewish policy in Bohemia. Jews, it will be recalled, had lived in urban enclaves in Bohemia until 1541, when they were expelled from the royal cities but allowed to remain in Prague. Henceforth, and despite the two temporary expulsions of 1557 and 1745, the Prague community expanded while the rest of Bohemian Jewry spread out in ever-widening circles in small towns and villages. Prague's subsequent ability to dominate Jewish affairs in Bohemia depended on its relative size, wealth, and security. By the middle of the seventeenth century, for example, the rural Jewish population had increased to a sufficient degree that the state came to recognize the *Böhmische Landesjudenschaft* as an independent entity whose main function was to collect and distribute Jewish tax monies. The only formal connection between the *Landesjudenschaft* and Prague Jewry at this time was through the office of the chief rabbi, Simon Spira-Wedeles.

The *Landesjudenschaft* consolidated its separate status during the last quarter of the seventeenth century, when fire, plague, and political indecision reigned in Prague. It was not until the second decade of the eighteenth century that Rabbi David Oppenheim (1664–1736) managed to extend his authority over all of Bohemian Jewry, which by that time had been divided among three chief rabbinates. Chief rabbi of Prague since 1702, Oppenheim assumed the two provincial rabbinical posts in 1713 and 1715, and won the title of *rosh yeshivah* in 1718. Meanwhile the state had also stepped in to impose "rationality" on the situation, creating positions of district rabbi (*Kreisrabbiner*) for the Bohemian provinces, abolishing the title of *Landesrabbiner* in 1749, and recognizing the chief rabbi of Prague as the top religious official for all of Jewish Bohemia. From this point until 1939, Bohemian Jewry retained a bifurcated communal structure—Prague on the one hand, the rest of Bohemia on the other—while the state recognized only the chief rabbi of Prague as the supreme religious authority.[29]

In Moravia Jewish autonomy operated along very different lines. Here the royal cities had expelled the Jews a century earlier than in Bohemia, and, unlike Bohemia, there was no single urban center that retained a permanent Jewish community. Moravian Jewry, rather, settled successfully in the small- to medium-sized towns of the nobility and did not have to disperse into the sparsely populated countryside. These patterns seem to have resulted in greater intercommunal cohesiveness than was the case in Bohemia, again similar to the situation in early modern Poland. As in Poland, Moravian Jewry created a supercommunal council, the Va'ad Medinat Mehrin, which operated under the supervision of the *Landesrabbiner* and whose principal functions included the collections of taxes, the representation of Jewish interests before the authorities, and legislation in matters affecting the larger Jewish community.[30]

Under the leadership of Chief Rabbi Menahem Mendel Krochmal, the Moravian *va'ad* began a project of assembling and publishing its legislative acts in 1651–52. The first installment consisted of 311 articles, or *takkanot* (hence the popular moniker *shai* [311] *takkanot*). To this were added pieces of communal legislation until the year 1748, the last year in which the supercommunal legislative council met. At the behest of the Habsburg state, which thought it necessary to establish limits to Jewish autonomy in Moravia, the entire collection was translated into German and published in 1754 as the *General Polizei-, Prozess- und Kommerzialordnung für die Judenschaft des Markgraftums Mähren*. The person who translated the collection was the famous convert Alois von Sonnenfels. The *Takkanot* of Moravia amounted to nothing less than a body of constitutional law governing the lives of Moravian Jewry. And although Maria Theresa insisted on certain amendments to this "constitution" in 1754, the principle of Jewish autonomy remained intact. The *va'ad* continued to function and enacted a new set of laws dealing with educational matters during the later part of the 1750s—laws that guaranteed the operation of *yeshivot* in Mikulov and other locations throughout Moravia. Moravian Jewry's strong sense of communal cohesiveness lasted well into the nineteenth century and helped to produce a Jewish "national" voice in Austrian politics in the midst of the emancipation process.[31]

Long-term demographic patterns have a way of turning into cultural destinies. One would do well to keep in mind, for example, the difference between Bohemian Jewry's pattern of rural dispersion around a large urban center and Moravian Jewry's settlement in noble towns when encountering various nineteenth-century developments in Czech-Jewish life. These would include: the rise of a Czech cultural and political movement among provincial Jews in Bohemia, the relative weakness of the same phenomenon in Moravia, Moravia's long-lasting tradition of Jewish self-government, and the fragile state of Jewish institutional life in the Bohemian countryside.

Enlightenment, Emancipation, and Nationalism

If political autonomy, social exclusivity, and traditional culture defined the parameters of premodern Jewish existence, the transition to what can be called the "conditions of modernity" would necessarily entail the dismantling of all three. For the Jews of the Czech lands, this process stretched from the 1780s to the 1860s. It was ushered in with a decade of sweeping educational, juridical, and occupational reforms but subsequently crept along at an inconsistent pace, full of starts and turns and reversals. Jews were not allowed to own landed property, for example, until 1841, and only in the wake of the Revolution of 1848 did marriage and residence restrictions disappear. Full legal emancipation was achieved only with the creation of the Dual Monarchy (Austria-Hungary) in 1867.[32]

The state, on the one hand, and the Jewish promoters of Enlightenment (the *haskalah*), on the other, acted as the principal agents of change in the 1780s. Emperor Joseph II (co-regent 1765–80, sole monarch 1780–90), like his mother before him, was determined to transform the disparate territories and unwieldy populations of the Habsburg monarchy into a centralized state with an industrial economic base in which the machinery of government worked rationally and efficiently and competing centers of power were gradually eliminated. He mobilized the upper levels of the bureaucracy to promote the interests of the state against those of traditional society, employing Enlightenment models of sovereignty, economic rationality, and reason of state to chip away at ancient privilege.

In the process the state extended its jurisdiction to spheres of activity that in the past had been the purview of the autonomous Jewish community. Eventually the state would curtail the juridical autonomy of the Jewish community, redirect occupational distribution, and even set a new cultural agenda for Jews. It would redefine the civil status of the community and, concomitantly, that of its members. In the emerging situation Jews would begin to relate directly to state and society as individuals whose status under law did not derive from a corporate identity.

Whether or not Jews would feel comfortable in their new position, as-similate to the language and behavioral patterns of the dominant cul-ture, or integrate successfully into majority society would remain open questions. But by this time the basic conditions for modern Jewish his-tory would have been put in place. There would be no return to the past.

Joseph II ushered in the era of conscious reform from above with the issuance of a *Toleranzpatent* for the Jews of Bohemia in October 1781 and for Moravian Jewry in February 1782. Similar legislation was ap-plied to Hungary in 1783, and the most far-reaching experiment of all— the *Toleranzpatent* for Galician Jewry—took effect in 1789, a year before the emperor's death. This legislation, though groundbreaking in its own right, represented but part of a much larger package of reforming measures that included the application of religious toleration to Aus-trian Protestants, the partial liberation of the peasantry from its ties to feudal land, and the institution of compulsory elementary education. Joseph's goals were to break down traditional societal privileges and to remove barriers to economic growth. He did not view the reforms as bequeathing any special advantages to the Jews. As he explained in a memorandum of October 1781: "It is by no means my intention to ex-pand the Jewish nation in the hereditary lands or to reintroduce them to areas where they are not tolerated, but only—in those places where they already exist and to the extent that they are already tolerated—to make them useful to the state."[33]

In order to render the Jews, as he put it, "more useful to the state," Joseph opened to them all forms of trade and commerce, encouraged them to establish factories, and urged them to engage more fully in the artisan crafts and in agriculture. Of course, for nearly two centuries the Jews of Prague had maintained their own craft guilds. One can only surmise that Joseph's advisors intended for this provision to apply mainly to the Jews of the smaller cities and towns, and its principal effect was to open the Christian guild network to Jewish participation. Whatever its ultimate intent, the law refrained from undermining the status quo in the shop or the countryside. It continued to bar Jews from owning rural property, and while Jews could apprentice them-selves to Christian masters and work as their journeymen, they could not attain the rank of master.[34]

The more far-reaching changes occasioned by the *Toleranzpatent* took place not in the area of economic activity but rather in the cultural and educational realm. Joseph II invited all of the Jewish communities of Bohemia and Moravia (and later Hungary) that were large enough to set up government-supervised schools of their own to instruct students in mathematics, geography, the German language, and morality. Parents who lived in communities that could not afford to construct their own schools could send their children to Gentile establishments. Meanwhile the doors of the universities and institutions of higher education were declared open for Jewish enrollment.

Following Joseph's death in 1790, the pace of reform slowed down considerably. From this point until 1848, the Viennese government withdrew from interfering in the affairs of Hungarian Jewry, and as a result, the new school system there collapsed. The Galician patent of 1789, which would have placed Jews on an equal political footing with other Galician subjects, also became a dead letter. But the core of the legislation survived and served, in truncated fashion, as the model for the Judensystemalpatent of 1797. Moreover, in both Hungary and Galicia, when the state decided to remove itself from Jewish education, members of the secular Jewish intelligentsia, the *maskilim,* filled the void. Thus Emperor Francis I may have abolished the *Normalschulen* in Galicia in 1806, but Joseph Perl established a model *haskalah* school in Tarnopol in 1813. And in Hungary, the *maskilim* of Pressburg (Bratislava) established an elementary school in 1820—which received government encouragement and official recognition—where both secular and religious subjects were taught.[35]

In Bohemia and Moravia, in contrast, the German-Jewish elementary school stayed in place and became a permanent feature of Jewish cultural life down to the end of the nineteenth century. Here the state retained a strong interest in promoting Jewish acculturation, and here, too, there was a party of *maskilim* influential enough to join forces with the state in promoting the new schools. Yet their success was not a foregone conclusion. The venerable Ezekiel Landau (1713–93), who had been chief rabbi in Prague since 1755, offered a major voice of conservative opposition. Over the decades he had helped to rebuild a community ravaged by political harassment and natural disaster (fire), and to reestablish Prague as the most prestigious Jewish community in Central Europe. At the same time he had amassed unrivaled political authority, becoming the undisputed spiritual head of Bohemian Jewry. Landau, the author of a major commentary on the Talmud as well as a famous collection of responsa (*Nodah bi-yehudah,* 1776), stood as an outspoken opponent of the Berlin *haskalah.* He railed against those, such as Naphtali Herz Wessely (author of the work *Divrei shalom ve-'emet*), who would raise secular studies to the level of the Torah or even higher.[36] And yet he acquiesced in the emperor's proposal. Fundamentally a pragmatist, Landau negotiated a package that did not pose a threat of radical change with Ferdinand Kindermann von Schulstein, the liberal-minded priest and educator whom Joseph had picked to oversee the project.[37]

Haskalah and reform, however, were not the only cultural forces that found expression among the Jews of Bohemia, Moravia, and Hungary. A competing voice was that of religious traditionalism, which refused to accommodate Jewish belief, practice, or educational models to the rising tide of European rationalism. Rabbi Moses Sofer (the "Ḥatam Sofer," 1762–1839) spearheaded the organized resistance to cultural reform. Born in Frankfurt am Main, he had been the head of the Prostějov (Prossnitz) *yeshivah* in Moravia from 1785 to 1794 and had served as rabbi in both Strážnice (Moravia) and Mattersdorf (Burgenland) before being appointed as rabbi in Bratislava (Pressburg) in 1806. There he established a *yeshivah* that quickly earned an international reputation as a major center for traditional Jewish learning. Though frequently under pressure from the leadership of the community, whose president, Wolf Breisach, was an outspoken advocate of reform, the Ḥatam Sofer succeeded in waging a vigorous and uncompromising campaign against religious and cultural innovation until his death in 1839. Thereafter his descendants—Abraham Wolf Sofer, Simhah Bunem Sofer, and Akiva Sofer—continued to direct the Pressburg *yeshivah* and to guide religious orthodoxy until the eve of World War II.[38]

Despite the best efforts of the absolutist monarchs, the Habsburg state remained relatively weak through the first half of the nineteenth century. It failed to develop either effective, centralized institutions or a strong political culture. Not only did the state not dominate society, but society itself in the Habsburg lands was becoming increasingly divided among linguistic, ethnic, and religious claimants. The emerging national movements of the Czechs, the Hungarians, the Germans, and others competed with the state for power while offering up vastly differing visions of the future. All of these factors—rapid Jewish acculturation in the absence of meaningful political change, the emergence of middle-class national movements, and the perennial weakness of Habsburg political culture—greatly complicated Jewish efforts at achieving mobility, status, and integration.

In Bohemia and Moravia, the Czech-German national struggle assumed greater and greater importance as the century wore on. Consequently, Jews faced the dilemma of reconciling an essentially German acculturation with the reality of an ethnically divided society. What type of community did Jews wish to join after the foundations of traditional Jewish society had broken away? Did the cultural reforms of Joseph II, the efforts of the state to recruit Jews to German high culture, effectively limit Jews to an Austrian-German identity?

As I hope to demonstrate in chapter 3, until the late 1840s linguistic and ethnic boundaries in the Czech lands were relatively fluid. The fact that Jewish graduates of secondary schools and universities had followed a German curriculum did not determine in advance that they would identify with an exclusively German-speaking community. Most Czech and Hungarian students, after all, had also been educated in German-language institutions. During the 1830s and 1840s, moreover, intellectuals in the Habsburg lands imagined a society in which democracy, national rights, and full emancipation for religious minorities coexisted. These were heady, if uncertain, times for Jewish students in Prague and Vienna. Some aligned with the young literary and national movements of the Czechs, the Hungarians, and the South Slavs. They contributed to journals such as *Ost und West,* which nurtured the folk cultures of East Central Europe while promoting constitutionalism and political reform. They translated the works of Slavic writers into German. Occasionally, as in the case of Siegfried Kapper (1821–79), they composed original works of poetry and prose in Czech. Or, as with David Kuh (1818–79)—the son of an old Prague-Jewish family—they used the pages of the German-Jewish press to exhort their fellow Jews to support the political and cultural aspirations of the Slavic peoples.[39]

But the efforts of Jewish students and intellectuals to promote Czech nationalism in the 1840s foundered on the shoals of hostility, misunderstanding, and popular violence. When industrial riots broke out in Prague and other parts of Bohemia in June 1844 (protesting the introduction of mechanization as well as the lowering of wages in the cotton printing sector), they were directed mainly against the businesses and homes of Jews. To make matters worse, the commercial middle class and the lower middle class as well as the nationalist press sided openly with the rampaging workers, leaving Prague Jewry to feel ever more isolated and vulnerable. David Kuh, who only weeks earlier had called upon the Jews of Bohemia and Moravia to join hands with the Slavic nations to promote democracy and political emancipation, now reported bitterly:

Textile workers rise up against their bosses, who happen to belong to the Jewish ethnic group [*Volksklasse*], cause damage and destruction to factories, and our dear cultivated and educated Czechs know of nothing better to do than to exhibit openly their own crude and crass Jew-hatred, accusing all Jews, as a single body, of fraud.... Oh Czechs, you call for freedom and independence at a time when you have dehumanized yourselves, when you have sunk to the level of beasts of prey.[40]

When Siegfried Kapper published his first collection of poems in Czech, *České listy* (Czech leaves), in 1846, the effort was greeted with scorn by one of Prague's most influential journalists, Karel Havlíček Borovský. Writing in *Česká včela*, Havlíček argued that the Jews constituted more than a religious denomination; they were also a distinct nationality. Hence they could not transform themselves by a simple act of volition into Czechs.

This bond that ties them [the Jews] together is stronger by far than the bond to the country in which they live. We hope that there is no need to prove the point that it is impossible to belong simultaneously to two fatherlands and two nations, or to serve two masters. Therefore anyone who wants to be a Czech must cease to be a Jew.[41]

Havlíček reproached those Jews who wanted to abandon their culture, including their "natural" language, Hebrew. To those who had already thrown Hebrew overboard he offered the advice that they cultivate German, as it had apparently become European Jewry's second mother tongue.

The final blow to this brief experiment in cultural rapprochement occurred in the wake of the Revolution of 1848. Popular violence directed against Jewish homes and businesses erupted once again in Prague. And once again Bohemian and Moravian Jewry were prompted to narrow their vision of the community into which they hoped to integrate—its contours and cultural boundaries. Havlíček's contention that the Jews of the Czech lands constituted their own nation did not find much of an echo among the Jews themselves. Jewish political strivings, social ambitions, and sense of identity throughout the nineteenth century had been predicated on the opposite notion—that a separate Jewish nationality no longer existed. If Jews did seem to take to heart one piece of advice, it was to complete their embrace of German language and culture, well underway since the first efforts at Jewish "modernization" in the 1780s. With the elaborate network of German-Jewish primary schools in place, secondary and higher education squarely within the German orbit, and a state apparatus that offered clear advantages to German speakers (west of Hungary), there appeared to be little to hold the Jews back from complete identification with Austrian-German liberalism. Nor, in the face of popular Czech antagonism, did there appear to be any alternative.

But the retreat to German culture was not to be permanent. Alternatives to the type of acculturation that had characterized the emancipatory period would begin to reveal themselves by the last quarter of the nineteenth century. In the 1870s and 1880s demographic and social factors within Czech Jewry combined with steady political pressure from the outside to initiate a new process of cultural affiliation. Tens of thousands of rural and small-town Jews who were conversant in Czech language and culture began to flock to the industrial centers of Bohemia and Moravia. A significant number of these families chose to send their children to the recently expanded system of Czech primary and secondary schools, especially those of the provincial cities that formed the heartland of the Czech national movement. As these young people began to enter the university or begin careers, they rebelled against prevailing cultural and political allegiances in the Jewish community. Little by little an extensive network of Jewish institutions emerged that dedicated itself to the achievement of a more genuine Czech-Jewish acculturation.

The first Jewish organization to challenge the liberal consensus of the mid-nineteenth century was the Spolek českých akademiků-židů (Association of Czech Academic Jews), founded by Jewish university students in Prague in 1876. It was joined in 1883 by the Or-Tomid (Eternal Light) Society, which aimed at creating a Czech linguistic vehicle for religious ceremonies and public ritual. When in 1893 the Národní jednota českožidovská (Czech-Jewish National Union) emerged—and with it the first Czech-Jewish newspaper, *Českožidovské listy*—the growing Czech-Jewish movement had come of age. For the next twenty-five years it would challenge both the institutions and the established practices of Bohemian and Moravian Jewry. Along the way the Czech-Jewish movement would close down the century-old network of German-Jewish schools that had been the hallmark of Jewish acculturation since the days of Joseph II. It would help to change the voting patterns and linguistic declarations of Bohemian and Moravian Jewry and would achieve no small success in transforming the overall national orientation of the Jewish community.[42]

An alternative to an exclusively Czech or German national affiliation—a "third way," if you will—presented itself with increasing co-
gency during the turbulent final half-decade of the nineteenth century.
Pockets of university students, businessmen, and young professionals
reacted to the general radicalization of political life in Bohemia and
Moravia by questioning the very premise of national assimilation, insisting that their ethnic affiliation was neither German nor Czech, but
Jewish. Many of the more creative minds of the younger generation of
Prague Jews—among them philosopher [Shmuel] Hugo Bergmann,
historian Hans Kohn, journalist Robert Weltsch, and writer Max
Brod—applied themselves energetically to the task of creating a modern
national Jewish culture appropriate to the multinational context of
Habsburg Central Europe. Most of these people emerged from the student Zionist organization Bar Kochba, which had been founded in
1899. A number were active in the influential Zionist weekly *Selbstwehr*,
published by Jewish nationalists in Prague from 1907 to 1938. All were
committed to the cultural and political renaissance of the Jewish people
both in Europe and in the land of Israel.

I have argued elsewhere that Prague Zionism and the Czech-Jewish
movement represented opposite poles of a single process of cultural
transformation.[43] This is not to say that the Jewish communities of Bohemia and Moravia possessed a single cultural profile. Moravian Jewry,
for example, exhibited patterns that were unique to its particular historical development. Less urbanized than Bohemian Jewry by the end of
the nineteenth century and more dominated by Viennese culture as
well, the Jews of Moravia tended to retain a greater allegiance to German language and culture. In 1900, more than 54 percent of the Jews of
Bohemia declared their language of daily use (*Umgangssprache* or *obco-
vácí řeč*) to be Czech; but only 17 percent of the Jews of Moravia made
the same declaration.[44] Also in sharp contrast to Bohemia, a large number of Moravian Jewish communities (twenty-seven in all) continued to
exist as autonomous political entities (*politische Gemeinden*) down to the
end of the Habsburg monarchy. Even the formal emancipation of 1867
and the liberal legislation that followed left the principle of Jewish
municipal rights intact in Moravia, rendering it the only place in
pre–World War I Europe in which emancipation and Jewish autonomy
were not considered irreconcilable conditions.[45]

Moravian Jewry's ability to combine political autonomy with emancipation certainly stands out as a curiosity in modern Jewish history.
And the origins of the *politische Gemeinden* in the mid-nineteenth cen-

tury remain somewhat mysterious. They may have emerged as the product of a long and successful history of centralized communal organization in Moravia. On the other hand, Jewish autonomy in modern Moravia may have resulted from a conscious ploy on the part of the government in Vienna to ensure a German majority in the Moravian Diet (*Landtag*). What is clear is that these "political communities" helped Moravian Jews to maintain a strong sense of national identity, distinct from that of both Czechs and Germans, down to the twentieth century. In 1921 the Jews of Czechoslovakia had their first opportunity to proclaim a German, "Czechoslovak," Hungarian, or Jewish national identity. Nearly 48 percent of Moravian Jewry chose to register as Jews; the largest bloc in Bohemia, nearly 50 percent, preferred to be identified as Czechoslovaks.[46]

Toward 1918

By the close of the 1860s the Jews of Bohemia and Moravia had experienced one modernization experiment: the restructuring of political and religious identities and of economic profile that had been set in motion by the reforms of the 1780s. Though still predominantly rural, Jewish society had long since abandoned most of its premodern forms. The community had no juridical autonomy; traditional Jewish education had fallen into disuse, as had the Yiddish language; and Bohemian and Moravian Jews no longer suffered from residential, demographic, or occupational restrictions. By 1914 a complex of social, cultural, and political factors had altered the face of Bohemian and Moravian Jewry once again. Demographic upheaval, migration, and urbanization; the realization of secular, universal education; Czech nationalism's challenge of German cultural and political dominance; and the general radicalization of national politics had elicited an array of Jewish responses and ultimately produced a new social and cultural entity: modern Czech Jewry.

Whereas Bohemian and Moravian Jewry had been predominantly rural and small-town, modern Czech Jewry was decidedly urban. Over a third of the Jewish population of Bohemia lived in Prague in 1910; close to 70 percent lived in towns of more than 10,000 people. Seven decades earlier there had been 347 separate Jewish communities in Bohemia alone, only twenty-two of which had a population of more than fifty. If Bohemian and Moravian Jewish culture had been colored largely by the German-Jewish alliance of the late eighteenth century (renewed after 1848), the Czech Jewish orientation was highly nuanced, increasingly alienated from Austrian-German liberalism, and self-consciously bilingual. Moreover, whether Czech or Zionist in political orientation, the culture of Bohemian and Moravian Jews after 1870 could only be elaborated in national terms. The arena of party politics certainly required this, but so too did the school system, the courts, the bureaucracy, and even voluntary associations and religious institutions.

By the first decades of the twentieth century, German-Jewish culture in the Czech lands was in full retreat. It was by no means dead, however. Jewish parents in Prague, Brno, and other large cities continued to send their children in significant numbers to German schools and universities. These were also the years in which the phenomenon known as *Prager Deutscher Literatur* broke through the confines of provincial culture and emerged as one of the truly great achievements of world literature. Writers such as Oskar Baum, Max Brod, Ernst Weiss, Franz Werfel, and Franz Kafka helped to define the contours of modern German letters. This great burst of literary creativity reflected not so much the confidence of these German-Jewish writers in the long-term viability of German culture, as their sense that they were standing at the end of a historical process. Theirs was to be the last generation educated before World War I, the last to enjoy the rewards accorded German speakers in the multinational empire, and at the same time, the first generation to represent Jewish aspirations in the new Czechoslovakia.

Franz Kafka (1883–1924) is today perhaps the most famous of all Prague Jews, his renown having surpassed that of the legendary Maharal. Clearly, Kafka possessed the ability to translate the turmoil and uncertainty of an inner consciousness into a universal language of psychological reality. Works such as *The Trial* and his masterly story "The Judgment" highlight the modern dilemmas of guilt (real and imagined), punishment (self-inflicted and meted out by society), and justice (seemingly undeliverable, certainly incomprehensible). Yet if Kafka produced universal and timeless art, he was also very much the product of his place and time. His father was a Czech-speaking dry goods merchant who had migrated to Prague from the village of Osek in 1881. Though educated in German schools, Kafka himself was fully conversant in Czech and maintained contact with Czech intellectual and political circles. He rebelled against the liberal middle-class culture of his father's generation, became attracted to Yiddish language and culture in 1911–12, and was drawn to the activities of Prague Zionism by his closest friends, Max Brod and Felix Weltsch. During the First World War, Kafka accompanied Jiří Langer (author of the mystical work *Nine Gates to the Chassidic Mysteries*) at least twice on visits to the courts of Hasidic rabbis. After 1918 he attended organizational meetings of the Jewish national school in Prague, where his sister Valli was a teacher. During his struggle with tuberculosis, he entertained visions of emigrating to Palestine. No one with this kind of personal history who had emerged from that peculiar cultural mixture that was Prague can be considered simply a German writer. Kafka was in many respects an isolated and unique figure, alienated from the world around him. On a deeper level, however, his life epitomized the very processes that were transforming Jewish life in Bohemia and Moravia. He was himself an emblem of modern Czech Jewry.[47]

In the autumn of 1918 both Prague Zionism and the Czech-Jewish movement stood poised to claim their rightful place as representatives of the new Czech-Jewish community. Both Jewish camps regarded the national unification of the Czechs and Slovaks, in the spirit of Wilsonian democracy and under the tutelage of Tomáš Masaryk, to be in accord with their own visions for the future. The Czech-Jewish movement, which had grown out of the dislocation of rural and small-town communities and the migration of tens of thousands of Jews to the cities, envisaged the creation of a cultural partnership with the progressive elements of the Czech nation. Jewish nationalism in the Czech lands, which owed its popularity not to the encouragement of any single national movement but to the national conflict itself, engaged in a campaign that—for all the differences—paralleled that of the Czech-Jewish movement. Zionism represented a deliberate turning away from the liberal German consensus of the nineteenth century, a revolt against the course of Jewish history in Central Europe since the period of Enlightenment and reform. Both movements were determined to rework Jewish culture so it would better fit the requirements of a post-imperial, national order. True, the "Czech" Jews for the most part remained loyal to Enlightenment rationalism and focused their energies on religious reform and refinement, while the Zionists spoke of "revitalization" and "renaissance," peppered with romantic imagery. But both Prague Zionism and the Czech-Jewish movement intended to engage the postwar order in order to effect a change in Czechoslovak society, to tame national tensions, and eventually to overcome the very conflicts out of which they had both emerged.

CHAPTER 2

Caution's Progress

Enlightenment and Tradition
in Jewish Prague, 1780–1830

In the light of contemporary disparities in economic and social development around the world, it is easy to lose sight of the fact that through much of the eighteenth and nineteenth centuries the division between East and West—wealth and poverty, power and insecurity, progress and reaction—was understood to apply to the European continent itself. And, as Robin Okey has argued, the countries of East Central Europe comprised the first world region outside of the West to attempt the social, economic, and cultural transformations to which the term *modernization* commonly refers.[1] Compared with the two great commercial giants of the mid-eighteenth century, England and the Netherlands, both Prussia and the Habsburg monarchy—not to mention Russia—suffered from economic backwardness and underdevelopment. They appeared to possess none of the prerequisites for industrialization and economic expansion, such as capital formation, an advanced state of urbanization, or an international trading network. Yet it was to these lands that the West first directed the twin challenges of capitalist transformation and political liberalism. If they could not hope to replicate the West, monarchs and government officials in East Central Europe could nevertheless try to mold reasonable facsimiles. Taking advantage of their wealth in human and natural resources, while applying fiscal incentives to areas targeted for development, the East European governments could set about the task of accomplishing their own modernization.

Although the monarchies and principalities east of the Rhine often tried to emulate Western patterns of economic and even cultural development, the process of adaptation was never complete. Absolutist rulers, while often "enlightened," were not usually prepared to allow the political and social accompaniments of a market economy to exist alongside more narrowly conceived inducements to economic growth and national consolidation. More often than not, government officials simply grafted an eclectic assortment of economic and social reforms onto a largely hierarchical and corporatist social structure. The lack of ethnic homogeneity in East Central Europe created both a more complicated demographic picture than in the West and an ever-growing potential for social conflict based on linguistic and cultural divisions. As a result, once these states did commit themselves, however uneasily, to "catching up" with the West, a new, regionally distinctive set of problems emerged, prominent among which were intense national rivalries largely unknown in the West.[2]

Just as the transition from a traditional to a modern society in East Central Europe followed its own course, so too did developments in Jewish society in these regions. Modernization in Jewish history consisted of factors both intrinsic to Jewish culture—and hence present over a wide range of local circumstances—and extrinsic to the normal functioning of the local community. This second group of factors consisted primarily of changes imposed on Jewish life from without, often at the instigation of central governments, but resulting from general social and economic developments as well. Specific features in this area of change depended heavily on local political, social, and economic conditions. Thus one can point to no single model of development that would be applicable to all situations. On the contrary, a comparison of similar transformations in different contexts reveals a more complicated pattern in which a small number of universal characteristics of Jewish "modernity" are intertwined with a much larger set of unique circumstances, varied timetables, and end results.

For Jewish communities in Germany, Austria, and Hungary the interplay of intrinsic and extrinsic factors usually took the form of a two-sided erosion of traditional Jewish existence. On the one hand, the independence, cohesiveness, and authority of the autonomous Jewish community broke down under the onslaught of governmental intrusion into its affairs and the steady curtailment of many of its legal functions and prerogatives. At the same time, proponents of the Jewish Enlightenment (*haskalah*), patterned after the European intellectual movement of the eighteenth century, agitated for cultural and educational change within the community according to the standards of Western rationalism and cultural tastes. The two sets of changes worked together in a variety of combinations to produce some of the basic features of modern Jewish history: the elimination of the independent, corporate status of the community; the weakening of rabbinic law (*halakhah*) as a norm for individual and group behavior; the emerging legal status of the individual Jew as citizen of the state; and the elaboration of extensive areas of Jewish and Gentile interaction.

In some instances, cultural change in the Jewish communities of Central and Eastern Europe sprang from direct contact with German-Jewish precedents. Both the friends and the opponents of *haskalah* in the Habsburg monarchy and Russia, for example, acknowledged the movement's German roots. To those Jews eager for a secular, rationalist orientation in Jewish culture, Berlin and Königsberg represented oases of intellectual creativity in a desert of medieval formalism and popular superstition. To those who, on the contrary, feared the caustic effects of manifestos such as Naphtali Herz Wessely's *Words of Peace and Truth,* the same names conjured up the specter of reckless cultural assimilation and religious indifference.[3] One could well argue that it was the dissemination of *haskalah* ideology to communities east and south of Germany that inaugurated the historic split between modernists and traditionalists—indeed between West European Judaism and East European Judaism—of the last century.

If we understand the question of influence to be one of providing a *compelling model* for change and development, then the question of the relationship between the Jewish communities of Germany and those of East Central Europe becomes more difficult. Prussia, after all, is part of East Central Europe. Therefore we must first determine in which circumstances German Jewry constituted an avant garde and in which circumstances it shared the characteristics of the region as a whole. We also must address the correlative question of whether the Jewish communities of Prague, Lwów, or Pest, for example, in the course of their respective modernizations were following cues set by German Jewry or by their own unique cadences. Finally, did the interplay of external and internal factors in the countries of East Central Europe produce a particular prescription for Jewish modernization that applied to the region as a whole and that was not necessarily indebted to the German example?

My goal in this chapter is to address some of these questions while focusing on the major cultural and social changes that were occurring in the Jewish communities of Prague and Bohemia during the late eighteenth and early nineteenth centuries. I first place the general evolution of Bohemian Jewish society in the context of Habsburg policy with regard to Jews and the promotion of social and economic development. This part concludes with an examination of the major external catalysts of change in Bohemian Jewish life: the reforms of the 1780s and 1790s. The chapter then looks at the redirection of Jewish cultural concerns in Prague under the impact of the *haskalah*. It deals primarily with the reception of the *haskalah* in Prague, the contribution of Prague Jews to the program of the *haskalah,* and the overall impact of the so-called Berlin school in the determination of both the tenor and the content of this program. In the last section I examine the practical application of one of the major cultural reforms of the period: the establishment of a secular Jewish school system. A joint government and community venture, the new Jewish schools of Bohemia succeeded in winning the support of a wide spectrum of opinion within the Jewish community. Not only did they play an important part in the acculturation and socialization of Bohemian Jewry from 1782 to 1869, but they also provide the historian with an excellent view of the operation of Enlightenment values in a community as well as insight into the process of cultural transformation.

Absolutism and Reform: The Effects of Partial Modernization

Prague's relatively continuous existence as a Jewish center throughout the medieval and early modern periods—in the face of the removal of the Jews from most royal cities of the region—resulted in the construction of a demographic profile unique to Bohemia. Unlike Germany (which by the end of the sixteenth century had only scattered Jewish settlements of relatively small size), unlike Moravia and Poland (where Jews lived by and large in compact settlements in the private towns and villages of the nobility), and unlike Hungary (where until the end of the eighteenth century the vast majority of the Jews were *Dorfjuden,* living in small clusters of families in isolated villages), no less than half of the Jewish population of Bohemia were densely concentrated at the center. The rest were dispersed in small villages and market towns, few of which contained enough families to support Jewish institutions of their own.[4] In the city of Prague the Jewish population grew from about 6,000 at the start of the seventeenth century to 7,800 in 1636, and finally to 10,000 or 11,000 by the beginning of the eighteenth century, making this Jewish community the third largest in the world.[5]

During this time, the Jewish population in the countryside also underwent unprecedented growth. A royal survey in 1635 indicated that there were some 14,000 Jewish "taxpayers" in Bohemia living outside of Prague (whether a taxpayer was the same as the head of a household is not clear). The first modern census of Bohemian Jewry, taken in 1724, established the number of Jews living in the countryside at 30,000.[6] This figure appears to have remained stable during the early decades of the Familiants Laws and in the immediate aftermath of the temporary expulsion from Prague. A new government census in 1754 revealed that the Jewish population of Bohemia stood at just under 30,000, one third of which was now concentrated in the capital.[7] Over the course of the next century the Jewish population would continue to both grow and disperse. A survey conducted by the Jewish communities in 1849 would detail no fewer than 1,921 localities outside of Prague in which Jews resided. Only 207 of these formed actual communities of more than ten families with a formal synagogue; 148 others managed to assemble a *Betstube* (prayer room) on Sabbaths and holidays by drawing on the resources of neighboring villages.[8] Clearly, the laws that had been designed to limit the size and scope of the Jewish population did not have the desired effects. Growth tempered by rural dispersion emerged the ultimate victor. On the eve of Bohemia's post-1850 industrial expansion, Prague maintained its position of preeminence among the Jewish communities, but the real potential for explosive growth lay in the countryside.

Though the political and economic decline of the Czech lands following the Thirty Years' War resulted in a worsening of the material conditions of Jewish life, it also called into play some of the very processes that would lead to Jewish modernization in the region. The depopulation of the cities and the abandonment of rural landholdings resulted in a shift in economic power from the cities to the countryside and from small freeholders to the landed nobility. At the precise moment that urban-based market economies were developing in Western countries such as England and the Netherlands, feudalism was enjoying a second wind in East Central Europe. The loss of population in the countryside induced the Bohemian nobility to increase the labor obligations of the peasantry and to make it more difficult than previously to leave the land. The decline in urban domestic markets left rural landlords intent on building up large stockpiles of raw materials to sell in

Germany, England, and the Netherlands. Nearly all finished products had to be imported. What small-time production did take place was based in the countryside rather than the city and involved a complicated network of merchant suppliers and domestic producers based on the "putting-out" system.[9] To make matters worse, foreign capital—primarily English—had penetrated the Bohemian linen industry by the end of the seventeenth century, and it was an English firm that succeeded in establishing the first large-scale linen factory in Bohemia in the first half of the eighteenth century.[10]

In the eyes of Habsburg officials, the country lagged visibly behind the West in economic development and, more important, had placed itself in a dangerously weak international position. Cameralist theory of the age held that national wealth and military strength were inextricably tied, that the key sources of a country's wealth lay in its population and its natural resources, and that commodities ought not to be sold outside of the country until they had become more costly finished products.[11] Proponents of mercantilism had periodically urged the government in Vienna to institute economic reforms along these lines as early as the late seventeenth century. But it was not until the second half of the eighteenth century (particularly in the last third) that such policies were applied with any consistency. At this point the state intervened directly to promote industry, limit foreign investment, and check the flow of natural resources from the country. It encouraged the growth of industry by offering subsidies and tax exemptions, removing the newer economic sectors from the purview of the guilds, and easing discriminatory restrictions toward Protestants and members of other religious minorities who were willing to establish new ventures. The state similarly sought to modernize transportation systems, abolish internal tariffs, and promote a unified customs policy.[12]

Much of this activity proceeded in a social and economic vacuum. No ready-made work force in the form of a large urban population existed. No international trading centers or investment banks were ready to lend financial support and commercial contacts. Nor had Austro-Bohemian culture produced to date the kind of individual entrepreneurial spirit that had emerged in some of the Protestant countries to the west and been responsible in large part for the private economic initiatives that had accompanied the beginnings of industrialization. At the same time, the government did not engage in any sweeping overhaul of traditional forms of social organization or methods of economic production. Ancient privileged orders continued to defend their prerogatives in the Diets and at the court. Government officials often worked at cross purposes to one another, defending privilege in one instance, promoting rationalization and uniformity in another. As a result, government-sponsored modernization never received an unambiguous mandate and, when it did move, appeared to do so at half speed.

The results of this partial modernization were likewise half-hearted. Aristocratic and middle-class *Fabrikanten* were recruited, internal tariffs within the two separate halfs of the monarchy were abolished, and textile manufacturing became a vital part of the Bohemian-Moravian economy. But the Habsburg monarchy still found it difficult to create a vibrant group of middle-class producers; the customs division between Austria and Hungary remained in effect until 1851, and the extent of industrial production in the country remained far below that of England. The picture in Prussia and other German states did not differ markedly. German cities had been more actively engaged in international trade than almost any Habsburg city. German ports were busier, their lines of transport and communication more efficient. With the exception of Saxony and Silesia, however, industrial production in the German states and in the Habsburg monarchy proceeded at about the same pace. Only after 1830, and especially after 1850, did the economic development of Germany break away from that of its southern neighbor. In the second half of the nineteenth century—during Germany's industrial revolution—the Habsburg monarchy made considerable progress of its own but could not match her northern neighbor in any of the key areas of output, number of plants, or technological sophistication.[13]

Half-heartedness notwithstanding, Habsburg efforts to catch up with the West while promoting national strength were to have a major impact on the course of Jewish life at the transition from the eighteenth century to the nineteenth century. Government recruitment of entrepreneurial talent, the easing of religious and social restrictions for those engaged in economic development, the promotion of universal education, and periodic assaults on the autonomy of medieval corporations loomed large as agents in this transformation. Yet, as with the general economic trends, change within the Jewish community appeared to proceed in an artificial context, spurred on by government initiative and Jewish visions of social integration and advancement, but deprived of wider social and cultural supports. As with general modernization, government policies concerning the Jews were often contradictory and self-defeating: supporters of feudal privilege clashed head-on with advocates of sweeping change; both punitive restrictions and the promise of social acceptance were dangled before the eyes of the Jewish population.

Joseph II, who ruled with his mother Maria Theresa as co-regent from 1765 to 1780 and then alone for the final ten years of his life, came to exemplify more than any other ruler the enlightened monarch, acting on rational principles to transform state and society. The nineteenth-century Jewish apologist Joseph von Wertheimer referred to his namesake as "a despot, like the spring, which breaks apart the winter's ice."[14] Joseph II had put in motion a number of political and economic reforms while his mother was still alive, but he stayed clear of direct involvement in Jewish affairs until he enjoyed complete control over the direction of government policy. Beginning in 1780 he began to act, and with his famous *Toleranzpatent* (issued for Bohemia in October, 1781 and for Moravia in February, 1782), he ushered in an era of conscious social, economic, and cultural reform.[15]

The edict represented but one small part of a much larger package of reforming measures, which included the application of religious tolerance to Austrian Protestants, the partial liberation of the peasantry from ties to the feudal domain, and the institution of compulsory elementary education. Joseph II's goal was to break down traditional societal privileges and remove barriers to economic growth—not to bequeath special privileges to the Jews, nor even to end the population and settlement restrictions under which they had been living since the early part of the century.[16] The emperor expressed his intentions from the outset in quite practical terms: "To make the numerous members of the Jewish national in my hereditary lands more useful to the state." He set out to transform the cultural outlook, social patterns, and occupational distribution of the Jews to better serve the interests of the developing state without altering the legal status of the Jewish corporation and without encouraging any further growth of the Jewish population.[17]

As we saw in chapter 1, the *Toleranzpatent* proved to be a disappointment in the economic sphere. Its provisions in this area had only a modest effect on Jewish social and occupational structures. Individual Jews did take advantage of the new mercantilism of the state and established industrial enterprises in the late eighteenth and early nineteenth centuries. But the occupational distribution of the Bohemian Jewish community remained fairly stable between the 1770s and the 1830s. No radical reshaping of the economic structure of the community occurred as a result of the edict. In the areas of communal autonomy, education, and popular culture, however, the Jewish legislation that poured out from Vienna in the 1780s and 1790s did create immediate and lasting results. The *Toleranzpatent* erased overnight the use of Hebrew and Yiddish in public records and business transactions. It encouraged Jewish communities to establish German-language, or "normal," elementary schools, with state-approved teachers and curricula. In areas where the Jewish community was too small to support a school of its own, Jewish children were welcomed to attend Christian primary and secondary schools. The universities of the monarchy, which had been removed from Jesuit control in 1773 and been completely secularized in 1782, were declared open to Jewish attendance.[18]

Subsequent edicts bolstered the cultural provisions of the early Josephine reform and further transformed the social and legal character of the community. The judicial autonomy of the Jewish community in civil and criminal matters was suspended in 1784. An ordinance of 1786 made the granting of marriage certificates to Jews dependent on the parties' ability to demonstrate that they had attended a *Normalschule*. Legislation the following year made mandatory the adoption of German personal and family names. In 1788 Jews were required to serve in the Austrian army. Finally, in 1797—in a law that was never completely enforced—the state required that all rabbis and cantors to be appointed by the Jewish community produce a degree in philosophy from one of the monarchy's institutions of higher learning.[19]

By the beginning of the nineteenth century government policy had made important strides toward altering the traditional complexion of Jewish life within the realm. It had declared a vested interest in the education, political loyalties, and economic contributions of its Jewish subjects. As yet, however, it was content to destroy the medieval autonomy of the Jewish community without incorporating the Jews into the social fabric of the state. Political reforms could raze the cultural defenses of the Jewish community but they left intact the ghetto walls.

Traditionalism and Change:
The Reception of the *Haskalah* in Prague

No amount of government interference could, by itself, effect a reorientation in Jewish cultural patterns. Significant changes in religious practice and belief, group attitudes, and shared knowledge and values required an extended period of time in which to evolve and were as much the result of subtle redirections and adaptations as of any articulated

program for change. The fact remains, however, that the reform measures of Habsburg officials coincided with the beginnings of a Jewish
movement for cultural readjustment, most audible in Germany, but
promoted by some members of the Prague and Bohemian Jewish communities as well. The *haskalah* movement in Prague found adherents at
first only within a small group among the wealthy and educated members of the community. In the context of Bohemia, Jewish Enlightenment may have been less a by-product of increased economic opportunity and social mobility than a prescription for such developments—not
so much an indicator of social transformation as an instrument for
change in its own right.[20]

If one were to divide the Prague *haskalah* into four stages, as Ruth
Kestenberg-Gladstein has done in her opus on the subject, one might
begin by remarking that in its earliest phase the movement took the
form of a received ideology.[21] The 1780s saw a handful of Prague Jewish
figures reacting to impulses whose origin lay outside of their own
community: following with interest such developments within the
Mendelssohnian circle in Berlin as the appearance of the *Bi'ur,* the
translation of the Pentateuch into literary German with an accompanying Hebrew commentary; subscribing to German-Jewish publications;
and even making original contributions to the mouthpiece of the German *haskalah, Ha-me'asef.* But participation in the Jewish Enlightenment at that point was limited by and large to the reception of signals
sent from abroad and the application of their messages to the context at
home.[22] During the 1790s Prague still seemed to be taking its cues from
Berlin. Now, however, Prague's home-grown *maskilim* (followers of the
haskalah) were beginning to react negatively to a number of aspects of
the German movement, including its open hostility toward Jewish law
and traditions and, significantly, the mocking disrespect that *Ha-me'asef*
editors had displayed toward the late Chief Rabbi Ezekiel Landau.[23]

In the later two stages of the *haskalah* movement in Prague (approximately 1800 to 1830), the city's *maskilim* appear to have succeeded in
striking out on their own and making some truly original contributions.[24] Yet something of a paradox was at work here. Though Prague
Jews were not directly imbibing the dictates of taste or the cultural in-
novations emanating from Germany, they were reacting to them
nonetheless. They may have been striving to achieve a style and vision
of their own, but their point of reference remained the German model.
Thus, while the Berlin *haskalah* put forward a program of radical religious and educational reform and displayed indifference to the role of

halakhah in Jewish life, the Prague *haskalah* insisted upon the sanctity of law and tradition. Prague's *maskilim* confidently pursued a policy of accommodation, weaving together European rationalism, respect for religious sensitivities, and loyalty to Jewish traditions. While *maskilim* in Berlin sought to further the prospects for political emancipation by eliminating national and ethnic components from Jewish culture, their Prague counterparts appeared to be remarkably free of such self-imposed burdens. Bolstered, perhaps, by the multiethnic realities of the Habsburg monarchy, Prague's *maskilim* proved to be more sensitive to the national context of Jewish existence and did not hesitate to portray their community as one nation among others.[25]

The tone of moderation and traditionalism, so characteristic of the Prague *haskalah,* was not necessarily unique to this city. Yet the notion of a conservative Enlightenment with quasi-national overtones may indeed have comprised the essence of Prague's contribution to the Jewish Enlightenment.[26] The sources of this conservatism lay in the areas of institutional leadership and what might be termed "cultural geography." Prague's rabbinate, under the direction of Ezekiel Landau and Eleazar Fleckeles, enjoyed tremendous prestige both at home and abroad. It is safe to assume that these men possessed a greater ability than their counterparts in Western Europe to either thwart or approve measures that could affect the nature of Jewish life in their community. Hence the attitude of such personalities toward the spread of the *haskalah* as well as toward the growing interest of the central government in Jewish affairs may have been crucial to the fortunes of change in Jewish Prague.

Ezekiel Landau entertained serious reservations about the social and political effects of Joseph's *Toleranzpatent* and condemned all efforts to upset the balance in traditional Jewish education. Yet (as will become clear in the section on the *Normalschule*) he determined from the beginning to exert his influence on the course of change rather than simply condemn it out of hand. Landau's critical views on the *haskalah* emerged in his sermons to the community. On the occasion of *Shabbat hagadol* 1782, which fell between the issuance of the *Toleranzpatent* and the opening of the Prague *Normalschule,* Landau made direct reference to the major events of the day. He lavished praise on the salutory intentions of the emperor; in the same breath he also warned his congregants not to alter their political conceptions, not to be overcome with pride and cease to treat with respect "the people of the state who own the land, for we are but strangers."[27] Having recently read Wessely's program for educational reform in the Hebrew pamphlet *Divrei shalom ve-'emet,* Landau remarked: "I have seen a world turned upside down.... A wicked and arrogant man has arisen from our nation for whom the Torah is not worth anything, for whom profane subjects are better than the study of Torah."[28]

Landau was willing to accommodate unavoidable changes in the political sphere and even to appropriate the technical expertise of Western culture, but no innovation in politics or education could be allowed to threaten the foundations of Jewish faith.

In truth, the substance of the thing—to improve manners and to know the grammar of the language of the Gentiles [*dikduk halashon ha-'amim*]—I, too, praise highly. And how good it is [for us] that the government has taken upon itself to accustom us to speak properly.... For he who fears the Lord, he truly understands [*einav berosho*]; he is able to hold fast to both matters [sacred and profane], but Torah is central. Nevertheless, he also learns this [Gentile] language [and] the correct manners to guide a person along the right way. Any [sacred] learning that does not include practical employment leads to idleness; indeed the essence of our activity is commerce, hence one needs to know language and writing.[29]

"The core is faith," Landau exhorted. Faith had to be protected from the incursions of rationalism and scientific inquiry. In his summation, Landau charged the Jews of Prague to submit both to God and the king, but to keep clear of all who would change the nature of Jewish belief and practice. The challenge of the age, he was convinced, was to educate oneself in Western science and language but to resist the temptation to apply the tools of the Enlightenment to the sacred body of revealed truths.[30]

For Landau the entire question of *haskalah* revolved around two sets of distinctions: sacred versus profane knowledge, and technical versus substantive change. It was on the basis of these sets of oppositions that he decided which cultural programs to support and which to oppose. The educational provisions of the *Toleranzpatent* received his approval primarily because he was able to insure that the new schools would exist only as supplementary institutions whose curriculum did not threaten the integrity of the traditional talmudic education. But he vehemently opposed programs such as Wessely's, which sought to transform the nature of Jewish education. He also disapproved of such ostensibly neutral enterprises as Mendelssohn's translation of, and commentary on, the Pentateuch (the *Bi'ur,* 1780–83). In a 1786 communication Landau explained that he had withheld approbation of the work precisely because Mendelssohn's translation had surpassed the bounds of what was necessary for a plain understanding of the Hebrew text:

I refused because in the work printed at the time the holy and the profane were joined together.... We fear that this foreign element will prove a stumbling block to Jewish children and lead to the neglect of the study of Torah.... The translator deeply immersed himself in the language, using as he did an extremely difficult German that presupposes expertise in its grammar.... It induces the young to spend their time reading Gentile books in order to become sufficiently familiar with refined German to be able to understand this translation. Our Torah is thereby reduced to the role of a maidservant to the German tongue.[31]

The strong positions taken by conservatives such as Landau may have engendered tension between the leadership of the Prague community and the early *maskilim*. Evidence of mild generational conflict, for example, does exist.[32] The remarkable thing about Prague, however, is that fathers and sons on the whole did not divide. In fact, from 1790 to 1810 Prague *maskilim* stood out as staunch defenders of the rabbinic leadership. The *maskil* Baruch Jeitteles (1762–1813) submitted a eulogy for Landau to *Ha-me'asef* following Landau's death in 1793. He then reacted with a bitter attack on the periodical when it ridiculed the eulogy and its object of praise. Later, Jeitteles joined forces with Rabbi Eleazar Fleckeles in denouncing the influence of Frankists within the Prague Jewish community.[33] Israel Landau, the late chief rabbi's youngest son, dominated *haskalah* publishing in Prague during the last decade of the century with works not only in philology and geography but also in popular *halakhic* education.[34]

Bohemia's proximity to the traditional societies of Poland, Hungary, and, indeed, Moravia also contributed to its traditional complexion. And the effects of the *Familiantengesetze*, which forced younger sons to emigrate in order to marry and establish households, intensified whatever ties geography alone may have produced. A network of intimate family connections extended from Bohemia to the east and north wherever younger family branches were able to establish themselves. Ezekiel Landau's immediate family provides interesting examples of such crosscommunal ties. His eldest son, Jacob, a rabbi in his own right who made his living as a merchant, settled in Brody, where his father had once served as *dayyan*. There he apparently maintained cordial relations with representatives of the Galician *haskalah*.[35] Israel Landau, though born and raised in Prague, married a Polish Jew with whom he had two sons. She apparently became alarmed at the "liberal" spirit of Jewish life in the city and pleaded with her husband to leave Prague and return with her and their children to Poland. Landau demurred; his wife demanded and received a bill of divorce (*get*). She then settled with the two boys in Poland, and her husband set out to find a new wife. This time he chose someone from a progressive Dutch-Jewish family.[36] One of the sons from the first marriage became a rabbi in Brody. A son from the second marriage, Moses (M. I.) Landau, established himself as a printer and publisher in Prague, producing works in Hebrew and German, including several volumes of the periodical *Kerem ḥemed*.[37]

Even when the *Familiantengesetze* themselves played no obvious role, Poland's proximity loomed large. The Landaus had long been one of the most powerful Jewish families in Opatów; at the time that Ezekiel Landau was approached by the Prague community to fill the vacant position of chief rabbi, he was serving in a similar capacity in Jampol, Podolia.[38] In the decades after 1754, students from Poland as well as other parts of Central Europe flocked to Prague to attend Landau's *yeshivah*. As late as 1840, Prague continued to look to Poland to fill its highest rabbinical post. In this year the Galician scholar Solomon Judah Rapoport was called to Prague from Tarnopol; he served the community for the next twenty-seven years.[39]

It would, nevertheless, be something of a distortion to conclude that the Prague *haskalah*, in its search for a "third way" between radicalism and traditionalism, set off on a course completely different from that of its German predecessor. The German *haskalah* itself was a multidimensional phenomenon, not all of whose features were either radical or anti-*halakhic*. More important, Prague's *maskilim* had neither the size nor the independence to maintain a distinct movement with its own publications. Only during one brief period, in 1802, did they manage to create their own organization, the Gesellschaft der jungen Hebräer, and produce their own journal, the *Jüdisch-deutsche Monatschrift*. Even then the enterprise lasted for only six months.[40] Thereafter, as in the 1780s and 1790s, the *maskilim* in Prague had to rely on outside publications both for reading materials and as vehicles for the dissemination of their own writing.

One such outlet, the periodical *Sulamith*, proved to be quite compatible with their conception of moderation in change. Published in Dessau by Joseph Wolf and David Fraenkel, *Sulamith* was to serve as the principal sounding board for Prague Jewish figures such as Ignaz Jeitteles, Peter Beer, M. I. Landau, and S. Löwisohn well into the second decade of the nineteenth century.[41] The editors intended the periodical to play the role of mediator both within the Jewish community—reconciling Jewish Enlightenment ideas with mainstream Judaism—and between Jews and the outside world. *Sulamith*'s task, in the words of Joseph Wolf, was to step forth "out of the midst of an oppressed nation" and act as "peacemaker between this nation and its opponents."[42] Though Dessau may have been in Anhalt and not Prussia, *Sulamith* was nevertheless a German enterprise that eventually provided the enlightened members of the Prague Jewish community with a sympathetic ear and a ready press.

Kestenberg-Gladstein has argued that the truly distinctive aspect of the Prague *haskalah*—that which most completely separated it from its Western namesake—was its national orientation.[43] The *maskilim* of Bohemia, according to this view, revealed a genuine appreciation not only for the multiethnic character of the Habsburg realm but also for the unique national qualities of Jewish existence. They peppered their treatises with German words such as *Nation* and Hebrew words such as *'am* (loosely translated as nation, or people), *'amei ha-'arez* (peoples of the land), and *'amei ha-'olam* (peoples of the world)—all of which are said to have resonated, to the contemporary ear at least, with national significance. And when members of the Gesellschaft der jungen Hebräer published historical studies in the *Monatschrift*, they raised preexisting ethnic sensibilities to a level of national pride, endeavoring to awaken in the hearts of their readers a true sense of belonging to "ihrer verachteten Nation" (their despised nation).[44]

One can easily be lured, however, into reading into the writings of the Prague *haskalah* more than was actually there. What better place than Prague, neatly situated between Western Enlightenment and Eastern traditionalism, to bring forth a unique brand of modern Jewish culture? A *haskalah* of this type would not only have tiptoed cautiously around the domain of the sacred in Judaism but would also have retained cognizance of that essentially national dimension of Judaism that was to survive the convulsive journey from ghetto life to Zionism. Such a reading, unfortunately, is fraught with dangers, not the least of which is anachronism. Terms of speech that in the second half of the nineteenth century betokened an anticosmopolitan view of group affinities often had no such connotation either before or during the *haskalah*.[45] Israel Landau's autobiographical introduction appended to his 1793 edition of *Iggeret 'orhot 'olam* (Epistle of the ways of the world) by Abraham Farissol provides a good case in point.

The younger Landau's ostensible purposes in composing the introduction were to describe how he had gone about the task of issuing a critical edition of this Renaissance work and to thank the people and institutions that had aided him along the way. The university libraries of Prague and Vienna had made a particularly strong impression. Landau was grateful to have been allowed to drink from the "wellsprings of knowledge" together with the non-Jewish subjects of the monarchy, and, in language borrowed from biblical and rabbinic literature, he prophesied about the future cooperation and peaceful coexistence of the peoples of the land:

There many from among the nations of the land meet; and permission is given to the Jews as well to turn here and there. To their questions they will find answers. There the waters of strife will be calmed. There fellowship and love will reign. Coming from all the nations, they sit together around the table, secure and serene, like fresh, green olive shoots.[46]

Landau in fact invoked long-standing terminology, such as *'amei ha-'arez,* in order to subvert that terminology's pre-*haskalah* meaning. What he meant to convey was that the experience of secular intellectual endeavor broke down divisions among ethnic groups. A common fellowship was achieved at such "neutral" sites of encounter as the library, where the universal, if ancient, ideals of peace, serenity, and love were to be realized. In this instance, as in others, his sentiments coincided neatly with the social vision of the German *haskalah.*

Hence one cannot speak of nationalism in the modern sense of the word—as a movement designed to express (and achieve) a congruence between political sovereignty and ethnic distinctiveness (real or imagined)—in reference to the thought of the Prague *maskilim.* When they were not speaking in traditional categories, they were invoking the basic ideals of the *haskalah.* Self-improvement through education and cultivation of the eighteenth-century ideal of virtue dominated the themes of Jewish writing in Prague. The practical bent of the Prague movement led to an emphasis on *Volkserziehung,* but the ultimate purpose of national education was not to accentuate feelings of Jewish distinctiveness. What mattered was *Bildung,* and tactics such as reaching out to the masses in their everyday language were aimed at bringing Jews closer to the aesthetic considerations and social values of the European Enlightenment. One might even invoke *gedolei 'am yisrael* (great Jewish figures), but one did so simply to demonstrate that models of virtue could be found in the Jewish past. These works stopped short of expressly articulating the conviction that Jews of the proper educational and moral standing were worthy of inclusion in the polite society of Enlightened Europe. But the message lay very close to the surface.[47]

In the end, an essential identity of interests linked the cultural programs of Berlin and Prague. The *haskalah* in Bohemia did possess unique features born of the political environment of the Habsburg monarchy and both a physical and spiritual closeness to the Jewish culture of Eastern Europe. Indeed, when interest in *Sulamith* waned after 1820, those *maskilim* who could still write in Hebrew found an outlet in the Vienna publications of the Galician *haskalah*. Still, on the question of the overall purposes of the *haskalah*, Prague and Berlin displayed a common front. Prague's representatives may have preferred to show more respect and deference to normative Jewish practice and beliefs, but this was a question of style or tone more than of substance. The German model exerted an inescapable influence on the Prague *haskalah*. The Gesellschaft der jungen Hebräer paid homage to Berlin in unambiguous terms when it chose to introduce its own publication with the motto of that city's association of enlightened Jews, the Gesellschaft der Freunde. The words were from Mendelssohn: "We are called upon and dedicated by our ancestors to be righteous, and, in our righteousness, happy; called upon and dedicated to strive for truth, to love *beauty*, to will what *is good*, and to do one's *best*; called upon and dedicated to worship and to do good deeds."[48]

Bildung in the Jewish Community: The Role of Educational Reform

The point at which government interference in Jewish affairs and the ideology of the *haskalah* most neatly coincided was in the area of educational policy. The promise of directing the scope and content of Jewish education for generations to come, of being able to mold attitudes and behavior, loyalties and beliefs, captured the imaginations of both Jewish illuminati and Gentile authorities. Central European *maskilim* were quick to pick up on Joseph II's call for the Jewish communities of the Habsburg monarchy either to establish state-supervised elementary schools of their own or else send their children to existing non-Jewish schools. *Maskilim* recognized in this call an invitation not only to alter the worldview of traditional Judaism but also to create a new kind of Jewish individual, educated in Western science and languages, committed to the use of reason in determining questions of truth and value, loyal to king and to country, and loving of his fellow citizen.[49]

The educational reforms, which were directed at the Jewish community after 1781, grew out of a general educational program that had already been set in motion during the reign of Maria Theresa. In 1774 a commission led by Johann Ignaz Felbiger established a new system of elementary education for the hereditary lands, and in the following year the ordinance was applied to Bohemia. Felbiger's *Allgemeine Schulordnung* called for the establishment of a *Trivialschule* (common school) in every village and market town in the countryside, at least one *Hauptschule* in every administrative district, and a *Normalschule* (teachers' training school) in every province.[50] The centerpiece of the new educational system in Bohemia was to be the Imperial and Royal Normalschule of Prague, opened in November 1775 at the site of a former Jesuit gymnasium in the city's Kleinseite (Malá Strana, or Lesser Town).[51]

The imperial government had made a tentative move to include the Jews of Bohemia in the new educational policy as early as 1776, when Maria Theresa suggested to the governor's office that Jewish schools, too, be established "nach dem Normallehrplane." At the time, Jewish leaders opposed the idea, arguing that the children needed all of the hours of the day for religious study and prayer.[52] By 1782, however, not only had the Jewish community ceased to oppose calls for educational reform, it now appeared to welcome them genuinely. A number of events had intervened in the meantime. Joseph II had succeeded his mother as sole ruler of the kingdom; in 1781 he had issued a decree for compulsory elementary education throughout the realm, and that same year he had bestowed his *Toleranzpatent* on the Jews of Bohemia.

Much of the credit for the success of the program lay in the adroit choice of supervisory personnel. Ferdinand Kindermann von Schulstein (1750-1801), a liberal-minded priest and educator, had been called to Vienna in 1774 to supervise the establishment of the new German schools of Bohemia. A tireless traveler who easily conveyed the depths of his own enthusiasm and commitment, Kindermann enjoyed wide-ranging success both in the Bohemian countryside and in Prague. In 1782 Joseph II chose him to oversee the establishment of the new Jewish schools as well. Kindermann approached his new role with no less determination than he had shown in the past and added a diplomatic skill that allowed him to disarm even the most wary conservatives.[53]

Almost from the start, Jewish lay leaders and notables scrambled over one another to demonstrate their readiness to accommodate the new decree. The Prague community began construction of a new building for its German school even before the government had resolved where the necessary monies were to come from. *Hauslehrer* (private tutors) selected to serve in the new teaching corps hurriedly learned the proper pedagogical methods at the Kleinseite *Normalschule*. And on 2 May 1782 the new school opened amidst great celebration. Morning services on this day included special psalms and prayers in honor of the monarch. A *Festgottesdienst* took place at the Maisel synagogue, where a prayer in verse, composed by the chief rabbi, was sung by a renowned Jewish vocalist from Mannheim. From the synagogue a ceremonial procession made its way to the new school building, where opening ceremonies were conducted. Count Karl Clary, the president of the royal *Schulkommission;* Deacon Kindermann; and the school director, Schindler, occupied places of honor, surrounded by dignitaries of the Prague Jewish community, including Ezekiel Landau, Stadtprimator Israel Simon Frankel, members of the rabbinical court, and communal elders. Speeches and laudatory addresses highlighted the occasion. Fireworks closed the day's celebrations.[54]

Not to be outdone, the *Landesjudenschaft,* represented by its president Joachim Popper and the *Landesdeputierten,* met with Kindermann during the winter semester of 1781-82 and easily resolved to carry out the reforms with dispatch. The Jewish leaders agreed that in places where the local community could not manage to build a new school building, German topics could be taught in the synagogue school at times when religious instruction (*Religionsunterricht*) was not going on. In general, the larger communities were to construct new schools. Those of middle size could contract with teachers in the Christian schools to teach Jewish children after hours. Families who lived in isolated villages would either have to make do with home tutors or send their children to the local schools. The rural communities chose to build thirty-four new establishments as a first step in the new educational venture.[55]

The apparent enthusiasm displayed by Jewish elites in Prague and Bohemia can be explained, in part, in terms of political lessons drawn from centuries of experience. Joseph II had sent signals that he intended to see the implementation of universal elementary education through to completion. The only prudent path for Jewish leaders was to show the willingness to comply. Some had already begun to show an interest in the educational and political programs of the *haskalah.* Encouraged by the *Toleranzpatent,* they saw in its educational provisions an opportunity not to be squandered. None of these factors, however, is sufficient to explain the near unanimity of support given to the school project in Bohemia. Indeed, the incursion of *haskalah* attitudes into the community had the potential of engendering open conflict. Yet the absence of public controversy over the schools distinguished Prague from communities in Galicia and Hungary, and the movement on the part of the rabbinical establishment in Prague from mere acquiescence to actual participation in the project further differentiated this Jewish center from others in East Central Europe.

For Ezekiel Landau to have concluded that the German-Jewish schools would pose no direct threat to the traditional sources of moral authority within the community was in itself a remarkable achievement. It could only have resulted from the careful diplomacy of Ferdinand Kindermann, from his ability to make potentially transformative reforms ride safely on a sea of moderation. Kindermann had resolved from the start to include the chief rabbi in his advisory council, to clear with him all details concerning the new curriculum, and to agree on the structural features of the new institution.[56] Subsequent negotiations between government officials and the rabbinic leadership produced results that could only have relieved traditionalists within the community. The German school was to consist of four classes, and students would generally not enter before their tenth birthday, thus providing time for them to receive a grounding in Torah before they came into contact with secular subjects. The hours of instruction were kept at a minimum: four hours daily during the summer months—with the exception of Saturday—and only two hours during the winter. The remaining time was reserved for religious instruction and prayer in the synagogue schools (*ḥadarim*), which continued to function alongside the *Normalschulen*. The government succeeded in establishing as a minimum requirement that students should remain in attendance at the German-Jewish schools until they had mastered the prescribed curriculum in reading, writing, arithmetic, and ethics.[57]

No differences existed between Jewish and non-Jewish curricula in technical subjects such as grammar, arithmetic, physical science, and geography. In fact, the same textbooks were used in both kinds of schools. On the other hand, the commonly used German language readers contained moral lessons drawn from Christian teachings and employed Christian religious imagery. At the start of the reforms, then, Kindermann faced the enormous task of adapting existing texts—with offensive passages excised—for use in the Jewish schools.[58] The effort proved to be quite trying, and Kindermann may finally have provoked the disapproval of rabbinical authorities. He alluded to this fact with some exasperation in a letter to Moses Mendelssohn:

What caused us some embarrassment at the time was the fact that the work was attacked the moment it was started.... The principal purpose in modeling the reader on part two of our own [reader] was to instruct Jewish youths in the social virtues and to guide them toward this end in community with others.... This surely is the great purpose: to make this nation more refined in manners and more sociable toward us, having hitherto been at such a distance.

We therefore tried to eliminate ... everything that was peculiar to the Christian religion. We inserted after every moral chapter ... a moral story by some highly reputed author, and we did this not only in order to make the tuition more concrete, entertaining, and comprehensible to the Jewish children, but also because ... the Jewish nation is descended from people who were fond of instruction by imagery and parable.

Altogether, our endeavor in the reader and in the entire constitution of this work of school reform was to start the thing in a manner suited to the spirit, mental capacity, and present needs as well as future destiny of this nation.[59]

The difficulties that Kindermann's efforts encountered were never completely resolved. Moses Wiener, who was hired to teach German grammar and composition, produced his own *Lesebuch für jüdische Kinder* in 1784, but it too apparently contained passages said to be "contrary to religion." It may have been of some consolation that Mendelssohn bestowed the work with his own approbation, and it never faced any serious challenge from the community. Wiener's *Lesebuch* remained the principal vehicle for linguistic and moralistic instruction until it was replaced by a new text in 1813.[60]

How popular, in fact, were the *Normalschulen*, and how effective were they as vehicles for the "reeducation" of Bohemian and Moravian Jews? Ludvík Singer, the Czech-Jewish historian (and Zionist) may have been overly optimistic when he characterized the new venture in the 1930s as "auffällig und segensreich" (noteworthy and prosperous).[61] Kestenberg-Gladstein, for one, has argued that neither Enlightenment reforms generally nor the German-Jewish schools in particular made great inroads in Prague before the 1820s.[62] She points out that the Prague school, unlike similar ventures in northern Germany, did not become a vehicle for the diffusion of *haskalah*, but maintained throughout its connection to the Orthodox Jewish establishment and pursued a narrow course of study in the technical arts and sciences. Traditional Jewish topics—Bible, Mishnah, Talmud, and Codes—were cut off from the *Normalschule* curriculum and shielded from the potentially negative effects of *haskalah* rationalism. The school's board of overseers, even when it included moderate enlighteners such as M. I. Landau and Juda Jeitteles, represented the traditional social and cultural elite of the community. It fought successfully to prevent the administration of the school from falling into the hands of radicals such as Peter Beer and Herz Homberg, preferring instead to hire Christian headmasters who would not attempt to influence the handling of Jewish subjects or impose the values of the more radical elements of the Berlin *haskalah*.[63]

Equally as important as the conservatism of the new schools was the fact that they did not stand as the sole vehicles for schooling (Jewish or otherwise) within the community. A Jewish family in Prague could choose from at least three different paths in the education of its children: traditional study in the *ḥeder* and *yeshivah;* private tutoring in the home (a favorite choice of the wealthy); the Jewish *Normalschule,* followed perhaps by a public, that is, Christian, *Gymnasium;* or a combination of these. Finally, there remained an untold number of children who refrained from attending any type of school. The first and last methods were not likely to produce the kinds of results desired either by *maskilim* or government ministers, although a ready pool of *maskilim* and educators emerged from the ranks of the *yeshivah*-educated in the 1770s and 1780s. Many of these people had been earning their living as private tutors when the provisions of the *Toleranzpatent* were announced. They quickly entered the teacher-training institute associated with the *Normalschule,* eager to be sent to small towns throughout the Habsburg monarchy to inculcate Jewish children with the new learning.[64] These private tutors could just as easily have transmitted *haskalah* attitudes and taught Western languages and science in the context of their former employment, and many undoubtedly did. In the end, we may never know whether private tutoring or communal education had the greater impact on the cultural transformation of Central European Jewry during this time, since neither statistics nor adequate biographical material is available to make a judgment on education in the home.

Moreover, in order to determine the number (and percentage) of Jewish children who attended the German-Jewish schools, we are left to rely on scattered printed sources that detail Jewish school attendance with varying degrees of completeness. Singer cites a semiofficial pamphlet of 1784 as well as a section of J. A. Riegger's *Materialien zur alten und neuen Statistik von Böhmen.*[65] Kestenberg-Gladstein bases her analysis on Johann Wanniczek's 1832 history of the school, which contained a *Schulbesuchkalender* for the years 1790 to 1831.[66] To these one can add a jubilee retrospective written by Herz Klaber and published in Prague in 1833.[67] The statistical information contained in these materials does not really allow for definitive conclusions; in fact, discrepancies exist among the published sources, and several short-term fluctuations in the curve cry out for explanation. The 1784 report, for example, sets the number of Jewish students at the Prague *Normalschule* at 347 and those in the Bohemian *Trivialschulen* at 584.[68] Government statistics for 1787 claim that 559 students were in attendance at twenty-five rural Jewish schools; in fifty-six additional localities, 278 Jewish children attended Christian schools. The first figure is said to represent an increase of 25 percent in one year, the second a jump of over 100 percent.[69] On the other hand, Wanniczek recounts that the Prague institution in 1790—which at this time also included a girls' school—attracted only 215 boys and 63 girls; over the next eight years, the number of students tended to drop and rise precipitously from one semester to the next.[70]

Some of the fluctuations in the fortunes of the *Normalschule* might be explained in terms of the ebb and flow of government interest in its own venture, some in terms of generational change. Under Joseph II and Leopold II—that is, until 1792—the state appears to have been eager to promote Jewish attendance. Beginning in 1786, for example, Jews who wished to acquire a marriage license had to demonstrate to the satisfaction of officials that they had attended a *Normalschule;* predictably, the schools were considerably more filled the following year than they had been in the recent past. And if, as Herz Klaber relates, attendance fell off once again between 1796 and 1812, the decline might well be attributed to government inattentiveness in the context of prolonged war with revolutionary and Napoleonic France.[71] Starting again in 1811, however, the state provided the German-Jewish schools with a number of important boosts. The first occurred with the appointment of the Bohemian-born *maskil* Peter Beer (1758–1839) as instructor in ethics at the Prague *Normalschule*—a position that offered Beer an ideal forum for the dissemination of Enlightenment attitudes concerning Judaism and Jewish history. At this time, too, members of the Jewish community who themselves had been educated at the *Normalschule* began to assume administrative and teaching positions. In 1812 two new overseers were named: Samuel Dormitzer, who also served as "Imperial and Royal" director of taxes, and Simon Hock, a businessman and amateur historian who had graduated from the *Normalschule* and had gone on to receive a doctor of law degree.[72] When Dormitzer stepped down in 1815 he was replaced by another graduate of the institution, the printer-scholar M. I. Landau, future head of the Prague Jewish community and grandson of Ezekiel Landau. In 1818 the radical *maskil* Herz Homberg, having already served the emperor as a teacher in Trieste and Galicia, was named instructor in religious ethics for Prague gymnasia students and Jewish private tutors—a sure indication of the breadth of Enlightenment indoctrination in the capital as well as of the greater participation of Jewish students in non-Jewish establishments.[73] Homberg's textbook of Jewish morality, *B'nei Zion*, had already been designated an obligatory part of the curriculum for all Jewish children; since 1813, prospective Jewish brides and grooms were required to pass an examination in the book before they could get a marriage license. Now all Jewish gymnasium students and private tutors (*Hauslehrer*) had to receive instruction in the teaching methods of *B'nei Zion* from Homberg himself.[74]

The real turning point for the schools may have taken place in 1815, when Anton Raaz, formerly director of the non-Jewish *Hauptschule* in Kutná Hora, was appointed director of the Prague Jewish school. Raaz approached his new job with energy and dedication and provided the school with both the organization and the sense of purpose that it seemed hitherto to be lacking. Since its origins in the rabbinate of Ezekiel Landau, as we have noted, the *Normalschule* had convened for only two hours per day during the winter months (from five to seven in the evening!); the rest of the day children studied "sacred" subjects in the traditional *ḥeder*. Under Raaz the hours of instruction were extended to four (eight to ten in the morning and two to four in the afternoon), and the "secular" school day gained pride of place on both sides of the lunch hour. With this simple act the *ḥeder* was pushed symbolically to the background. Before another fifty years had elapsed, it would virtually disappear from the cultural landscape.

With Peter Beer, Anton Raaz, and Homberg's *B'nei Zion* firmly in place, attendance at the *Normalschule* jumped considerably. Already in 1812 an *Elementarklasse* had been added to the four existing *Knabenklassen;* four years later the community added a two-class *Trivialschule* in an enlarged school building. By 1818, the first-year class in the *Mädchenschule* had grown to over 200 and had to be divided into two groups. In 1822 attendance in general grew so large, particularly in the lower classes, that the administration was forced to institute double sessions.[75] Attendance figures for the Prague school, which stood at only 144 students in 1809 and at less than 400 in 1814, now soared and soon reached an annual average of between 700 and 800 students. Wanniczek has reported the total enrollment for the years 1790 to 1831 to have been 17,800—an annual average of 424.[76] Not all students who registered at the Prague school studied there for a full five years, and so it is impossible to know just how many Jewish youngsters passed through its doors during this time, but the number may have been as high as 6,000. Indeed, participation in the *Normalschule* in Prague may have been higher than Jewish attendance in comparable schools in Berlin and Frankfurt. Only a systematic comparison of the several cities will yield compelling results, but we do know that as late as 1812 Berlin sent 215 students, out of a school-age population of 900, to its Jewish school, while Frankfurt sent 120 from a population of 558.[77] The figures in both cases represent 20–25 percent of the pool of school-age children. Yet, one might well argue that the yearly average of 424 students in attendance at the Prague institution constituted as much as 40 percent of the eligible Jewish children in that city.[78] Clearly, the majority of Prague's Jewish children did not attend the community school, but neither did the vast majority of those of Berlin or Frankfurt. Throughout this period wealthier families preferred to hire private tutors to teach in their homes; public education remained in large part the domain of the poor and the dispossessed.[79] At the same time, it would be a mistake, I think, to presume that the "informal" education of well-to-do children incorporated only traditional subjects and methods of instruction. Here too, opportunities abounded for the Enlightenment project to encroach upon the values and ideals of the premodern community. When one keeps this in mind, one begins to understand how pervasive Jewish acculturation may have been well before emancipation.

Attendance, of course, is but one of a variety of factors one would want to consider in judging the role of the new schools in directing social and cultural change. Did the focus of the new schools remain as narrow as it had been at its inception, or did it broaden to include new areas of instruction? If so, with what consequences? How long did the traditional *heder* and *yeshivah* continue to operate alongside but independently of the *Normalschule?* When did Jewish students begin to abandon the former in favor of an exclusive concentration on secular education? Finally, at what point did Jewish youth begin to attend gymnasia and universities in large numbers, and where did such students receive their elementary education? As for the expansion of the

Normalschule curriculum and the encroachment of secular studies on traditional Jewish education, I can attempt only tentative conclusions based on scanty information. I have found no indication that the new school system ever sought to compete directly with the *heder* and *yeshivah* by teaching traditional subjects according to the *haskalah* approach. Thus Ezekiel Landau's fears in this regard never materialized. The progressive members of the community appear to have been content to let the traditional educational tract wither of its own accord as it attracted fewer and fewer students over the decades. Indications of "benign neglect," coupled with moderate increases in the Jewish component of the curriculum, appeared during the early nineteenth century. In 1809, for example, the board of overseers succeeded in having Hebrew taught at the school after hours and "under certain [unspecified] conditions." [80] With the publication the following year of Peter Beer's *Toldot Yisrael* (History of Israel), Jewish school children throughout the kingdom were fed a steady diet of biblical and ancient Jewish history. The text of the work was in Hebrew, but it was accompanied by a Hebrew-lettered German translation and notes by the author in the same language and script. [81] Finally, in 1815 the school day (which up until now had been relegated to the late afternoon) was divided into two parts extending from eight A.M. to four P.M. Such a move could have greatly reduced the stature of the *heder* as an equal partner in the education of the young. But it may also have simply reflected a decline in the *heder* long since in evidence. [82]

Whatever the actual chain of events, by the time Solomon Judah Rapoport was appointed chief rabbi in 1840, Prague's once-famous *yeshivah* had sunk into obscurity. The decline in traditional Jewish education had run its course in a little over half a century. Prague's rabbis in the 1780s and 1790s had taken great pains to warn Jewish parents that they must resist the temptation to reduce the amount of time devoted to the study of sacred matters in order to introduce their children to the new secular sciences; by 1870, a Jewish gymnasium student in Prague who supplemented his general studies with classes at the Talmud Torah had become a rarity. [83]

One interpretation of the relationship between government policy and cultural change among the Jews of Bohemia and Moravia would be to link both the successes and the shortcomings of the "modernization" programs to the inconsistent efforts on the part of Habsburg officials to promote political and economic development generally, to achieve—if you will—parity with the West. According to this line of argument, government programs that were designed to promote Habsburg industry and create an educated and productive citizenry were doomed to fall short of English, French, and even German achievements because of the semifeudal nature of Habsburg society and the lack of adequate institutional and cultural supports. Political determination alone could not achieve social and economic transformation. Similarly, the absence of what Jacob Katz has called "semineutral society"—areas in which Jews and Gentiles could establish new social relationships on the basis of common interests and shared values—rendered the process of Jewish modernization in Bohemia incomplete, if not tenuous, throughout much of the nineteenth century. London, with its liberal Protestant spirit and highly developed economy; Paris, the home of European rationalism and political democracy; and even Berlin, with its literary salons and progressive bureaucratic corps—all offered Jews the opportunity to participate in meaningful ways in the larger society of the Gentile world. Prague did not. Here political and cultural reforms went adrift, unable to drop anchor in a receptive environment.

Such an answer, however, fails to satisfy completely. The Habsburg monarchy did, after all, enjoy its own industrial revolution. It never managed to pull itself even with the West (and it eventually slipped far behind Germany), but it nevertheless achieved a respectable position between the highly developed and underdeveloped countries of Europe. The transformations that occurred within Bohemian Jewish society compared favorably to developments in the West. The political élan of revolutionary France may have eluded Prague; the pace of change may have been more gradual, its leading advocates more circumspect, than in Berlin. The fact remains, however, that beginning with the 1780s Bohemian Jewish society began a transition from which there was to be no return. The dismantling of communal autonomy left a political vacuum that could only be filled by the state. The new educational structure combined with the widening of economic opportunities to overhaul both the civic horizons and the social aspirations of Bohemian Jews. As in most Central European communities, acculturation preceded political emancipation by a half century or more. But civic emancipation, true to its role as handmaiden of economic advancement, was achieved during the early stages of Habsburg industrialization only gradually—as Habsburg culture would have it—between 1848 and 1859.[84]

If Prague failed before 1848 to provide avenues for Jewish and Gentile social interaction comparable to what had developed in Germany, it nevertheless offered alternatives that were better suited to the Habsburg context. Bohemian Jews looked to the agents of change themselves—the state, the schools, and the economic world—as domains outside of the traditional community where they might participate and be received as individuals. The social clubs of the Prague bourgeoisie eventually opened their doors as well. Beginning in the 1850s, Jews constituted a large and crucial element in such civic institutions as the German casino. Seven decades of Germanization had made them indispensible allies in the politics of ethnic defense.[85] Later, in the post-emancipatory period, growing national strife in Bohemia together with the massive immigration of Czech-speaking Jews from the countryside would alter the face of the community once more.

CHAPTER 3

The Social Vision
of Bohemian Jews

Intellectuals and Community in the 1840s

Introduction

For the Jews of the Habsburg monarchy, political emancipation and social integration were often frustratingly difficult processes. The problem
derived in part from the conservative, hierarchical nature of Austrian
society, compounded by the government's inability—or unwillingness—to match the wide-ranging transformations that it did encourage
in the cultural sphere with commensurate political reforms. Thus, while
Jews in Bohemia, Hungary, and lower Austria by and large accepted the
educational and occupational reforms of Joseph II and his successors—
constructing state-supervised primary schools along the model of the
German *Normalschule;* placing their sons in *Gymnasien* and eventually
universities; patterning behavior, dress, and language on middle-class
urban models; establishing many of the early textile plants in the
monarchy—tangible improvements in their legal and political status
lagged behind. Marriage and residence restrictions, for example, were
erased only in 1848, while the last barriers to free economic activity did
not come down until 1859. Full legal emancipation was achieved only
with the creation of the Dual Monarchy in 1867.[1]

The relative weakness of the Habsburg state and the disintegrative
effects of competing social and political forces contributed further impediments to Jewish integration. The Habsburg monarchy lacked both
effective centralized state institutions and a strong political culture. Its
territories comprised a multitude of distinct societies defined by language and ethnicity whose traditional structure and complexion, by the

middle of the nineteenth century, were in the process of breaking down under the challenge of modern nationalism. The emerging national movements, meanwhile, competed with the state for power while offering alternative visions of society and, in so doing, complicated Jewish efforts for mobility, status, and security.[2]

The combination of these factors—lagging reform, weak political culture, emergence of middle-class national movements, and a relatively high rate of Jewish acculturation—produced what might be called an episode of uncertainty among Habsburg Jewry. The decade of the 1840s offered no clear vision of social integration, no obvious program of political emancipation, no determined cultural path. These were years of experimentation in both politics and the arts, and the as-yet-undelineated boundaries of ethnic affiliation created—for the moment at least—extensive opportunities for the testing of cultural possibilities. How in the end was political emancipation to be achieved? In what kind of society would the Jews find acceptance? What were the linguistic and cultural boundaries of such a society likely to be? Given that both assimilation to non-Jewish cultural patterns and integration into the larger social environment were commonly held goals of Habsburg Jewry, what was unclear to many was which cultural patterns and which larger community offered the best prospects for fulfillment.

The present chapter focuses on six Bohemian Jews born between the years 1815 and 1822: Moritz Hartmann (1821–72), Siegfried Kapper (1821–79), Isidor Heller (1816–79), Simon Hock (1815–87), David Kuh (1818–79), and Leopold Kompert (1822–86). With the exception of Simon Hock, all were recipients of a gymnasium education during the 1830s and studied at universities at the start of the 1840s; hence they had mastered the "high culture" of the Habsburg state. All pursued writing—including both journalism and belles lettres—as a vocation, but typically had to subordinate this passion to a career in one of the liberal professions. To varying degrees they all looked to politics as the arena in which both personal designs for advancement and more universal visions of progress might be achieved. Because of their status as acculturated Jews, deprived to a large extent of the fruits of their intellectual training, they fit what Paul Mendes-Flohr has suggested are the main attributes of the modern intellectual: they were "cognitive insiders" while at the same time "axionormative dissenters."[3]

This "generation of the 1840s" was the first in the history of Bohemian Jewry to pursue gymnasium and university education in a sustained fashion; the first also to pass through the revived and expanded system of German-Jewish primary schools dominated by committed *maskilim,* including Peter Beer, Herz Homberg, and later, Wolfgang Wessely.[4] This generation's quest for social integration took place in an atmosphere in which nationalism was tied to political liberalism and democratic reform and at a time when promoting the claims of the various nationalities within the Habsburg monarchy appeared to be perfectly compatible with the struggle for Jewish emancipation. The cultural, linguistic, and political identity of this generation was sufficiently fluid to allow for wide-ranging experimentation and "border-crossing." Not only did the writers in question comfortably combine German and Czech loyalties; they also were involved in the national revivals of other Habsburg populations, most notably the Hungarians and the South Slavs.

The concept of community existed as a problematic ideal for Jewish intellectuals who stood midway between alienation from traditional Jewish society and comfortable situation in a non-Jewish environment. Yet it is also the number and variety of "communities" offered up by this compact group of writers that is interesting and that calls out for explanation. What did the large number of possibilities mean in terms of Jewish mobility and integration in the mid-nineteenth century? Did their visions of community indicate a break or continuity with the "classical assimilationism" of the post-*haskalah*? Lastly, how did the political experiences of this generation during the 1840s affect its notions of community, on the one hand, and real prospects for integration, on the other?

Family Culture and High Culture

Nearly all of the biographical treatments of the six individuals under consideration comment that they were born to middle-class Jewish families.[5] The term "middle," of course, is of limited descriptive value for the early nineteenth century, since it could encompass almost any occupation from artisan to rabbi—from the proprietor of a stall in the flea market to the owner of a factory in one of the suburbs of Prague. One needs to look for more precise measures in order to locate these families within their contemporary Jewish social settings. One criterion might be the attitude of the family toward primary and secondary education, as well as its means of providing these. Although I am forced to rely on incomplete biographical data, the families in question did seem to distinguish themselves in at least two ways: they did not, by and large, belong to the wealthiest stratum of the community, for whom it was fashionable to substitute private tutoring in the home for primary schools; on the other hand, almost all of them sent their sons to classical secondary schools (gymnasia), which did cost money and for which the families underwent considerable material sacrifices.[6]

I have no specific information on the schools attended by David Kuh, other than the fact that they were in Prague and included a classical gymnasium. Similarly, one can only assume that Leopold Kompert was educated in the German-Jewish school in Mnichovo Hradiště (Münchengrätz) before being sent by his father, a wool merchant, to the Piarist gymnasium in nearby Mladá Boleslav (Jungbunzlau).[7] Isidor Heller, who was born in Mladá Boleslav, was apparently groomed to become a talmudic scholar and studied simultaneously in the gymnasium and the *yeshivah*. We do not have precise information concerning his earlier education, however, and so cannot determine whether he only attended the traditional *ḥeder* or also the *Normalschule*.[8]

Moritz Hartmann appears to have made a number of starts and false turns before ending up—like Kompert as well as Heller before him—in the Piarist gymnasium in Mladá Boleslav. Born in the Czech village of Daleké Dušníky, he spent short periods of time at a (presumably Jewish) *Normalschule* in Březnice, the *Hauptschule* in Neukollin, and the Altstädter gymnasium in Prague; he also received home tutoring at times. Finally, in 1833, Hartmann traveled the long distance from his home to Mladá Boleslav, where his maternal grandfather, Isaac Spitz, was rabbi. Boarding at his grandfather's house, Hartmann attended the Piarist gymnasium for the next five years.[9]

Siegfried (born Salomon Israel) Kapper grew up in Smíchov on the outskirts of Prague. The eldest of nine children, he received his earliest education, at age five, from his father in the spirit of the *haskalah*. The father taught from the Hebrew Bible, using the text as a springboard to secular learning: the creation story led to a presentation of the rudiments of astronomy, geography, and natural science; from the story of the Pharaohs the boy was introduced to world history.[10] In the Kapper household Enlightenment rationality appears to have coexisted happily with folk culture of various forms, ranging from the Jewish stories of a mendicant musician, who was a frequent guest in the home, to the Czech folktales and songs of the street. Kapper's biographer, Oskar Donath, has shown that he received his first formal schooling at a two-grade Czech *Volksschule* in Smíchov (which was in reality bilingual, or "utraquist," in common parlance); for the next two years he went to a Jewish school that met at the Klaus Synagogue in Prague. What is unclear is whether Kapper attended only *ḥeder* or the *Normalschule* as well. But since Donath describes the school as a place where Kapper learned Hebrew and "perfected his German," the answer is probably the second.[11]

Simon Hock's early life and education offer an important contrast to those of his five contemporaries. Probably as a result of his mother's piety, Hock attended neither a *Normalschule* nor a gymnasium. Instead, he followed a fully traditional educational course: *ḥeder* until age ten, followed by study at the *yeshivah* of Rabbi Judah Loeb Schlesinger, the last of its kind in Prague by mid-century. Whatever Western education he received he acquired on his own, risking parental opposition along the way. Hock's father apparently was the more open of the two parents to secular education. Following his mother's death when he was fourteen, Hock undertook an intensive campaign of self-education, serving at the same time as tutor to his younger siblings.[12]

The quest for "secular" knowledge on Hock's part took place within the limits of acceptable religious behavior. He did not break with his family over this issue; he never took part in a regular course of study at a non-Jewish secondary school; and he appears to have remained loyal to normative religious practice for his whole lifetime. While other Jewish youth of similar economic backgrounds entered the gymnasium world of high culture, Hock labored in the world of commerce, at first with a maternal aunt and later with his father. Though committed to scholarship and writing, he pursued these ends as an avocation and not as a profession.[13] His "enlightenment" occurred outside the main institutions of acculturation that linked the Jew to the state and its high culture. Perhaps as a result of this, he never experienced the estrangement from Jewish tradition that so marked the careers of his five compatriots. In many respects he serves as an instructive contrast to them, their personal dilemmas, and their imaginative resolutions to the problem of community.

For Kuh, Kapper, Hartmann, and company, the road from the local Jewish community to the larger society led through a five- or six-year course of study at a gymnasium and invariably brought in its wake a break with the traditional culture of their childhood surroundings. One of the more striking examples of this emerges from the early career of Moritz Hartmann. Hartmann, it seems, was sent to the gymnasium in Mladá Boleslav precisely because his grandfather, Isaac Spitz, was the rabbi there, and he continued to live with the grandfather throughout his gymnasium years. Otto Wittner claims, perhaps rightly, that Hartmann cherished the memory of those years in his grandfather's house and that his grandfather served as a model for sympathetic characters in later works of fiction.[14] The fact remains, however, that Hartmann broke with Judaism during the very time that he lived with his grandfather. According to the version recounted by Hartmann himself, when he was thirteen years old he took a walk in the woods and ostentatiously tossed his pair of phylacteries—used by Jewish men in morning prayer—into the trees.[15]

In the case of Siegfried Kapper, it was his father who had already moved far beyond the confines of the traditional Jewish community, both literally and figuratively. Joseph Kapper was listed in official registers as a peddler (*Hausierer*), but Siegfried Kapper reveals in his unpublished "Autobiographie" that the father's career was considerably more interesting than might otherwise be suspected. For besides a peddler, Joseph Kapper was also, at various points in his life, an artisan, a soldier in the French army, and a teacher at various Swiss institutions (under the name Fischer).[16] In the autumn of 1830—after one year of lessons with his father, two years at the Czech *Volksschule* in Smíchov, and two years at the Prague Jewish school—Siegfried Kapper entered the Piarist gymnasium in Prague's Malá Strana (Kleinseite). Kapper's six years at the gymnasium proved to be the formative intellectual experience of his life. During his final two years he studied with the writer and poet Johannes Zimmermann. It so happened that the Malá Strana gymnasium during this time played a key role in the elaboration of romantically inspired Czech cultural nationalism. Václav Svoboda was one of its most influential professors—though probably not one of Kapper's teachers; in 1817 Svoboda had almost certainly aided the ethnologist Václav Hanka in the preparation of the controversial literary forgeries known as the Dvůr Králové and Zelená Hora manuscripts, which purported to consist of fragments of ancient Czech poems. It was not until the 1880s that the manuscripts were proven beyond doubt to have been nineteenth-century fabrications. In the meantime Kapper could take comfort, together with other young Czech intellectuals, that the early Czechs had also possessed a rich literary past.[17]

To say that the gymnasium and university years represented the crucial cultural experience for Jewish intellectuals of the 1840s is not to imply that the experience was unambiguously positive or free of conflict. Most accounts of life at the Piarist gymnasia in Bohemia indicate that the professors were uninspiring, the educational atmosphere was stifling, and the main pedagogical technique was memorization.[18] Jewish students, moreover, found that they had to overcome considerable hostility on the part of both teachers and fellow students if they were to succeed in their studies. One of Moritz Hartmann's teachers, a former Jesuit, was fond of remarking to his class that Jews ought to be studying haggling (*Schacher*) rather than Latin.[19] Moritz, the main character in Leopold Kompert's novella *Die Kinder des Randars* (written in 1847), which bears strong autobiographical features, is also subjected to religiously inspired humiliations at the Bunzlau (Mladá Boleslav) gymnasium. When he arrives to register at the school, the rector pointedly asks the boy's mother whether she wishes the boy to be addressed as "Moses" or as "Moritz." On the fourth day of school Moritz is ordered to kneel before the teacher's desk as punishment for arriving late to class. When the boy protests that he must not kneel, the professor threatens to "lock him up." Moritz in the end kneels.[20]

Despite these antagonisms and the tedium of the classical curriculum, the gymnasium experience provided Jewish students with their first prolonged exposure to the literary culture of Central Europe as well as to local patriotism. It was at Mladá Boleslav that Hartmann and Kompert were first introduced to Goethe, Heine, and the German romantic poets; at the gymnasia of Prague that Siegfried Kapper and David Kuh first learned to appreciate the role of the Czech literary revival in the evolution of Bohemian cultural life. It was during their gymnasium years that Jewish students first mastered the high culture that promised an avenue of social mobility, faced the prospect of literature (especially poetry) as a vocation, made the first lasting friendships with non-Jews, and conceived of the possibility of entering into common political cause with non-Jewish society. By the time our figures began their university careers, they were firmly committed to a life of letters, to which their actual courses of study and subsequent professions may have related only tangentially.[21]

The University and the Wider World

During the years 1837 to 1840 most of our circle of Bohemian Jewish intellectuals made their way to Prague to embark upon university study. Siegfried Kapper entered the philosophical faculty in the autumn of 1837. Moritz Hartmann arrived in the city in the winter of 1838, took classes at the Neustädter Gymnasium in order to complete the sixth and final form (the second "humanistische Klasse"), and entered the university in the autumn of the same year, where he was joined for a short while by his gymnasium classmate Leopold Kompert.[22] By this time Isidor Heller, recently returned from France, was back in Prague for his second try at university study. I do not know where David Kuh began his university career—very likely Prague as well—but by 1840 he was a student in Vienna.[23]

If the tedium of classroom instruction in the gymnasium could not deter students such as Hartmann, Kapper, and Kompert from acquiring both an education and an introduction to the world of literature, the walls of the university were unable to contain them once they arrived in Prague. Numerous facets of intellectual life, including literary creativity, took place outside the confines of the university, especially in nearby cafes. One cafe in particular, the Roter Turm, served as a meeting place for a group of writers and poets—influenced by Byron, Heine, Lenau, and the German romantics—that adopted for itself the name Young Bohemia. Among the more active members of this group stood Heller, Hartmann, and Kapper; Alfred Meissner, the son of a German-speaking physician from Teplice and later Karlovy Vary (Karlsbad); Friedrich Hirschl, a Hungarian who later magyarized his name to Szarvady; and the physician Friedrich Bach. Of these, only Meissner was not Jewish.[24]

The poets of Young Bohemia took from the German romantics their love for lyrical poetry and their appreciation for the interconnectedness of language, landscape, and heroic striving. Heine and Börne in particular served as models for the application of literature and cultural criticism to political and social ends. At the same time, Rudolf Glaser—described by Otto Wittner as "the librarian of one of Prague's largest institutes and a writer of no apparent importance"—provided Young Bohemia with its first literary opportunity.[25] His journal *Ost und West,* which appeared between 1837 and 1848, provided the Young Bohemia group with its first important public forum, publishing hundreds of their poems, essays, and literary translations.

Ost und West was committed to a unique political program, which came to be regarded as emblematic of the liberal, biethnic, "Bohemian" consensus of the decade that preceded the Revolution of 1848. It expressed a political and cultural aesthetic that cultivated original lyrical creations as well as the "folk" literature of the peoples of East Central Europe and combined this with liberal politics in the service of constitutionalism and reform. The name of the journal itself, which may have derived from Goethe's remark, "Orient und Occident sind nicht mehr zu trennen" (the East and the West will no longer be divided), suggested a mediating mission for Austria, and particularly Bohemia, in both realms.[26]

In addition to Kapper, Heller, and Hartmann, the Jewish contributors to *Ost und West* included L. A. Frankl, Friedrich Bach, Ignaz Kuranda, Gustav Karpeles, David Mendl, and Wolfgang Wessely. Kapper in particular immersed himself in the role of *Vermittler* (mediator), translating more than forty pieces of the "national poetry" of the Czechs, Slovaks, and Moravians (whose literature occupied a distinct category in the journal). As purveyor of Czech and Slovak literature to the German reading public of Europe, Kapper occupied a position second only to the poet Karel Sabina.[27] Meanwhile, Kapper, Heller, Hartmann, and Mendl used the pages of *Ost und West* to publish their own original works, which bore such titles as "Ost-Westlicher Divan," "Concordia," "Der Utraquist," and "Chorgesang der Wiener Studenten-Legion." Wessely, a teacher at the Prague *Normalschule*, offered an anthology of rabbinic aphorisms in the spirit of Herder.[28] *Ost und West*, it seems, provided the young Jewish poets of Bohemia with more than a literary forum. It served as a "society of letters" whose middle-class constituents shared with the Jews not only a common educational and social background but also a political vision of Central Europe as ethnically pluralistic and democratic at the same time.

None of the Jewish students examined in this chapter managed to complete his university studies in Prague. Financial pressures forced most to seek outside employment as private tutors—interrupting their studies for longer or shorter periods—but the main reason appears to have been dissatisfaction: dissatisfaction with the university and impatience with Prague as a provincial city.[29] Indeed, next to poetry, *Wanderlust* and quest constituted the main themes of the 1840s, both during and after the university years. Moritz Hartmann might have left Prague altogether in 1838 in favor of Leipzig, where censorship laws were much less severe, but for the fact that he could not obtain a residence permit. In 1840 he finally went to Vienna, where he attended the university, shared a room for a while with David Kuh, and continued to write for *Ost und West*, but now also for L. A. Frankl's *Sontagsblätter*. In 1842 he began a trip that took him to Trieste, Venice, Switzerland, Munich, and ultimately back to Vienna. For two years he managed to hold the position of tutor (*Hofmeister*) in the house of Prince Schwarzenberg. He eventually gave this up as well in order to make his way back to Leipzig in search of a publisher for his by-now-considerable poetic opus. From there he proceeded to Brussels, where he oversaw the publication (in Leipzig) of his first book of poems, *Kelch und Schwert*. He spent some time in Paris and Germany and then returned to Bohemia in 1847, where the following year he was put on trial for some political writings just as the Revolution broke.[30]

The peregrinations of Hartmann's colleagues were no less daunting. Isidor Heller did not return to Prague until 1838, after his application for membership in the French Foreign Legion was turned down by the commander in Nancy. He later lived in Vienna as a teacher; edited a literary journal, *Der Ungar*, in Pest; left Pest in 1847 after an unhappy romance; converted quietly to Protestantism; moved to Leipzig, where he wrote short stories and political articles; and returned to Pest at the end of March 1848 to edit a new political journal, *Der Morgenröthe*.[31]

Siegfried Kapper completed the two years of "philosophical studies" in the summer of 1839 and proceeded to enroll in the medical faculty upon the urging of his father. But by now he had reached a dead end in Prague, forced to devote all of his time to private tutoring. His luck was no better the next year even though he managed to inherit Hartmann's teaching position with the wealthy Mauthner family. And so, in the autumn of 1841 we find Kapper too in Vienna, where he made a valiant effort to resume his medical studies.[32] From this point until he received his medical degree in 1847 Kapper lived a relatively sedentary existence in Vienna. But after 1848 he left the confines of both liberal Vienna and nationalist Bohemia for years of work and travel in the South Slavic lands of Serbia, Croatia, and the Banat.[33]

Leopold Kompert put up with university life in Prague for less than a year—in 1838—before escaping to Vienna. He soon found a position for himself as *Hofmeister* to a wealthy merchant with five children, a job that made it impossible for him to continue his formal studies but did improve his material circumstances and gave him some time to devote to poetry and fiction. He began his *Wanderjahre* in 1840, taking off on a ship up the Danube, living for a while in the villages of the Hungarian plain, and eventually making his way to Pressburg (Pozsony, Bratislava) where he befriended the publisher of the *Pressburger Zeitung*, Adolf Neustadt. While publishing his first stories in the *Pressburger Zeitung* and the *Sontagsblätter*, Kompert also signed on as *Hofmeister* for the family of Count Andrássy. Not until 1847, after learning of the death of his mother, did he decide to resume university study.[34]

Significantly, the one person not to travel at this time was Simon Hock. His quest for Western enlightenment, for a broadening of cultural horizons, took place not only in the context of the established Jewish community but also within the confines of the city of his birth. Hock joined forces in 1835 with other Jews who were traditional in religious practice but "enlightened" in outlook to create an association that would promote "a united stylistic form" in keeping with "the scientific progress of the age." His collaborators included Koppelmann Lieben; Daniel Ehrmann, who later served as rabbi of numerous Bohemian communities; the future physician Moritz Kuh; Guttmann Klemperer, later rabbi in Tábor; and Josef Schack.[35] They called their new association Aurora to suggest the dawning of a new age, yet it was essentially conservative in its attachment to Jewish culture—Mendelssohnian in tone one half-century after the master's death.

Simultaneously, Jewish *Wissenschaft* exerted a growing influence on Hock and his friends. In 1835 Leopold Zunz came to Prague to serve as preacher of the recently dedicated Reform synagogue. Though he stayed for only one year, he was replaced by Michael Sachs, a conservative reformer and scholar who had a major impact on Jewish life in Prague before leaving for Berlin in 1844.[36] Hock attached himself to Zunz, Sachs, and later Solomon Judah Rapoport (who became chief rabbi of Prague in 1840) and became an ardent *dévoté* of mid-century *Wissenschaft*. He began to write journalistic pieces in the 1840s for the *Allgemeine Zeitung des Judenthums* and *Der Orient*, dealing alternatively with the conditions of Jewish life in Prague and the Reform movement in Germany (which he opposed). It was during this time also that Hock conceived of his plan to produce a massive history of the Jews of his city. Though he did write an important study based on tombstone inscriptions in the ancient Jewish cemetery, he never completed the larger project, and the manuscript that he was working on ultimately was lost.[37]

It is tempting to view the impressive amount of travel undertaken by young Jewish intellectuals in the 1840s as an indication of a broader cultural restlessness. Removed from the villages of their parents or ancestors, alienated as well from the entrenched Jewish community of Prague, filled with social and intellectual ambitions but as yet unemancipated and unintegrated into the non-Jewish environment, the Jewish students expressed their lack of rootedness symbolically by wandering. By contrast, Hock's sedentary existence reflected a sense of comfort and satisfaction with his identity both as a Jew and as a European. He apparently had achieved in his life a happy synthesis of traditional Jewish culture and European science and rationalism, represented by his dual interest in German stylistics and *Wissenschaft des Judentums*. Though implicitly loyal to the Habsburg state, Hock was also a Jewish patriot committed to preserving the history of the community in Prague, transmitting knowledge of the Jewish past, and assuring the cultural health of the community in the future.

But if this picture is correct in its rough outline, it fails to account for two important points. The first is that the wanderings implied the hopeful outlook that there was still a world open with possibilities. Kompert, Kuh, and Heller might have felt stifled by the immobility of Prague, but they could take advantage of Hungary's occupational opportunities, relative political freedom, and national experimentation. Siegfried Kapper could sample from the folk cultures of Bohemia, Moravia, and Slovakia—before going on to those of the South Slavs— because he felt that they were promising fields of participation between Jews and non-Jews.[38] The second point is that the travels were not aimless; they invariably led to (and sometimes back to) Vienna. Students and intellectuals of all nationalities gravitated to Vienna in the years preceding 1848. This university city and imperial capital offered—for a few heady years, at least—a place of opportunity par excellence, where politics and culture could be wed and untold visions of community born.

Community and Ethnic Strife

It was in Vienna, too, that the cross-cultural ventures of *Ost und West* bore an interesting fruit. In 1843 Václav Bolemír Nebeský (1818–82), who may already have struck up an acquaintance with Bohemian Jewish students in Prague, arrived in Vienna to study medicine.[39] Here he formed a close relationship with Siegfried Kapper and David Kuh and with them embarked on a project that combined elements of political liberalism, incipient Czech nationalism, and the struggle for Jewish emancipation.

Nebeský's early life paralleled that of his Jewish colleagues in some telling ways. Born to a Czech father and a German mother, he attended mainly German schools—including the gymnasium in Litoměřice (Leitmeritz)—although the family spoke Czech at home. He was exposed to German and classical literature at the gymnasium and later took up Greek and German philosophy in Prague. Before arriving in Prague in 1836 he apparently knew very little Czech history and literature; these he acquired as part of his extracurricular intellectual formation in the university environments of Prague and Vienna.[40] Nebeský belonged to a group of Byronist Czech poets, which included Karel Sabina and K. H. Mácha, who had joined literary romanticism to political activism and also showed an interest in Jewish cultural themes. At some point Nebeský became convinced (perhaps after reading Herder) that the Czech nation could reap enormous benefits if it were able to recruit the potential talent of Central European Jewry. He appears to have been struck, in particular, by the role that Heinrich Heine and Ludwig Börne played in the cultural politics of Germany. In any event, he, Kapper, and Kuh hit upon the idea of launching a newspaper campaign designed to elicit the support of Bohemian and Moravian Jews for the Czech national movement.[41]

Before the end of 1843 Nebeský was able to report to a friend that the first article in the campaign was ready to appear in print:

A good article, excellently written; it will work terrifically. One can already sense this a little among the Jews of Vienna. I am going to continue to work in this direction. We could get a lot of help [*gute Kräfte*] from the Jews; they are an excellent, wonderful people, full of spirit and action. They have already helped the Germans a lot. Would that they would help us, too![42]

One cannot say with certainty what article Nebeský was referring to: possibly the three-part series by David Kuh that ultimately appeared in the *Allgemeine Zeitung des Judentums* in April 1844; possibly the anonymous *Berichte* from Prague that began to appear in *Der Orient* in February.[43] But the February report, probably written by Kuh, does appear to have inaugurated the official campaign.

The dispatch from Prague opened with the words: "The position of the Jews in a country in which the nationality struggle is taking place, and with it the language struggle, is a difficult one." Neutrality in such a situation is impossible, and the Jews must choose a side to support, "something which they ought not to do and yet must."[44] Choosing sides, the writer admitted, was accomplished more easily in Hungary, where the Magyars clearly had the upper hand, where the government—despite itself—tended to support the supremacy of the Magyar language; where the landed aristocracy was independent and not merely a shadow of the regime. In such a situation, Jews benefited from magyarization. "The Magyar values and loves anyone who speaks Hungarian well."[45]

But for the Jews of Bohemia, the article continued, where the government repressed the "Slavic element" and where the local elites had only just begun to cherish their language and local culture, the situation was different. Here the regime ruled in the full sense of the word; the aristocracy had no real political power; its *Landtag* was but a silent monument to an ancient freedom. What political strategy was open to Jews who lived in this type of context "between Scylla and Charybdis"? The reporter's advice was to ignore discretion: "Not [to be] petty, cowardly, or self-interested, but to be true sons of your fatherland!"[46] In this instance, "fatherland" referred not to the empire as a whole but to the smaller Czech "state" within it. This political community stood at an undetermined distance between the ghetto and the emancipating central state. And the Jew owed loyalty to this intermediate body in the name of his own geographic origins, the linguistic culture of his early environment, and, above all, the new flag of nationalism. "The Jews should help to set in motion the machinery of nationality—language; attach themselves to those people who are occupied with scientific research into the Czech language in order to appear as Czechs to their (unfortunately one cannot as yet say fellow- ...) citizens." The report closed by singling out the efforts of Siegfried Kapper "and a few other Jews" who involved themselves in Czech language and literature, thus serving as a model to be followed by others.[47]

In the 14 May 1844 issue of *Der Orient* the same reporter wrote of efforts on the part of some within the Prague Jewish community to establish a teaching position in Czech language in the city's *Normalschule:* "If these words are actually put into practice, then this is very welcome news, and this step promises much good for Bohemian Jewry generally. Common research efforts in language and literature will lead to an intellectual rapprochement between Jews and Christians, and the intellectual interaction will also make the social bond stronger."[48] He ridiculed the "feeble-minded" (*Schwachköpfe*) within the Jewish community who opposed the teaching of Czech in Jewish schools on the grounds that it would antagonize the government authorities. "I need only refer these 'timid sirs' to our own beloved provincial governor (*Landeschef*), who himself has given many indications of how highly he values the language of his subjects."[49]

The major thrust of the newspaper campaign consisted of two parallel series of articles: David Kuh's "Ein Wort an Juden und Slaven," which appeared in the *Allgemeine Zeitung des Judentums* on 1, 8, and 15 April 1844; and Nebeský's "Něco o poměru Slovanů a židů" (Concerning the relations between Slavs and Jews), which came out in the Czech-language newspaper *Květy*. Kuh's argument for a new involvement of Jews in the national movement of the Czechs derived from both the principle that nationality is a culturally determined phenomenon and the observation that the German national movement has gained much strength through the participation of "foreigners" in its cultural life.

What has made the Germans so great intellectually, what has positioned them as the most educated and thoughtful people on the earth, is that they, for the most part, have never neglected the spirit....
Frenchmen and Jews, Danes and Slavs have vied with one another to carry the stones for the building of the German temple of glory.

But who, Kuh asked, has bothered to help the Slavs?[50]
No one, of course. But here Kuh added a rhetorical touch that revealed an optimism that would elude him in the future. He identified himself with that Czech nation that stood isolated from the rest of Europe: "What we are and what we shall become we are and shall become only through ourselves."

Among our heroes and wise men, our poets and artists, there is not even one from a foreign tribe (*Stamm*). But nations are not to be divided into full- and half-blood races, and it is the highest triumph of a particular cultural direction when foreign geniuses and foreign powers subordinate themselves to it and serve it in joy.[51]

Kuh placed much of the blame for the lack of participation of outsiders in Czech cultural life with the Czechs themselves. They simply were not interested. And yet the potential for Jewish-Slavic cooperation in East Central Europe was so great—Kuh mentions that the vast majority of Europe's Jews lived in Slavic lands—that neither side should miss the opportunity of joining forces. "Take hammer and trowel in hand and eagerly and ceaselessly cultivate the education of the nation, the [building] of common bonds, and the reconciliation of hearts."[52]
In the second installment of the series Kuh shifted his focus to questions of prejudice and persecution and adopted a dramatically different

tone. Whereas his first article had been marked by hope and optimism, the second tasted of bitterness and disappointment. Kuh admitted to being frustrated at the lack of improvement in the political, economic, and social condition of the three hundred thousand Jews (his count) living in the German Confederation. And he spoke with stubborn pride of this people who had withstood a millennium of Christian persecution only to wake up to new strength and vitality; certainly they must possess unusual qualities.[53]

Curiously—given the ultimate purpose of the articles—Kuh's next remarks, addressed to Czech intellectuals, were laced with scorn and anger.

If only a single one of you, Slavic intellectuals (*Gelehrten*), would admit to this; if only one of you would step ahead of the crude masses and emancipate himself from Jew hatred; this one person would make a beneficial, eternal impact not only on the Jews, not only on his own people, but indirectly on the whole world.

You kill so much proud hope, so much budding talent, you West Slavs, through the stifling swamp air of your stupid hatred and your contempt. Do you think you are only killing the Jews? No, you are robbing yourselves, you are suppressing the spiritual blossoms that were to have borne fruit for you.[54]

Almost three times as many Jews lived among the Slavs as among the Germans, Kuh argued. They might some day form a mighty and powerful middle class that could be of service to the young Czech nation. Why should one deliberately alienate them, reject their services? If the Czechs should close their doors to Jewish participation, if they should waste the opportunity at hand, they could not lay the blame at the door of the Jews,

who have had to battle the greatest, heaviest, and most adverse impediments in order not to doubt humanity; who have had to struggle ... not to lose faith in themselves and in their inner freedom.... Do you want to accept the fact that [the Jew] rightly turns his back on you in disgust ... and allies with the German nationality and German culture?[55]

In the end, the Jews were not asking so much from the Slavs. Not relief from burdensome taxation, not civil equality, not political emancipation—the Czechs were not in a position to grant any of these things. All that the Jews asked for was a measure of love and esteem, "which man has the sacred right to demand from his fellow man, his own likeness."[56]

It is difficult not to be both moved and puzzled by the stridency of Kuh's remarks. The articles were intended for a Jewish audience: why was it necessary to direct so much pent-up emotion at the Slavs, whom, after all, one wanted to court? And why remind the Jewish readers of the *Allgemeine Zeitung des Judentums* of the centuries of hatred and persecution that the Jews had suffered at the hands of their hosts?

In fact, the final article in the series did much to balance the score. Kuh directed his attention this time to the Jews, and lashed out at them, one could say, with equal fury: "You, West Slavic Jews, who are so proud of your cleverness and your intellect, who are so proud of the sciences, who even tend exotic plants ... I ask you whether you have sunk so low through oppression that you must wait until someone raises you up and comes close to you?"[57]

Kuh seems to have subscribed to a variation on the "mission theory" of Judaism, arguing that the Jews were called upon "to realize the highest and most noble ideals," but also—together with the Western Slavs— to serve as spiritual intermediaries between Eastern and Western Europe. He called upon the Jews to abandon old cultural forms in the name of a new, better order for all Central Europeans: "You must become actively involved, sacrifice much, tear down much in order to achieve even more, in order to build more grandly." And a prime symbol of the revolution in Jewish culture would be the wish on the part of some within the Prague Jewish community to cultivate the Czech language and to teach it in their schools. "Then the time will surely come when you will no longer have to go begging to your brethren in Germany in order to quench your thirst for European learning and culture, which rages in you still so vehemently."[58]

Kuh's articles in the *Allgemeine Zeitung des Judentums* have frequently been cited—together with Siegfried Kapper's *České listy* (1846) and Moritz Hartmann's *Kelch und Schwert* (1845)—as marking the high point of Czech-Jewish cultural collaboration before 1848. Hartmann and Kuh's subsequent defections from the Czech camp, accordingly, are typically understood as representing a sudden about-face, explained partly by the anti-Jewish violence that erupted in 1844 and again in 1848, and partly by the unhospitable reception of Kapper's work on the part of Czech intellectuals such as Karel Havlíček Borovský.[59] Doubtless, the events of 1844 and 1848—as well as the critical reviews of Kapper's Czech writings—did cause much disappointment. But the entire Kuh-Kapper-Nebeský venture was shot through with ambivalence and mistrust from the beginning. Kuh used the pronoun "we" only once when referring to the Czech nation, at the very beginning of the first essay. In the second part, while analyzing Czech attitudes toward Jews, he steered clear of the first-person voice altogether. In the concluding part, ostensibly a criticism of Jewish behavior, the "we" that bound the writer to his subject was certainly implicit. One might add that the angry, accusatory tone of Kuh's second article overwhelmed the series as a whole. He never really shook himself loose from it, even as he tried to "even the score" in the last segment. What was to have been a criticism of Jewish cultural behavior and an exhortation to change ended with yet another denunciation of the anti-Jewish behavior of European Christian society, especially in the Slavic lands. Kuh held out hope for an eventual reconciliation between Jews and Slavs, but he did so in the manner of an Abraham bickering with God over the fate of Sodom and Gomorrah. "I am convinced that the well-intentioned and appropriate words of a single one among the Slavic intellectuals will travel like lightning among your [the Jewish] masses, will rouse them and win them over to a great European nation, and, in so doing, provide salutory reconciliation to both parties."[60]

Perhaps Nebeský was to have been that single Slavic intellectual ready to receive the Jews of Central Europe. Even his overture, however, was more cautious than warm. Responding to Kuh in *Květy*, Nebeský found himself essentially repeating Kuh's criticism of the Jews, reproaching them for never having taken part in the national strivings of the Slavs. To the contrary, he added, the Jew's attachment to "foreign elements" had undermined the Czech "national element." This "tragic isolation," as Nebeský put it, which was harmful to both sides, ought to stop.[61] That Nebeský desired and valued Jewish participation in Czech culture was nevertheless clear. Jewish-Czech cooperation, he wrote, would be "a nice development for humanity": "It was no nation of mean spirit that played such a role in the history of mankind, in whose language the Bible, the book of books, was written; a nation that withstood the wildest storms of the most tragic centuries while maintaining its character, its religion—the oldest in the world."[62]

It was one of fate's cruelties that industrial riots should have broken out in Prague and other parts of Bohemia so soon after the start of the Czech-Jewish courtship. The riots were carried out primarily by textile workers protesting the introduction of mechanization in the cotton printing industry and the nearly simultaneous drop in real wages. Jews had played a conspicuous role in the development of textile production—particularly in cotton printing—throughout the Habsburg monarchy. One of the largest firms in Bohemia, the Porges family's cotton printing plant in Smíchov, just outside of Prague, employed 569 workers in 1835; by 1843 it employed 700. In 1835 there were 117 cotton processing plants in Bohemia, of which fifteen of the largest were located in Prague and owned by Jews. By the 1840s the Epstein and Porges families alone produced more than 10 percent of the entire Austrian output in printed cotton fabric. The Porges brothers were also the first to introduce steam engines into the printing process and were granted titles of nobility for their troubles.[63]

A string of bad harvests in the early 1840s had resulted in a general rise in prices. At the same time factory owners responded to a crisis in the industry by holding down wages. But the immediate background to the events of June 1844 involved the introduction of machines—the so-called perrotin—into the cotton printing factories. When the Porges brothers introduced the perrotin in their plant in Smíchov, they also lowered wages. Venting their anger at the predominantly Jewish factory owners, the Prague textile workers went on a rampage and destroyed machinery in plants owned by the Porges, Dormitzer, Brandeis, Schick, and Epstein families.[64] Soon the riots expanded beyond the bounds of industrial protest and spilled over into acts of violence against Jews generally. On 21 June a mass meeting of cotton workers at which anti-Jewish speeches were made was broken up by the police, but it quickly reformed as a mob that streamed into the Jewish quarter, destroying market stands and shops and attacking individual Jews. Eventually the military and the police intervened to restore order. Riots erupted several days later as well, this time led by some two thousand railway workers.[65]

To complete the isolation of Prague Jewry, the commercial middle class and the lower-middle class sided wholeheartedly with the rioting workers in the aftermath of the June storm. Non-Jewish merchants and shopkeepers presented a petition to the government in Vienna urging that it enforce existing restrictive legislation on Jews and also limit their economic activity. The petition signaled the start of an anti-Jewish movement among Prague's *Kleinbürgertum,* which lasted at least until 1848 and reached its peak in 1847 in a campaign that involved eighteen hundred masters from virtually every guild in the city.[66]

Following closely on the heels of the Kuh-Kapper-Nebeský initiative as they did, the riots of 1844 transformed the cautious skepticism of some Jewish intellectuals into outright disillusionment. Dispatches from Prague that reached the offices of *Der Orient* in Leipzig seethed with bitterness at the actions of the Czech mobs. The reports were written by two different individuals, both anonymous. The tone and style of the first set of reports, however, closely resembled Kuh's series in the *Allgemeine Zeitung des Judentums* and at one point were appended with the initials "D. K." Another set of dispatches, more conservative in tone but equally critical of Czech actions, carried the signature "24." I cannot be certain about the authorship of the articles, but there are good reasons to believe that the first set—reports dated 23 and 24 June and 10 and 22 July—was written by David Kuh and the second—particularly the long report of 26 June—by Simon Hock.[67]

A pained sarcasm dripped from the opening lines of Kuh's dispatches and continued throughout the series. It derived from what he saw as the complicity of the educated middle classes in the anti-Jewish excesses. "The blessed Libuša and yet another queen will be shedding tears of joy in their graves," he wrote, "that their loyal subjects have maintained the ancient Jew-hatred [*Judenhass*] down to the year 1844. If the wandering Jew [*der ewige Jude*] is a fable, eternal Jew-hatred is certainly no myth."

Textile workers rise up against their bosses, who happen to belong to the Jewish ethnic group [*Volksklasse*], cause damage and destruction to factories, and our dear cultivated and educated Czechs know of nothing better to do than to exhibit openly their own crude and crass Jew-hatred, accusing all Jews, as a single body, of fraud.... Oh Czechs, you call for freedom and independence at a time when you have dehumanized yourselves [*da Ihr Euch entmenscht*], when you have sunk to the level of beasts of prey.[68]

Kuh laid the blame for the anti-Jewish riots—which he labeled "the crude acts of crude men"—at the doorstep of national and religious fanaticism. He lashed out in particular at Professor Svoboda of the Malá Strana gymnasium who, it will be recalled, was not only a fervent nationalist but also had a role in promoting—and perhaps producing—Václav Hanka's "medieval" Czech manuscripts of Zelená Hora and Dvůr Králové.[69] He accused Svoboda of fomenting anti-Jewish sentiment, of humiliating Jewish students in front of their Christian colleagues, in the end, of "preaching a Crusade against the Jews." Foreshadowing his subsequent attack on the authenticity of the manuscripts—while hinting at a political rationale for his stand—Kuh sarcastically suggested: "the creature Sv——a, by the way, is an expert in the Czech language. Perhaps he is preparing the Prague scene for a Bohemian epic, wherein he and his beloved Czechs can shine in glory."[70]

Ultimately Kuh understood the riots of 1844 to be a by-product of the absence of emancipation, both Jewish and Christian. When the "birth pangs" of Czech nationalism first began to be heard, he wrote—after the dust had settled and the troops had left—the Jews thought to themselves that real freedom might be coming to Bohemia.

It was as though we could already see the Jews sitting in the newly built city hall; in uniform, marching along with their fellow citizens; occupying numerous chairs at the university. We didn't think at all about the little things—like living in the Christian [parts of the] city, opening shops in the marketplace, and the like. That was then, but no longer. We've [since] lived through the dark Middle Ages.[71]

The initial shock came in the form of the fury of the mob. But if the mob knew only to vent its anger at the Jews, one ultimately had to deplore the type of state that did not teach its subjects any differently, that capitalized on social and political inequality to pit one disadvantaged group against another. The educated classes, with their "refined Jew-hatred," cynically chose to encourage and manipulate the discontented masses. Yet it was the "patriarchal" state, which distributed privileges like candy to favorite children and under which groups measured well-being in terms of their advantages relative to other social groups, that endangered the security of the Jews the most. Only complete Jewish and Christian emancipation could end the cycles of violence against Jews.[72]

Simon Hock's reporting from Prague contained neither the political radicalism nor the cynicism of David Kuh's. To be sure, Hock also railed against the violence and deplored the "retreat to the Middle Ages." What he was witnessing was "once again a war of might against right, of force against humanity [Menschlichkeit], of blind hate against reason." The order of the day was no longer progress but reaction. In the past, governments had withheld civic rights from the Jews; now "the people" scoffed at their human rights.[73] But the overall tone of Hock's reporting was conservative and even pious. He thanked "the eternal Guardian of Israel, who has never abandoned us," and also the "watchful and wise authorities" for intervening to restore order, thus preventing the riots from causing more harm than they did. In fact the flowery, exaggerated language with which he expressed his thanks to the government causes one to wonder if the remarks were not intended as irony.[74]

Also unlike Kuh, Hock's dispatch of 26 June contained an internal critique of recent events based on a strong sense of Jewish ethnic solidarity. His target was Prague's wealthy Jewish families, who in the past, pursuing status and mobility, had turned their backs on the rest of the community. These people now found themselves under attack by the very Gentiles whom they had tried to court. "At the hour of need the Christian friend—who before had only a handshake and a smile for you—now had ready a kick and a sneer. Your poor coreligionists, however, whom you had kept at a distance, unfortunately were beaten up on your behalf."[75] Perhaps in the future, Hock wrote, Jewish notables would not look down on their Jewish brothers from atop "a half-Christian isolation stool" in contempt. Rather, as their forefathers had done, wealthy Jews would attach themselves ever more forcefully to the Jewish community; "tie the knot that binds them to their coreligionists ever more tightly; make the interests of the community their own; strive for its well-being as for their own; and base their own pride and worth on the realization of this obligation."[76]

Narrowing of Vision: The Retreat to German Culture

In the weeks and months that followed the June riots the voices that only recently had called for a common Czech-Jewish political front fell silent. Doubt-ridden and inconsistent from the beginning, the vision of a new community based on common Jewish and Czech interests could not be sustained in the face of popular violence combined with the tacit collusion of Czech elites. One of the few individuals who continued to urge Czech-Jewish unity during the second half of 1844 and throughout 1845 was the little-known Ignac Schulhof. Writing in *Der Orient* in September and October 1844, Schulhof maintained that the promise of Jewish integration to Czech society was not dead (one anti-Jewish professor did not an entire society make) and insisted on the immersion of Bohemian Jews in Czech language and culture.[77] Siegfried Kapper also refused to lose faith, at least for the moment. He busied himself with writing poetry and in 1846 published the first collection of poems in the Czech language to be written by a Jew, *České listy* (Czech leaves, or Czech letters). Kapper's poetry explored the themes of Jewish longing and hope, to which he added an imaginative identification of the Jewish and Czech nations, matching tragedy for historical tragedy and offering the vision of a common future.[78]

Whatever hope Kapper may have had of a positive reception of *České listy* by the educated Czech public, however, was quickly derailed by the leading Czech journalist of the day, Karel Havlíček Borovský (1821–56). Havlíček reviewed Kapper's book in *Česká včela*—which he edited—in November 1846. In the review he criticized Kapper, not for his poetry but for the idea that Jews could regard themselves as Czechs:

The Jews who live in Bohemia frequently count themselves among our nation, they frequently call themselves Czechs. This is a completely false point of view. With regard to Jews one should bear in mind not only their creed and religious confession ... but primary consideration should be given to their origin and nationality (*národnost*).

How can Israelites (*Israelité*) belong to the Czech nation when they are of Semitic origin? ... Thus one cannot claim that the Jews living in Bohemia and Moravia are Czechs of the Mosaic religion; rather one must consider them to be a separate, Semitic nation, which simply happens to live among us and sometimes understands or speaks our language.... Undoubtedly all Jews—whatever country or part of the world they may live in—consider themselves as a nation, as brethren, and not solely as coreligionists. And this bond that ties them together is stronger by far than the bond to the country in which they live. We hope that there is no need to prove the point that it is impossible to belong simultaneously to two fatherlands and two nations, or to serve two masters. Therefore anyone who wants to be a Czech must cease to be a Jew.[79]

Though laced with an undertone of resentment toward the Jews of Bohemia-Moravia, Havlíček's piece in *Česká včela* also contained remarkable perceptions on the nature of Jewish cultural life in his country. His rejection of Jewish assimilation into the Czech community was based not on religious prejudice but on a Herderian idea of the sacredness of distinct, national cultures. Nor did his lack of interest in a Czech-Jewish alliance mean that he opposed the granting of political rights to the Jews. In fact, he came out in favor of Jewish emancipation in the 1850s.[80] But the Jews, in Havlíček's view, constituted a distinct nation bound together by ancestry, history, language, and religion. And of Kapper's putative Czech patriotism he wrote: "With one eye he looks at Jerusalem—the Land of Promise—with the other, at the Czech fields, which he claims to love. However, his poems clearly reveal that he loves still more what is truly his own—which is only natural and praiseworthy."[81]

Havlíček—unlike other, more sympathetic reviewers—appreciated the role of traditional Jewish themes in Kapper's writing, including the power of Jewish yearnings for redemption. Poems with titles such as "Forever Eastward" (*K východu*), "Son of Sorrow" (*Ben-Oni*), and "The Ninth of Ab" (*Na devátý ab*) lent poignancy to the rest of the volume and its call for Czech-Jewish union. Kapper sought to harness and redirect the age-old longing for Zion that had been the expression of Jewish hope for many centuries.

> New cities rise from the ruins of ancient lore,
> New nations come and others pass unnamed
> Old gods must will their reign to gods unknown before,
> And forests whisper now, where once thundered seas untamed.[82]

But the old longing remains potent, even as the poet searches for a new haven. As long as the Jew—the boy with coal-black wavy hair in the poem "Ben-Oni"—is rebuffed by the world around him, he cannot help but remember the distant "Star of Zion":

> I do not ask of You to end my woeful bane,
> To guide my steps, to aid me to return
> To the distant shrine for which I long in vain,
> Where the Star of Zion ne'er again shall burn.

> For the Rose of Sharon I no longer pine,
> Nor for the fruits from a sloping Jordan hill,
> Its milk and honey I gladly will decline,
> Its pleasant days, and nights so cool and still.

> My plaintive prayer is free from all regret,
> For wasted joys and sweetness spent in vain,
> If but for once in life I could forget
> The bitter drops of my fellow-men's disdain.[83]

The juxtaposition of Zion and Europe, of the landscape of Palestine and Bohemia's Czech countryside, also surfaces in Leopold Kompert's novella *Die Kinder des Randars*. The itinerant beggar (and prophet?) Mendl Wilna is a favorite guest of the innkeeper Rebb Schmul. For hours Mendl Wilna regales the family with his "holy error" (*heiliger Irrtum*): stories of Jerusalem and of its imminent rebuilding. On Sabbaths the beggar takes Rebb Schmul's son to the fields surrounding his village and there—standing in the landscape of the Czech countryside—speaks at length of his "distant fatherland": "[He] described to him the lands that he had just traveled through or entertained him with fables and sacred tales. He never spoke a word about his own home [Heimat]."[84]

In a chapter entitled "Wo ist des Juden Vaterland" Kompert portrays the inner conflict of divided loyalties and cultural affinities in the young

gymnasium student Moritz. Cultural conflicts born of the classroom itself engender in Moritz a longing for Mendl Wilna's Jerusalem, on the
one hand, and a desire to merge with the Hussites—the national heroes
of his Czech friend Honza—on the other.

Moritz also read history, but he was struck by a different spirit. As a Jew he
did not understand the nature of the religious struggles of Bohemia; it was
all the same to him if one took communion of one or both kinds. . . . But
the political significance seized him mightily. Here he saw a battle for good
and freedom and independence; here his own feelings could join in.
Jerusalem and Bohemia! The same night spirit enveloped the two giant
corpses with the silence of the grave.[85]

As Havlíček would have it, the longing for Zion, the positioning toward the East, represented more than a pious memory (or a "holy error"); it was a living reality that helped to define the ethnic distinctiveness of Jews. And he reproached those Jews who wanted to abandon
their culture, including their "natural" language, Hebrew. To those who
had already thrown Hebrew overboard, he offered the advice that they
take up German, as it had apparently become European Jewry's second
mother tongue.[86]

Havlíček's reply to Siegfried Kapper did close the door on the brief
experiment in Czech-Jewish literary and cultural cooperation. The fact
that it was sandwiched between anti-Jewish riots in 1844 and 1848
seemed to emphasize the finality of the rejection. Equally significant,
however, was the fact—often overlooked—that Havlíček had been Václav Bolemír Nebeský's closest collaborator and confidant throughout
the 1840s. Nearly all of Nebeský's early pronouncements on Czech-
Jewish cooperation had appeared in Havlíček's paper *Česká včela;*
Nebeský himself took over the editorship of the paper in 1847. One
must conclude, then, that Havlíček gave his tacit approval to the
Nebeský-Kapper-Kuh initiative in 1843 and 1844 and that he himself decided to put a stop to it by attacking the work of Nebeský's closest Jewish ally in the same organ that had started it all.[87]

Havlíček's contention that the Jews of the Czech lands constituted
their own nation did not find much of an echo among the Jews themselves. Jewish political efforts, social ambitions, and sense of identity
throughout the middle decades of the nineteenth century were predicated on the opposite notion—that a separate Jewish nationality did
not exist in Central and Western Europe. Intellectuals, industrialists,
and tradesmen alike desired political rights, economic opportunity, and

social advancement above all. The order of the day simply did not leave room for Jewish cultural nationalism. If Jews did seem to take to heart one piece of advice, it was to complete their embrace of German language and culture, well underway since the first efforts at Jewish "modernization" in the 1780s. With the elaborate network of German-Jewish primary schools in place, secondary and higher education squarely within the German orbit, and a state apparatus that offered clear advantages to German speakers (west of Hungary, at least), there was little to hold Jews back from complete German acculturation. Nor, in the face of Czech popular antagonism, did there appear to be any alternative.

In the summer of 1844 Moritz Hartmann wrote to Alfred Meissner in Prague, expressing the outrage that was by now common among Bohemian Jewish intellectuals. He also unwittingly offered an apt metaphor for the shrinking cultural horizon of his fellow Jews. In an allusion to his already completed book of poems, *Kelch und Schwert* (parts of which glorified the democratic and social ideals of the Hussites), Hartmann wrote: "When one hears about revolution, like the one your fellow Praguers had, the best thing for a person to do is to become a loyal citizen and make his volume of poetry smaller by half."[88]

—Pfui! What a miserable pack of hounds! There is no idea of national consciousness there, of proletarian sentiment, of historical memory, or of a view to the future. Miserable, pitiful, petty materialism. The fleamarket their Bastille, the ghetto their St. Denis ... if it were to come down to it, I would be the first volunteer for Austria, in other words for Germany.... My friend, the time has come for us in Bohemia to stand as Germans; that will be our post in the future.[89]

Gradually, between 1844 and 1850, the Jewish intellectuals of Bohemia did make up their minds to "stand as Germans," combining an adherence to German culture with an ongoing commitment to democratic politics. Only Siegfried Kapper, David Mendl, and Ignac Schulhof retained their pro-Czech sympathies to varying degrees. Kapper, in fact, did not respond directly to Havlíček's devastating review of his work. He simply stopped writing original prose and poetry in Czech, devoting himself instead to the more appreciated calling of translation. Kapper earned his medical degree in 1847, took part in the revolution in Vienna in March 1848, became a doctor of surgery in 1851, and practiced for a number of years in Croatia, Serbia, and the Banat before returning to his native land in 1854. His literary output after 1847 consisted of translations from Czech and from Serbian, travel accounts (*Südslavische Wanderungen*, 2 vols., 1853), and fiction in German. He, like Kompert, now chose Jewish themes for his fiction, seeking to recapture the quality of life in the towns and villages of Bohemia both before and in the face of the disappearance of traditional Jewish society. He published, among other things, ghetto stories, a Bildungsroman based on Jewish gymnasium life in Vormärz Bohemia, and a novel about a Jewish family in the Bohemian countryside.[90]

During the 1848 revolution in Prague, Moritz Hartmann made good on his promise to promote German progressivism. He attended the Frankfurt Vorparlament as a trustee and was then elected to the National Assembly from Leitmeritz (Litoměřice), where he sat on the far left. When Austria recalled its delegation to the Frankfurt Assembly, Hartmann sought refuge in Stuttgart; when that city was occupied by Prussian troops, he began a prolonged period of travel, pausing for a number of years in Switzerland and in Paris, but visiting England, Scotland, and Ireland as well; serving as a war correspondent on the Crimean front; then on to Germany once more and France, Switzerland, and Italy. A democrat and lover of German culture, Hartmann's true *patria* was Europe; his feet, however, rarely found rest.[91]

Isidor Heller was back in Pest in March 1848, where he edited the political journal *Die Morgenröthe*. But this, his second stay in Hungary, also ended abruptly. By the end of May he was forced to abandon both Pest and the paper as the result of articles that he had written against the government of Louis Kossuth—articles that protested Hungary's policies toward its national minorities. Returning to Vienna in June 1848, Heller wrote lead articles under his real name for *Der Freimütige*. As a political moderate he was able to remain safely in Vienna until December, at which point he made his way to Frankfurt, and from there to Berlin. Heller finally managed to get himself into trouble in 1852. The Prussian authorities reacted to a brochure that he had published entitled *Sendschreiben eines Österreichers an die deutsche Nation*, in which he accused Prussia of being a hinderance to German unity, by giving Heller twenty-four hours to leave Berlin. Ensconced once more in Vienna, Heller found a receptive audience in Austrian government circles, served as private secretary to Baron Bruck (in Constantinople!), wrote on foreign affairs for the *Österreichische Zeitung*, and eventually edited the paper *Der Fortschritt*. In his political writings Heller argued for freedom of religion, equality and autonomy for the nationalities of the monarchy, but against the "overreaching" of nationalities beyond the reasonable bounds of autonomy.[92]

Simon Hock lived through the Revolution of 1848 in Prague, apparently uninvolved in revolutionary activity per se. He contributed articles to the *Österreichisches Central-Organ für Glaubensfreiheit*, criticizing the Jewish community for failing to respond to the events of 1848 by democratizing its own structure. But he himself did not lead a revolt in the Jewish streets. Rather, after marrying in 1849, he became involved in the day-to-day affairs of the Prague community (helping to write its new statutes in 1850), and settled down to his life-long vocation of investigating and writing the history of the Jews of Prague. In 1856 he collaborated with Koppelmann Lieben to bring out a collection of 170 gravestone inscriptions from the Prague Jewish cemetery, together with accompanying biographies. Though he never fulfilled his ambition of publishing a complete history of Prague Jewry, he remained committed to the writing of local history throughout his remaining years.[93]

Interestingly, David Kuh rebounded from his disillusionment with Czech nationalism by trying his hand as an actor with a German theatre troupe traveling through Moravia. Tiring of this, he began a career in journalism and found himself in 1848 in Pest, trumpeting the cause of Hungarian independence in the pages of an obscure German paper. He soon started his own (German) paper in the Hungarian town of Pécs (Fünfkirchen), where he supported Kossuth's politics and agitated against Hungary's Slavic populations. When the Hungarian revolution collapsed, Kuh was sentenced to six years in prison but was released in 1850 following the proclamation of a general amnesty.[94]

At this point Kuh returned to his native city of Prague, founded first the *Prager Zeitschrift für Literatur* and then the more successful *Tagesbote aus Böhmen,* achieved respectability, cofounded the German Independent Party, and served in the Bohemian Diet (1862–73) and finally in the Austrian Reichsrat (1872–73).[95] In the autumn of 1858 Kuh's paper, the *Tagesbote,* published an anonymous attack on the authenticity of the Dvůr Králové manuscript, which, it will be recalled, had been "discovered" in 1817 and purported to represent an early example of Czech national literature. The charge elicited a storm of protest from the Czech middle class. František Palacký himself launched a public campaign against Kuh, asking sarcastically how his "Börsen-Blatt" (clearly implying *Judenblatt*) suddenly became interested in literary issues. Czech nationalists pressured the by-now-elderly Hanka to initiate a libel suit against Kuh. The sensational trial took place in the summer of 1859 and coincided with the rebirth of political life in Bohemia following the collapse of neo-absolutism. Kuh, it seems, was indeed found guilty of libel, though he ultimately would be vindicated. In the 1880s Tomáš Masaryk would be under attack by loyal Czech nationalists for publishing the very same claim about the manuscripts in his journal *Athenaeum*. By Masarayk's time, however, the charge of forgery proved incontrovertible.[96]

Christoph Stölzl wonders openly why Kuh, who apparently remained on friendly terms with Nebeský and other Czechs in the 1850s, should have taken it upon himself to launch an attack on the famous "Czech manuscripts." Surely the answer to this question is not hard to find. It lies in the anti-Jewish uprisings of the 1840s and in Kuh's reading of both the origins and the shortcomings of middle-class nationalism. The modern Czech movement, he noted, had been born and nurtured in the gymnasia and universities, the very places where he and his generation had come to love the "other" language and culture of Bohemia. There they had created their own vision of an alternative society, an open, meritocratic community whose benefits were to be enjoyed fully by both Czechs and Jews. Cultural nationalism, however, was itself the by-product of an uneasy tension that existed between the Enlightenment rationalist tradition and the romanticism of the nineteenth century. It always carried the danger that myth and fanaticism would replace reason and tolerance in the effort to further the national cause. Siegfried Kapper's Malá Strana gymnasium had been the setting for the Hanka forgery of 1817, aided and abetted by the influential professor Václav Svoboda. Perhaps inevitably, it was the same Svoboda who incited his students to violence against Jews during the riots of 1844. His was a *trahison des clercs* that inevitably alienated Kuh and most of his fellow Jewish intellectuals from the Czech cause as a whole.

Kuh sought the ultimate revenge in 1858. His charge that the Czech manuscripts were fakes implicitly discredited the romantic-intellectual stream of the Czech national movement. He was also able to punish Václav Svoboda and all other Czech intellectuals who had either supported or condoned the violence of the 1840s. Stölzl, I think correctly, points to the significance of the fact that the person who launched the attack on the sacred icons of Czech national renewal was the same one who fourteen years earlier had tried ("with ... an almost religious idealism") to bring Jews and Czechs together.[97] With the campaign in the *Tagesbote* Kuh symbolically closed the chapter on a brief experiment in the modern history of Czech Jews. But he also did more. As Moritz Hartmann had suggested in 1844, Kuh was making the book "smaller by half," signaling the retreat of educated Jews and intellectuals from Czech concerns.

The retreat was not to be permanent, however. Beginning in the last third of the century, demographic and social factors would prove to be more important determinants of cultural affiliation than the political experiences of the monied and educated elite. The removal of family and occupational restrictions in the 1840s and 1850s had been followed by a steady growth in the rural and small-town Jewish populations of Bohemia. By the 1870s and 1880s tens of thousands of Jews—provincial in origin and conversant in Czech language and culture—flocked to the larger cities and towns of the crown land, there to pursue jobs in industry, banking, and commerce and to feed their children on the expanded networks of secondary and higher education. The first Czech-Jewish student association was founded in Prague in 1876, the first Czech-Jewish religious association five years later; the first political organization of Jewish Czech nationalists emerged in 1893, and with it came a Czech-language Jewish newspaper. At the same time that Jews from the Czech provinces were overwhelming the traditional community in Prague and other urban centers, the Czech national movement itself was usurping the power of German elites in virtually all public spheres.[98]

Consequently, the sociopolitical context in which Jewish life was carried out, in which cultural choices and alliances were made, bore only the remotest resemblance to that of the 1840s. The popular violence and political insults of that decade were largely forgotten, but not because the Czech populace no longer vented its fury on the Jews, nor because the political relationship was now free of tension. If anything, the 1890s witnessed a great deal more violence against Jewish life and property and much greater political pressure directed by Czech nationalists toward Jews. But in the 1840s both the German elites and the Habsburg house held sway in Bohemia. Until at least the 1870s the Jews of Bohemia could afford to follow a "narrow" vision of community—one that essentially excluded both the Czech nation and Jewish ethnic nationalism—because the German Habsburg option was still alive. By the twentieth century the social vision of Czech Jews was compelled to widen as the former options were closed.

CHAPTER 4

Pursuing the Golem of Prague

Jewish Culture and the Invention of a Tradition

Introduction

The Babylonian Talmud, Sanhedrin 65B, reads:

Rava said: If the righteous wished, they could create a world, as it is written [Isaiah 59:2]: "It is your iniquities that have separated you from your God" [i.e., made a distinction between you and God]. Rava created a man and sent him to Rabbi Zera. Rabbi Zera spoke to him but he [the man] did not answer. Then he [Rabbi Zera] said to him: You are from the companions [i.e., a creature created by the rabbis]. Return to your dust.

Rabbi Hanina and Rabbi Oshaia spent every Sabbath eve studying the *Book of Creation (Sefer Yezirah)*; a third-grown calf was created for them, and they ate it.

An observation:

Prague's oldest existing synagogue, the thirteenth-century Altneuschul (Staronová synagoga), to this day follows an idiosyncratic—and apparently unique—liturgy during Friday evening services. Psalms 92 (the psalm for the Sabbath day) and 93 are said in their entirety and then *repeated* before the cantor issues the formal call to prayer (*Barekhu*).

A modern rendition of the Golem story reads:

Der Golem

During the reign of Rudolph II there lived among the Jews of Prague a man named Bezalel Löw, who because of his tall stature and great learning, was called "der hohe" [the Great] Rabbi Löw. This rabbi was well versed in all of the arts and sciences, especially in the Kabbalah. By means of this art he could bring to life figures formed out of clay or carved from wood, who, like real men, would perform whatever task was asked of them. Such home-made servants are very valuable: they do not eat, they do not drink, and they do not require any wages. They work untiringly; one can scold them, and they do not answer back.

Rabbi Löw had fashioned for himself one such servant out of clay, placed in his mouth the Name (a magic formula), and thereby brought him to life. This artificial servant performed all of the menial tasks in the house throughout the week: chopping wood, carrying water, and so on. On the Sabbath, however, he was required to rest; therefore, before the day of rest had begun, his master removed the Name from his mouth and made him dead. Once, however, the rabbi forgot to do this and calamity ensued. The magic servant became enraged, tore down houses, threw rocks all around, pulled up trees, and carried on horribly in the streets. People hurried to the rabbi to tell him of the situation. But the difficulty was great; the Sabbath was already at hand, and all labor—whether to create or to destroy—was strictly forbidden. How, then, to undo the magic? The rabbi's dilemma with his Golem was like that of the sorcerer's apprentice and his broom in Goethe's poems. Fortunately, the Sabbath had not yet been consecrated in the Altneu synagogue, and since this is the oldest and most honorable syna-gogue in Prague, everything is set according to it. There was still time to re-move the Name from the crazy youth. The master hurried, tore the magic formula from the mouth of the Golem, and the lump of clay dropped and fell in a heap. Alarmed by this event, the rabbi did not wish to make such a dangerous servant again. Even today pieces of the Golem are to be seen in the attic of the Altneu synagogue.[1]

• • •

The oft-cited passage from the tractate Sanhedrin, many scholars have argued, constitutes the literary core of the Golem legend in Jewish cul-ture, the tale of the artificial being created from earth and clay and brought to life through the miraculous combination of letters.[2] The an-ecdote concerning Rava and his colleagues is embedded within a larger discussion, which sets forth permissible versus nonpermissible forms of magic. It is apparent from the tone of the story, as well as from more explicit statements that follow, that the Talmud views the activities of the rabbis in question as perfectly acceptable. Righteousness, one might infer, involves more than moral perfection. Ultimately, it constitutes both a striving after and an imitation of God, an effort that for the truly righteous has no limits. The rabbis have extended the sentiment in Isa-iah—that human sinfulness erects a barrier between God and his crea-tures—to suggest the obverse: that in the absence of sin, individuals can in fact become Godlike, even to the extent of creating life. Apparently, however, even the most righteous would-be creators of life suffer a major limitation to their art. Though their creatures can apparently understand the spoken word, they are denied the power of their own speech. Thus when Rabbi Zera could not get Rava's creature to respond to him, he immediately suspected that it was in fact an artificial creation made by one of his colleagues and ordered it to "return to its dust."

The Golem motif has undergone a long and meandering evolution from antiquity to our own times, when the tale seems to speak of cybernetics and artificial intelligence while retaining strong elements of doom that hark back to Faust and Frankenstein.[3] What we know as the *Book of Creation (Sefer Yezirah)*—one of Judaism's earliest mystical texts, dating anywhere from the third to the sixth century C.E.—may or may not be the work referred to in Sanhedrin 65b. In seeking to understand the secrets of creation, the *Sefer Yezirah* proposes "thirty-two paths of wisdom," consisting of combinations of the ten basic numerals and the twenty-two letters of the Hebrew alphabet.[4] At least one modern scholar argues that the *Sefer Yezirah* is not merely a speculative work, but rather has as an underlying goal the actual creation of artificial life.[5] This conclusion may remain a controversial one for some time. It is eminently clear, however, that a number of medieval Jews who read the work understood it in this practical light. The most prominent example of this trend is the twelfth- and thirteenth-century rabbi Eleazar of Worms, one of the exemplars of German-Jewish pietism. Eleazar's commentary on the *Sefer Yezirah* went so far as to enumerate instructions for the actual creation of a Golem. The kabbalistic writings of Abraham Abulafia of Spain and the so-called *Pseudo-Saadya*—a thirteenth-century text of French-Jewish origin—similarly testify to the interest of medieval Jewish mystics in the "practical" arts of creation.[6]

Among early modern Jews, tales of the creation of life by pious individuals seem to have been most common in Poland, where beginning in the seventeenth century, an important new motif was added. The creature of the rabbis was understood to be not only a servant who performs all sorts of physical labor for his master, but also a source of danger. One of the earliest literary depictions of this theme comes from a non-Jewish source, Christoph Arnold, who reports in a letter written in 1674 on the practice of Golem-building among Polish Jews.

After saying certain prayers and holding certain fast days, they make the figure of a man from clay, and when they have said the *shem hamephorash* [the explicit—and unmentionable—name of God] over it, the image comes to life. And although the image itself cannot speak, it understands what is said to it and commanded of it; among the Polish Jews it does all kinds of housework, but is not allowed to leave the house. On the forehead of the image they write: *emeth,* that is, "truth." But a figure of this kind grows each day; though very small at first, it ends by becoming larger than all those in the house. In order to take away his strength, which ultimately becomes a threat to all those in the house, they quickly erase the first letter *aleph* from the word *emeth* on his forehead, so that there remains only the word *meth,* that is, "dead." When this is done the Golem collapses and dissolves into the clay or mud that he was.... They say that a *baal shem* [literally, master of the Name (of God)] in Poland by the name of Rabbi Elias made a Golem who became so large that the rabbi could no longer reach his forehead to erase the letter *e.* He thought up a trick, namely that the Golem, being his servant, should remove his boots, supposing that when the Golem bent over, he would erase the letters. And so it happened, but when the Golem became mud again, his whole weight fell on the rabbi, who was sitting on the bench, and crushed him.[7]

That Arnold's report is based either on the first- or second-hand testimony of Polish Jews is supported by the individual details of the account as well as by its reverberations in the Hebrew literature of the period.[8] The Rabbi Elias in question is Elijah of Chelm (d. 1583), an important talmudic scholar, kabbalist, and wonder-worker who possessed secret knowledge of the "Holy Names" of God. It is not surprising that Jews should have attributed to popular healers (*ba'alei shem*) the ability to create life, since both healing and the act of creation, according to the mystical tradition, involved the purposeful manipulation of words and letters. Zevi Hirsch Ashkenazi, a descendent of Elijah of Chelm, told a similar story to his son Jacob Emden (1697–1776), the leading German rabbi of the eighteenth century. Yet this tale, recorded by Emden in his autobiography and elsewhere, omits the wordplay that had occupied a central position in the accounts of Christian Hebraists (i.e., *emeth* and *meth*) and also allows a less drastic fate to befall his ancestor Rabbi Elijah. In Emden's version, the Golem does not crush and kill his unfortunate creator but only renders him cut and bruised.[9]

Sometime between the seventeenth and the nineteenth centuries—precisely when is not clear—the Golem tradition among European Jews appears to have taken a decisive turn, attaching itself to the life and career of Prague's most famous Jew after Franz Kafka, Rabbi Judah Löw ben Bezalel (ca. 1520–1609), known in Western literature as "the great (*der Hohe*) Rabbi Löw," and in traditional Jewish culture by the acronym *Maharal*. Judah Löw was active in Prague during the reigns of the Habsburg emperors Maximilian II (1564–76) and Rudolph II (1576–1612), a period often referred to as the Golden Age of Czech Jewry, during which time imperial policy demonstrated remarkable tolerance toward Jews and Protestants alike, Jewish cultural life flourished, and the Jewish population—particularly in Prague—grew significantly.[10] The Maharal presided over one of Europe's great talmudic academies, pioneered important reforms in Jewish education, and produced a large literary oeuvre that bestowed pride of place to Judaism's homiletical tradition (*'aggadah,* or narrative tradition). But no evidence suggests that he ever engaged in activities associated with the creation of a Golem. While he does appear to have had an interest in the speculative side of Jewish mysticism, Judah Löw is not known for having been a devotee of the so-called "practical kabbalah"; and unlike Elijah of Chelm, Judah Löw was not a *ba'al shem.*[11]

Nevertheless, virtually every literary evocation of the Golem legend since the first half of the nineteenth century has incorporated two new elements: Judah Löw is understood to be the Golem's creator and Prague's Jewish Town is portrayed as the locus of events. Precisely, it is the Prague of Rudolph II that is recalled, the capital city of one of Europe's most eccentric, cosmopolitan, and tolerant monarchs, patron of the arts and the occult sciences, supporter of the astronomers Johannes Kepler and Tycho de Brahe, and suspected Protestant sympathizer.[12] When Rudolph became emperor in 1576, he moved the imperial court from Vienna to Prague, which then, in the words of Frances Yates, "became a center for alchemical, astrological, magico-scientific studies of all kinds.... Prague became a Mecca for those interested in esoteric and scientific studies from all over Europe." It was, again in her words, "a melting pot of ideas, mysteriously exciting in its potentiality for new developments."[13]

It is possible that the modern version of the Golem tale settled on Prague as the locus of events because of a general knowledge that it was there during the age of Rudolph that occult science and magic, humanistic pursuits and textual study, appear to have coexisted in a creative mix the likes of which were rarely seen—even in Renaissance Europe. To posit this hypothesis, however, is to answer very little. The Golem tale, after all, is one of many built around the life and personality of Judah Löw. Rudolph may represent little more than the rabbi's alter ego; he may simply be the Gentile king in a story created by and for Jews. And one still would like to know where this version of the legend originated. Did it constitute a piece of the "local knowledge" of Prague Jews, generated in Bohemia and recounted as a form of self-understanding; or was it shared simultaneously by a number of different local cultures? Did both Jewish and Gentile communities "know" and transmit—hence remember—the tale?

The only hard piece of evidence we have linking the Maharal to the intellectual universe of Rudolph's court is a brief entry in a Hebrew chronicle written by the Maharal's contemporary and fellow resident of Prague, David Gans, in 1592.[14] A student of both the Cracow luminary Moses Isserles and Judah Löw, Gans had taken the unusual step for a Jew of his era of devoting himself mainly to the "secular" sciences: mathematics, astronomy, geography, and history. Around the year 1600 he made the acquaintance of two of Europe's leading astronomers—the Dane Tycho Brahe and the German Johannes Kepler—both of whom were living in Prague at the time and enjoying the patronage of the imperial court. Gans managed to visit the two in their "observation rooms" on at least three occasions, and he wrote about the encounters in his own work on astronomy, *Neḥmad ve-naʿim* (Delightful and pleasant).[15] His chronicle of world history, *Ẓemaḥ David* (The offspring of David), was completed in the aftermath of a century of cataclysmic events that included the expulsion of the Jews from Spain, the rise of the Ottoman Empire, the Protestant Reformation, and the wars of religion in Central Europe; the book ended with a summary of the year 1592 and with profiles of some of Prague's luminaries. It is in this context that he wrote the following:

Our lord the emperor ... Rudolph, may his glory be exalted, in the full measure of his graciousness and correctness sent for and called upon our master Rabbi Löw ben Bezalel, received him with a welcome and merry expression, and spoke to him face to face [literally, *peh ʾel peh*, mouth to mouth] as one would to a friend. The nature and quality of their words are mysterious, sealed, and hidden [*setumim, ḥatumim, ve-neʿelmim*]. This took place here in the holy community of Prague on Sunday, the third of Adar, 352 [1592].[16]

In view of the fact that the encounter in question involved a member of Gans's own community and purportedly took place not only in his own lifetime but in the months preceding the completion of his work, it would be reasonable to suppose that Judah Löw and Rudolph II did meet on at least one occasion. The nature of the interaction and the content of their discussion, however, cannot be retrieved. Judah Löw may have preferred to keep the details confidential, or he may have been enjoined by the imperial court to do so. It is also conceivable that Gans wished to intimate with his choice of words—"mysterious, sealed, and hidden"—a topic of conversation relating to mysticism and the occult sciences, whether Jewish or Gentile. Any conclusions are necessarily speculative, but there is no evidence to suggest that Gans's account of the royal meeting encouraged, in the short run, a *local* tradition tying the Maharal to practical kabbalistic arts.

Precisely when a body of legend and popular wisdom developed around the figure of the Maharal remains largely an enigma, but the degree of our indecisiveness depends to a large extent on the methods we use to attack the problem. If one were to proceed as a literary historian (following the lead of Gershom Scholem, Moshe Idel, Sigrid Mayer, et al.) what one would look for are paper trails—formal written stories linking the Maharal to the creation of a Golem. On this point the record seems clear enough: nothing appears during the Maharal's lifetime; nor is anything found from the seventeenth or early eighteenth centuries, when tales of Golem-making circulated among both Jews and non-Jews, but mainly in connection with Elijah of Chelm.

When Moses Meir Perles (1666–1739), a descendant of the Maharal, produced *Megilat yuḥasin,* the first biography-cum-genealogy of his illustrious predecessor, in 1727, the theme of Golem-making was likewise absent—although Perles did include other traditions associated with the life of the Maharal.[17] The first written source that gives voice to a Maharal Golem legend does not appear until 1841—about which more will be said later. All of this leads the literary historian to conclude that the story of the Golem of Prague is a quite modern creation. It could not have existed before 1730 or Perles would have known about it, yet we can be fairly certain that it enjoyed popular currency in Prague before 1840. Thus, as Gershom Scholem writes, the Golem legend "was transferred from R. Elijah of Chelm to R. Löw at a very late date, apparently during the second half of the eighteenth century."[18]

The rough coincidence of timing and geography has led Vladimír Sadek to speculate that it was Polish Hasidism that generated the modern connection of the Golem legend to the Maharal and to Prague.[19] He observes that the Beshtian Hasidim and their pietistic predecessors venerated the Maharal and saw him as a spiritual precursor. Ze'ev Gries relates, moreover, that some of the same publishing houses that were responsible for the diffusion of Hasidic books in the late eighteenth century and early nineteenth century also reissued the works of Judah Löw. The Koznitzer Rebbe, R. Israel ben Shabbetai, is a case in point. An enthusiastic publisher of works on *halakhah* and Midrash and a great admirer of the Maharal—whose works had been out of print for generations—R. Israel reprinted many of these, accompanied by his own commentaries.[20]

It is one thing, however, to acknowledge an elective affinity between Polish Hasidism and the Maharal and quite another to establish a role for Hasidism in the Golem saga. One major obstacle to making such an argument is the fact that the Prague Jewish community (as opposed to that of Moravia, for example) appears to have been largely cut off from and immune to Hasidic influence until the First World War. Although preemancipatory Czech Jewry enjoyed close ties to a number of Polish-Jewish centers, none of these was in an area dominated by Hasidism. The first documented appearance of Hasidim in Bohemia occurs after 1914, when refugees from Galicia—among them the entourage of the Belzer Rebbe—streamed into the country.[21] More problematic still is the relationship of Hasidism to the theme of Golem-making. Moshe Idel calls our attention to the "obvious absence of the golem legend" in the formative years of Polish Hasidism. "Hasidic literature," Idel writes, "richer in legends than all the Jewish mystical literature, ignored this peculiar type of legend." Tales of Golem-making may have been excluded from Hasidism's early repertoire, he suggests, because of the assumption at the core of Hasidic thought that spiritual perfection is attainable not through miracle or magic but through the mystical performance of prayer and the *mizvot*. When R. Menaḥem Mendel of Kotsk was told about the powers of a wonder-worker, he is said to have responded, "Can he also make a Hasid?"[22]

An alternative to the literary-historical approach might be found in ethnography and the study of folklore. What the ethnographer wishes to know is not when literary texts were produced but what a culture "remembers" and recounts, especially through oral transmissions. But how to get at these memories? Communal and family traditions can often be inscribed in decorative art, tombstone carvings, communal record books, family Bibles, and the like; if one cannot always work backwards from these sources to original expressions of beliefs or ideas, one nevertheless can see in them evidence for the presence of a given motif in the general culture of the community. One window of opportunity for ethnographic observation was opened up in the 1720s when the Prague Jewish community embarked on a renovation of the Maharal's tombstone and, more or less simultaneously, a rabbinical descendant of Judah Löw—Isaiah Katz, who served as rabbi of Ungarisch Brod (Uherský Brod) in Moravia—instructed the secretary of the Prague Jewish community, Moses Meir Perles, to write the family chronicles.[23] As noted earlier, Perles's work, *Megilat yuḥasin,* makes no mention of a Golem tradition and, although legends involving the Maharal's grave may already have been in circulation at the time, the decorative accompaniments to the new tomb do not allude to a Golem theme.

I should also mention two other folkloristic possibilities that have yet to yield much fruit. One was brought up by Vladimír Sadek in the context of his argument in favor of a Hasidic origin to the Maharal-Golem tale. Sadek observes that Hasidim accord the gravesite of the Maharal the same treatment that they would give the final resting place of any *zaddik,* making pilgrimages to it and placing on it prayers and petitions.[24] Anyone who has visited the old Jewish cemetery in Prague knows that this is true. But it is no less obvious that thousands of non-Hasidim—both Jewish and Christian—also visit Judah Löw's grave every year and engage in comparable behavior. The problem is that we do not know when this practice began or who started it. It is possible that the folklorists are right in looking to the early eighteenth century, sensing that the renovation itself was either an indication of a kind of "Maharal cult" or an act of "invented tradition." But it may also be that the Maharal's grave did not attract pilgrims until the early twentieth century, when Jewish refugees from Eastern Europe reminded Prague Jewry of its own cultural history by seeking out the graves of numerous rabbis, all of whom were part of the living memory of Polish orthodoxy—if no longer of Czech Jewry.

To date neither ethnography nor literary history has succeeded fully in explaining the convergence of the Golem legend with Prague and the Maharal. Admittedly, Scholem and Idel have established the Polish tradition associated with Rabbi Elijah of Chelm as the most likely immediate predecessor of the Prague venue. And folklorists are probably correct in guessing that some type of new, or renewed, veneration of the Maharal took root in Prague around the 1720s or 1730s. This was during a period of rapid growth and development of the Jewish community: the residents of the Jewish Town made up nearly half the population of Prague's Staré Město (Altstadt) and about 28 percent of the city's five districts combined during the first decades of the eighteenth century.[25] It was also a time in which David Oppenheim (1664–1736) consolidated unprecedented political and religious authority, occupying—at various times and in combination—the positions of *rosh yeshivah,* chief rabbi of Prague, and chief rabbi of Bohemia. The rabbinical establishment in Prague during the second, third, and fourth decades of the eighteenth century appears to have been deeply implicated in kabbalistic studies. Frederic Thieberger claims that Oppenheim himself was a kabbalist, but one can point to other figures as well: Naftali Kohen, a great-grandson of the Maharal and former chief rabbi in Frankfurt am Main, who moved to Prague after 1711; and Jonathan Eibeschütz (1690–1764), a charismatic preacher and *rosh yeshivah* who was known to have dealt in amulets and who, later in life, stood accused of being a secret follower of the "false Messiah," Shabbetai Zevi.[26]

But there are crucial connections that have yet to be drawn. It may well be that rabbinic elites in Prague in the 1720s and 1730s—in particular the students and faculty of the city's *yeshivot*—fostered a magical-kabbalistic reinterpretation of the life of the Maharal. If this was indeed the case, then it is to the traffic between Poland and Prague in students and teachers that one needs to look for the transmission of the early modern Golem tale to the Bohemian capital. Continued human and intellectual commerce after 1740 might explain the internalization of Maharal traditions within Polish Jewry—especially Hasidism—which one finds by the nineteenth century. A venue of the 1720s or 1730s would also imply that in producing a Maharal cult the elite circles in Prague were actually engaged in a process of historical projection, in which the mystical pursuits and cultural fashions of the present were attributed to an earlier, heroic age and to an older historical figure.

And what does one make of the custom maintained by the Altneuschul of repeating Psalm 92 on Friday evening? The skeptical impulse—probably correct—would lead one to view the practice as relatively recent (i.e., post sixteenth century), the justification for which was sought in the evolving cult of the Maharal. It is possible that the repetition originated from practical, perhaps even *halakhic,* considerations. Here I am drawn to the claim made by the ethnographer and biblical scholar J. J. Schudt in his compendium *Jüdische Merckwürdigkeiten* (1714–18), purportedly on the basis of Jewish testimony, that Prague's Altneuschul possessed an organ.[27] If this claim is true, and assuming that it was generally agreed that the *halakhah* did not permit the playing of an organ on the Sabbath, the practice in the Altneuschul may have been to allow musical accompaniment for the introductory Psalms (95 through 99, and 29) on Friday evening but not once the Sabbath had formally begun. Psalm 92, which is introduced as "A Song for the Sabbath Day," might well have been viewed as a liturgical demarcation between the sacred and the profane—sung once to the accompaniment of the organ and once without as the prayer that marked the start of the Sabbath in the synagogue.[28]

The crucial point seems to be that while the organ eventually was removed from the Altneuschul—possibly during the rabbinate of Ezekiel Landau (1713–93)—the custom of repeating Psalm 92 remained. And it is around this ethnographic curiosity that the Golem narrative turns. Landau, who was born and raised in Opatów (Poland), and who assumed the chief rabbinate of Prague in 1754, may have played a dual role in the reinvention of the Golem tradition: insisting on the removal of the synagogue organ and reinforcing the connection between Polish and Bohemian rabbinic culture. By the 1830s and 1840s, when ethnographers set out to collect the stories that Prague Jews told about themselves, the community had "mythologized" the practice of repeating the ninety-second Psalm, locating its justification in a heroic narrative, a legend associated with the venerable rabbi of the Prague Renaissance.

I readily admit that the limb onto which I have just climbed is unsteady and that more research is needed before feelings of vertigo can be reasonably eliminated. A proper research agenda might take the following tacks: a reexamination of Jewish communal records in Prague in the eighteenth century, particularly as they relate to *yeshivah* life and the rabbinate; a rereading of the writings of Oppenheim, Eibeschütz, and Landau; and a new effort to get at the popular culture of both Jewish and non-Jewish Bohemians. The opening up of libraries and archives in East Central Europe in the last few years should be helpful to a certain extent. But much of what is called for involves a new reading of old materials with an eye to a new set of questions.

What we do know is this: the first literary records of the Golem of Prague come to us by way of nineteenth-century ethnography and folklore—relatively new fields of inquiry in the 1830s, inspired by a mixture of Enlightenment criticism, Herderian anthropology, and budding romantic nationalism. Jakob Grimm, of the famous brothers who were among the major practitioners of these arts in Germany in the early part of the century, published a version of the Polish legend in the journal *Zeitung für Einsiedler* in 1808. He was, however, apparently unaware of any association of the Golem theme with the city of Prague.[29] The first individual to transmit in written form a tale told by Prague Jews concerning the Maharal and a Golem of his creation was the non-Jewish journalist and folklorist Franz Klutschak (1814–86). He published his story in 1841 in a Prague monthly devoted to the investigation of world cultures that went by the name of *Panorama des Universums*.[30] Omnivorous in its interests, *Panorama* offered cultural/anthropological pieces on Europe and Austria (separate rubrics), Asia, Africa, America, and Oceania, as well as examples of "narratives, legends, and folktales" from different parts of the world. In 1838 Klutschak had published a set of short pieces called "The Old Jewish Cemetery of Prague and Its Legends," the opening story of which also dealt with the Maharal, though not as the creator of a Golem.[31] His story "Der Golam [*sic*] des Rabbi Löw," which appeared three years later, formed one of four tales that Klutschak offered under the heading "Legends, Fables, and Stories from Bohemia: Partly newly told, partly retold, by F. K."[32]

A Jewish physician by the name of Leopold Weisel (1804–73), who lived most of his life near the town of Domažlice in southwestern Bohemia, worked during this time as a kind of partner-in-arms to Klutschak. Weisel's career is testimony to the fact that the self-conscious recovery of oral traditions is a decidedly *modern* act in which secular intellectuals, in the throes of social and cultural change, seek to save something of the traditional society that is fast slipping away forever. He acquired his medical education in Prague—probably between 1824 and 1830—during which time he lived in the Old Jewish Town and supported himself as a private tutor for a number of Jewish families. Sensing that he stood at a historical turning point, he took it upon himself to capture the rich folk traditions of the ghetto, apparently by interviewing older residents and recording their stories.[33]

Weisel occupied himself in the 1830s and 1840s with the collection and dissemination of the folk wisdom of Jewish Prague, publishing his earliest efforts alongside those of Klutschak in *Panorama des Universums*. In 1838 his "Die Pinchasgasse: Eine jüdische Volkssage" appeared, a tale about a poor peddler who lived in Prague "over two hundred years ago," who traced the streets of the city with a pack over his shoulder by day and "studied the law" by a dim lamp in his dirty room at night.[34] The story was reprinted in 1847, along with four other tales collected by Weisel together titled "Sagen der Prager Juden" and included in the immensely popular collection *Sippurim: Eine Sammlung jüdischer Volkssagen*, published by Wolf Pascheles.[35] Among the five stories retold here by Weisel was his own version of the Golem legend, a minor classic of brief fiction and the benchmark for subsequent retellings until the eve of the First World War.

These two modern renditions of the Golem tradition were published six years apart, yet they build upon rather different narratives. Interestingly, Klutschak's is the longer and more elaborate of the two, written with an eye for descriptive detail in lyrical German prose.[36] By contrast, Weisel's rendering is sparse and unembellished. The Klutschak tale proceeds as a prose piece that is annotated with ethnographic and scholarly observations and punctuated with "insider" information and terminology.[37] Thus the designation "der Hohe Rabbi Löw" alternates in the text with the more homey (and Yiddish) "Rabbi Liwa"; the Altneuschul, the narrator tells us—"as is well known"—was built by the angels immediately after the destruction of the Temple in Jerusalem. Though the story is narrated in a distinct voice, it is equally apparent that the storyteller has his informants within the Prague Jewish community. The tale is offered as an example of authentic Prague-Jewish folk tradition.

The story is also remarkable for the completeness with which it accounts for circumstances and motivations in the Golem narrative. Klutschak offers a compelling explanation, for example, for the Faustian element of power run amok, which occupies a central position in all modern versions of the Prague account. With one foot in the practical Kabbalah and the other in popular psychology, he writes that "fortunately, the Golem was not aware of his magical powers," and that Rabbi Löw was able to devise ways to keep his creature under control.

He prepared for each of the seven days of the week a talisman that held the strength of the Golem in check and directed its will only toward good; and when the Rabbi went to the synagogue in the evening [literally, in the evening at the start of the day], he would remove the old *shem* (talisman) from the mouth of the Golem and exchange it with a new one.[38]

Similarly, Klutschak's narrative accounts for Rabbi Löw's absence from the synagogue on that critical Friday evening, the reason for the rabbi's ordering first the stopping and then the repetition of Psalm 92, and the fact that the Sabbath had not yet officially begun. Relying, once again, on one layer of Jewish folk tradition to explain another, Klutschak has the cantor urging an early start to the Friday evening service so that the souls in purgatory might cool themselves off in the brooks and streams, an enjoyment that was prohibited to Jews on the Sabbath day.[39] Attending to a sick and dying daughter, Rabbi Löw had decided not to pray with the community that evening; but he was brought running to the synagogue when the cries of people watching the Golem start to tear apart the building reminded the rabbi of his failure to provide the Golem with a new talisman. The reason for the violence lay in the simple fact of consciousness: the creature was becoming aware of his own power.

By the time the Maharal arrives at the Altneuschul, the Golem is tearing at its walls; the doors to the Holy Ark (which Klutschak knows—and makes certain that his readers know that he knows—rested in the eastern wall of the Altneuschul) have fallen off, and the candelabra has fallen to the ground, so that all is darkness "as though the end of the world were approaching." At this point, practicality reigns. The Maharal orders the prayers halted so that he can put the proper talisman in the mouth of the Golem. Once peace is restored and the candles rekindled (which can only be done on a weekday), the Jews "laud the wisdom of Rabbi Löw, who has saved them from destruction, and pray more ardently than ever the first [*sic*] Psalm and the Sabbath prayers; [they] send a prayer to Jehovah with such fervor for the recovery of the great Rabbi's daughter that Jehovah calls upon the Angel of Death ["malach Hamawod" (*sic*)], whom He has already sent to the Rabbi's house, to return."[40]

Weisel's "Der Golem," though spare and impoverished compared to Klutschak's tale, is the better known of the two and appears to have served as the basis for subsequent borrowings. For all of its brevity, the author does provide a few bits of extraneous information, which afford the reader a small window onto Weisel's self-conceived ethnographic mission. When he writes, in a brief introduction to "Sagen der Prager Juden," that "countless tales are attached to the old synagogues and the narrow streets; and nearly every tombstone in the large, old cemetery offers up material to one tale or another," he betrays his own indebtedness to the romantic movement. At the same time, he assures the reader that he transcribed the stories as he heard them "from the mouth of the old," thus attesting to his reliability as a transcriber of folk traditions.[41]

Weisel introduces his story with a tantalizing aside that relates directly to my inquiries in this chapter: he excuses the brevity of the story that is to follow with the observation that this "popular tale" (*Volkssage*) has already been used by various writers. "It seems to me superfluous," he writes, "to rework such a well-known story. I shall present it briefly if only so that no one should think that I did not know it."[42] Weisel clearly means to indicate that *this particular* Golem story enjoyed wide circulation in his day, both as a piece of literature and as a tale told by the Jews of Prague. He hardly deemed it worthy of reproducing because it already was widely acknowledged as belonging to the folkloristic treasury of Jewish Prague. Weisel's statements in this regard make me more confident in assigning a date for the provenance of the Prague tale that is a good deal earlier than what most literary historians have allowed up to now.

The efforts of Weisel and Klutschak to retrieve—and ultimately recast—Jewish Prague's folk traditions in literary language were echoed beyond the confines of the Jewish community. The writer Václav Bolemír Nebeský—who was discussed in the last chapter—a romantic poet of the Byronist mold, published a Czech version of Prague Jewish tales for the literary journal *Květy* in 1844.[43] As we know, Nebeský had formed close ties to Jewish university students in both Prague and Vienna and had become convinced of the desirability of recruiting Jews to the cause of Czech nationalism. His collection of Jewish legends in the Czech language appeared in the same year in which he joined forces with Siegfried Kapper (1821–79) and David Kuh (1818–79)—both Jewish writers of Prague—to launch a newspaper campaign in both the Czech and German press designed to create a Czech-Jewish cultural alliance.[44] The effort to "capture" Jews to the cause of Czech culture and politics achieved only moderate success before the 1880s. Nevertheless, the various literary codifications of Czech folklore that occurred in the nineteenth century, including Josef Svátek's *Pražské pověsti a legendy* and Alois Jirásek's *Staré pověsti české*, reserved an important place for the Jewish stories that the writers-cum-ethnographers of the 1830s and 1840s had so assiduously collected.[45]

What united these various endeavors was the desire to uncover and disseminate the cultural memory of the Czech nation, to put forward a "usable past" that could be employed in the service of the construction of a collective identity. A cultural program of this type inevitably combined anthropological investigation and creative embellishment, with equal importance ascribed to the oral traditions of the older generation and to the literary imagination. In adopting Weisel's "Sagen" for their own rewritings of Czech folk culture, the modern authors of the Czech nation were, in effect, claiming Jewish Prague as part of their own inheritance. Why did they do this? Did non-Jewish Czechs have their own memory of Judah Löw and Prague's Golden Age? Did they "remember" the Golem tradition in the same way that the Jews of Prague did or differently? Did this adoption of Jewish lore as something that was simultaneously Jewish and Czech indicate the existence of a significant area of shared culture? Perhaps in appropriating part of Prague's Jewish past the Czech nationalist writers were deepening their own claim to Bohemia itself, thereby strengthening their challenge to German cultural, economic, and political domination. When seen as part of the process of creating a "usable past," the discovery of the Maharal and his Golem among the oral tales of the Czechs themselves added to the antiquity and legitimacy of the Czech national position. Both the Jews and the Czechs were "there" before the Germans; they shared the same wise men, the same legends, the same monsters.

The recovery of myth and legend in the nineteenth century provides evidence for the fact that oral traditions can in a very real sense *follow* literary traditions—even invented ones. The stories of the modern Czech masters were avidly read—their renderings of the Jewish past "remembered"—and over the ensuing decades both assimilating Jews and educated Gentiles recounted the same legends. Thus, when the Czech sculptor Ladislav Šaloun was commissioned to erect statues outside the newly constructed Town Hall in Prague's Staré Město in 1912, he produced two figures, both drawn from the folklore of the city. One was a knight—the so-called Iron Knight—of Czech lore. The other was the Maharal, depicted in a frankly modernist (and unlikely) pose, flanked by his granddaughter (who is unclothed). The granddaughter is handing Judah Löw a flower in allusion to a well-known Czech—and Jewish—tale concerning the master's ultimate demise at a very advanced age: death, whose designs the Maharal had been able to thwart for so long, hides in the fragrance of the rose.[46]

A final example of the role of literature in the production of popular wisdom: the story that *everyone* knows about the Maharal and the Golem (reproduced in film and in plays and even in contemporary Czech anthologies) is the newest of them all. In the decade immediately preceding the First World War, the Jewish world was treated to a series of publications based on sensational manuscript "discoveries" that were said to have been uncovered at the "imperial library" of the city of Metz in eastern France. The first such work, *Sefer goral ha-'assiryot* (Book of lots of tens), which appeared in 1904, purported to describe a system whereby through various manipulations of Hebrew letters people were able to receive oracular answers to their queries. This was followed in 1905 with the publication of a commentary on the Passover Haggadah said to have been written by the Maharal. The work that elicited the most interest, however, appeared in 1909 under the title *Sefer nifla'ot Maharal 'im ha-golem* (Book of the wonders of the Maharal with the Golem). The publisher of each of the "manuscripts" was Yudel Rosenberg (1859–1935), a Hasidic rabbi and *dayyan* living at the time in Warsaw. Rosenberg claimed to have received all three manuscripts from one Hayyim Sharfstein, whom he later described as a relative, and even reproduced letters purported to have been written by Sharfstein in the introductions to two of the works—letters that described the difficulties that he had had copying by hand from the worn and faded pages of the forgotten works and that alluded to other "discoveries" that he would soon make available to Rosenberg. Not surprisingly, perhaps, there is no "imperial library" in Metz and there was no Hayyim Sharfstein. The author of all three works in question (including the oft-reprinted *Haggadat ha-Maharal*) was Yudel Rosenberg himself.[47]

Rosenberg claimed that both the Haggadah commentary and *Sefer nifla'ot Maharal* had been written down by the Maharal's son-in-law, R. Isaac Katz (Issac ben Samson ha-Kohen, d. 1624). In fact, much of the Haggadah commentary (which went under the names *Divrei negidim* and *Leshon limudim*) was derived from the Maharal's work on the exodus from Egypt, *Gevurot ha-Shem;* the rest was Reb Yudel's.[48] As far as *Sefer nifla'ot Maharal* is concerned, the narrative is laced with historical inaccuracies, improbabilities, and terms and concepts that make sense only in a *Polish* context.[49] This story, too, is Reb Yudel's, yet people continue to read and remember it not only as a "genuine" account, but as the *only* account of the creation of the Golem that they know! Subsequent twentieth-century authors have adopted Rosenberg's forgery wholesale. Hebrew writer and folklorist Micha Yosef Ben Gurion anthologized it in his *Mekor Yehuda* (Fountain of Judah). The Galician-born writer Chaim Bloch adapted Rosenberg's stories (or should we say Rabbi Isaac Katz's stories?) to German prose, a project which *he* claimed to have produced through "ethnographic research" on the Russian front. Bloch's collection was soon translated into English and was widely distributed in the United States for many years under the title *The Golem: Legends of the Ghetto of Prague.*[50] *Nifla'ot Maharal* was also adapted by the Yiddish poet H. Leivick for his drama entitled "Der Goylem." As recently as 1980, Judaica Press of New York published a work by the Brooklyn-based writer Gershon Winkler entitled *The Golem of Prague,* an unabashedly romantic and pious rewriting of Yudel's "invented tradition," which promoted itself as "a new adaptation of the *documented* stories of the Golem of Prague" (my emphasis).[51]

What has gone largely unnoticed in the almost automatic acceptance (and retransmission) of Rosenberg's twentieth-century rendering of the Golem legend is the fact that this version constitutes a radical rewriting of the tale. Here the story of the creation and adventures of the artificial being is embedded within a larger narrative of Christian accusations of Jewish "ritual murder." The motif of the blood libel is inscribed in Rosenberg's subtitle "Lekhol ha-'otot veha-moftim asher pa'al ha-ga'on ha-gadol Maharal mi-Prag 'al yad ha-golem asher bara le-hilaḥem neged ha-'alilat [*sic*] dam" (All of the signs and wonders that the great and wise Maharal of Prague effected with the aid of the Golem, which he created [in order] to battle against the blood libel).[52]

I suspect that most twentieth-century readers of these tales do not appreciate the irony that the supposed need to build a monster out of clay in order to defend the Jews against popular violence inspired by the Christian accusation of Jewish ritual murder would *not* have made much sense to a Jew living in the Prague of Rudolph II and the Maharal. The Jewish community in Rudolph's capital at the end of the sixteenth century simply did not face any serious accusations of ritual murder, and I know of no evidence to suggest that the Maharal dispensed much, if any, energy defending his people against this libel. The salience of the ritual murder motif, which serves as the architectural underpinning of the entire collection of stories—and, indeed, which constitutes Yudel Rosenberg's chief literary contribution to the legend—is the strongest evidence by far of the work's twentieth-century provenance. It was the Europe of Reb Yudel, not of the Maharal, that witnessed a proliferation of accusations—and even formal, criminal trials—against Jews on the charge of ritual murder. Starting in 1882 in Hungary and continuing down to the eve of the First World War, Central and Eastern Europe served up a half-dozen sensational murder trials, each prosecuted by agencies of the modern state, in which the case against the Jewish defendants hinged on a modern reworking of the old canard that Jews require the blood of innocent Christians for their religious rites.

Viewed, then, from the perspective of the twentieth-century, Yudel Rosenberg's rendition of the Golem tale functions—on two levels—as wishful thinking. The Maharal's creature of clay does not act as a mere servant to perform menial tasks at the bidding of his master. Like the superheroes of comic-book culture, the Golem rescues the community from powerful enemies who would do it harm. But beyond the wish for a supernatural resolution to human conflict, Rosenberg's *Nifla'ot*

Maharal gives expression to another pious hope: As the long-lost manuscript of R. Yitzhak Katz, it is supposed to silence all of the modern
"doubters" within the Jewish fold—the rationalists and sceptics, who
had cast doubt on the authenticity of the folkloristic accounts of the
Maharal's powers.[53] Rabbi Yitzhak's Maharal is a Jew of the old school,
unsurpassed in wisdom, adept at the secrets of Kabbalah, dignified in
his dealings with the non-Jewish world, and a strict defender of *halakhah*. He personifies for Yudel Rosenberg the bedrock faith of earlier
generations of European Jews, and he, too, is a redeemer of Israel.

In the well-known version the Golem does his job, saving the Jews
of Prague from the certain catastrophe that would have resulted from a
false accusation of ritual murder. But the purpose of this story was not
to instill hope and confidence in its readers. It was a cautionary tale of a
type quite different from the original legend. At least as far back as the
seventeenth-century Polish rendition, the source of danger had always
been understood to reside within—within the confines of community,
and in the very process of the creation of artificial life. Throughout the
twentieth century, the tale has been remembered as a distortion, as if it
had always been concerned with the danger posed by the outside
world. Much has been lost, I think, in the translation; much can also be
inferred with regard to the changing nature of the Jewish-Gentile relationship in East Central Europe.

CHAPTER 5

On Myth, History, and National Belonging in the Nineteenth Century

Myth, Ethnic Identity, and Discourses of the Nation

Anthropology, classical philology, and religious studies have brought distinct analytical traditions to bear on the study of myth in human culture. Classicists have tended to view myth primarily as an epic literary genre, an account of "the gods," which purports to transmit cultural information based on the preliterary, oral traditions of a people. It is understood to represent a bridge between orally transmitted epic tales and sagas and the more sophisticated genres of history, philosophy, and rhetoric. Anthropologists of the early part of this century who did ethnographic field work among so-called preliterate populations understood myth to be a primary component of orally transmitted cultures. They looked to oral narratives about "the gods" that were transmitted in social settings or accompanied the performance of public ritual in order to reveal the conceptual but nonrational underpinnings of the societies in question.[1] Comparative religionists, for their part, appear to have been equally impressed by both classicism and anthropology. While acknowledging myth to be a fundamental form of religious expression, a sacred mapping of encounters between the human and the divine, they also have tended to share the assumption that myth belongs to "prehistoric" time and that only echoes of this type of consciousness remain in the written texts of the major religions.[2]

In their rough outlines all such approaches involve significant modernist biases. The classicist perceives the mythic literary stratum to be both historically bounded and superceded by types of writing that accord more with our own sensibilities. The association between myth and "primitive," or between myth and "preliterate," in much of the ethnographic literature attests to a similar conceit concerning progress and the rationalization of culture. And both students of and apologists for religion in the nineteenth century isolated the philosophical and ethical strands within religious traditions as representing higher—or later—stages of development. What is implied throughout is that myth as a system of knowledge reflecting a particular type of cultural sensibility is inaccessible, and when it is "retrieved" it is done so as the result of an atavistic act, a retreat to the dark, the savage, and the irrational.

If we wish, then, for the study of myth to be made relevant to questions of ethnicity and modern nationalism, it must first be removed from the classical paradigms within which it has typically been viewed. Myth should neither be tied to a particular literary genre nor relegated to a single stage in an assumed evolution of human consciousness; it ought to be contingent not upon form or time, but rather upon content and function. It should be understood as reflecting a particular type of social knowledge, that is, a system of meaning, constructed and transmitted in social settings, in which the realm of direct experience is related to, explained by, and patterned after a metaphysical, timeless, or sacred reality. Maurice Leenhardt has written that in those cultures in which individuals actively participate in their myths, landscape, topography, and art mediate between visible and invisible realities, between the individual and divinity. If one were to expand upon this concept of participation, one might view myth phenomenologically as the production of a "sacred geography" of time and space, travel through which orients the individual (and the group) to realities and significances that are understood to lie beyond the bounds of both, that is, beyond historically bounded time and locally marked space.[3]

In the modern world one of the key areas in which the social production of myth is to be found is in the constitution of collective identity through ritualized memory. Ethnic communities, argues Anthony Smith, "are nothing if not historical communities built up on shared memories." And of the complex of symbols and values that make up a group's identity, it is the myths of origin and descent that work best to orient the group in its temporal and spatial environment.[4] Ethnic groups, of course, also evolve various "signs" of cultural distinctiveness, such as language, religion, kinship systems, and so on. But "in the last resort, it is the belief in the common and unique origins of the community, and in its liberation from all ills, past and present, that justifies and sustains the other cultural dimensions or 'signs' of individuality."[5] Smith also makes the point that there is nothing "obvious" or straight-forward in the transition from ethnic consciousness, as such, to modern nationalism. State formation, the creation of modern bureaucratic structures, scientific revolutions, new paradigms for the organization and evaluation of knowledge, and new methods for its production and dissemination intervene in such ways as to militate against any simple extension of pre-Enlightenment ethnic solidarities to the arena of mod-ern politics.[6] Nor, as Benedict Anderson points out, do all ethnic com-munities take the decisive step of imagining themselves as nations. But where such processes do take place, information that is transmitted through myth again serves as an important stimulus to group solidarity and self-knowledge. Because modern nationalism encompasses not only the imaginative construction of communities of affinity but also contests for political power involving other human groups as well as states, the myths that these communities cultivate and hold dear are also likely to convey critical pieces of information about the "otherness" of other groups.

It is also true that in the post-Enlightenment West the production and dissemination of myth was rendered problematic precisely because rationalism, the scientific method, and historical criticism seemed to offer stronger and more compelling paradigms for truth. If myth was not entirely pushed aside, it nevertheless acquired a new epistemologi-cal status as the repository for "subjective" truths and values. Mythic knowledge was able to occupy an almost sacred place by virtue of emo-tional attachment alone. A nation loved its myths because they were *its* myths.

By the same token, history and myth should, in theory, stand as competing if not incompatible sources of knowledge. Even in the men-tal universe of the ancient Greeks, as Paul Veyne explains, historical crit-icism and speculative science presented powerful challenges to mythic knowledge because, in contrast to myth, they operated on the assump-tion that truth and falsehood composed epistemological opposites.[7] As it turns out, both history as a discipline and historians as professional experts have been deeply implicated in the production of myth for na-tionalist purposes. One reason for this mixing of genres lies in the issue of "authority" within knowledge systems. Much of the power of myth, according to Veyne, derives from the unimpeachability of its source, not from its correspondence to daily experience. Similarly, people in modern societies display blind trust in statements of truth that they could never—or would never choose to—verify in their own lives.[8]

By the early nineteenth century, what Anthony Smith calls historicism—the conviction that all of reality, including sacred institutions, has an origin in time and that the nature and purpose of things are revealed in the record of their evolution—occupied a position of cultural authority once reserved for divine inspiration. In uncovering the "origins" of societies and institutions and documenting their careers over time, historians also assigned meaning, coherence, and moral value "to what might otherwise so easily be seen as unrelated pieces of cultural information."[9] In this context, the discovery and analysis of medieval manuscripts assumed particular importance. "Of special interest," writes Andrew Lass, "were those documents that could be argued to be local in origin, documenting the country's 'historical dawn,' upholding the particular qualities of the national character, the 'original' lives of its folk, its struggles and heroic deeds."[10] It might well be argued—as some have—that those historians who became so deeply invested in the modern quest for origins were engaging in public behavior that violated their own "scientific" ethos. Eric Hobsbawm understands this phenomenon as part of the general tendency of modern institutions and political movements to "invent" traditions—practices organized around ritual or symbol that are designed to express a presumed continuity with the past. Invented traditions, however, almost always emerge in response to a sense of radical disjuncture with the past; the continuities that they reveal are themselves figments of the imagination.[11] For Ernest Gellner the imaginative virtuosity of nationalist intellectuals is of no intrinsic interest, as it simply lays bare the "false consciousness" that is inherent in all national ideology.

Its myths invert reality: it claims to defend folk culture while in fact it is forging a high culture; it claims to protect an old folk society while in fact helping to build up an anonymous mass society.... Nationalism tends to treat itself as a manifest and self-evident principle, accessible as such to all men, and violated only through some perverse blindness, when in fact it owes its plausibility and compelling nature only to a very special set of circumstances, which do indeed obtain now, but which were alien to most of humanity and history.[12]

All national historiography, William McNeill has suggested, with its inevitable blending of ideology, truth, and fabrication, constitutes myth or, to use his coinage, "mythistory." "We are free with Herodotus, or saved with Augustine, or oppressed with Marx, as the case may be."[13] The role of the historian in the production of a nation's history is not simply to "[portray] the people they write about as they wish to be." The construction of "mythistory," in fact, involves a compelling psychological contradiction. Having usurped the authority of priest and theologian as arbiter of truth, the modern national educator employs the methods of historicism in a project that is profoundly ahistorical. For the narratives that he or she produces are intended to reveal essences and qualities whose origin in time is so remote as to defy precise location, and which are not themselves subject to change and development. The nation and its heroes are imagined to reach beyond history to sacred time; and history itself, defined as a field of contest, failure, and struggle, is to be overcome even as it is fulfilled. The nation meets its destiny with the aid of a map provided by the historian.

Yet, Lass reminds us, the critical tradition of the Enlightenment—to which modern historical scholarship also belongs—also contained the tools and assumptions that could be used by others to question and even discredit the orthodoxies of the national awakeners. To common assumptions about the distinction between "fact" and "fiction," for example, one might add the tendency to define myth as something mistakenly presumed to be true but which is in fact false, derived from polemics born of the Age of Reason. Thus, the same analytical methods that might claim to establish the historical truth of a document could just as easily—in the hands of someone else—raise doubts about its authenticity.

My goal in this chapter is to capture two moments in the modern historicist creation of myth. The first is an episode of historical fabrication that took place during the early decades of the Czech national movement, an example of the conflation of genres—myth, history, ideology—that appears to feature prominently in the cultural activity of modern nationalism. The second concerns the first modern effort on the part of Bohemian Jews to produce a history, as well as a historical mythology, that would be tied to place, delineate the connections between Jews and non-Jewish Bohemians, and serve as an ideological guide to political behavior in the present. The two moments connect on a number of levels: The earlier project, in orienting Czech intellectuals and middle-class professionals to a specific narrative of the past, directed their relations in the present with Germans and Jews. Jews, in turn, informed to a large extent by these same texts, responded to them in a variety of ways, depending on personal history, friendship circles, and political events. In the end, part of the Bohemian Jewish intelligentsia participated in the public subversion of Czech myth even as a new effort to write its Jewish analogue was beginning.

Documentary Forgery and the Delineation of Community

As we have seen, the themes of state building, secularization of culture, professional recruitment, and construction of nationality began to take shape in the Czech provinces of the Habsburg monarchy during the last quarter of the eighteenth century. Maria Theresa's somewhat tentative efforts at political centralization and educational reform during the 1770s, followed by Joseph II's self-conscious "modernization from above," had the overall effect of liberalizing economic life, encouraging population movement from the countryside to the cities, and creating a multitiered school system—based on the principle of universal education for boys and girls—from which male graduates were recruited to fill places in an expanding state bureaucracy.[14] By the second and third decades of the nineteenth century the sons of wealthy Czech-speaking peasants were filling the ranks of the secondary school teaching corps, editing newspapers and journals, practising the professions, and climbing the ladder of state civil service.

It was this second generation of Czech-speaking intellectuals that first imagined the contours of what was to become the modern Czech nation. Josef Jungmann (1773–1847)—gymnasium professor, linguist, and translator and after 1834, prefect of the Altstädter Gymnasium in Prague—played a central part in elaborating what the boundaries of the national community were to be.[15] Up to this time parts of the Bohemian nobility and urban population, as well as most of the peasantry, had been conscious of a premodern ethnicity of descent, the content and shape of which were not precise. It was not even clear whether or not one actually had to speak the Czech language in order to be included in this collection of individuals. In 1806 Jungmann sought to clarify the issue of membership in the nation with the publication of two programmatic articles that appeared under the general title "Concerning the Czech Language" (*O jazyku českém*) in the periodical *Hlasatel český* (Czech speaker), edited by Jan Nejedlý. In these pieces Jungmann divided the population of the Czech lands into two distinct groups—Czechs and Germans—on the basis of linguistic preference: "A Czech [person] is only one who speaks and writes in Czech, not one who proclaims himself to be Czech but speaks German." At the same time he resuscitated an older theory of the fundamental unity of the Slavic languages and, by extension, the national unity of Slavic speakers. The combination of these two prescriptions, which were not logically consistent, created a scenario of "belonging" that was both odd and compelling.[16]

On the one hand, inclusion in a national group resulted from linguistic choice. On the other, participation in a linguistic culture carried primordial implications: it cut one off from groups and individuals living in geographic, temporal, and social proximity; it conferred kinship to cross-national populations and their linguistic cultures; and it militated in general against an understanding of national affiliation as contingent. By insisting that not all Bohemians were Czechs but that all Czechs were related intimately to all Slavs, the Jungmannian vision of national community asked one to believe that a Czech speaker from Prague had more in common with a Russian speaker from the Ural mountains, for example, than with a German speaker from Prague. Moreover, the linguists' proclamation that the territory of the Czech lands was divided between intrinsically different groups implied that the realization of the national aspirations of the Czechs could not be accomplished simply by "fulfilling history"—that is, by ultimately bestowing political power on the people resident in those lands—for it was historical change that had perverted the ancient and natural state of affairs in the first place. The key was to push beyond history to "origins."

What Antonín Měšťan calls the "myth of linguistic affinity" also colored Jungmann's major scholarly project, the five-volume Czech-German dictionary published between 1834 and 1839. Here Jungmann purposefully introduced numerous expressions from Polish, Russian, and Serbo-Croatian in order to prepare the ground for the expected emergence of a pan-Slavic language. It was also during this period of romantic activism on the part of linguists and literary scholars that the concept of Slavic literature gained currency. Individual literatures of Slavic peoples were understood to represent regional components of a unitary expression, a pan-national literature whose specific characteristics allegedly differentiated it from that of other European peoples.[17]

Slavic affinity and German difference, then, stood as the fundamental, binary truth of the "national awakening." As I have argued, the insistence on a preferred language as the carrier of national identity necessarily excluded large numbers of Bohemian residents from the imagined community, even if those residents were related by demonstrable family ties to Czech speakers or possessed Czech surnames. Equally problematic to the educators and intellectuals, however, was the fact that, up to now, this work of separation had been carried out largely in German. Czech was rarely used as a scholarly vehicle before 1830; Josef Dobrovský (1753–1829) published his pathbreaking *History of the Czech Language and Literature* in German in 1792; Pavel Josef Šafařík's (1795–1861) *History of Slavic Language and Literature according to All Dialects* also appeared in German in 1826. Even the monumental *History of the Czech Nation* by František Palacký (1798–1876) appeared first in German under the title *Geschichte von Böhmen* (1836–45).[18] It was Jungmann who first broke with the convention of writing scholarly works in German when he published his *History of Czech Literature* in Czech in 1825.

To the extent that the Czech national vision was promoted by individuals whose own linguistic patterns were ambiguous, the enterprise encompassed from the start a degree of psychological tension. Not surprisingly, much of the early scholarship—as well as the modern myth-making—of the Czech intellectuals undertook to sharpen the linguistic divide, promote "Slavic" culture, celebrate the national language, or highlight specific periods of the national past (especially pagan antiquity and the Hussite revolt) in which the lines of Czech language and culture appear to have been more clearly drawn. Scholarly activists of the post-Jungmann generation were particularly eager to discover relics and monuments of a glorious Czech past. Most visible in this group were Václav Hanka (1791–1861), a student of Dobrovksý and librarian at the National Museum of the Kingdom of Bohemia, who affiliated with Jungmann after his arrival in Prague in 1814; the romantic poet and writer Josef Linda (1789–1834); and Václav Alois Svoboda (1791–1849), who began teaching in 1821 as a professor at the Malostránské Gymnasium in Prague.[19]

Between 1816 and 1830 members of this exclusive circle appeared to have made a number of spectacular archeological discoveries in which previously unknown medieval Czech manuscripts were unearthed. The "Lay of Vyšehrad" (*Píseň Vyšehradská*), a Czech ballad said to date from the thirteenth century, constituted the first discovery, announced by Josef Linda in 1816. In September 1817 Hanka reported the discovery of another medieval manuscript—this one consisting of both fragmentary and complete poetic works—in the cellars of the cathedral of Dvůr Králové in northeastern Bohemia (and thus named the Královédvorský, or Königenhof, manuscript). In November of the same year the National Museum in Prague "anonymously" received a package of four manuscript pages (known subsequently as the Zelenohorský manuscript) that purported to date from an even earlier period than the first two discoveries. Finally, in 1828 Hanka claimed to have discovered an interlinear translation of the Gospel of John dating back to the eleventh century. These discoveries generated great excitement as well as debate in Czech philological and historical circles. They managed to serve simultaneously as sources of an ancient literary culture, objects of scholarly investigation, generators of national pride, and wellsprings of myth, both ancient and modern.[20]

The twentieth-century scholarly consensus concerning the Czech manuscripts holds that they are forgeries. Brilliantly devised and artfully constructed, they nevertheless represent an extreme form of invented tradition whose purpose was to secure the Czech national movement to an ancient foundation of literary culture and myth. In most cases the discoverers of the documents were also their authors. Hanka and Linda appear to have divided most of the labor between themselves, although there is some difference of opinion as to who was responsible for the lyrical sections, who for the epic, and who made sure that everything was transcribed into a plausible Old Czech.[21] Some have suggested that one cannot rule out the possibility that the venerable Jungmann himself was involved. Significantly, it was the new "secular clergy" of philologists and historians who established the "truth" of the manuscripts. They did so on the weight of their own authority and by appealing to the methods of discovery and critical analysis that were the hallmark of their fields of expertise.

As William Harkins has suggested, Hanka, Linda, and company may have been moved to fabricate early medieval literary sources in an attempt "to give the Czechs their own mythology and antiquity."[22] One Czech literary historian, speaking to a French audience in the early twentieth century, tried to capture the psychological underpinnings of the whole effort:

There was a great cry of joy among patriotic circles. The early Czechs were after all not rude barbarians, since they had a poetry that was so rich and varied. One could tell this from the scattered pieces that had been found, which made up only an insignificant fragment in comparison to what must have been lost! They thus possessed not only a poetry but—according to the Judgment of Libuša—also a written legislation, a beautiful mythology, and sacred rites that were both very poetic and highly developed. And they had always been convinced patriots, for the hero of one of the poems expressly said: 'It is not good for us to look for truth among the Germans.'[23]

While the Czech manuscripts project can easily be understood as the presumed need among romantic "national awakeners" to establish pride of place and antiquity of origins, it also promoted a polemical definition of Czech national identity. The net effect of the manuscripts was to demonstrate that the Czechs were both different from and superior to their German-speaking neighbors. "Unlike other forgeries," writes Milan Otáhal, the Czech manuscripts "not only expressed the Romantic love of antiquity and folk poetry, but they were specifically designed to prove the superiority of Czechs to Germans, to prove their distinctiveness and maturity."[24]

The epic poems of KM [Královédvorský ms.] describe battles against foreigners and Germans; foster hatred against these groups; stress the antagonism said to exist between Germans and Czechs. 'Though a German wail and plead, kill him still,' reads one of the lines of ZM [Zelenohorský ms.] ... [which] stresses the fully developed social order of the old Czechs, their mature judicial system and advanced culture. Its mood is again anti-German. When Chrudos appeals to the Germanic law of primogeniture, not valid in the Czech lands, others condemn him almost as a traitor.[25]

James Macpherson, the eighteenth-century Scottish poet, had ushered in the modern era of historical fabrication in 1760 with the publication of his *Fragments of Ancient Poetry* (said to contain songs in Gaelic of the ancient bard Ossian, dating from the second or third century).[26] The Englishman Chatterton followed suit in 1768 when he published in a Bristol newspaper a medieval tale that he claimed to have discovered in a church. Remarkably, at least one antagonist in the Czech manuscript affair acknowledged his British precursors without apology. Václav Svoboda, in defending the manuscripts from scholarly criticism, went so far as to argue for the acceptability of forgery in the name of the nation:

We would be happy if we had another Chatterton among us, and paying little heed to the historical accuracy of his work, we would beg him to compose as many such works as possible.... We are deeply convinced that an inspired Chatterton has far more to contribute to our culture than men who depopulate centuries of our history with excessive criticism.[27]

Although no less an authority than the venerable Dobrovský (the excessive critic referred to above) had raised doubts about the authenticity of the manuscripts as early as the 1820s, few among the Czech academic and literary elites wanted to hear them; the manuscripts, in the words of Otáhal, "were becoming untouchable."[28] The manuscripts went on to inform two generations and more of scholarly, literary, and artistic endeavor. Painters depicted scenes from them on their canvases; their motifs reverberated in the poetry of Neruda, Vrchlický, and Zeyer. The historian Palacký greeted the appearance of the manuscripts—which he first read in 1819—with "inexpressible joy."[29] Indeed, his magisterial *History of the Czech Nation* would have been inconceivable without its overall conception of the eternal struggle between Germans and Czechs, which was borrowed wholesale from the manuscripts. Not surprisingly, Palacký's history closed with the loss of "Czech" sovereignty and the capture of the Bohemian crown by the Habsburgs in 1526.[30]

When new voices of skepticism concerning the manuscripts' provenance and antiquity began to be raised in the 1850s, they were met with an overwhelming chorus of disapproval and disbelief. As Otáhal reminds us, "precisely because the Manuscripts had become sacrosanct, anyone who doubted their authenticity, though a good Czech, faced merciless persecution."[31] Only after 1886, when the historian Jan Gebauer published a "reappraisal" of the manuscripts in Tomáš Masaryk's periodical, *Athenaeum,* did a "progressive" scholarly consensus emerge that rejected them as authentic.[32] In the interim, the Czech manuscripts had narrated and reinforced a particular vision of the past: one of an independent Czech society, tied to nature and geography and based on a rich literary culture, in which individuals who were larger than life preserved the community while confronting hostile forces.

Writing the Jews In: Politics, Historiography, and Communal Identity at Mid-Century

One of the most prominent populations to have been implicity written out of the Jungmann-Palacký conception of community were the Jews. Though Jews had been permanent residents in the Czech lands since the tenth or eleventh century, they could not have shared many of the key, mythic experiences ascribed to the Czech nation: its pagan antiquity, the conversion to Christianity, and the combined resistance to Catholic Rome and to German overlordship that was embodied in the Hussite revolt.[33] Equally problematic was the linguistic commitment that Jungmann had insisted on. Urban Jews down to the nineteenth century were conversant in German while their rural and small-town counterparts conducted many of their daily affairs in Czech; the principal language of both communities, however, was Yiddish.[34] Beginning in the 1780s the state-mandated secular school system educated the vast majority of Jewish children (girls as well as boys) in the German language, in accord with the centralist principles of the absolutist state, even in the predominantly Czech-speaking regions of Bohemia and Moravia.[35] As a result, even the most patriotically inclined Jews of the 1830s, 1840s, and 1850s—that generation of secularized intellectuals that included Moritz Hartmann (1821–72), Siegfried Kapper (1821–79), Leopold Kompert (1822–86), and David Kuh (1818–79)—with few exceptions expressed their Bohemian loyalties in German.[36]

If it did not occur to most Bohemian Jews that the history of the region was to be understood as an unremitting clash between two incompatible nations, they can perhaps be forgiven. Jewish students and professionals maintained the belief through most of the 1840s—later than most Germans and Czechs—that attachment to Bohemia was compatible with loyalty to Habsburg Austria and that both could be expressed in the German idiom. For Jewish writers and artists of this generation, one way of expressing their attachment to place, their *Landespatriotismus*, was to act as linguistic and cultural mediators who would bring to Europe's attention both the artistic works and the political aspirations of the Czechs. In 1843–44 Kuh and Kapper collaborated with the Czech poet Václav Bolemír Nebeský in a bilingual newspaper campaign designed to create an alignment of Jewish and Czech identities and interests. Echoes of this project can also be found in the German translations of the Czech epics produced by Moritz Hartmann in 1847 and by Siegfried Kapper in 1859.[37] As we saw in chapter 3, however, the pre-1848 experiment in Czech-Jewish rapprochement failed to produce a sympathetic response. What Jews witnessed of Czech popular protest in 1844 and again in 1848 caused mainly shock and alarm (much of the violence had been directed against Jewish homes and property); the protests had the overall effect of tightening the Jewish embrace of the central state as the main promoter of acculturation, social mobility, and security.[38]

Recall Kuh's dispatches from Prague published in the wake of the 1844 riots, the anger and sarcasm that he directed at the Czech-speaking, educated middle class, who, he felt, had tacitly encouraged the anti-Jewish excesses. The one person whom Kuh singled out for criticism was Václav Svoboda, the associate of Hanka's and professor at

Prague's Malá Strana gymnasium who once had gone so far as to argue for the acceptability of documentary forgery in the name of national rebirth. Kuh had accused Svoboda of fomenting anti-Jewish sentiment, humiliating Jewish students in front of their Christian colleagues, and, finally, of "preaching a Crusade against the Jews."

In the aftermath of the 1848 revolution—following a two-year stint in prison for his participation in the Hungarian revolt—Kuh edited what was to become one of the leading German newspapers in Prague, the *Tagesbote aus Böhmen*. It was in the pages of this newspaper that Kuh launched in 1858 what, for him, must have been sweet revenge. He arranged to have a series of unsigned articles published under the headline "Handschriftliche Lügen oder Paleographische Wahrheiten" (Handwritten lies or paleographic truths), which accused Hanka in no uncertain terms of being a forger. Not surprisingly, the articles provoked a storm of indignation from the Czech side. Palacký, you will recall, had begun the counterattack by asking how it was that Kuh's "Börsen-Blatt" had suddenly discovered a taste for literary history and by emphasizing the anti-Czech motivation behind the *Tagesbote* initiative. He then went on to publish three studies that proved the authenticity of the manuscripts.[39]

The Czech defenders of the manuscripts were not entirely wrong in questioning the motives of their detractors. It is now clear from the archival record that it was the head of the Prague police who first came up with the idea of issuing a public debunking of the manuscripts in the German press; his motive was to undermine the ideological foundations of Czech nationalism.[40] From the police chief's standpoint, Kuh was an obvious conduit who required little cajoling. He viewed the anti-Jewish riots of the 1840s as a betrayal, one that was made all the more painful because of the apparent collusion of middle-class academics and professionals. As incubators of the middle-class nation, the gymnasium and the university constituted the places where Kuh and others of his generation had come to love the "other" language and culture of Bohemia, but they were also the sites of twin conspiracies: the project to create a "usable" Czech past and the recent rhetorical campaign against Prague's Jews. To complete the circle of distrust, it seems that Kuh's Czech critics—ignorant of the role that the police had played in the affair—suspected that the author of the articles in the *Tagesbote* had been none other than the original promoter of Czech-Jewish cooperation, Nebeský.[41]

Bohemian Jewish writers began to make their own contributions to the public contest over local history and memory in the wake of the political liberalizations of 1860 – 61. The Austrian government had responded to a serious financial crisis as well as to humiliating military defeat at the hands of the Italians in 1859 by relaxing censorship, providing for much greater freedom of association, allowing for representative parliaments at the imperial and regional levels, and instituting locally elected city and town governments.[42] Although formal Jewish emancipation was not enshrined constitutionally until 1867, specific legislation between 1859 and 1861 had already removed most remaining economic and civic disabilities, and Jews both voted in local and parliamentary elections and ran for public office (often successfully).[43] During the municipal elections of 1861 and the elections for the Bohemian Diet in 1863, the newspaper *Národní listy* and other organs of Czech national opinion openly criticized Jews for lending their support to German political domination as well as for harming the Czech nation socially and economically. Riots lasting several days broke out in Prague in August 1861. Ignored by the city council and its first Czech nationalist mayor, Václav Pštross, the disturbances were ultimately brought under control by the police (who answered to the imperial governor of Bohemia), but not before 1,312 window panes from Jewish homes and stores had been destroyed.[44]

In the midst of the 1863 election campaign, a minor pamphlet war erupted, which involved at least two opposing visions of Bohemian Jewish history and possibly as many as three points of view. The debate began with the anonymous publication of a small book entitled *Die Juden in Böhmen und ihre Stellung in der Gegenwart* (The Jews in Bohemia and their situation in the present). Authorship of the book generally has been attributed to Markus Teller (1814 – 75), a Prague Jewish physician, journalist, and political activist who served as Prague correspondent for the liberal Viennese press.[45] Two decades earlier, according to Christoph Stölzl, Teller had appealed to the Jews of Bohemia to produce a history of their own in which they might find a *Landesrecht* akin to that which was being promoted by both Germans and Czechs.[46] To the 1863 pamphlet he suggestively appended the motto: "Jede Zeit hat ihre eigene Geschichte" (Each age has its own history).

Die Juden in Böhmen displayed both in tone and in argument the strong influence of the Prague *haskalah*. Rationalist and liberal, committed to ideas of progress and science, and quoting frequently from

Lessing, Schiller, the Bible, and Prague *maskil* Ignaz Jeitteles (1783–1843), the work sought to create an overall image of the Jews as improvers and developers whose secular "mission" had been as the carriers of knowledge and science (*Wissenschaft und Intelligenz*) to the civilized world.[47] The myth of origins that it invoked operated on two levels. First, it interpreted Jewish settlement patterns in the diaspora in terms of the degree of civilization of potential host countries, explaining that thriving Jewish communities were to be found among peoples who were inclined toward advancement and knowledge—small wonder, then, that so few Jews had settled in early medieval Europe. Second, it also tried to establish that Jewish settlement in Bohemia predated that of the Czechs themselves. Thereafter Jews rendered exemplary service to the Czechs—a favorite theme of Teller—aiding them in the struggles with their pagan neighbors in the eleventh and twelfth centuries, participating in the advance of science during the Renaissance, and defending the country against the Swedes during the Thirty Years' War.[48]

Teller's account of Jewish origins in Bohemia laid the foundation for all subsequent arguments in the book. Most importantly, it oriented the Jews in their geographic and temporal milieux, found for them a place in the history of the region, and traced lines of connectedness both to the population of Bohemia and to the Austrian state. When the two strands of the story—antiquity and mission—were played off against each other, a tension resulted in the historical narrative that could only be resolved in the future. The Jewish fate was linked to that of Bohemia as a whole. But because Jewish identity and well-being depended also on a general commitment to rationality, progress, and scientific advancement, it was incumbent upon Jews to work to realize these goals in the Bohemian context, thereby linking *home* and *mission*.

On the basis of these twin themes, Jews could assess what was right and what was wrong with their relationship to their Czech-and German-speaking neighbors. What was wrong was that the "services" of the Jews often went unappreciated, unrewarded, or worse. In the High and Late Middle Ages, when the Jews' work had been accomplished, they were subjected to expulsions and periodic readmissions. In modern times, "religious fanaticism and mob hysteria" (*geistlicher Fanatismus und Pöbelwahn*) combined to wreak havoc on Jewish life and property. The Jewish attachment to place, however, remained steadfast. "Love for the native soil attached them to their new homeland (*Heimat*) and despite struggles and cycles, despite all the injustice, which they experienced in huge measure, they remained true to their freely chosen fatherland and contributed in not a few ways to its development."[49]

The bulk of *Die Juden in Böhmen* focuses on the modern experience of Bohemian Jewry, the Jews' "civic and moral improvement" (to borrow the liberals' phrase that Teller also used) under the aegis of the tutelary state. From this point on in the historical narrative, the theme of Austrian benevolence assumes a preeminent position alongside those of place and progress. Teller judges contemporary political movements in terms of their accommodation to progress, rationality, and loyalty to the state, implicitly obliging the Jewish reader to gauge his or her political involvement in the same way. In the last chapter, he contemplates the predicament of Bohemian Jewry in the midst of the intensifying Czech-German ethnic conflict. How were the Jews to respond to calls from the Czech national camp to support its cause and its candidates? The National Party had even come out in favor of Jewish emancipation in 1861.

Through this paper promise [*dieser Versprechen auf dem Papiere*], they thought, the Jews would—had to—hurry over to their party, swear an oath on their flag. But the thoughtful Jews did not do this, above all because every Jew is mindful of the second verse of chapter eight in Ecclesiastes ["Keep the king's command, and that in regard to the oath of God"]. The hard-tested Jews, who weigh on the past and the future, wanted first to become convinced that what was promised would also be realized.[50]

And so the Jews did not "throw themselves completely into the arms of the nationalists." In response the Czech press launched a litany of complaints against them: Jews were characterized as ruinous to the nation, poisoning it with their brandy, demoralizing it with their peddling, ruining it with their money exchanges, and pulling it down with their rejection of nationalism.[51]

What is striking about Teller's account is the reluctance with which it acknowledges the "national question" in Bohemia. He applies the term *die Nationalen* (literally, "the nationals") to the Czech nationalists specifically, suggesting that before the emergence of a Czech ethnic consciousness, there had been no nationalism in Bohemia. This picture of an ethnically indistinct homeland before the middle of the nineteenth century stood in sharp contrast to the one that was being promoted in Czech history and myth. The latter held that the entire sweep of local history comprised a contest that pitted Czech against German and freedom against coercion. To be Czech, according to this view, corresponded to an existential reality; to side with the Czechs was to act with honor and integrity. In contrast, Teller's "Austro-Jewish" myth understands Czech ethnicity to be a modern choice, a divisive act of political will not necessarily demanding imitation. Jews in the end were to steer clear of both national extremes and to uphold the government, "which stands above the parties, effects law and justice, and has, in fact, up to now been hindered by [political] parties from according the Jews their full rights, their unrestricted equality with the other inhabitants of Bohemia."[52]

Die Juden in Böhmen engendered a swift response in the form of a rival brochure, which offered a radically different vision of the Jewish past. *Die Juden und die Nationalen* promoted itself as a "counterpart" (*Gegenstück*) to *Die Juden in Böhmen* and although also published anonymously, claimed to be written by a Jew.[53] Imitating the language of the first pamphlet, it drew attention to the ambiguous characterization of the Czechs as *die Nationalen* even as it set out to redefine and reimagine the Czech-Jewish relationship.

True to its billing as "counterpart," *Die Juden und die Nationalen* accords neatly with the worldview of the Czech manuscripts and of Palacký's history, even to the point of expressing the same anachronisms. While *Die Juden in Böhmen* argues that Jewish settlement in Bohemia predated that of the Czechs, *Die Juden und die Nationalen* portrays a Bohemian antiquity in which Jews and Czechs coexisted prior to the entry of Germans, with their ubiquitous policy of cultural and linguistic coercion.[54] Jews, according to this story, had coexisted with the Czechs and had done so happily. Jews were subjected to the same policies of Germanization as the Czechs and, like the Czechs, had to endure periods of religious intolerance that were essentially alien to the region's traditions. "German mores and language entered Bohemia together with the kings of the House of Luxembourg. Chivalry declined, both the nobility and the Germans devoted themselves to German culture [*Deutschtum*], the old Bohemian law gave way to bloody strife and horror, and the Jew felt (1389) that old Czech virtue had begun to disappear."[55]

Though intolerance and religious fanaticism reached high levels during and after the Hussite wars of the late fourteenth century and the fifteenth century—the violence from these conflicts spilling over onto Jewish lives—the struggles themselves, the reader is reminded, were precipitated by the oppressive policies of Rome and the Empire. Periodic persecutions of Jews were to be viewed as "the fruit of the times and of general savagery, but not of Jew-hatred." In this account, "actual, systematic oppression" of Jews (as well as real hatred toward them) first began with the "humiliating and degrading" Jewish laws that were issued during the regime of the *German* (i.e., Habsburg) emperor, Ferdinand I. Even during the time of general lawlessness and savagery, this author proclaims, the Czechs showed far more tolerance than the Germans.[56]

As myths of origin are designed to isolate the era of harmony and perfection that existed before history—that is, before human struggle and failure—so the one offered by *Die Juden und die Nationalen* locates Eden in a Czech landscape. It establishes a mutual identity of Czechs and Jews and a common fate at the hands of a German Pharaoh. In the distant past, the aspirations of most Bohemian Jews had been Czech, the Jews themselves spoke Czech in their daily lives, and "only in the aftermath of the Germanizing frenzy *(Germanisierungswut)*" did Czech "gradually disappear from mouth and memory."

Religious intolerance did not lie in the Czechs' character; it only entered their spirit when one tried to graft them onto a German shoot and thus make them into a hybrid, and when fanatical monks tried to fill the up-to-now humane and good-natured Slavs with bestial anger *ad majorem Dei gloriam* [for the greater glory of God]. In the end, however, the Czech of this time did not entirely renounce his national character, but always treated the Jews more tolerantly and humanely than did the Germans.[57]

In contrast to the general consensus concerning the authorship of *Die Juden in Böhmen,* historians have not ventured to identify the anonymous writer of *Die Juden und die Nationalen.* The author presents himself or herself simply as a Jew from the Czech-speaking countryside. This claim, however, cannot be accepted at face value. There were no prominent Jews in 1863—even in the provinces—who spoke in the idiom of this booklet. It would be another two decades, in fact, before a popular movement would begin to take root within Bohemian Jewish society that sought to align Jewish and Czech identities.[58] Another curiosity, in my view, is the fact that the author of *Die Juden und die Nationalen* cites no Jewish sources; makes no reference to the liturgy, calendar, or sacred texts of Judaism; mentions none of the names of the leadership of Bohemian Jewry, past or present; and appears not to identify with any particular trend or movement within the community. All this, too, is in stark contrast to *Die Juden in Böhmen.* The author is conversant with, and echoes, the main outlines of Czech historiography. He or she identifies with the nationalist tendencies of the 1848 Revolution, the unification of Italy, and the Polish uprising of 1863. As an apologia, in fact, *Die Juden und die Nationalen* justifies Czech political behavior and not the positions taken by Jews. These observations lead me to conclude that *Die Juden und die Nationalen,* in all likelihood, was written by a non-Jew—possibly a patriotic Czech liberal, perhaps someone close to the circle of historians and ethnologists associated with the Bohemian Museum in Prague. Neither documentary fabrication nor police plant, this text occupies instead the category of pseudepigraphy.[59]

If one accepts this conclusion, then *Die Juden und die Nationalen* needs to be reread as another Czech origin myth, albeit one about Jews, ascribed to them, and intended for a Jewish audience. The Czech author of this narrative has, in effect, "written the Jews in" to the Jung-mannian account of ethnic solidarity and linguistic differentiation. He or she has posited a Jewish antiquity in the Czech lands that is coterminous with that of the Czechs, identified the Jews as belonging to the Slavic linguistic family, and ascribed to them the same calamity of cultural and linguistic oppression at the hands of the Germans. However one reads the text, it is impossible to arrive at an unproblematic identification of Jew and Czech. Read as a Jewish piece, *Die Juden und die Nationalen* voices alienation from the Czechs to the degree that they have succumbed to religious intolerance and persecution, even though it is acknowledged that such behavior is ultimately foreign to the Czech character. As a Czech narrative, it targets the Jews of Bohemia for protection and criticism simultaneously, appearing to defend the Jews against the political charge of Germanization even as it chides them for behaving in such a way as to render the accusation believable.

We know the Jews of the countryside well and can thus repeat with good conscience that *all of the demonstrations of the Jews in support of Czech culture (Čechentum) of which we spoke above represent the true and genuine expression of belonging and of sympathy for the nation in whose midst they live.* Whoever claims otherwise—be he Jew or Christian—is *an enemy of the Jews.* [Emphasis in the original.][60]

One cannot help but wonder whether, when the writer claims to "know the Jews of the countryside," this is a knowledge of self or of "other." In any event, the last sentence contains a clear warning for Jews as well as for Christians: It may be unreasonable to expect the Jews to simply throw off centuries of German acculturation "like an old dress" and acquire Czech as one would "the multiplication tables."[61] On the other hand, their recent political behavior—maintaining German schools and supporting German liberal candidates—is indefensible.

It is unfortunately true that in no other large city (*grössern Orte*) in the world in recent times has the Jew been shown such crude enmity. But it is also true that nowhere else in the world has the Jew shown such little regard for the majority of his fellow citizens as in Prague. The Jews of Prague allow hollow ranters not only to deliver ruthless speeches against the Czechs but also to libel them. "The Jews are German!" call out Prague Jews from newspapers; "the Jews are German and must remain so," resounds from speakers' podiums.[62]

The political message here is ominous and potentially unfriendly. What started out as an enterprise in inclusion and imaginative sympathy has turned into rebuke. The underpinnings of "myth-history" have given way to straightforward ideological criticism. According to your own ideology of assimilation, the writer says to the Jews of Prague, you are members of that nation in whose midst you possess the right of settlement. Since the city of Prague is predominantly Czech, you must be as well.

The texts of the 1863 pamphlet war offered radically different prescriptions for Jewish political behavior based on divergent constructions of the Bohemian Jewish past. If *Die Juden in Böhmen* comprised the cultural and political credo of the Austro-Jewish consensus of the nineteenth century, *Die Juden und die Nationalen* articulated the counterposition of the Czech-Jewish opposition. It is safe to conclude that during the 1860s the latter pamphlet made virtually no impression on its intended audience. Austrian centralism was too attractive a vehicle for integration and mobility—and the memories of Czech popular violence toward Jews were still too vivid—for the Jews to be budged very far from their accustomed linguistic, social, and political patterns. It seems to me, moreover, that *Die Juden in Böhmen* rang truer to the ear as a *Jewish* statement. Though utterly conventional and occasionally self-righteous in tone, it spoke from within the matrix of recognizable Jewish experience. Its historical sketches corresponded generally to group memories, and its public myth of Jewish "service" to the nations of Europe—tied to notions of science, rationality, and progress—accorded with the conceits of the time. *Die Juden und die Nationalen,* in contrast, offered a rival historical myth and a new measurement of identity that had no resonance in Bohemian Jewish culture. It represented a compelling way for Czech liberals and political activists to look upon themselves and, by extension, at Jews, but it did not yet correspond with Jewish memory or experience.

By the 1880s, however, this pseudepigraphical history would be adopted by Czech-speaking students, professionals, and white-collar workers—the sons and daughters of small-town and rural Jews who had migrated to Prague and other larger cities in the 1850s, 1860s, and 1870s. Its images of ancient Czech-Jewish coexistence and cultural reciprocity, Czech tolerance, German-inspired religious persecution, and forced Germanization would be reproduced in Jewish manifestoes, works of fiction, and historical writing. The most visible repository of this "reconstructed" history is the volumes of the *Czech-Jewish Almanac* (*Kalendář česko-židovský*) published by the Association of Czech Academic Jews (Spolek českých akademiků-židů) from 1881 to 1939. August Stein's "Židé v Čechách" (The Jews in the Czech lands), published in the *Almanac* in 1881/82, visualized a "fusion of Czech culture and Judaism" (*češství a židovství*) that echoed nearly every sentiment of *Die Juden und die Nationalen*. The fiction of Vojtěch Rakous (Adalbert Österreicher, 1862–1935) reproduced the experiences of village and small-town Jews whose universe was as quintessentially Czech as that of any Prague worker or National Liberal ("Young Czech") journalist. At the turn of the century Czech-Jewish lawyers, physicians, and academics would forge a political alliance with Tomáš Masaryk and the progressive wing of the Czech national movement that would last until the German occupation of Czechoslovakia.[63]

That an entire ethnic reorientation—a dramatic accommodation to new linguistic, social, and political realities—should have been built at least partly on the cultural foundations of what amounted to a forgery is perhaps not surprising. Mythical histories, invented traditions, and false attributions have been a common feature of the modern nationalist enterprise; and ultimately, the influence of *Die Juden und die Nationalen* was much more modest than that of the Czech manuscripts. In the final analysis one ought not to look too closely at the provenance of a sacred text. As William McNeill reminds us, "flattering historiography does more than assist a given group to survive ..., for an appropriately idealized version of the past may also allow a group of human beings to come closer to living up to its noblest ideals. What is can move towards what ought to be, given collective commitment to a flattering self-image."[64] The value of myth is not that it is true, but that it is self-validating.

CHAPTER 6

Education and
National Conflict

Germans, Czechs, and Jews

Introduction

National movements typically have sought to link the political with the cultural, to achieve sovereignty or power for a particular group—defined variously in terms of language, broadly shared cultural traditions, and a sense of shared historical destiny—that is imagined to be cohesive and able to act in concert on the stage of history.[1] Because of the equation of culture and politics in modern nationalism and, just as importantly, because of the role that the technical and professional intelligentsia has played in promoting nationalism's claims, the issue of public education has often been paramount. It was the local school that helped to transform a dialect or peasant language into a vehicle of high culture and that paved the way for the sons of the peasantry to enter the occupations and professions of the new industrial age. It was the school that prepared one for a bureaucratic career under the auspices of a centralizing state. And if integration into the larger state and society proved impossible or unsatisfactory, it was again to the local high culture of the school that the disaffected intellectual or professional turned in search of an alternative political community.[2]

Nowhere has the link between education and national politics been more prominent than in the Czech lands of the Habsburg monarchy during the second half of the nineteenth century. Self-conscious Czechs and Germans of all political stripes stressed the preeminent role played by the school in determining the outcome on various fronts of the national struggle between the two groups.[3] Universal education in the national language was understood by the growing Czech middle class to constitute a major prerequisite to ethnic mobility and power. The Habsburg school system prepared the sons of migrating peasants and petty merchants for careers in industry, the bureaucracy, and the professions. At the same time, it was important to Czech nationalists that the schools not serve an assimilatory or denationalizing function (as they once had), and that they not be used to create a "German presence" in regions that otherwise would have possessed no ethnic German element.

A number of issues were at stake in the late-nineteenth-century debates surrounding education: the sheer number of schools that offered instruction in the national language; attendance figures for these schools; and of course, the curriculum that they offered. Czech and German national politicians at times presumed that this single institution held the key to the ultimate determination of the most pressing national issues, such as the right to conduct business with the government and the courts in one's own language, the ability to gain employment and achieve social mobility, and the hope of determining one's own future and that of one's children. Karel Adámek, a Young Czech economist and political activist, gave voice to these preoccupations in his study of contemporary Czech life:

The blossoming of Czech education was and must remain for all time the principal political goal of all genuine patriots and true friends of the people, of the whole nation.
... The question of schools is raised high above the interests of parties and of individuals; [it is] certainly the most widespread, important national and cultural question.[4]

Similarly, a German study at the beginning of the twentieth century accused the Prague city council of setting up public kindergartens in the city not only to provide a necessary service to working parents but, more importantly, "to win over the children at this most tender age to the Czech nation."[5] Because of the demographic weakness of the German community of Prague, all of the publicly funded kindergartens were Czech-language institutions. German nationalists, for their part, feared that the children of working-class Germans who attended such schools would lose the opportunity (and the desire) to speak German on a daily basis and consequently would "be completely lost to the German people."[6]

The Austrian government itself did much to raise the school issue to a level of primary importance. Imperial legislation of 1868 and 1869 established a clear separation of church and state in the area of public education, removed state-supported primary and secondary schools from the purview of local parishes and religious orders, and opened both the faculty and the student body of such schools to people of all religions.[7] Moreover, in creating a new network of state-supported primary and secondary schools throughout Cisleithania, it placed the school under the direct control of the provinces. Thus, local autonomy in cultural affairs—a by-product of the constitutional reforms of the 1860s—combined with the state's interest in promoting compulsory, secular education to produce a situation in Bohemia, as well as elsewhere, in which notables from competing national camps vied with each other to determine the cultural makeup of their region.[8]

The government also helped to politicize education when, beginning with the census of 1880, it chose to measure the ethnic composition of the monarchy solely in terms of language. Before 1869 government censuses had employed what might be called ethnographic criteria in delineating the various nationalities of the Habsburg lands. In other words, they accepted the existence of ethnically distinct populations as well as the right of individuals to identify with them.[9] This practice ceased with the census of 1869, which was taken two years after the *Ausgleich* with Hungary. Franz Josef's ministers mistakenly believed that in the agreement with Hungary they had solved the major nationalist challenge to the empire, and they simply refused to measure national affiliation in the new census. By 1880 the government had been unburdened of this illusion but now chose to defuse the nationality issue by claiming to be interested only in the "everyday language" of the local population, and then only for "administrative" purposes, so that the courts, government offices, and schools might serve the needs of the population.[10]

What the Austrian government agreed to measure in the censuses of 1880 and after was *Umgangssprache* (in Czech, *obcováci řeč*), which can be translated loosely as everyday, or colloquial, language. The president of the Central Statistical Commission explained that the term was meant to indicate "that language which the population of local towns and communities actually spoke."[11] If this had really been the case, however, the government would have sent teams of observers throughout the monarchy who would later map the country's linguistic divisions on the basis of first-hand experience. In fact, individuals were allowed to declare their *Umgangssprache* to census takers, with the restriction that only answers that corresponded to languages actually used in the region in question (hence, *landesüblich*) would be counted.

On the one hand, then, the government opened the door for the political exploitation of the census returns, encouraging the various national movements to let it be known what language a sometimes multilingual population should give as its "everyday" tongue. In so doing, Vienna increased the premium that national leaders placed on cultural and linguistic institutions like the schools. If Czech and German politicians agreed on anything, it was on the role that the school played in determining an individual's primary linguistic preference. On the other hand, some groups—the Jews in particular—lost the status of separate nationality that they had enjoyed in the mid-century censuses. In the case of some groups, the language that they might have spoken was not *üblich* in a particular region. As for the Jews, the process of emancipation had reduced their Jewishness to the realm of religion in the eyes of official Austria. The census takers could not accept a declaration of nationality that was not couched in linguistic terms, but they also refused to recognize Yiddish as a separate language—even in Galicia—and instead included it in the German category.[12]

The Growth in Primary and Secondary Education

The liberalization of political life in the 1860s and the restructuring of the schools coincided with other dramatic developments in the social and economic conditions of the Czech lands. Chief among these were the demographic revolution in the countryside, the beginnings of large-scale industrialization, and the waves of Czech migration to the cities, especially to Prague. The population of the Czech lands grew from 6,956,000 in 1857 to 8,640,000 in 1890; by 1910 it had reached well over 10,000,000.[13] Prague meanwhile grew from 204,488 in 1869 to over 442,000 in 1910.[14] The lion's share of this increase resulted from in-migration from the Czech-speaking towns and villages of Bohemia. A special study of the Central Statistical Commission determined that 115,235 residents of Prague's districts one through seven in 1900 were native to other parts of Bohemia, and 92 percent of these came from districts that had Czech majorities.[15] During this time Bohemia-Moravia became not only the most highly industrialized region of the Habsburg monarchy after Lower Austria, but also one in which illiteracy had been virtually eliminated. There were 3,650 elementary schools (*Volksschulen* or *národní školy*) in Bohemia in 1860, 3,875 in 1865, and 4,636 by 1885. Barely 611,000 students enrolled in 1860; by 1885 the number had reached 899,385. For the twenty-year interval 1865–1885, the number of primary schools in Bohemia grew by 19.7 percent, the number of teachers of academic subjects by 29.9 percent, and the number of registered students by 47.4 percent.[16] Among those who declared Czech as their daily language in the Austrian census of 1900, nearly 94 percent could both read and write. Close to 92 percent of Austrian Germans could do the same.[17]

The expansion of secondary and higher education in the Habsburg monarchy in the second half of the nineteenth century was equally impressive. Gary Cohen points out that Austrian enrollments in these two areas, in comparison to the total school-age population, were "among the highest in Europe." The number of students attending *Gymnasien* and *Realschulen* in the western half of the monarchy grew from 25,630 in 1851 to 140,545 in 1910. Over roughly the same period of time, the number of students enrolled in technical colleges increased by a factor of five, and those in universities by a factor of six.[18] In geographical terms the regions that benefited the most from the expansion of secondary education in the 1860s and 1870s were Lower Austria (including Vienna), Bohemia, and Moravia. If we highlight Bohemia, we see that in 1861 there were twenty-three *Gymnasien* and *Realgymnasien* (10 Czech, 6 German, and 7 bilingual or "utraquist") and eight *Realschulen* (4 German, 4 Czech). By 1884 the number of *Gymnasien* had risen to fifty-three (31 Czech, 22 German) and the number of *Realschulen* to sixteen (7 Czech, 9 German). Altogether some 9,500 students enrolled in secondary schools in 1861. In 1884 the number stood at just under 21,000.[19]

Czech national leaders in particular could point with pride to the major advances that had been made since the beginning of the Constitutional era in educating Czech children in their own language and culture. In 1864 there were some 3,200 Czech-language elementary schools in the Czech lands. This number jumped to 4,129 in 1884 and to 5,439 by 1914—an increase of 68 percent over the 1864 figure.[20] In Bohemia alone more than 560,000 children (72.5 percent of the school-age population) attended Czech primary schools (*obecné* or *měšťánské školy*) in 1885. Meanwhile, the number of students attending Czech *Gymnasien, Realgymnasien,* and *reálky* (*Realschulen*) grew from 4,273 in 1861 to over 14,000 in 1884.[21]

Relatively few children attended private elementary schools—only 26,339 in all of Bohemia in 1884–85, or about 2.8 percent of the total school-age population.[22] Nevertheless, leading figures within the Czech national movement voiced dissatisfaction with the pace of national education in the Czech lands. They worried in particular about the persistence of German schools in regions that had overwhelmingly Czech populations and about the movement's inability to attract a high percentage of students to Czech schools in predominantly German regions. For example, 5,296 children attended German public schools in predominantly Czech regions, while only 2,131 went to Czech schools in German districts. Only 612 children attended Czech schools in urban areas other than Prague, but 7,410 went to German schools in large cities, including 3,662 in Prague alone.[23]

The situation in secondary and higher education was even more troublesome. In 1883–84, 17.8 percent of the students in Prague's German gymnasium, 27.6 percent of the students in the German gymnasium in Smíchov, and 17.6 percent of those in the German gymnasium in the southern Bohemian city of České Budějovice, were Czech nationals. Moreover, Czechs comprised 35.3 percent of the student body at the German *Realschule* in Prague, 30.7 percent of the school in Litoměřice, and 35.4 percent of the one in Karlín.[24] Before 1882 there was only one university in Prague, and it was attended by Czech students as well as by Germans. Thereafter the institution was divided into separate national branches. Over the course of the next decade, virtually no self-declared German nationals received their education from the Czech university, yet Czech students continued to choose the German branch in significant numbers. During the winter and summer semesters of 1889–90, for example, Czechs comprised 19.4 and 21.4 percent, respectively, of the total student body of Prague's German university.[25] A similar situation prevailed in the city's technical institutes. During the academic year 1880–81, 99.5 percent of the students who attended the Czech *Polytechnika* were themselves Czechs. On the other hand, approximately 35 percent of the students at the German *Technische Hochschule* were Czech nationals.[26] This situation improved only slightly by the end of the decade, when Czechs comprised 24 percent of the student body.[27]

Such "incursions" of German influence into Czech national life were partly the result of uneven development. As late as 1886, one state-supported German middle school existed for every 25,000 Germans in Bohemia, but the Czechs could boast only one middle school for every 119,000 of their own nationals. Hence there simply may not have been enough Czech institutions to accommodate all of those who desired a secondary education.[28] Perceptions about the quality or ultimate utility of a German education also played a role. A significant minority of the population that lived in the Czech regions of the country—who may even have considered themselves ethnically Czech—nevertheless insisted upon a German language education for their youth because it was seen as providing a more useful vehicle for professional and social advancement.

The provincial school boards operated under legal mandate to establish, oversee, and support with public funds schools that taught in the language of the local population. The state had no obligation to erect or support schools for groups whose numbers did not reach a minimum level within a given district.[29] In such cases, the children went to either public schools in the language of the majority population or privately funded institutions in their own language. The question of minority schools, then, served as a rallying point for nationalists of all stripes. Community leaders on the one hand would attempt to organize support for the establishment of private schools in order to protect the "national integrity" of beleaguered minorities. On the other hand, the same leaders would berate the representatives of rival national groups who hoped to accomplish the same ends for their own members. What was protection in the eyes of one was incursion in the eyes of the other.[30]

The Austrian Germans were the first to organize in order to secure minority schools for their children. The Deutscher Schulverein emerged in the spring of 1880 to establish minority schools and support them until they could meet the minimum standards for public subvention. The Czechs in Bohemia responded almost immediately with an institution of their own, the Ústřední matice školská (Central School Foundation). In 1887 the Schulverein claimed 120,000 members divided among over one thousand local groups. By 1902 it was spending 4.3 million kronen to run twenty-six of its own schools and another two million kronen to subsidize forty-one others.[31] The Matice školská, meanwhile, had some thirty thousand contributing members in 1900. In twenty years it had dispensed some four million gulden (eight million kronen) in school aid, and ten thousand Czech students had enrolled in its private schools.[32]

Jewish Children, Jewish Schools

ELEMENTARY EDUCATION

Recently emancipated and thus stripped of their ancient national identification, the Jews of late-nineteenth-century Bohemia found themselves in a doubly precarious situation. Their population of 92,745 represented only 1.5 percent of all of the people of Bohemia in 1900, hardly enough to tip the statewide balance of power between Czechs and Germans, which stood at approximately 60 percent to 40 percent.[33] As in all of Central and Eastern Europe, however, the percentage of Jews in the larger cities and towns was much higher. The 18,986 Jews who lived in the inner city of Prague in 1900 comprised more than 9 percent of the total population and almost 8 percent if one includes the inner suburbs.[34] And although Jews did not make up as much as 5 percent of the population in the rest of Bohemia, their presence in individual school districts could help to determine whether or not a given school would exist or, alternatively, be given state support.

But the real difficulty for the Jews of Bohemia lay in their long identification with German language and culture. This identification dated back at least to the 1780s, when Joseph II launched an important set of cultural and social reforms within the Bohemian Jewish community. Not all of the laws of the 1780s and 1790s had a great deal of effect on the Jews. At least three, however, were of lasting significance: the ordinance of 1784, which ended the juridical autonomy of the Jewish community; the provision in the *Toleranzpatent* of 1781 that directed that all business and communal affairs be recorded in German; and, most important of all, the *Toleranzpatent*'s mandate for the establishment of Jewish *Normalschulen,* a network of secular schools supported by the Jewish community but supervised by the state in which the language of instruction was German. Through the *Normalschulen* the Jewish children of Bohemia were weaned away from Yiddish (and sometimes Czech), educated in the spirit of the German Enlightenment, and chanelled through the non-Jewish, German system of secondary and higher education.[35] This type of Jewish elementary school served as a universal medium of acculturation and Germanization and was a ubiquitous feature of Bohemian Jewish life until the end of the nineteenth century.

Since all elementary education before 1868 was connected to the Catholic Church, it is not surprising that the Jews of the Czech lands should have felt little inclination before this time to abandon their separate school system. But with the secularization of the schools, the raison d'être of the *Normalschule* would appear to have vanished. Did Jews close their schools at this point in recognition of the completion of emancipation?

The answer, interestingly, is no. The Jewish communities of Bohemia still maintained 114 private elementary schools in 1884–85. True, the total population at these schools was only 4,470—approximately one third of the entire Jewish school enrollment in Bohemia and barely 17 percent of the 26,339 children who attended private elementary schools of all types in the province.[36] Truly damnable in the eyes of Czech nationalists, however, were the following facts: ninety-six of the schools (84 percent) were located in Czech-speaking towns and villages, not including Prague; all but one of these institutions employed German as the language of instruction; and over 97 percent of the Jewish children who were enrolled in private schools attended German-language institutions.[37]

Clearly, during the early years of the national educational system, Jews in small towns and villages did not place much stock in Czech schools. Some did, to be sure—enough to create a critical mass of Jewish student supporters of Czech national culture. But the large majority, for reasons of traditionalism, religious conservatism, loyalty to the Austrian state, or expediency, chose to keep in place the old system of privately run Jewish schools—at least for the time being. On the other hand, while such traditionalism may have held true for the Czech countryside, it did not necessarily extend to the areas of new Jewish settlement, in particular the industrial centers of northern and western Bohemia. Most of these places had no official Jewish community before the 1850s or 1860s and thus did not possess long-standing private Jewish schools. In those cities and towns with large German-speaking populations, Jewish children tended to go to the state-run German-language schools. In some cases, formerly Jewish institutions were taken over as state-run schools.[38]

Surprisingly little has been written about the precise state of affairs in Prague. Primary accounts do not detail the fate of the Jewish *Hauptschule* (and its subsidiary schools) following the secularization of public education at the end of the 1860s. My sense is that it was converted to the category of "private school recognized under public law" and gradually acquired a mixed Jewish and Gentile population. Apparently the Schulverein also helped to maintain some of its branches. Only a close examination of the manuscript records of the Prague Jewish community, however, will yield a definite answer. We do know that on the eve of the 1860s educational reform, the Jewish community of the city maintained fifteen private elementary schools, ten for boys and five for girls.[39] Another source holds that the Prague Jews supported five such schools in 1885, but is silent on the existence of German-Jewish schools in Prague a decade later.[40] What is clear is that the large majority of Jewish children in Prague avoided private education altogether in favor of the municipal school system and that most of this majority chose the German track. In 1890, 97 percent of the Jewish children attending public schools went to German-language institutions. In 1900 the figure stood at 90.5 percent, and in 1910 it was still 89 percent. Over the course of this period, the Czech cause made very small but steady progress both in terms of absolute numbers and as a fraction of the Jewish aggregate.[41]

SECONDARY AND HIGHER EDUCATION

The Josephine reforms of the late eighteenth century had provided for a system of secular Jewish schools at the primary level only. The Jewish communities of the monarchy were not expressly prohibited from establishing private middle and upper schools, but none chose to do so. Jewish parents who wished to send their children to classical *Gymnasien* in preparation for the university selected from among existing private or state institutions. Most of the former, particularly in places like Prague, were administered by Christian religious orders, but this fact does not appear to have deterred Jewish attendance. Jewish students in Bohemia, as in most parts of Europe, attended secondary schools with far greater frequency than their non-Jewish counterparts. Thus in 1880 the 1,716 Jews who attended *Gymnasien* and *Realgymnasien* in Bohemia represented 11.5 percent of the student population, and the 586 who attended *Realschulen,* 10.6 percent.[42]

Because Jewish middle and upper schools per se did not exist in Bohemia, Jewish separatism—as it were—could not have been an issue for Czech nationalists. This did not mean that the secondary and higher education patterns of Jews had no political importance, however. Their conspicuously large presence in schools at this level meant that the "national" choices that Jews made carried extra weight. This was particularly true once the Austrian government began to award the benefits of cultural autonomy on the basis of precise nationality ratios. For their part, Jewish middle-school students appeared to "vote with their feet" in favor of the German minority. In 1882–83 (the first year for which accurate statistics are available), some 83 percent of all Jewish secondary school students attended German-language institutions. By the middle of the decade the figure settled at about 80 percent, with the remaining 20 percent going to Czech schools. More significantly, the 1,931 Jewish students who attended German-language secondary schools represented 23 percent of the student body in these establishments, while the 403 Jews attending Czech schools constituted a mere 3.2 percent.[43]

Not surprisingly, Jews also tended to pursue higher education at a considerably greater rate than their percentage within the population at large.[44] Hence, as was the case with the middle schools, Jews constituted a conspicuous presence in the universities and technical colleges of Bohemia, particularly in the German institutions. By 1863 Jews made up 10 percent of the student body at the University of Prague. During the winter semester of 1880–81, 11.7 percent of the student body at Prague's still-unified university and 17.9 percent at the German *Technische Hochschule* were Jewish. Many other Bohemian Jews completed their schooling in Vienna.[45] In the winter semester of 1885–86—three years after the University of Prague was divided into separate German and Czech establishments—the 404 Jews in attendance at the German branch comprised 26 percent of the total student body. The 50 Jews who registered with the Czech university represented but 2.5 percent of that body. They did represent 11 percent of the Jewish university students in Prague, but their presence in an institution of over 2,000 students went virtually unnoticed alongside the Jewish attendance in the much smaller German school.[46]

The Propaganda Offensive against Czech Jewry

The cultural behavior of Bohemian Jewry—their identification with both the German language and the privileged German minority—provided much grist for the propaganda mill during the last quarter of the nineteenth century. For one thing, the Jews offered an easy explanation for some of the shortcomings of the Czech national movement. They represented an irritating anachronism, a stubborn remnant of the imperial past that refused to take cognizance of the new *national* basis of social, political, and cultural life. If private elementary schools continued to flourish in the Czech countryside, denying the largely anticlerical Young Czech movement its vision of a secular and fully national school system, the fault lay with the Jews, who continued to maintain communal institutions that dated back to the times of enlightened absolutism. If the German nationalists were able to threaten the integrity of the

Czech regions of Bohemia through the agency of German minority schools, they owed their good fortune to Czech Jews who were both ambiguous in their national orientation and obsequious in their devotion to the Habsburg monarchy. And finally, if Czech nationalism failed to transfer to the cities of Bohemia the cultural dominance that it had achieved so decisively in the countryside, the blame once again could be placed at the doorstep of the Jews, who unlike their non-Jewish counterparts appeared as eager to trade national-cultural allegiances as they were to change domiciles.

Karel Adámek, for one, held such views. He charged in *Z naší doby*, his important work on contemporary Czech politics, culture, and economic life, that the Jews in combination with the Austrian bureaucracy were "certainly ... the strongest German factor in Slavic circles." Moreover, the Jewish elementary schools, "like the schools of the [German] Schulverein, [were] a dangerous lever in the Germanization of Czech cities and communities."[47]

This was not a new attack. Public opinion in the Czech lands had by this time equated Jews with the German minority for decades. As we have seen, on the eve of the Revolution of 1848, the patriotic Czech journalist Karel Havlíček Borovský rejected an overture for Czech-Jewish cultural collaboration put forward by the Jewish poet Siegfried Kapper on the grounds that the Jews comprised a separate ethnic entity; if anything, they could ally themselves more naturally to the German nation than to the Czech.[48] At the end of the nineteenth century, however, such accusations against the Jews emerged from an entirely different perception of their role in the country's national relations. The seemingly age-old German-Jewish alliance was no longer accepted as part of the natural state of affairs. Czech opinion held that the Jewish communities in the Czech countryside ought to have resembled more closely the cultural environment in which they were located: Jews ought to have behaved like Czechs; they ought to have demonstrated loyalty to the language and culture with which in their day-to-day activities they appeared to be completely at home. Above all, now that a national, secular system of primary education was in place, they ought to have been sending their children to local public schools.

Some within the Czech national movement accused the Jews of not only insensitivity toward Czech national aspirations but actual collusion with the rival German national movement. Karel Adámek, once again prominent in his criticism of Czech Jewry, claimed that the German Schulverein went so far as to base its "operational plan" for the Czech countryside on the maintenance of private Jewish schools. To support this contention, he quoted the remarks made by a certain Dr. Kraus at the General Assembly of the Schulverein in 1882:

In Bohemia there is a whole array of private German schools, with and without public legal status, which are maintained in purely Slavic localities by the Jewish religious communities there. We must look upon these schools in the purely Czech countryside as rare linguistic islands that must be preserved, since in such regions these schools are often the only seedbeds of German culture.[49]

Adámek then rattled off the names of Czech communities where private German schools were subsidized by the Schulverein: Holešovice, Libeň, and Josefov within greater Prague; Pardubice, Příbram, Slaný, Nové Benátky, Jičín, Nový Bydžov, Zbraslav, Čáslav, and elsewhere.[50] Singling out several specific examples of German-Jewish treachery, he cited the case of Heřmanův Městec, where the formerly private Jewish school had been transformed into a public German establishment because Jews there *"freely* chose the German nationality" (emphasis in the original); and the private German school in the town of Nymburk, which had 230 students in 1884–85, although according to the 1880 census the town had 5,126 Czech residents and only 226 Germans. Of the 230 students enrolled in the school, only 39 could legitimately be called "German" (the designation is never specifically defined). "What would the Schulverein schools look like," Adámek asked rhetorically, "if they were not attended by Jewish and Czech children?"[51]

Josef Kořán, Czech journalist and deputy in the Bohemian Diet, appealed directly to the heart of the Czech-Jewish community when he used the pages of the *Kalendář česko-židovský* (Czech-Jewish almanac) to pressure Jews to de-Germanize their communal institutions. The first thing that had to go, naturally, were the German-Jewish elementary schools. Not only did they prevent Jewish children from developing the proper Czech national sentiment, but they also stole non-Jewish children from the national camp; for alongside the 4,073 Jewish children in the Czech towns and villages who in 1885 continued to be educated in German schools attached to the Jewish religious community were 192 Catholics and 17 Protestants.[52]

Kořán challenged Bohemian Jewry to admit to the untruthfulness of many of the rationalizations that they used to justify this cultural behavior. "The supporters of these schools," he wrote, "would certainly object to us that they are only intended for children to be educated in German from a young age, that they, however, are not educated in anti-Czech thought."

But the mere existence of the schools is conclusive proof that Jews who establish and support them do not think as Czechs, have no love for our language, have no confidence in the victory of our cause, and even the knowledge of Czech [carries] less weight than the knowledge of German. These schools are a living protest against our national and political endeavors; indeed they are actually—even if their supporters did not have this in mind— demonstrations against our Czech culture.[53]

Some within the Jewish community, apparently, had argued that Jews were merely supporting confessional schools and not German schools per se. If that were so, Kořán asked, why were many of these schools interconfessional, particularly in Prague, where there were five German-Jewish establishments? If they existed primarily for religious instruction, one would have expected to find them in German as well as Czech regions of the country. But such was not the case. There were only ten Jewish schools in all of the German-speaking towns of Bohemia together, proof enough that they existed primarily to perpetuate German culture among the Jews.

The Czech-Jewish Response

Those Bohemian and Moravian Jews who identified with Czech language and culture—represented in the public sphere by organizations such as the Spolek českých akademiků-židů (Association of Czech Academic Jews [SČAŽ])—were already sufficiently uncomfortable with the linguistic favoritism of the formal Jewish community to want to do something about it. They did not need the prodding of Czech nationalist politicians, whether friends like Kořán or opponents such as Adámek. Jewish Czech nationalists such as J. S. Kraus had been agitating for the closure of the German-Jewish schools in the pages of the *Czech-Jewish Almanac* (*Kalendář česko-židovský*) since the early 1880s.[54] Kraus went so far as to offer a new reading of Bohemian Jewish history to account for the schools. Not only were they to blame for the abnormal assimilatory pattern of the Jews since the Enlightenment (the absorption of "state culture" over and against local, national culture), but they had been forced upon an unwilling population. Traditional Jewish society, therefore, had been no less a victim of a despotic policy of Germanization than traditional Czech society.

Nevertheless, the Czech-Jewish movement was prodded, and none too subtly. And it is impossible to determine precisely which motives most influenced Jewish behavior in this hazy and tumultuous period in Czech-Jewish relations. The Czech-Jewish activists *were* committed nationalists; they naturally stood in opposition to the cultural policies of the Jewish establishment; yet they were also recipients of a barrage of criticism from Czech national quarters.

Driven by a complex of factors, then, the Czech-Jewish movement during the last decade of the nineteenth century increasingly turned away from purely cultural tasks and toward the establishment of a political machinery to effect change within the Jewish community. Beginning in 1893 with the founding of the Czech-Jewish National Union (Národní jednota českožidovská), followed in 1894 by the creation of both the first Czech-Jewish newspaper (*českožidovské listy*) and an overtly political Czech-Jewish organization (Politická jednota českožidovská), the by-now-veteran activists of the SČAŽ took aim at the Jewish communities of Prague and Bohemia. Their purpose was no longer simply to educate and to cultivate national feeling; rather, they intended to mobilize the Czech-Jewish population to political action, to challenge the structures of Jewish life that had resulted from Jewish emancipation in the Habsburg monarchy.[55]

The establishment of the Czech-Jewish National Union signaled a subtle shift within the still relatively new Czech-Jewish movement. Whereas the student leaders of the SČAŽ had displayed no single political orientation, their faculty advisors and outside supporters generally had been devotees of the National, or Old Czech, Party. Members of the urban upper-middle class inspired by František Palacký and F. L. Rieger, they had tended to affirm the conservative nationalism that the Old Czechs typified. Those who became active in Czech politics themselves, such as Bohumil Bondy, Alois Zucker, and Josef Žalud, ran for office as Old Czech candidates.[56]

Many of the recently graduated lawyers, doctors, businessmen, and journalists, however, supported the rivals of the Old Czechs—the National Liberal Party, or Young Czechs.[57] Jakub Scharf, Maxim Reiner, Ignát Arnstein, and others—all veterans of the Czech-Jewish student movement—tended to be supporters of the Young Czechs. They took it

upon themselves to broaden the base of Czech-Jewish activities by creating a state-wide coordinated network of Jewish patriotic societies. In
establishing the Czech-Jewish National Union, they took as models the
various voluntary societies that had been created by the Young Czechs
during the previous decade to mobilize opinion and bolster nationalist
policies in Prague and in the countryside. One of these, the Central
School Foundation (Ústřední matice školská), we have already encountered as the great rival of the German Schulverein. But also important
were the several national unions (*národní jednoty*) that had been established to improve the material and cultural situation of Czech families
living in mixed or predominantly German areas.[58]

Like the SČAŽ before it, the Czech-Jewish National Union sought
to "spread the news" of the Czech national movement to every corner
of the country. To do so it relied not only on public lectures and social
gatherings but also on the creation of an institutional network consisting, before the year was out, of a central organization flanked by thirty-
four district chapters.[59] Like the Central School Foundation and its
subsidiary organizations, the Czech-Jewish National Union considered
one of its principal functions to be the furthering of Czech national
education. Yet its manner of operation was quite different from that of
its Czech counterpart. The Central School Foundation had emerged to
meet the challenge of the German Schulverein essentially by mimicking
it, by performing parallel functions of its own, but in German areas.
The Czech-Jewish National Union, on the other hand, constituted a
power that could actually negate the effects of the Schulverein in the
Czech lands. Instead of simply providing increased opportunities for
Czech children, the National Union attempted to make Czech education universal in areas where a *Jewish* minority had in the past dissented
from the norm.

Through its fortnightly newspaper, *Českožidovské listy* (Czech-Jewish
press), the Czech-Jewish National Union called for the closing of all
German-language Jewish schools in Prague and the Czech countryside.
"We want to work so that every Czech Jew will become completely
Czech," wrote the editors of *Českožidovské listy* in its opening issue, "will
feel, think, speak, and act as every other loyal Czech."[60] The modern
Czech Jew, the paper argued, felt himself to be part of the nation in
whose midst he lived, whose culture he shared. He had no reason *not* to
send his children to local Czech schools, and to persist in the old practice of maintaining separate Jewish schools was to commit an affront
not only against the Czech people but against the "modern Jewish

spirit" as well.[61] As for the argument that it was important for Jews living in the Austrian monarchy to know German to insure success in business and professional careers, *Českožidovské listy* referred to a speech by the Prague physician and Young Czech politician Emanuel Engel: this could be accomplished through the establishment of special language schools that would be private enterprises, "not connected with either you or your faith." As for himself, Engel admitted he was not so radical as to believe that one did not need to teach German to one's children. But he challenged the Jews of Bohemia to work toward a time when it would become less and less important for them to do so.[62]

The Demise of the German-Jewish School

Between 1894 and 1907 *Českožidovské listy* reported with great interest on the concerted efforts of the Czech-Jewish National Union to purge the German-Jewish elementary schools in the countryside. One by one it rattled off the names of small-town and village communities like a gunfighter from the Old West carefully taking aim and picking off rows of standing targets: Benešov, Tábor, Hradec Králové, Kutná Hora, Mladá Boleslav, Plzeň, Slaný, and so on. Josef Kořán, the Young Czech deputy who had admonished Czech Jews in the pages of the *Kalendář česko-židovský* in 1886, made a second appearance in 1896 to report on the progress made over the past decade. Apparently, nine *new* German language schools had been established in the Czech countryside between 1885 and 1894, but twenty-five had been closed.[63]

Kořán's 1896 report revealed that in all of Bohemia—German areas included—the number of German-Jewish schools had declined from 113 in 1885 to 90 ten years later. The number of Jewish children enrolled in such schools fell by 39 percent—from 4,239 to 2,587—while the number of Catholic students in German schools dropped during this period by only 9.4 percent and the number of Protestants by 23.5 percent.[64] Not only did a greater percentage of Jews switch from German to Czech schools, but virtually all of the establishments that succumbed during the 1890s were schools whose student body was exclusively Jewish. Those that had a mixed Christian-Jewish student body enjoyed greater stability and resistance to closure.[65] The Jews of Bohemia, then, appeared to have responded more completely than either German Catholics or German Protestants to the urgings of the Czech national movement. The truth of the matter was that Jews had fewer options than either Catholics or Protestants; Jews felt less secure in their patterns of cultural behavior, more vulnerable to political attack. The ideology of the Czech-Jewish movement, moreover, provided a cognitive structure through which to abandon cultural choices that were deemed no longer workable. These choices, after all, were themselves understood to be recent historical fabrications, experiments of the emancipatory process in Central Europe, not sacred practices.

Typically, notices of school closings in *Českožidovské listy* were brief and matter-of-fact, though colored with the editors' obvious satisfaction. Thus one reads in the 1 February 1898 edition of the paper of recent events in Zbraslav on the southern outskirts of Prague:

German-Jewish school closed. From Zbraslav *Hlas národa* [daily paper of the Old Czech Party] announces that the local German school, which has been maintained by the Jewish religious community, will be closed at the end of the school year. Jewish students attending this school will go next year to the Zbraslav public elementary schools.[66]

The newspaper was careful to add the last sentence to this brief notice. It was not enough to point out that the Jewish community had given up its practice of maintaining a separate primary school. One had to add that the families in this community would be taking the subsequent proper step of enrolling their youngsters in public Czech schools. They would not be seeking other German alternatives.

Occasionally the editors of *Českožidovské listy* came across Jewish responses to Czech nationalism that they could not wholly endorse, as they appeared to have been made half-heartedly or without sufficient understanding of the nature of the undertaking. One such case occurred in Humpolec early in 1898. The Jewish leaders of this small town decided not to close the local Jewish school but rather to change its medium of instruction from German to Czech. *Českožidovské listy* greeted the news with reservation, acknowledging the progress that this change signified but complaining nevertheless that the period of time required to achieve a complete linguistic transition would be too long. The editors sought to gently cajole the Jewish community. If it insisted on maintaining what the paper called a confessional school, at least it could begin instruction in Czech before the end of the calendar year.[67]

Where gentle persuasion would not work the National Union resorted to all-out attack. Such was its tactic with the city of Kolín in East Central Bohemia, which had one of the larger provincial Jewish populations at the time. In March 1898 *Českožidovské listy* devoted a series of columns to what it called "the situation in Kolín." It contended that the German-Jewish school there maintained its existence against the wishes of the majority of the city's Jews, against the statutes of the community, and thus "as a provocation to the entire Czech nation without regard to faith."[68] To support its charges, the paper published an open letter signed by sixty voting members of the community:

It was pointed out in the Jewish communal council that on the question of schools, [in the light of] present-day—in many respects, changing—conditions, *neither* the council *nor* the board of deputies *any longer represents* the thinking of the majority of Jewish citizens, and that therefore this citizenry must be given the opportunity to express its desires and aspirations in this regard.... We therefore demand that the larger directorate of the religious community be convened so that it might speedily decide upon the closing of the existing German school. [emphasis in the original][69]

The German-Jewish school of Kolín had educated 147 children in 1894–95. Within six months of the start of the campaign in *Českoži-dovské listy,* it had closed.

In 1906 the Czech-Jewish National Union announced with satisfaction that as far as it knew, fifty-two German-Jewish schools in Czech linguistic districts had closed since the organization first began its campaign in 1893. At least two public German schools, which were frequented primarily by Jewish students, likewise were closed, and in at least two other localities the German-Jewish private schools had been replaced by Czech-Jewish institutions.[70]

In point of fact, the extent of German-Jewish school closings since the early 1880s far exceeded the claims of the political leaders of the Czech-Jewish movement. Whether or not these institutions disappeared as a result of Czech-Jewish political pressure, however, is open to question. We know that the movement specifically targeted a number of towns for school closings and in most cases was successful. However, the data also show that Jewish schools in rural Bohemia began to close of their own accord during the 1880s and early 1890s, most likely because of declining enrollments.

The figures that follow reveal the steady progression in German-Jewish primary school closings between 1884–85 and 1910. At the start of this period some 4,500 children attended Jewish-sponsored German-language schools throughout Bohemia, over 88 percent of which were located in Czech-speaking districts, including Prague. By the end of this period, the number of children attending the German-Jewish schools had shrunk to 154. Of the 114 private schools that had existed in 1885, only five remained.

The pace of school closings during the first decade of political agitation (1885–95) was brisk. The number of German-Jewish schools dropped by about 21 percent, the number of students attending them by 42 percent. This, it will be recalled, was a period in which a small number of new schools were actually opened while others were being closed. Moreover, in many places where the schools did not actually close they nevertheless lost a high percentage of their enrollment. The Jewish school in Benešov, for example, had 60 students in 1885; a decade later the number stood at 26—less than half. Mladá Boleslav dropped from 105 to 67; Jičín, from 67 to 31; Brandýs from 52 to 30.[71] Even the important German-Jewish school in Kolín, the special target of Czech-Jewish criticism in 1898, had been losing population well before it became a political cause célèbre.[72]

The Jewish population of Bohemia had indeed been shifting away from the small towns and villages and toward the larger urban areas since the 1860s and 1870s, and the aggregate Jewish population did begin to fall after 1890. In neither case, however, was the pace of decline as rapid or as dramatic as that suggested by the statistics on primary school attendance. One cannot escape the conclusion that Jewish parents in the Czech countryside began to remove their children from the German-Jewish school system of their own accord, long before the demise of that system would offer them no choice. And they took this action in more and more places and with growing frequency as the end of the century approached.

During the half-decade from 1895 to 1900 ethnic conflict in the Czech lands in general intensified, but this period also witnessed an outbreak of popular violence directed specifically against Jews in the Czech countryside, in the German towns in the Sudetenland, and in Prague. It was indeed one of the most explosive periods in modern Czech history. And during this time a virtual tidal wave of school closings engulfed rural and small-town Jewish communities. Depending on which statistics one follows, the number of German-Jewish schools in this short period fell by as much as 69 percent and the number of students by 35 percent. Only twenty-eight schools remained open in 1900. A decade later the German-Jewish school and, to all intents and purposes, the traditional German-Jewish alliance in the Czech countryside was finished.[73]

In the meantime Jewish children were swelling the ranks of public elementary schools in Bohemia. A total of 2,770 Jewish children attended public schools in Czech districts in 1880; in 1890 the number was 4,791; by 1900 it had reached 6,131. During the same years the number of Jewish students in public schools in German districts declined (probably because their population in these districts was dropping): in 1880 the figure stood at 5,908; by 1900 it had slipped to 5,137.[74]

Changing Patterns in Secondary and Higher Education

Despite its obvious victory in the redirection of elementary education, the Czech-Jewish movement failed to have as strong an impact on other areas of educational life. Changes in the patterns of Jewish attendance at the secondary-school and university levels did occur, but they tended to take place gradually. Educational patterns at the highest levels showed remarkable stability through the first decade of the twentieth century. Gustav Otruba has compiled and published data comparing Bohemian middle-school attendance for 1882–83 and 1912–13. Over this period the yearly total of Jews attending Czech-language *Gymnasien* and *Realgymnasien* rose from 355 to 539; the Jewish share as a percentage of the entire student body climbed modestly from 3.3 to 4.5 percent.[75] Over the same period of time Jewish attendance at German-language *Gymnasien* and *Realgymnasien* declined slightly, from 1,481 in 1882 to 1,225 in 1912. As a percentage of the whole, however, the decline was more profound. The 1882 figure represented 24 percent of the German student body, the 1912 figure only 15.8 percent.[76]

Thus, a twofold process appears to have been operating. On the Czech side, Jewish attendance increased gradually both in terms of absolute numbers and percentages. On the German side, the weight of Jewish presence was felt less and less—on the one hand, because the real numbers of Jewish students were falling, and on the other, because their relative numbers were declining even faster.[77] In the last analysis, the ratio of German-Jewish to Czech-Jewish gymnasium students provides the sharpest indication of the extent of cultural change within the Jewish community itself. And this measurement indicates clearly that progressively fewer and fewer Jews who received a classical secondary education were choosing to attend German schools. In 1882 close to 81 percent of Jewish gymnasium students took part in the German-language system. By 1912–13, however, this figure had been pared down to 69.4 percent—still the majority, but shrinking.[78]

The patterns of higher education among the Jews of Bohemia—attendance at universities and technical institutes—proved the most resistant of all to change. Between 1863 and 1881 Jews were able to increase their percentage at the University of Prague by only a small amount, from 10.3 to 11.7 percent—again because the increase in Jewish numbers was more or less offset by a parallel rise in the general student population.[79] Once the university split into separate German and Czech branches, Jewish attendance figures at the two institutions resembled those of the middle schools but were even more pronounced. Thus, in 1889–90, the 478 Jews who went to the German university constituted more than 30 percent of the student body, while the 42 Jewish students at the Czech university represented a mere 1.7 percent of that institution.[80] Here too, the actual number of Jews who attended the German university declined somewhat over the next two decades, while the absolute number of Czech-Jewish students rose. Percentages, however, remained about the same as the total population at the German institution dwindled while the reverse process occurred on the other side of the ledger. Thus we find that during the winter semester of 1899–1900, 413 Jews were enrolled at the German university, 74 in the Czech university, but the respective percentages were 31 and 2.4. In 1910 Jews continued to constitute about 20 percent of the German institution and only 2 percent of its Czech counterpart.[81]

Since we know that the Jewish population of Bohemia declined after 1900 and that even before this time the Jewish rate of growth did not keep pace with that of the population at large, the only true test of the effectiveness of Czech-Jewish acculturation with regard to higher education is one that measures attendance figures as a percentage of total Jewish enrollment. Yet even from this perspective, the results could not have been promising for patriotic Czech Jews. Between 1885 and 1901 as many as 92 percent—and never less than 82 percent—of Jewish university students in Prague enrolled in the German university. Perhaps some consolation could be taken from the fact that this figure was declining in steady, albeit minute, fashion over the course of the 1890s.[82]

Both the German and the Czech technical institutes (Technische Hochschulen and Polytechniky) succeeded in attracting ever-larger numbers of Jewish students between 1880 and 1900. But here again, the Czech establishment could barely compete with the German school in popularity among Jews. Between 1881 and 1886 an average of 73 Jews attended Prague's Technische Hochschule each year; this was 25.4 percent of the student body. The number of Jewish students dropped somewhat for the remainder of the decade, but rose to 122 (26.2 percent of the student body) for the years 1896 to 1901, and jumped to 216 (30.5 percent) between 1901 and 1904. The Czech institution showed a similar curve, with attendance dropping for some reason during the second half of the 1880s but then rising dramatically in the 1890s. Between 1896 and 1901 an average of 27 Jewish students attended the Prague Polytechnika, forming 2.6 percent of the student body as a whole. Over the next four years the average grew to 34, but the Jewish share in total attendance dropped slightly, to 2.3 percent.[83] As we have found in every other case, minor change over time is perceptible when the attendance records are considered from the point of view of total Jewish enrollment. The ratio of German to Czech enrollment hovered between 9.5 to 1 and 12 to 1 for the first part of the 1880s. In 1897–98 the ratio stood at less than 4.5 to 1 and remained fairly steady in subsequent years.[84]

Conclusion

The Czech-Jewish movement would have been the first to confess that it fell short of its stated goal of transforming Jewish educational patterns in Prague and Bohemia in the short term. Its only shining success came with the virtual elimination of the German-Jewish primary schools in the small towns and villages. This development resulted not only from secular demographic and social trends in the countryside but also from the sustained pressure applied by both Jewish and non-Jewish Czech activists on individual Jewish communities. The Czech-Jewish movement offered no such political program with regard to secondary education, relying instead on indirect persuasion and the natural inclinations of Czech-Jewish youth to do the job. Nevertheless, inroads were made in the patterns of Jewish gymnasium attendance; the percentage of German-Jewish students to Jewish students generally did drop, but by modest amounts and without causing any major disruptions.

Attendance patterns for higher education proved to be the hardest shell to crack. When it came to university and technical college education, Bohemian Jewry opted for perceived quality, utility, and prestige over other considerations by very wide margins. The German institutions of Prague enjoyed international renown. The education and training that they provided could be applied in many other parts of Europe on the strength of the German language. And the German university was, for all intents and purposes, the heir to the ancient institution founded by Charles IV. To have deliberately chosen the lesser-known, relatively untested, provincially oriented Czech university would have required most Prague Jews to turn their backs on the very premises upon which a Jewish university education rested: the pursuit of scholarly achievement, the criterion of utility, and the promise of social integration and economic mobility.

In the long term, the thousands of Jewish young people who abandoned the traditional German-Jewish school in favor of a Czech education helped to move the Jewish community toward a fundamental cultural reorientation. These sons and daughters of Czech-Jewish townspeople and villagers formed the backbone of postindustrial urban Czech Jewry. Their "secondary acculturation"—accomplished in part at the hands of the Czech national movement—had weaned them away from the social and cultural patterns of the emancipation period. The twentieth-century community was to display a more attenuated national profile, one that accommodated both Jewish nationalism and Czech patriotism and one in which Czech language and culture found their pride of place. If after 1918 Czech Jewry could feel at home in the new Czechoslovak Republic and achieve a high degree of social integration, it was in no small measure thanks to the cultural shifts of the 1870s, 1880s, and 1890s, of which the German-Jewish school was a principal casualty.

CHAPTER 7

Jan Hus and the Prophets

Fashioning a Czech Judaism
at the Turn of the Century

Emancipation, Language, and Religious Forms

In 1867 the Prague Jewish community laid to rest its venerable chief rabbi of twenty-seven years, Solomon Judah Rapoport. In the same year construction was completed on a new, domed synagogue on Geistesgasse, built in the so-called Spanish style of Reform Judaism. When Rapoport first came to Prague from Galicia at the age of forty-three, the city had very much the air of a provincial Austrian capital, modest in size, unprepossessing, and dominated by a Gentile, German-speaking elite. Its Jewish population continued to labor under numerous disabilities, including residential and occupational restrictions, the formal *numerus clausus* of the Familiants Laws, and extraordinary taxation. The linguistic balance in the city was then at the threshold of transition: although the migration of Czech speakers from the countryside was well underway—the majority entering the workforce as artisans, shopkeepers, and industrial workers—the Czech presence was just beginning to be felt at the political level.[1]

The religious life of the Jewish community in 1840 was also being remapped after some six decades of gradual reform, during which time Enlightenment schools and normative religious patterns coexisted in a kind of uneasy truce. Rapoport himself seemed to embody Bohemian Jewry's compromise between East and West, modernity and tradition: a native of Lwów (Lemberg), he arrived in Prague from Tarnopol in Eastern Galicia (according to one account, dressed in the traditional costume of Polish Jewry).[2] A defender of orthodox practices in the controversies surrounding the German rabbinical conferences of the 1840s, Rapoport was at the same time a leading exponent of the historical study of Judaism (*Wissenschaft des Judentums*), the author of important biographical essays on tenth- and eleventh-century *ge'onim* (heads of Babylonian talmudic academies), a contributor to the Hebrew periodical *Bikkurei ha-'ittim* (First fruits), and editor of the journal *Kerem ḥemed* (Vineyard of delight).[3]

It was in 1867, finally, that the Dual Monarchy of Austria-Hungary was established and the principle of Jewish political equality was inscribed in the Austrian constitution. In many respects the year must have had the feel of a turning point: the twenty-year process of Jewish emancipation was now complete; the old order of Jewish disabilities and religious orthodoxy had ended; and a new era, full of potential for social, economic, and cultural advancement, had begun. At the same time—though not consciously—the new dualistic state would establish the framework for the numerous ethnic struggles that were to challenge the political order on both sides of the Leitha River up to the First World War.

None of these developments—least of all the transformations in religious life—happened overnight. The Jews of Prague and Bohemia had been engaged in a gradual though inevitable process of cultural and social modernization since the 1780s, one of whose consequences was the steady erosion of traditional Jewish practices, including religious observance and attendance at *ḥadarim* and *yeshivot*. By 1850 virtually every Jewish child attended German-Jewish primary schools (*Normalschulen*), which were run by the local Jewish community though supervised by the state. Many went on to *Gymnasien* and universities, and only those young men who wished to train specifically for the rabbinate occupied places in Prague's once-famed talmudic academies. Lastly, as the available memoir literature readily attests, the thousands of Jews who migrated to Prague from the countryside during the last third of the nineteenth century arrived in a metropolis whose Jewish population showed a marked disregard for the outward signs of religious piety.[4]

Lack of concern for normative Jewish practice, however, did not necessarily mean that the Prague community on the whole was receptive to the type of religious reform that had won over many cities in Germany in the nineteenth century. The Spanish synagogue at this time was, after all, the only one of some twenty congregations in Prague to adopt the characteristic features of Reform worship. And even this institution chose to follow the moderate format associated with Viennese Judaism, which included the retention of most Hebrew prayers and the intro-

duction of a choir and of sermons in German.[5] Two or three more synagogues would adopt such modern features in their services before the
end of the century, but religious innovation in a formal sense would not
proceed any further.

Jewish religious life in the countryside, in contrast, appears to have
barely been affected by even this small amount of change. Here traditional patterns of religious observance and worship lasted at least
through the first half of the nineteenth century. What village and small-
town Jews of Bohemia lacked in formal religious knowledge and cultural sophistication they made up for in simple piety and a retention of
traditional forms of behavior that owed more to habit than ideology.[6]
Institutional life and public ritual in the countryside did share at least
one important element with that of the cities, however: the propensity
to employ German for all discourse outside of the formal liturgy (for
which the original Hebrew was preserved). German had served as the
principle cultural vehicle in the modernization of the Jewish communities of Bohemia since the period of Joseph II.[7] By the early nineteenth
century, it had already become the everyday language of nearly all Jews
in the larger towns and cities. The community-run schools used it for
instruction in all subjects, and certainly no one was surprised to hear
German either spoken among congregants in places of worship or used
in the sermons and choral music of the Reform synagogue.

On the other hand, small-town and village Jews lived in small clusters and were heavily dependent on the non-Jewish population for all
forms of social and economic intercourse. Hence the language of the
workaday world tended to be Czech. In the nineteenth century German
receded more and more to the private domain, reserved for discourse
within the family or among coreligionists. Yet Jews maintained the language in highly visible public institutions, such as schools, synagogues,
and community councils, until the last quarter of the nineteenth century with a steadfastness that appeared to many to be singularly out of
place. The popular Jewish imagination tended to associate German
with Enlightenment and religious toleration, with the social and cultural reforms that had been inaugurated during the reign of Joseph II—
indeed with the very process of Jewish emancipation in the Habsburg
monarchy. Moreover, the German language's long association with
public worship seemed to have endowed the language with an almost
sacred quality.

Small-town Jews in particular were thought to assign what some
called a "holiday" status to one of the languages of Bohemia and a
weekday status to the other. The Czech-Jewish humorist and story

writer Vojtěch Rakous (Adalbert Österreicher, 1862–1935) caricatured this predilection in his short piece "Jak se u nás němčilo" (How we spoke German at home).[8] The memoir recounts how Rakous's father, a village Jew who spoke not a word of German during the week, would return from prayer in the neighboring town on Saturdays, having picked up a few words of German and Yiddish here and there, and would proceed to speak only German for the rest of the day. Rakous's mother barely understood a word, yet listened silently and attentively to everything her husband had to say: "Father would explain each German or Yiddish word with such genuine piety, as though he were standing in the synagogue in front of the altar; and mother took in every word with awed reverence. These words may have been compensation for the Jewish worship, which she neither heard nor saw in the synagogue."[9]

In a similar vein, the Prague Jewish lawyer Maxim Reiner once complained that he often came across Jews who publicly professed the Czech nationality, but who nevertheless conversed among themselves in German once they entered a synagogue. It was, he suggested, as if German were more conducive to holy occasions than their everyday language.[10] Cognitive dissonances such as these played a part in the creation of the first Czech-Jewish associations in Prague, such as the Spolek českých akademiků-židů (Association of Czech Academic Jews), which was begun by Jewish university students and a few academic advisors in 1876, and eventually in the establishment of a formal Czech-Jewish political movement. The SČAŽ advocated what it called the "national assimilation" of Jews into Czech life and during the first quarter-century of its activity consistently sought to purge public Jewish institutions in predominantly Czech-speaking areas—particularly the schools and synagogues—of all associations with German cultural dominance.[11]

Before the 1880s Jewish Slavophiles in Bohemia and Moravia had made only sporadic attempts at synchronizing Jewish liturgy and ritual with Czech language and culture, the religion of their fathers and mothers with the idiom of Jan Hus. One early experiment grew out of the Young Bohemia literary movement of the 1840s, itself inspired in part by Jewish intellectuals. Hynek Kraus, a postmaster in the town of Luštenice (near Mladá Boleslav), published the first Czech-Hebrew *siddur* in 1847. Kraus's prayerbook sought to fill the needs of those Czech Jews who, even by this time, may have felt more at home in the Czech language than in German.[12] Ultimately the book was to have little impact on Czech-Jewish life. It was not widely distributed, and, apparently, its numerous printer's errors and linguistic archaisms rendered it unusable within a few decades.[13]

Of more lasting significance was the work of Rabbi Filip Bondy (1830–1907), a student of Solomon Judah Rapoport and Aaron Kornfeld and a graduate of the University of Prague. Bondy served the Jewish communities of Kasejovice (1859–68) and Brandýs nad Labem (1868–76), traveling through many small towns and villages, preaching in Czech, and conducting religious services to Czech accompaniments. His early determination to use the Czech language as a vehicle for the popular diffusion of religious ceremony and education may have caused eyebrows to be raised within the Jewish community. A number of people, however, were undoubtedly heartened and impressed by Bondy's actions. Vojtěch Rakous, whose sister was married in a ceremony conducted by Bondy, was one. He ironically remarked of the occasion, "It was certainly the first time in my life that I understood every word that was spoken from such a mouth."[14]

Bondy had directed his efforts at de-Germanizing the context of public ritual in order that Jewish ceremony would become more understandable to village and small-town Jews. The SČAŽ meanwhile sought to employ similar means in order to heighten the national sensitivities of all Czech Jews—particularly those of the cities—as well as to showcase the cultural inroads made by their movement. In general, the smaller, largely isolated Jewish communities of the countryside tended to be quite receptive to the program of the SČAŽ. They yielded readily to the pressure that was brought to bear by the movement's so-called rural secretaries. Jewish institutions in the capital proved to be much more resistant to change, and consequently the SČAŽ decided to circumvent Prague's established congregations by creating a Czech-Jewish presence in the area of public worship without necessarily challenging the legitimacy of the existing synagogues.

A number of the leading members of the association formed a new organization in 1883 called Or-Tomid (Eternal Light), devoted to promoting "prayer in Czech and in Hebrew." The founders of Or-Tormid, themselves having emerged for the most part from small towns and villages, acknowledged the general unpopularity of Reform Judaism in the Czech lands and declared that they had no intention of "reforming" Judaism as such. In truth, they do not appear to have drawn much inspiration from either the German or the Viennese reform movements. An early programmatic statement of the organization explained: "[The society] ... does not want to change any [part] of that which up to this time has been performed in worship services in Hebrew. Only that which up to now has been conducted in German—such as sermons, the prayer for the royal family, occasional talks, public announcements, declarations, etc.—will from now on be given in Czech."[15]

In 1886 Or-Tomid began to hold services on a regular basis and called upon Filip Bondy to serve as its spiritual head. Within a few years this arm of the Czech-Jewish movement had outgrown its original quarters. Josef Žalud, a professor of law at the Czech University and éminence grise of the movement, announced in 1892 that a fund was being established for the creation of a Czech-Jewish "temple," the construction of which he likened to that of the recently completely Czech National Theater. In both instances the physical structure was to assume an importance equal to that of the cultural enterprise going on within its walls; it was to be a visible symbol of patriotic sentiment and national determination.[16] Or-Tomid became a showpiece of Jewish sincerity toward Czech language and culture, and non-Jewish dignitaries frequently were invited to join Jewish worshippers in the new building on Jindřišská Street near the center of Prague as the contents of Judaism were transferred ceremoniously from a German to a Czech vessel.

During the 1880s and 1890s Or-Tomid and the SČAŽ embarked on an ambitious publishing campaign designed to create as quickly as possible—often through simple translations of German originals—a sacred literature in Czech. Hynek Kraus, the author of the 1847 Czech-Hebrew prayerbook, issued a book of prayers for women in 1881 based on a centuries-old adornment of traditional Jewish homes, which up to now had been available only in German or Yiddish.[17] Cantor Mořic Kraus made Herculean efforts to help transform Jewish worship in Bohemia into an entirely Czech and Hebrew affair through a whole series of translations and occasional readings. His contributions began with an 1885 translation of the Yizkor, or memorial service, and culminated at the end of the decade with the publication of the first Czech-Hebrew Passover Haggadah.[18] In between he published a variety of miscellaneous pieces: *Psalms and Prayers on the Birthday of His Majesty [the Emperor]; The Five Prayers for Sabbath and Holidays; Funeral Prayer;* and *Czech Prayers for Public Worship at the Synagogue of the Or-Tomid Association.*[19] Easily the most important and influential of the volumes that rolled off the presses of Or-Tomid was the 1884 Czech-Hebrew prayerbook compiled by August Stein.[20] In his introduction to the work, Stein made conscious reference to the larger political implications of his undertaking. The new prayerbook, he hoped, not only would serve the needs of the young Czech Jew, who spoke Czech both inside and outside of the home, but also would carry the message to the Czech people with renewed emphasis that the only thing that separated them from their Jewish neighbors was religious faith, not language or ethnic identity.[21]

The most remarkable aspect of the Czech-Jewish religious reforms of the 1880s may have been their superficiality. The activists within the SČAŽ and Or-Tomid seem to have been content merely to tinker with the linguistic forms of public worship and ritual. Once Judaism had acquired a "Czech face," as it were, they considered their job to have been completed. One could argue, on the other hand, that the superficiality of early Czech-Jewish reform was born of optimism. Activist Czech Jews saw nothing in the content of their religious culture that would stand in the way of their swift integration into modern Czech society. Nor did they view any major obstacles within Czech society itself that would bar their acceptance as full and equal members.

A Czech-Jewish Response to an Alienating Environment

This sense of optimism was forced to confront hard realities in the political arena in the 1890s. The first half of the decade saw the emergence of general industrial unrest, economic boycotts against both German and Jewish businesses, mass demonstrations in favor of universal suffrage, and eventually, popular violence directed at Jewish homes and property.[22] Hostility born of political frustration and psychological insecurity often deflected to the Jewish population of the Czech lands, which may have offered an inviting target because of the very ambiguity of its ethnic status. Accusations against Jews of ritual murder began to be heard in provincial towns, often to the accompaniment of popular demonstrations and the threat of violence. While the revival of the blood libel in an industrial society such as that of Bohemia and Moravia may have shielded people from the need to face certain social realities, such as child abuse or suicide among young single females, the rationalizations made by some public officials in the wake of the anti-Jewish accusations bestowed an unreal, almost comical, quality to the events of the day. One Czech weekly reported that the Jews had brought the rioting on themselves through their economic behavior and their support of the German cause. A medical officer who examined the body of a dead servant girl discovered in Kolín seems to have concluded that the root of the problem lay in the maintenance of a German-Jewish primary school in that town.[23]

The last half-decade of the century produced enough social conflict to shatter the confidence of any integrationist movement. Developments during these years also raised painful questions about the long-term compatibility of Jewish and Czech interests, to say nothing of the prognosis for the evolution of a Czech-Jewish religious idiom. The troubles began with the elections to the Austrian Reichsrat in 1897, when the Young Czech Party organization in Prague nominated a vocal antisemite, Václav Březnovský, to run in the city's new fifth curia.[24] Czech-Jewish leaders faced the unpleasant prospect of choosing among a Social Democrat, a clerical candidate, and a Czech antisemite for endorsement. When the Jews of Prague swung their support to the Social Democratic candidate, who ultimately lost a run-off election to Březnovský, segments of the nationalist press lashed out at them with vengeance.

Following the elections, the Austrian Prime Minister Casimir Badeni issued a pair of language ordinances that were designed to meet many of the demands of the Czech nationalists while insuring that the Czech lands remained an integral part of the monarchy. The proposed legislation would have required that all civil servants in Bohemia and Moravia show proficiency in both German and Czech or face dismissal, and it provoked a storm of protest by Austrian Germans. German deputies in the Reichstag resorted to filibuster and other obstructionist tactics in an effort to thwart the new legislation and to bring down the Badeni government. Mass demonstrations and popular violence erupted in the streets of Vienna and Graz, as well as in the German towns of northern and western Bohemia, where the targets of unrest were not only Czech student groups but also Jews.[25]

At the end of November Badeni resigned. This act set in motion a new series of violent demonstrations, this time in Prague and the Czech countryside. In the three days following Badeni's resignation the streets of Prague served as a battleground for rival armies of urban agitators. German university students taunted Czech crowds with boisterous renditions of patriotic songs, such as "Wacht am Rhein," and open-air marches to their civic center, the German Casino. Czech-speaking mobs marched in retaliation to the New German Theater and bombarded it with stones; violence broke out in residential neighborhoods; eventually the army had to be called up to restore order.[26] On the second day of demonstrations, masses of people attacked German-owned stores, coffeehouses, and private homes near the fashionable Příkopy (Graben) and Wenceslaus Square. The crowds destroyed every plate of glass on the New German Theater, attacked the German *Schulverein* school in the Královské Vinohrady district, and smashed the windows of synagogues both there and in Žižkov. Vienna now increased the military presence in Prague from two to four battalions of sharpshooters and added two battalions of infantrymen.[27]

After the third day of rioting the government declared a state of martial law, but not before the synagogue in Smíchov and many private homes and institutions had succumbed to the popular fury. Miraculously, the riots had not resulted in any deaths. Nevertheless, they produced something of a trauma within the ranks of the Czech-Jewish movement, to say nothing of the rest of the Bohemian Jewish community. The carefully constructed plans and cherished hopes of countless Czech-speaking Jews lay strewn along the sidewalks of Prague and tens of smaller communities, together with the shards of glass and broken furniture from Jewish homes and shops.

The liberal Czech press did nothing to soften the blow of what became known as the "December storm." *Národní listy*, closely associated with Young Czech policies, reported that the Prague disturbances had been precipitated by German and Jewish provocations, that the coffeehouses from which German students had taunted the Czech population were mainly frequented by Jews, and that "Semitic" faces could be seen outlining the doors of the cafes.[28] Among Jewish observers, even the most charitable had to conclude that the Czech national establishment had abandoned the Jews in their hour of need. The less sanguine began to fear that something much worse was happening.

Czech Jews barely had a chance to recover from the shocks of 1897 when a new calamity struck. On 1 April 1899 in the eastern Bohemian town of Polná, a nineteen-year-old dressmaker named Anežka Hrůzová was found murdered in a quarter of the town inhabited by poor Jews. Leopold Hilsner, a Jewish vagabond of apparently unsavory character, was arrested and charged with the crime. The prosecutor, in determining the probable motive for the killing, emphasized the fact that the girl's body—which obviously had been stabbed or punctured—lay, as the indictment read, in "an insignificant pool of blood, no bigger than a hand."[29] During the course of the ensuing trial, both Catholic and liberal newspapers charged that Hilsner had killed a young Christian woman in order to make use of her blood for ritual purposes. As the body was discovered in early April, generally the season in which Passover falls, they presumed that the blood was used in the preparation of Passover *matzot*. To exacerbate matters, the opportunistic Young Czech politician Karel Baxa—who years later became mayor of Prague—volunteered to represent the dead girl's family at the trial. His frequent evocations of the imagery and vocabulary of Jewish "ritual murder" contributed greatly to the sensationalism of the proceedings.[30]

Had the outpouring of popular antisemitism in 1897 and 1899 been confined to the fringes of respectability, leaders of the Czech-Jewish movement would have greeted it with stoicism. They might have agitated for a speedier implementation of school closings and a more thorough bilingualism in the public life of the Jewish community, but they would not have doubted for a moment the correctness of their overall cultural and political strategy. It was clear, however, that *Národní listy* and part of the leadership of the Young Czech Party had colluded in the attacks against the Jews. This realization stripped the Czech-Jewish movement of its confidence. How was it to answer the charges of opponents that Czech liberalism had abandoned the Jews of the Czech lands? Indeed, what could the Czech-Jewish National Union or the Association of Czech Academic Jews offer their own members by way of consolation?

Given the depth of their commitment to Czech national culture, most Czech-Jewish leaders showed remarkable independence and courage in reacting to the crisis of the late 1890s. When the "*Svůj k svému*" (each to his own) campaign of anti-German and anti-Jewish boycotts achieved its full force under the direction of the group Národní obrana (National Defense), leaders of the Czech-Jewish movement rose one by one to denounce it. Many admitted that they had been prepared to weather the storm in the name of national economic development and full autonomy, had the boycott been applied strictly on an individual basis against German nationals or clear supporters of the German national camp. But the tactic had been applied indiscriminately to Jews as a whole, ruining the livelihood of thousands in the process. Thus Czech Jews publicly withheld support for the economic program of the national movement.[31]

Eduard Lederer (1859–1941), an attorney educated in both Prague and Vienna who was to assume a leading position in the Czech-Jewish movement after the turn of the century, began to question openly the basis of the Jewish–Young Czech alliance shortly after the elections of 1897.[32] The national liberals, he acknowledged, spoke for the majority of the Czech nation, and until recent weeks, Jews had found in them a natural ally. But memories of Březnovský's nomination and election and the provocative behavior of *Národní listy* hovered over the heads of Czech Jews like a cloud. The "liberal" parties in the Czech lands were abandoning liberalism. Worse yet, they either ignored or belittled the accomplishments of the Czech-Jewish movement. The social democrats, in Lederer's view, were not much better. They considered the nationalist activity of the Czech Jews to be antiquated and a barrier to modern development. Only the left wing of the liberal camp, made up of the Realists and the Progressives—and represented by their respective newspapers, *Rozhledy* and *Samostátnost*—offered some cause for optimism. These circles may not have jumped and cheered for Czech Jews, but their journalists did at least write respectfully about Lederer's movement and considered it a legitimate political force.[33]

In the immediate aftermath of the December riots Lederer lashed out at the Young Czechs, laying the blame for the violence in no uncertain terms at their feet.[34] Subsequently, Maxim Reiner, leader of the Czech-Jewish Political Union, publicly denounced the Young Czech Party for having flirted with Vienna's racial antisemites in collusion with the Christian Social movement. He expressed dismay that the mouthpiece of Czech liberalism, *Národní listy,* had gloated over the two convictions of Dreyfus in France and had accused Dreyfus' supporters of having perpetrated a Jewish cabal. In a revealing moment of self-criticism, Reiner admitted that the Czech-Jewish establishment had seriously underestimated the effects of radical groups such as Národní obrana, whose agitation throughout Prague and the Czech countryside helped greatly to prepare the ground for the December storm. Yet the Czech political press was no less myopic. A considerable portion of it had been content to pay lip service to the official program of the Young Czechs, which abjured antisemitism, while it encouraged the actions of the antisemitic movement.[35]

Reiner's analysis of the political relations of the Czech-Jewish movement followed a pattern that was characteristic of the difficult time in which he was living. He began with a litany of charges and accusations against the Czech nationalist establishment but ended with counterbalancing arguments that invariably started with the word "nevertheless." Reiner proclaimed that his movement would hold fast to this long-standing position of working as Czechs for Czech national rights. But at the same time it would insist that Jews achieve full equality and freedom within Czech society.

We wish to be equals among equals in both rights and duties. We shall gladly lend our strength to the service of the nation. We want to fulfill this obligation and shall, conscientiously and resolutely as in the past. On the other hand we do demand that we and our actions—our persons and our deeds—be judged according to truth and justice, not with glasses clouded by hatred.[36]

· · ·

The fact that their movement was facing an important crossroads was clear to all of the participants in Czech-Jewish politics on the eve of the new century. The younger generation of Czech-Jewish intellectuals, represented chiefly by Lederer and Viktor Vohryzek (1864–1918)—a Pardubice physician—realized that the marriage to the Czech National Liberals had soured irretrievably. But they were reluctant to sue for a formal divorce. The preferred tactic during the initial regrouping of the Czech-Jewish movement was to "shake things up," to cajole and admonish, to challenge assumptions. Lederer, for example, caused a small furor in 1898 when he published an exposé in the pages of *Českožidovské listy* on the Jews and Social Democracy.[37] While the piece did not go so far as to advocate a formal split with the Young Czechs, it *did* urge Czech Jews to question the political orthodoxies of the recent past and to show greater sympathy for the just causes of Czech workers.[38]

It was only in 1900, when Viktor Vohryzek used the pages of the same newspaper to publish a long and influential piece entitled "Epištoly k českým židům" (Letters to Czech Jews), that the foundation was laid for a reworking of the Czech-Jewish relationship. Vohryzek's point of departure marked a definite shift in Czech-Jewish rhetoric and apologetics. He proposed that when all was said and done, the causes of Jewish suffering and persecution everywhere lay not in some misdirected historical evolution, in poorly conceived governmental policies, or in the stubborn refusal of Jews to assimilate. The problem of antisemitism lay not in Jewish behavior—collective or individual—but in human nature. It was a question of ethics and of psychology, arising, as did other forms of hatred, from atavistic instincts in humankind:

Just as the child, who has hardly learned to move about, breaks and destroys everything that comes into his hands; just as the hunter chases down and destroys game, not out of need, but for amusement based on destructive instincts; so too does the person who possesses power destroy those who are weak—as a pastime, for his own whim and amusement.[39]

Hatred was a basic human instinct, no less than love. By arguing that the chief causes of antisemitism lay within human nature and did not derive from any particular behavior on the part of Jews, Vohryzek was delivering two important messages to his readers. The first was that Czech Jews were not the agents of their own misfortune. They had done nothing to warrant or "deserve" the violence that had been directed at them, as neither "recent history" nor patterns of cultural allegiance could ultimately account for such behavior. The second point was that, in the last analysis, antisemitism was a Czech, not a Jewish, problem. It reflected a weakness in the character of the Czech people (an argument that Masaryk was also to make), one that was exploited by nationalist politicians for selfish and shortsighted purposes. In the last analysis, it was the Czech "soul" that suffered from antisemitism's poison.[40]

By way of conclusion, Vohryzek advised Czech Jewry to do two things. First, it ought to wait out the decline of the liberal party:

If the Czech nation were once again to return to Hussite liberalism, I would not hesitate to proclaim that we would soon succeed in reaching that point in which all Czech Jews would be in the Czech camp as loyal sons; but it would have to be a sincere liberalism, not the comical preelection kind in which Jews cannot and do not believe.[41]

No one expected a return to the ideals of the Czech Reformation to be accomplished soon. In the meantime, Jews were to prepare an "antidote" to the poison that had infected the Czech nation. "Our antidote is the strengthening of all progressive influences ... the battle against hypernationalism and clericalism. The antidote is the struggle against the dark."[42]

Vohryzek called upon Czech Jews, in the meantime, to learn how to defend themselves—to straighten their backs, as he put it—and not "fall down in the dust before every journalistic bandit." They had to act with dignity and pride in order that basic human consideration dictate the conduct of others toward them.[43] This is not to say that there was not a great deal wrong with the nature of Jewish cultural and economic life in the Czech lands. Vohryzek felt that it was just as incumbent upon Jews to examine their faults as to defend their rights. In his opinion, Jews still pursued dangerous and unsavory economic occupations such as money lending and the production and distribution of liquor. Jewish life required a thorough, ongoing reform—a renewal based on the spiritual purposefulness, social ethics, and progressive outlook of the prophets of the Old Testament. But the issue of internal reform and redirection, Vohryzek warned, was for Jews to face on their own. Society at large was in no position to pass judgment.

Between 1900 and 1905 this dissenting wing of the Czech-Jewish movement set about the task of redefining the nature of the Czech-Jewish relationship. Its efforts invariably took the form of both a search for new political alignments and a reevaluation of the moral and intellectual significance of the movement itself. Eduard Lederer's *Žid v dnešní společnosti* (The Jew in contemporary society), published in 1902, contributed to the new debate. The work consisted, on the one hand, of a definitive apologia for Bohemian Jewry, which sought to lay to rest once and for all the false charges that had been leveled against it. Second, it attempted to provide the Czech-Jewish movement with a consistent intellectual direction, a program that might carry it into the twentieth century.

The single most important development in the creation of a new Czech-Jewish identity occurred in 1904 with the establishment of the independent newspaper *Rozvoj* (Development). Published single-handedly during its early years by Vohryzek—first in Pardubice and after 1907 in Prague—*Rozvoj* grew out of the cultural activities of a Jewish youth organization in Pardubice of the same name. The group's organizers—all graduates of provincial Czech *Gymnasien*—gave expression to the tensions of postliberal, postemancipatory Central Europe. They announced the need to address in particular two cultural challenges: that of Zionism, which was gaining popularity among small-town merchants and professionals, and also that of an as-yet-undefined religious revival, which stood in stark contrast to the rationalist heritage of the Enlightenment.[44]

The *Rozvoj* circle differed from its predecessors in the Czech-Jewish movement on virtually all counts but one—the desire to instill greater Czech national sentiment among Jews. In its sensitivity to the inroads being made by Jewish nationalism in Central Europe, its concern for a thorough economic and social restructuring of Czech Jewry, and its allegiance to the progressive branch of Czech liberalism represented by the Czech People's Party of T. G. Masaryk and Jan Herben, *Rozvoj* proved to be more responsive than the old guard to the political and cultural realities of Czech-Jewish life, more astute and independent politically, more willing to borrow from the successes of rival cultural affiliations.

Rozvoj invited Czech-Jewish intellectuals to redefine the goals of the assimilationist movement, to address issues that previous Czech-Jewish leaders—in their haste to achieve specific social and political objectives—had failed to resolve. Wasn't it Masaryk, after all, who had challenged Czech Jews to define precisely what type of assimilation they envisaged for their coreligionists? How far was the merger of Czech and Jewish culture to go? The editors of *Rozvoj* felt it was time that a concrete response be forthcoming, one that took into account such questions as the future of Judaism itself as well as the ethical basis of the Czech-Jewish relationship.[45]

An interesting by-product of the *Rozvoj* circle's rejection of Czech liberalism and simultaneous discovery of Masaryk was the priority that it now gave to questions of religion and ethics. Vohryzek, in the paper's introductory column, went so far as to suggest that the failure to investigate the religious underpinnings of modern culture had been the greatest mistake of the Czech-Jewish movement to date.[46] Czech Jews, he argued, had overestimated the power of secular, liberal nationalism to effect a successful integration of Jews into Czech society. Moreover, they had seriously underestimated the residual strength of traditional antisemitic attitudes within the overall Czech population. Nationalism devoid of a religious foundation operated outside the bounds of morality and ethical purpose, for it was religion that both transmitted and made manifest the ethical component in culture; religion defined the ultimate ideals of national activity.[47]

Rozvoj's religious agenda was problematic on several counts. As we already have seen, it ran counter to the confident universalism of the founders of Or-Tomid and the old guard of the SČAŽ. Its insistence on uncovering the religious underpinnings of community in a national setting not only challenged the conventional wisdom that no changes in Jewish belief and practice were needed to move Bohemian Jewry into the mainstream of Czech national culture; it also was suggestive of the variant of ethnic particularism that equated ethnicity and religious confession. Are we dealing here with an anachronism, a call for Jewish religious reform long after similar enthusiasms had played themselves out in other parts of Central Europe, or perhaps with a manifesto for Jewish ethnic renewal, for the construction of a non-Zionist Jewish identity tied to a Czech milieu?

The answer, I think, is no on both counts. If the younger wing of the Czech-Jewish movement was voicing sentiments that were fashionable in certain academic and nationalist circles, it did not understand those attitudes to be exclusivist. The spiritual redirection called for by Vohryzek and his colleagues was imagined to advance, rather than im-

pede, the larger goal of Jewish integration. Their "antisecularist" manifesto (admittedly a curiosity, given the casual attitude of many in the
movement regarding Jewish religious practice) was part of a larger
strategy to cut the wind from the sails of both the new antisemitism
and modern Zionism. A revitalization of the religious element in national life, they reasoned, would rehabilitate the purely religious definition of Jewish distinctiveness—a definition denied by both racial antisemites and Jewish nationalists. It might also provide a much-needed
boost to the involvement of Jews as Jews in the Czech national revival.
Since the real value of a people was determined by its spirit, that is, its
religion, a demonstration of the spiritual "worthiness" of Judaism—in
fact, of Judaism's universal appeal—might increase the desirability of
Jewish cooperation in the eyes of the Czechs.[48]

The chief concern of the assimilationists, however, was to correct the
excesses of Czech national politics. In this regard they found Masaryk's
oft-expressed call for an infusion of the spiritual values of the Czech
Reformation of the fifteenth and sixteenth centuries—exemplified in
the figure of the reformer and martyr Jan Hus—most appealing.[49]
When Eduard Lederer argued in *Žid v dnešní společnosti* that *all* of society needed to operate along radically different lines, that the idea of social justice as expressed in the Gospels must temper that of nationality,
he was echoing the views of the Czech philosopher. The Czech Reformation, as reformulated by its turn-of-the-century interpreters, was understood to rest on the foundations of religious and social democracy,
the primacy of peaceful means and intentions, and the insistence on political and social justice.[50] Both the *Rozvoj* and the Masaryk circles, then,
were in basic agreement that true national renewal could emerge only
from a moral regeneration.

Masaryk made repeated references to the moral challenge posed by
Hus to all national movements in a well-known speech delivered in
1910: "The leaders of our reformation have but one message for us all,
repeated and reechoed over our land: regenerate, reform the individual;
regenerate, reform the whole people."[51] It was this call for reform that
Lederer and Vohryzek had picked up on. *Rozvoj* dedicated many pages
during its early years to a wide-ranging discussion of the moral transformation of Czech society. It did so not only out of devotion to
Masaryk, but also because Vohryzek felt that Jews had a special contribution to make in this area. Czech Jews, he argued, were in a position
to draw upon the resources of rabbinic and biblical Judaism, as well as
nineteenth-century philosophy, to aid in the creation of a new moral

consensus, a religious and philosophical synthesis that would "unite us in a single cultural whole."[52]

Pessimism concerning the present state of Czech-Jewish relations thus combined in the writings of Lederer and Vohryzek with the hope for a future reconciliation. The Czech-Jewish relationship could still be salvaged; with renewed effort from both sides, a future based on autonomy and freedom, cultural symbiosis and ethical perfection, could still be reached. "The Czech nation may have spurned us for the moment," Vohryzek mused, "but it needs us urgently; and the day will come when it will acknowledge that."[53]

Lederer expressed a similar vision in the closing pages of *Žid v dnešní společnosti*. The Czech-Jewish experiment could be saved were it to be mounted on a new ethical foundation, modeled on the teachings of Hillel, Jeremiah, and Jesus of Nazareth:

The demagoguery of our day, countenanced from above and below, eventually will peter out. It is a fever that does not consume society, an illness out of which the people will emerge healthier than before.... A wave will once again roll that will lead society out of the depths of today's decay to a level of higher consciousness [*nazírání*]. Likewise, antisemitism—one of the manifestations of this demagogic fever—will pass simultaneously with it; and of its effects only a few fires on the field of culture will remain, nothing more.[54]

The "Galician" Specter

According to the *Rozvoj* circle, Czech Jews would not be able to contribute to the expression of a new moral aesthetics for the nation at large until they had tended, as it were, to their own house. Judaism was said to be in drastic need of change, both as a religion and as a system of practical ethics. Curiously, this generation of Czech-Jewish intellectuals possessed much the same combination of ethnocentrism and low self-esteem that had characterized the early Reform movement in Germany. "There must be a moral improvement of the whole," wrote *Rozvoj*'s editors in 1904, "in order for there to be fewer transgressions on the part of individuals."

The better the totality, the more noble the moral idea that governs the whole, the more "perfect" is each individual, the more infrequent, then, the lapses of isolated individuals.[55]

Both Lederer and Vohryzek called for far-reaching reforms within Czech Judaism, but they did not always share the same attitude toward the faith of their fathers. Often their remarks alternated between vigorous anti-Orthodox polemic and prophetic statements about what a reinvigorated and progressive faith of the future might look like. Lederer seems to have been a moderate. He was reasonably familiar with the sources of traditional Judaism, citing them frequently in his works and with a certain sense of intimacy. Likewise, he showed himself to be more eager than some of his colleagues to defend the reputation of the classics of rabbinic literature—the Mishnah, Talmud, and Midrash—as storehouses of ethical teachings and wisdom, rather than as mere legal compilations.[56]

Vohryzek, for his part, made a point of despising Orthodox Judaism. He urged his readers to fight against the kind of religion that conceived of a purely national rather than a universal God and that did not allow for the development of faith on the basis of reason.[57] In an article with the unlikely but revealing title "Away from Galicia," Vohryzek condemned what he labeled "clericalism" within Judaism and argued that the restrictions that were placed upon the individual by Jewish law no longer were valid.

A progressive person is one who proclaims: in the fullness of your heart you do not believe this; you are unable to observe this. You are leading a struggle for existence, and these laws are a hindrance for you; they complicate your domestic life and make it more expensive. It [the law] is a deadweight that would throw your already burdened ship down into the high sea.

"Orthodoxy is our principal enemy," he concluded, "and we cannot spare anyone who proclaims it."[58]

One wonders to what "orthodoxy" Vohryzek, in the end, was referring? The Prague Jewish community may not have been particularly responsive to the ideology of German Reform, but by the turn of the century it was nevertheless largely indifferent to Orthodox practice. No rabbi since the death of Solomon Judah Rapoport could be said to have wielded much power and influence in the city. In any event, the leading representatives of the Prague rabbinate, Nathan Ehrenfeld, Alexander Kisch, and Heinrich Brody, were all Western, university-educated clergymen—not at all representatives of Galician orthodoxy.

Nor could Vohryzek have seriously feared an influx of Galician rabbis to the Czech lands. The first Jews to arrive in Prague from Galicia in any numbers came as refugees during the First World War. Vohryzek's real concern lay with the need to formulate a philosophy of Judaism that would match the categories of Masaryk's religious thought and that might serve as a partner in the cultural transformation of the Czech nation. "We acknowledge Masaryk's watchword," Vohryzek wrote, "that a new philosophical-religious synthesis is needed in which our world can be united."[59] For Masaryk and other Czech intellectuals, anticlericalism, and especially anti-Catholicism, had constituted important elements of national self-awareness. If they frequently called upon the Czech people to reconstruct the intellectual tradition of Jan Hus, Jan Amos Komenský, and the Czech Reformation, they did so not only out of a concern for religious and social freedom, democracy, and justice but also because Protestantism itself highlighted the historical distinctiveness of the Czech nation.[60]

Vohryzek applied similar rhetorical imagery to his analysis of Judaism. Galicia served much the same function for Vohryzek as Rome did for Masaryk's philosophical allies. It was made to represent an obscurantist, backward, and repressive culture, which may or may not in fact have existed in Prague but on whose doorstep one could lay responsibility for the thus-far unhappy integration of Jews into the Czech nation. Judaism then, like Czech culture, required a "reformation" of its own in order that Czech Jews might join progressive Czech nationalists in a new, symbiotic relationship, a joint effort in the redirection of the national spirit.

In essence, I think, Vohryzek and his colleagues set out to reform an abstraction. The Czech-Jewish Reformation of the turn of the century constituted a largely formal internalization of Masaryk's religious critique, which originally had been aimed at Roman Catholicism. Unequipped on the home front with a cultural villain on the scale of the Church, Czech-Jewish intellectuals invented a not-entirely-believable Jewish analogue. Hussite liberalism, too, could not easily be translated to a Jewish idiom. It was not, after all, the same as nineteenth-century Reform Judaism, which had never really moved Bohemian Jewry. What, then, was to be the agent of Jewish renewal?

Though it was a bit of a reach, Czech-Jewish publicists claimed to have discovered in the work of Moritz Lazarus—a neo-Kantian professor of philosophy at the University of Berlin—the spiritual synthesis that they were looking for. His *Ethik des Judentums,* published in 1898, had set out to demonstrate the ethical foundations of Judaism on the basis of classical and rabbinic Jewish texts alone. Lazarus had argued that morality—God's Law—is accepted in a Kantian affirmation of duty, because human beings strive to resemble the moral quality of the Divine. Lazarus insisted that it was possible to isolate a fundamental principle that composed the essence of Judaism: "Because the moral is divine, therefore you shall be moral, and because the divine is moral, you shall become like unto God."[61]

Armed with Lazarus' definition of an unwavering ethical core at the heart of Jewish teaching, Vohryzek called for a paring away of the rotten exterior of the faith to get to its wholesome fruit.

The meaning of our religion, as Lazarus has demonstrated, is the hallowing of the name of God, *kiddush ha-shem* [quoting the Hebrew], the raising of man to divine status [*zbožnění člověka*, in Vohryzek's Czech]. All of our thoughts and deeds must be a celebration of His name—not a benefit or a profit, but rather a reaching out for the highest goal.[62]

The question, Vohryzek thought, was whether or not all aspects of Judaism allowed for the moral perfection of the Jew. His answer, predictably, was no. Certain practices actually inhibited the individual from achieving this goal. Consequently, it was incumbent upon the Jew to distance himself from them. "Only he who believes and acts according to his convictions can be [called] a good person."[63]

This morally honed Judaism of the future, with its emphasis on the hallowing of the name of God through ethical behavior, was to perform a specific function in Czech society. *Rozvoj* endowed it with Hillel's well-known dictum: "Do not do unto others what is hateful to yourself." The paper interpreted this to mean: believe in and support human progress; struggle against asceticism and the suppression of one's humanity. "Everyone belongs to our camp; everyone is our brother. That is our confession of faith."[64] This version of Jewish neo-Kantianism was meant, on the one hand, to serve as a vehicle for the improved integration of the Jew into Czech society, but it was also intended to have an impact on Czech society itself. The Czech-Jewish elite was to help direct the nation along a more moderate course, to lead it away from the hypernationalism of the past toward a new, humanist vision:

The national patriotism of the Jews has a precisely determined path: it is and must be humanistic. Humanistic in this sense: that it must not deny the legitimacy of other nations in the face of its own individuality. For Jewry this is a ready-made cultural and political program ... and it is allotted to the Jew as his own, let us say, political station—in other words, his religious-cultural mission.[65]

Such descriptions of the role of Judaism in the Czech future possessed a decidedly messianic flavor. In the end, Judaism's task amounted to nothing less than the modulation, even the sublimation, of the national impulse. Judaism was to provide the basis for the resolution of national tensions, for the wiping out of ancient prejudices. It is both paradoxical and revealing that the redefined and reshaped Jewish culture, once it was redirected toward Czech society, would result in the blunting of the very conflicts that had spawned it in the first place. This, ultimately, was to be the "missionary" task of Czech Jewry: to mediate the national struggle, to eventually overcome nationalism and arrive at a humanistic solution to social conflict.

If *Rozvoj*'s political message offered a clear challenge to prevailing attitudes and policies within the Czech-Jewish movement, the religious views of Vohryzek's wing ultimately did not. The reformulation of Judaism along the lines of Masarykian—and neo-Kantian—moral philosophy consisted for the most part of a formal intellectual exercise and remained the property of a narrow cultural elite. In the 1880s Or-Tomid had circumvented the established religious institutions of Prague in order to realize structural changes in Jewish worship. A generation later, Czech-Jewish religious thought again operated in a sphere of its own, but now in the absence of any institutional supports. Just as Vohryzek had been content to issue a "decontextualized" critique of Czech Judaism, which ignored social realities, he now demonstrated equal indifference to the prospect of actually implementing his cultural program in a concrete fashion; somehow the combination of independent, creative thinking and journalistic exhortation would simply work their magic on the Czech and Jewish populations.

From the point of view of the day-to-day practice of Judaism, then, the Czech-Jewish reform "in the image of Hus" was rather sterile. It produced numerous echoes on the printed page—Otakár Kraus's rehabilitation of the Berlin Reform movement and Bohdan Klineberger's massive opus on religious sensibility, for example—but had little direct impact on organized religious life.[66] Its ultimate significance lay in the larger arena of Czech politics and political culture. Here the *Rozvoj* circle successfully accomplished both a practical and a philosophical realignment, which enabled the Czech-Jewish movement to participate with confidence in progressive Czech nationalism. Admittedly, religious thought represented but one element in the transformation of Jewish society in the Czech lands in the late nineteenth century, a process that involved important demographic, linguistic, educational, and occupational changes as well. It was, however, this post-positivist obsession with the religious dimension in culture that signaled most profoundly the Czech-Jewish dilemma at the turn of the century. It articulated the frustrations of Jewish assimilation in a postemancipatory, ethnically contentious environment. In continuity with the Jewish messianic tradition, it also held out hope for a peaceful resolution to national strife. It offered the vision of a multifaceted society taming its nationalist demons, acting in concert for the good of the whole.

CHAPTER 8

Death and the Nation

Ritual Murder as Political Discourse
in the Czech Lands

Introduction

The title of this chapter begs for some explanation. Let me begin by proposing that the term *discourse* describes a cognitive system, a set of logical propositions, metaphors, and symbols whose overall effect is to impose order and meaning on experience, to provide a "mapping" of reality according to which the objects of experience are applied to a discrete, limited, and knowable set of (culturally specific) meanings. Preexisting knowledge of the world is, in many respects, inseparable from perceptions of that world; it informs, directs, and molds perception and may also undergo modification as a result of—or in the course of—experience.

When I speak of "ritual murder" as political discourse, I mean to suggest that this particular type of constructed knowledge about Jews, which had a vociferous career in Central Europe from 1882 to 1914, assumed an important role in the elaboration of politics and political relationships in the Czech lands, in the determination of group boundaries, and in the definition of allegiances. The general theme of "Jewish ritual murder" in the decade 1892 to 1902 (marked at one end by the ritual murder trial in Xanten, in the Prussian Rhineland, and at the other by the Hilsner trial) functioned on one level to locate, define, and express the larger theme of "Jewish danger" that can also be traced around the same time in other parts of Central Europe and in the Russian empire. In so doing, it offered commentary on such contemporary themes as Jews and criminal behavior, Jews and sexual danger in the modern world, the vulnerability of traditional social structures and values in an industrial age, Judaism and human cruelty, and the challenges to Christian hegemony in the modern world.[1]

On the one hand, much of the debate surrounding "Jewish ritual murder" in late-nineteenth-century Central Europe led logically to the conclusion that the political emancipation of the Jews—which was largely complete by 1871—had been a mistake and that its resulting social and cultural effects had to be opposed. In so doing, this "conversation" about Jews made a psychologically compelling case against the Enlightenment values of tolerance and social integration and in favor of some kind of resegregation of society; it condemned the rapid social and cultural transformations associated with industrialization and urbanization; and it sought to rehabilitate both Christianity and the Church by recasting these as victims of violence and disorder, as martyrs to the overturning of the traditional values of love and family. On the other hand, in Bohemia and Moravia, however, discourse on Jewish ritual murder also functioned as an indirect commentary on the national conflict between Czechs and Germans. The largely indeterminate position of Jews in the nationality controversy, the fact that they were neither obviously German nor obviously Czech, helped to produce the commonly held suspicion that Jews were unreliable partners in the struggle. This judgment soon merged with "new information" concerning the Jews and ritual killings—the result of a conflation of discrete blocks of social knowledge—to produce a mixture in which one set of symbolic associations tended to confirm the "truth" of the other.

It is worth asking in this connection whether the combination in the Czech lands of these two types of socially generated and communicated knowledge about Jews made any substantive difference. Did it make the ritual murder accusation itself more compelling? What effect did it have on the "national" position of Jews in the Czech lands? Did it contribute generally to the radicalization of the Czech-German national competition? Or did it amount to little more than a curiosity?

It seems clear that a preexisting set of propositions on Jews as Germanizing elements in the Czech countryside led some activists in Czech society (from the National Liberals to the more radical national socialists) to take a particular interest in the growing, European-wide discussions on Jewish ritual murder. They then allowed this new information to modify their own understanding of "national community"—and of the many dangers that it faced—creating long-term logical conflations of the two types of knowledge. This meant, on the one hand, that neither the supposed ritual murder of a servant girl in Kolín in 1893 nor the Hilsner case six years later (the Habsburg monarchy's most famous ritual murder trial) could fully be understood in the absence of nationalist symbols and metaphors, and on the other hand, that each set of knowledge contributed to the establishment of a structure of plausibility (one might say irresistibility) for the other. My understanding of the intersection of ritual murder discourse and political culture in the Czech lands is not intended to imply that the *locality*—the dynamic situation in small towns and villages—is not in many respects crucial in the elaboration of "knowledge" of Jewish ritual murder. Indeed, an anthropology of place remains the indispensable starting point for all studies of this phenomenon.[2] Still, one can consider the career of the modern ritual murder accusation from a number of contexts. What this chapter seeks to explore are the questions: What happens to this social knowledge when it is dislodged from its local moorings? And, on what structures of plausibility does it rely for its success as a cognitive system?

A Rhetoric of Politics and of Blood:
Ritual Murder Discourse in the 1880s and 1890s

In the aftermath of the Tiszaeszlár ritual murder investigation in Hungary in 1882 and the convening of the first Antisemitic Congress in Dresden in September of the same year, Habsburg district captains (*Bezirkshauptmänner* or *okresní hejtmanové*) began to report to the Bohemian governor's office in Prague on anti-Jewish activities that were taking place within their own jurisdictions.[3] The district official in Karlovy Vary, for example, reported to the governor's office in 1883 with some alarm about the distribution of some thirty to forty copies of the printed manifesto of the Dresden Congress.[4] Numerous reports in 1883 tracked the distribution in Bohemia of August Rohling's *Meine Antwort an die Rabbiner, order Fünf Briefe über den Talmudismus und Blut-Ritual der Juden,* including a Czech translation of the work.[5] A letter of 7 May 1883 by the leadership of the Jewish community complained about the effect that Rohling's pamphlet was having on Czech-Jewish relations; it cited a placard from Mladá Vožice that read: "the Jews need blood for their *challah* bread" (*židi potřebujou krev do barchesů*).[6] The following month, several agencies, including the Prague *Polizeidirektion* and the State's Attorney (*Vrchní zastupitelství*) in Prague, argued in reports to the governor's office that the Rohling brochure constituted a breach of the public order. Eventually the governor revoked the license to print it.[7]

It was not until the 1890s, however, that discussions of Jewish ritual murder became commonplace in the Czech lands. A number of factors seem to have contributed to the widespread dissemination of this new knowledge. Although the decade opened with the victory of the National Liberal—or Young Czech—Party in the parliamentary elections of 1891, leading the way to a decade and a half of Young Czech dominance in the Diet and among Czech representatives to the Reichsrat in Vienna, this shift in political power did nothing to calm political passions or moderate ideological positions. In many respects it led to a radicalization of the Czech-German national debate. At the same time, the party found it very difficult to achieve and maintain any kind of ideological consensus, and it suffered numerous factional splinterings.[8] The 1890s also witnessed the emergence of Czech economic nationalism in the form of anti-German and anti-Jewish boycotts (the movement commonly known as *Svůj k svému,* "each to his own"); the extension of previous political efforts to achieve linguistic parity for Czech in the territory of the Kingdom of Bohemia; and the final push in an intense pressure campaign, directed at Czech Jews, to shut down the German-Jewish *Normalschulen* in the Bohemian countryside. These were in many respects years of crisis, a time when the political integration of Czech Jewry seemed in doubt.[9]

During this time a good deal of "news" of Jewish ritual murder began to filter in from outside the country. In the spring and summer of 1891 word of an alleged ritual murder on the Greek island of Corfu was widely reported. Although the rumors quickly were proved false—the victim in question had in fact been Jewish—this did not prevent extensive rioting from taking place on the island.[10] The fact that radical Czech newspapers had sought to capitalize on the events in Corfu is apparent in the criminal case brought in Prague against one such paper, *Naše zájmy,* and its editor, Jaromír Hušek. Hušek was charged with "incitement against a religious community" (*popuzování proti náboženské společnosti*) for his front-page story in the 23 May 1891 edition of the paper, which was printed under the banner headline "Murder of a Christian Girl in Corfu." The story, laced with such epithets as "Jew synagogue" (*židácká synagoga*) and "kike" (*židák*), purported to be the testimony of a Czech sailor from Dalmatia. It testified, in the editor's introductory words, to "the danger of talmudic teaching and of the entire Jewish nation."[11]

The sensational arrest and trial of Jews on the same charge in the Rhineland town of Xanten in 1891–92 followed closely on the heels of the events in Corfu and quickly surpassed both Corfu and Tiszaeszlár in the popular imagination. The Xanten affair became the focal point for the emergence of a small industry of antisemitic, propagandistic literature and may also have been the chief inspiration behind the rapid rise in the number of local ritual murder accusations that appeared in the Czech press starting in 1892. When the Prague Criminal Court ordered the confiscation of the 15 June 1892 issue of *České zájmy*, it cited two inflammatory articles. In its "Miscellany" column the paper had reported that "wherever Jews are in the majority"—such as in one small town in Bukovina—"they murder Slavic people without mercy." Another article judged to be deliberately provocative concerned "the usurer Popper." Pieces on such topics as "The Jews according to the Talmud," "On the Murder in Xanten," and "Jewish Impudence in the Czech Jerusalem—Rakovník," escaped specific censure.[12]

The Viennese priest Josef Deckert may have done more than any other person in his time to promote "knowledge" of Jewish ritual murder as a centerpiece of contemporary political rhetoric. His 1893 tract, *Ein Ritualmord: Aktenmäßig nachgewiesen*, which had been inspired by the events in Xanten, was widely distributed throughout Bohemia before it was finally confiscated by the state. Playing on his dual authority as priest and Catholic historian, Deckert countered "enlightened" dismissals of Jewish ritual murder with an appeal to what he claimed to be irrefutable legal and historical evidence of such crimes.[13] The brochure thus comprised a self-consciously modern defense of the ritual murder accusation. Deckert met the charge of the "irrationality" of the ritual murder accusation by arguing for the historicity of memorialized events. He upheld the believability of the accusation—in its traditional forms—by appealing to history as a scientific discipline.

In Deckert's view, it was the case of Simon of Trent—murdered in 1475 and subsequently beatified and for whose death six Jews were burned at the stake and two strangled (after converting to Christianity)—that provided the most direct, "irrefutable" historical and legal evidence of the Jewish propensity toward this type of criminal behavior.[14] Alternatively paraphrasing and quoting from the interrogation record of the Trent investigation and trial, Deckert characterizes the denials of various Jewish defendants as "stubborn lies," but accepts at face value the confessions extracted by means of torture. He thus puts forward as a plausible motive for the crime the explanation offered by one defendant: that the dried blood of the Christian child was applied as a powder to heal the circumcision wounds of Jewish boys.[15] When Deckert deviates from his "historicist" mission to quote at length from the recollections of the court physician Johannes Tiberinus, he reveals what he understands to be the theological and political truth lying at the heart of the enterprise.

See here, my fellow Christian, how once again Jesus is crucified between two thieves. See what the Jews would do if they had power over Christians. The glorious, innocent martyr, Simon, hardly weaned from the mother's breast and not yet able to speak, has been crucified by the Jews as an insult to our faith. Listen, you who allow so cruel a race [*eine so grausame Menschenrasse*] to be tolerated in your cities, how daily they curse the holy Eucharist and the saintly Virgin Mary, uttering scandalous, sinful words, which they follow with expressions of open contempt for the Roman Church.[16]

In the murder of Simon, then, the Jews of Trent not only reenacted the crucifixion of Christ and added to their scandalous treatment of the Eucharist and the Virgin Mary, but were also issuing a warning as to what Christians might expect if the Jews were ever allowed to exercise power in their midst.

In his own brief conclusion to the tract, Deckert returns to his stance as naive observer of "empirical reality." Was this murder in fact a "ritual murder," he asks? The question, of course, is rhetorical. When one acknowledges the timing of the act (on the eve of the holiday of Passover), its location (the synagogue), the circumstances under which it was carried out, and the purposes to which the blood of the child was put, what other conclusion can one draw? "One has to admit that this was, indeed, a ritual murder; otherwise, I would not know what meaning to attach to the term."[17] Deckert seems willing to concede that no explicit written law of the Talmud commands Jews to commit ritual murder. "Rather, it is a question ... of a secret teaching transmitted orally by the 'sages' of the Jewish people, the traces of which are frequently revealed in the trial records."[18] Deckert goes so far as to admit that most Jews—Orthodox as well as Reform, Hasidic Jews as well as Karaites—may know nothing of this esoteric teaching. But those who are guilty of this crime must be called to account.

Deckert does not close his survey of Jewish ritual murder before directing a biting criticism at contemporary Jewry. Why is it, he asks, that whenever a Christian child is murdered "in the form of a ritual slaughtering" (*in Form des Schächtens*) and a Jew is accused of the crime,

"Jewry" summons all of its influence to hinder the investigation and trial, to hush up the whole affair, or to rescue the proven criminal from the punishing arm of the law? What do the Jews have to hide? Through such behavior they are only inviting the suspicion that they feel collectively guilty or "that they know more about the secret teachings of the Talmud than they dare to admit."[19] Repeating his conviction that the murders of Christian children *by Jews* do not derive from acts of anger, lust, or robbery but concern specifically the blood of children, he tosses in one last rhetorical question: to what end?

His protestations to the contrary notwithstanding, Deckert's pamphlet worked precisely to spread guilt by association, and Habsburg officials in Bohemia and Moravia were justly concerned about its impact on public order.[20] Tensions were already high in the summer of 1892 in places like the Moravian town of Kojetín, where the disappearance of a Christian servant employed by a Jewish family gave rise to a rumor that she had been murdered for religious purposes. The town's Jews were physically mistreated as a result, and windows in many Jewish homes were smashed; but apparently, when the girl's body turned up in the river without any marks of violence on it, relations returned to normal.[21]

A more serious case of rumored kidnapping and ritual murder surfaced in Kolín in Bohemia in March and April of 1893. This, too, involved the disappearance of a young Czech female servant who had worked for a Jewish employer. Although the young woman had disappeared in March, it was not until 11 April 1893, the day on which the body of a young woman was pulled out of the Elbe river, that the district captain (*okresní hejtman*) reported the incident to the governor's office in Prague.[22] According to the local official, the victim—who was identified only by the last name Havlínová—had "disappeared without a trace" while in the service of a Jew named Reitler. Although the girl's aunt (named Machovská) had testified to the fact that Havlínová had been contemplating suicide, the district captain had asked the State's Attorney in Kutná Hora to initiate a criminal investigation because the word on the street—spread largely by the newspaper *Polaban*—was that this was a case of Jewish ritual murder. The judicial investigation, however, could make little headway in the absence of physical evidence of an abduction, suicide, or murder. When the body of a young woman was pulled from the river, it was identified as that of the missing girl by her aunt. News of the discovery resulted in renewed popular excitement: again there was talk of Jewish ritual murder; again the newspaper *Pola-*

ban—at the time the mouthpiece of the Progressive party in Kolín—took a leading role in spreading this view.[23] The district captain wished to report, however, that a medical examination of the body had demonstrated the rumors to be groundless: the girl had ended her own life.[24]

On 12 April, the following day, the Habsburg official in Kolín sent another dispatch to Prague. We now learn that the servant girl had been missing for six weeks before the body was recovered and that the optimism of the previous day had been unwarranted. Popular demonstrations had taken place on the night on April 11 in response to rumors that the medical team that examined the corpse had found stab wounds on the body! Mobs gathered in the city's Jewish quarter, where they were joined by unemployed textile workers. Fearing that rioting could take place in the vicinity of the Ringplatz, the local police called in reinforcements from the Gendarmerie. Eventually the crowds were dispersed. The district captain expressed concern that similar disturbances might take place during the girl's funeral and in the nights ahead. A telegram of 13 April indicated that rioting had in fact taken place.[25]

As I shall demonstrate below, the alleged kidnapping and ritual murder in Kolín played a key role in the ties evolving among local political strategies, nationalist rhetoric, and the symbolic language of anti-semitism. At this point I would simply underline the fact that in the Kolín case, as in Corfu but unlike Kojetín, conspiratorial interpretations of the events in question appeared to enjoy greater plausibility in local knowledge than what may be called the ostensible or empirical record. In Corfu, the "empirical" contradiction of the accusation of ritual murder consisted of the fact that the victim in question had herself been Jewish (though she had died a violent death). The local resolution to this dilemma rested on the conviction that the girl had, as it were, only been masquerading as a Jew. In fact, she had earlier been kidnapped from her Christian family of origin and was subsequently raised in a Jewish family in preparation for her eventual sacrifice.[26] Local wisdom in the Kolín case directed skepticism at the coroner's examination of Havlínová's corpse and disbelief at his conclusion that the only violence she had suffered had been at her own hand. Such sentiments were clearly echoed in the newspaper *Naše zájmy*. In an issue that was confiscated by the Prague Criminal Court the paper ridiculed the notion that the girl had simply "disappeared" or that she might have had reason to commit suicide. Responding indirectly to the sexual connotations of suicide among young unmarried women, *Naše zájmy* countered that Havlínová had been "in all respects a happy and respectable girl."

And in an aside revealing the self-confirming role of collective memory in such episodes, it continued, "because the local population remembers other such mysterious cases, it considers this, too, to be a case of ritual murder."[27]

Nation, Economic Struggle, and Jewish Ritual Murder

The appearance in 1892 in provincial cities across central Bohemia of placards bearing the slogan "*Nekupůjte od židů*" (Do not buy from Jews) can be said to have marked the beginning of the campaign known as *Svůj k svému*.[28] Proponents of economic nationalism in the Czech political camp—many of whom came from the ranks of the Young Czech Party—argued that as long as German speakers occupied a dominant economic position in the country, the political balance of power would not shift. Hence, in order for Czechs to realize the vision of political and cultural autonomy cherished by their national spokespersons, they would have to seize economic power as well. In theory all "Germans" were targeted for commercial boycott; Jews, however, whose national allegiance could not be measured with certainty, seemed to attract particularly harsh criticism. In fact they performed a dual role, paralleling the split function of the boycott movement itself. Ostensibly viewed as undifferentiated supporters of German hegemony, Jews constituted a compact, accessible, and politically vulnerable economic target—a facsimile of the Austrian Germans. But the boycott also worked as a cultural ban, ostracizing from the nation elements that were considered to be ethnically indistinct or uncertain. The act of ostracism should be seen, then, as an effort to define, to clarify the boundaries of community, to remove doubt.[29]

A three-part series on "*Svůj k svému*" in the newspaper *Polaban* in 1893 attempted to make a coherent case for Czech economic nationalism and to rally popular support around the campaign. So provocative, apparently, was its message that the paper's editor at the time, Josef Hejnic, was charged by the Kutná Hora court with anti-Jewish agitation. At times the entire platform seemed to boil down to the injunction to not give money to one's enemies, "who would then use it as a massive weapon against our nation."

Should we not guard against sending money away for the most expensive things, if not out of the country, then in any event out of the Czech countryside, [against allowing] capital to accumulate in the hands of foreigners and enemies, mainly Jews?[30]

The Jews, *Polaban* emphasized, are not merely problematic; they are "our greatest enemy" (*největších našich odpurců*).[31] As has been noted, in the language of Czech economic nationalism both Jews and Germans occupied the categories of *cizinec* (foreigner) and *nepřátel* (enemy)— terms that were used somewhat indiscriminately and to which the implied category of self (*vlastní já*) or native (*rodák*) stood in opposition. The condemnation of Bohemian and Moravian Jews was in some respects more severe than that directed at "Germans" (i.e., German Gentiles), because for Jews living in "Czech" towns and villages to identify with German elites required an "unnatural" or perverse willfulness. The rhetorical structure of the campaign was significant, I believe, because it provided a set of categories into which ritual murder discourse could eventually move without much difficulty. The perpetrator of ritualized violence against adolescent Czech women was both *cizinec* and *nepřátel*, even if his family had been native to Bohemia-Moravia for centuries and even if his principal language was Czech. The victims, whether individuals or the nation as a whole, were personified as women, their dual status as "self" and as daughter confirmed by their victimization. Finally, the exhortation not to "let money flow" out of the country alluded to the powerful image of life-blood.[32]

The themes of economic nationalism, linguistic competition, and antisemitism combined frequently in the writings of provincial newspapers; often such writing landed their editors in court, and occasionally, in jail. The editors of two papers that were allied for a time with the Young Czech Party, *Polaban* and *Kolínské listy,* both published in Kolín, made frequent appearances before a judge and prosecutor at the Kutná Hora regional court. *Polaban*'s editor, Václav Nevídek, was forced to appear on at least six occasions in 1885 alone because of articles that agitated against Jews, Germans, the army, and the state.[33] *Kolínské listy*'s editor, Václav Řezníček, was brought to trial in July 1886 on the charge of making antisemitic statements (*protižidovské výroky*). At issue was an article entitled "The Jews and Our National Struggle," whose characterization of the Jews of Bohemia as "the most fanatic opponents of the Czech nation" constituted, in the opinion of the court, "a general inclination to violate public peace and order." Appealing the court's verdict, Řezníček argued that his article had in no way advocated hatred against the Jews as a religious community (*náboženské společnosti*), but had merely offered statistical data on the Jews of the Czech lands according to the most recent Habsburg census. The court rejected his appeal, noting that the offending article contained not only statistical material but the specific observation that the Jews "with very few exceptions stand among the ranks of our enemies, in fact, belong to the most fanatical of the enemies of our nation."[34]

Such cases were followed by a whole series of prosecutions against *Kolínské listy* and *Polaban* that lasted well into the next decade. By 1891 and 1892, editors for the two papers were making court appearances seemingly every other month, occasionally for circulating articles that had already been confiscated. The titles of the contested stories give some indication both of the symbolic structure of antisemitic discourse at the time and of its intersection with extremist constructions of Czech national identity: "The Jews and Cannibalism" (1886); "The Germanizing of Kolín Jews" (1891); "The Jewish Benefactor of the Peasant" (1892); "On the Blue Star" (1892); "Why Do They Have It In for Us?" (1892); and "Do We Need to Protect Ourselves against the Jewish Seder?" (1892).[35]

Thus, in the decade preceding the Hilsner affair, a significant corner of Czech national opinion and action—representing the intersection of "progressivist" dissent within the Young Czech Party, the ideology of economic nationalism, and provincial small-town interests—had elaborated a set of axiomatic propositions about Jews in the Czech lands. The coherence of these claims rested on an assumed relationship between twin Jewish conspiracies: the politics of national obstructionism coincided with and could be explicated by an inherent, ritually inspired criminality. It is instructive to note in this context a report of the district captain of Mladá Boleslav in December 1892, in which he attributed a palpable anti-Jewish mood in the town to the political choices of the local Jewish population. The district official tied recent anti-Jewish disturbances to a newspaper campaign in the Young Czech press instigated by radical elements within the party who had been incensed that Jews in Mladá Boleslav had voted for the more conservative Old Czech candidates in recent municipal elections.[36]

The report from Mladá Boleslav also takes note of a rumor of Jewish ritual murder that was circulating in the neighboring town of Nové Benátky over the disappearance of another local servant girl, Josefa Urbanová. Attached to the file in the Central State Archive in Prague is a copy, written in another hand, of the words to a Czech song that was apparently making the rounds, the first five lines of which are translated here. "Kindly take note," the informant wrote at the top of the page:

Song about the Jews

[1)] When a girl is sixteen every Jew will grab for her, but once she is old no Jew will have her[.]

2) They must have Christian blood, and if they do not get it, they'll stink a lot.

3) Josefa Urbanová was a proper girl, she never did anything bad,

4) Then all of a sudden the Jews ran up to her and tied her up; on the spot the butcher rose up and kosher-slaughtered Josefa.

5) And if they get enough blood, the Jews bring out a skin [?]; they quickly pour it in and at night take it away.[37]

Here the themes of sexual predacity and ritual murder are starkly juxtaposed, with the kosher butcher acting simultaneously as rapist and ritual leader. The song continues for several more stanzas, in the course of which a new character is introduced: another "upstanding" lad unwittingly becomes party to the Jews' evildoings. While tavern songs and popular ditties voiced traditional premodern attitudes toward Jews, tending more toward the scatological than the political, it is nevertheless true that they flourished now in a highly politicized climate. In an atmosphere of rhetorical hyperbole, vocabulary and imagery from separate discourses could easily intersect or serve as mutual points of reference. The medical officer who examined the body of the servant girl from Kolín might serve as a case in point: according to an article that appeared in the newspaper *Naše doba,* he is reported to have claimed that the root of all the troubles concerned the existence of a German primary school maintained by the local Jewish community.[38] When the Czech weekly *Krakonoš* commented on the rioting in Kolín in 1893, it suggested that the Jews had brought the rioting on themselves through their economic behavior and as a result of their support for German national interests:

It is difficult to determine whether or not the rumor that has spread among the people has a basis in fact, or whether it can be explained as provocation. It is not an easy thing to determine the cause of death of the victim, whose body lay in the water for many weeks. Whatever the case may be, the simple fact that as a result of the rumor—perhaps unfounded—agitation started amongst the people against the Jews and quickly grew wider is proof that there simmers among our people anger and hatred against the

Jews. [The] bubbling over [of this hatred] simply took the form of a rumor that the girl in question had been murdered by Jews.

Our people has plenty of cause to be dissatisfied with the behavior of the Jews from a political, national, and economic point of view, and this is where one must look for the main causes and explanations of the recent anti-Jewish unrest in the Czech lands. The vast majority of Jews stand in the way of our political and national endeavors, and where they do nonetheless identify with us, one cannot depend on them. Deep down [in their bowels] they are all either blatantly or secretly supporters of the German liberal party; indeed, among German journalists—our enemies—there are none fiercer than the Jews.[39]

Papers like *Naše zájmy* were determined to connect economic nationalism and perceptions of Jewish ritual murder to a discourse on women. On 23 April 1893, in an issue that was confiscated by the court, Jaromír Hušek wrote that the events in Kolín should have made clear to all patriotic, antisemitic Czechs that it was necessary to stop buying from Jews and that prudent families should no longer allow their daughters to work for Jewish families. This was the simplest way to prevent what had occurred in Kolín from happening again.

Our nation should not allow its daughters to serve among Jews. In this way the whole incident that took place with Havlínová could not happen; neither rumors nor riots against the Jews would occur, because it would not be possible for suspicious news about the death of a servant girl to develop [in the first place]. And if it were spread, no one would believe it.[40]

Economic and sexual exploitation went hand in hand with national and religious enmity, and all four themes combined to deepen the suspicion of Jewish implication in a new wave of criminality. Moreover, editors like Hušek sought to mold and define the nation partly by controlling the behavior of Czech women. Hušek also pursued a dual strategy in his reportage of ritual murder. One track dictated that he profess a skeptical neutrality bordering on condescension; the other, that he emphasize the social meaning of the accusation. Legendary accounts of Jewish ritual murder may indeed be "fabulous," he admitted, but it is not the content of popular belief that is at issue. The problem is economic power, or political unreliability, or linguistic treason, or the exploitation of adolescent women. Remove the underlying causes of social tension, and the epiphenomenon—belief in Jewish ritual murder—will whither away of its own triviality.

Echoes of liberal condescension combined with nationalist critique can also be found in the local histories of Polná (the hometown of

Leopold Hilsner and site of Bohemia's most famous ritual murder case) written by the educator and museum director, Břetislav Reyrich. In an unpublished history entitled "The Jews and Polná," Reyrich consistently criticizes the local Jewish population for maintaining German loyalties despite the clear identification of the majority of the population for Czech culture.[41] Commenting on the conversion in 1874 of the two-grade German-Jewish school into a public establishment, he writes: "In the midst of Czech political development, this school stood as the symbol of civic discord in Polná for a quarter of a century. Because of declining numbers of Jewish children, Czech children were also accepted there, and thus the school was given the name *přebejvárna* [surplus storage]."[42]

In a tourist guide to Polná published in 1927 Reyrich comments that the German-Jewish school had been better endowed in the 1870s than the town's two five-grade Czech schools. When the Young Czechs took over the government in 1894, with the election of Rudolf Sadil as mayor, they improved Polná in a number of ways. Among Sadil's accomplishments were "paved streets, unified numbering, the new banks of the fish pond, the establishment in the upper town of a shoe factory, and the tearing down of the former German school."[43] It should be mentioned in this regard that despite Young Czech rhetoric to the contrary, the majority of Polná's Jewish population had declared its primary language to be Czech as early as the census of 1890.[44]

Despite his national grievances against the Jews, Reyrich expresses genuine regret in his local history of Polná over the ruining of Jewish-Gentile relations that ensued in the wake of the Hilsner trials of 1899 and 1900—relations, he asserts, that in the past had been "tolerable" (*snešitelné*) if not exactly friendly. He offers several explanations for this breakdown. The fact that the two female victims of the murders attributed to Hilsner had been residents of a neighboring village (rather than of Polná itself) encouraged what he calls "peasant antisemitism." Urban, or bourgeois, antisemitism, on the other hand, was supported by "the German orientation of some Jews, the bloody incidents [i.e., riots] in Jihlava, the struggle against the former German school in Polná, and even by the provocations of several imprudent Jewish students affiliated with fraternities."[45] Reyrich also places a large portion of the responsibility for Jewish-Gentile tensions during the Hilsner investigations and trials on the Jews themselves. Jews, he argues, responded to the attacks of the antisemites "so inelegantly" (*tak nevybraně*) that they helped to produce a period of genuine intercommunal tension, "a time of mutual irritation, complaint, and court convictions against both sides for libel and violence." As an example of the "undignified" responses taken by some Jews, Reyrich refers to renewed popular demonstrations that took place on 9 and 10 June 1899, during which three hundred people rioted, marched on the Jewish quarter, and broke eighty-one window-panes. Apparently some Jews had the temerity to pour refuse on the rioters from behind the broken panes of glass.[46]

In the end, Reyrich seems to accept the proposition that Jews as a group do not commit murders for purposes of blood ritual. At the same time, his attitude throughout the historical narrative is decidedly anti-Hilsner. He is convinced of Hilsner's unsavory character and of his guilt in the murders of the young women, Anežka Hrůzová and Marie Klí-mová. He has a habit of identifying individuals with ethnic tags: for example, the two people named by Hilsner between his two trials as coper-petrators (later denied by him)—Erbman and Wasserman—are "Jewish beggars" (*židovští žebráci*). And he is critical of Jews as a group for devoting so much time, *money,* and energy defending a scoundrel like Hilsner, who deserved much less sympathy than his unfortunate victims.[47]

It is also remarkable how the rational, if uncompromising, voice of economic nationalism and linguistic struggle can slip into an irrational register for rhetorical effect. Thus the same issue of *Naše zájmy* that establishes the psychological connection between the observation of national enmity, on the one hand, and perceptions of ritual criminality, on the other, goes on to argue that the very fact that "the people" believe in the truth of Jewish ritual murder is reason enough to take the accusation seriously:

This is really a very significant marker [*příznak*] of the whole affair: that the people believe all of the news of Jewish ritual murder. And not just the Czech people, but every Aryan nation, proof of which [can be found in] the riots that followed the murder of Eszter Solymosi—where the Hungarian people believed it; the storm that accompanied the murder in Xanten—when the German people believed it and rioted; and after the murder of the Christian servant girl in Munich who had been abused by the Jew Moyžíš Richter, who was convicted unanimously three times by Galician juries of the crime of murder and sentenced by the court three times to death by hanging. Another major storm broke out following the death of a Christian girl on the island of Corfu, where the Greeks believed in it and rioted; and riots—not only by Aryans, but also on the part of Moslem Arab-Semites—following an attempted Jewish murder in Port Said.[48]

Radikální listy, the paper of the left-of-center Czech Progressives, re-ported on Polná in a similar vein.

And now this conclusion: what was the motive of the murder? The ritual murder legend has a powerful and persistent hold on all of public opinion. You fight believing it, you cannot admit that, at the end of the nineteenth century, a race exists whose religion demands, or allows, murder for reli-gious ends.
    You fight believing it, but the strength and persuasive force of circum-stances is overwhelming. Never up till now has all the evidence testified [so clearly] for ritual murder.
    If ritual murder exists, then Polná is a case in point.[49]

Conclusion

The editors of *Radikální listy* and *Naše zájmy* accomplished for national-ist reportage what Josef Deckert had achieved for historical argument: a logical operation that equated public testimony with historicity. Each of these sources vested historical authority in public opinion and collective memory. Social knowledge of Jewish ritual murder, whether ancient or formed in the recent past, became part of the historical record. It was a curious romanticism masked as naturalism that functioned as a rhetori-cal bridge between the mythic and the pragmatic. Its ultimate accom-plishment was to facilitate the merger of disparate political discourses — to remove on at least a superficial level the contradiction between the modernist appeal to reason and "progress," and the atavistic resort to the conspiracy myth of the dangerous and ultimately unknowable other.
    At the level of provincial politics, where shopkeepers, small-time en-trepreneurs, and middle-class professionals strove to achieve relative ad-vantage for the Czech nation-in-the-making, credit for the assiduous juxtaposition of these two types of social knowledge about Jews goes to the radicalized wing of the Young Czech establishment. Provincial crit-ics of centrist complacency, student radicals affiliated with the "Progres-sive" movement, national socialists, and radical state-right activists un-derstood the symbolic codes of ritual murder, sexual licentiousness, and national treachery to be mutually dependent and interchangeable. I have attempted to demonstrate that although their constructions pro-ceeded from a liberal epistemology of reason and empiricism, they found the romantic impulses of struggle against the natural order and

attachment to the vital truths of the "people" equally compelling—
hence the rhetorical swings between skeptical detachment and the un-
critical acceptance of popular sentiment and collective memories. It was
not psychological predisposition alone, however, that allowed these
groups to embrace contradictory systems of knowledge. A kind of romantic historiography that equated popular testimony with historicity
allowed for the reformulation of myth as empirical knowledge; it
offered a naturalistic portrait of human beliefs that rendered the distinction between "rational" and "irrational" irrelevant. Ultimately, it could
be argued, both types of knowledge derived from the same reasonable
premises.

Ritual murder discourse added important psychological dimensions
to the rhetoric of economic nationalism. Jews were not only stranglers
of the nation but also sexual predators and murderers in a literal sense;
they bled the bodies of their female victims just as they bled the nation
dry; they were enemies not only of the cause, but of the very communities in which they lived. The equation worked in the other direction as
well: the roles assigned to the Jews in the radical discourse of Czech-
German national struggle both accommodated and confirmed those
that were imagined for the Jews in contemporary ritual murder discourse. Political "realities," then—together with history, collective
memory, popular wisdom, and scientific analysis—provided a context
that translated the ritual murder accusation from the realm of fantasy to
that of the mundane. In so doing, they rendered the accusation eminently plausible, as a hidden manifestation of general, national enmity.

Whether or not this combination of symbolic systems made the ritual murder accusation *more* compelling in the Czech lands than in other
parts of Central Europe cannot fully be answered. Caution and skepticism may well be the only acceptable responses to such a question. I
would point out, however, that in both the Tiszaeszlár and the Xanten
trials, the Jewish defendants were ultimately acquitted. Hilsner was
found guilty and sentenced to death—not once, but twice.

CHAPTER 9

Masaryk and Czech Jewry

The Ambiguities of Friendship

Introduction

The relationship between the Jews of the Czech lands and Tomáš G. Masaryk (1850–1937), the national educator and politician who was to become the first president of Czechoslovakia in 1918, revolved around a pair of paradoxes. On the one hand, Masaryk enjoyed a reputation among both Jews and non-Jews as a staunch opponent of antisemitism, a relentless critic of the "blood libel," and a defender of Jewish political rights.[1] Yet, as this chapter will attempt to demonstrate, the record of Masaryk's dealings with Jewish leaders, as well as his writings on Jews, leaves little doubt that his attitudes were in fact highly ambiguous and, at times, overtly negative. The other paradox concerns the nature of the political alliance that was forged between Masaryk's Realist party and the Czech-Jewish movement—the wing of the Jewish community that had committed itself both to the promotion of the Czech national cause and to the assimilation of Jews to Czech culture. Following the radicalization of Czech politics at the end of the 1890s, it was largely Masaryk and the Realist party who commanded the loyalties of Czech-nationalist Jews. Yet Masaryk and other leading intellectuals could not shed their fundamental ideological discomfort with the idea of Jewish assimilation and, hence, with the prospect of Jewish participation in the Czech national movement.

Masaryk, in fact, felt himself to be much closer in temperament to the European Zionists than to the leadership of the Czech-Jewish movement. His frequent endorsements of Jewish national positions and the tactical support that he and Eduard Beneš lent to the Czech Zionists after World War I produced genuine consternation in the Czech-Jewish camp. When the Czechoslovak state formally recognized Jewish national autonomy in the constitutional documents of 1920, it dealt what was at least a psychological defeat to some of its most fervent Jewish supporters. After decades of painstaking work promoting Czech national culture and Czech political loyalties among the Jews, the Czech-Jewish movement had to face the predicament of an independent Czechoslovakia that supported the principle of Jewish cultural autonomy.

This chapter will explore the ambivalent relationship between Masaryk's Realists and the Czech-Jewish movement and attempt to explain the uneasiness felt by Czech nationalists toward the Czech-Jewish partnership. In so doing, I shall consider the intellectual and emotional factors that determined the attitude of Masaryk and others toward the Jews, the role of residual antisemitism in the relationship, and the significance—both social and political—of the Realists' flirtation with Zionism. Lastly, the question of whether the ambivalence toward Jewish assimilation had any real effect on Jewish integration into interwar Czech society will have to be examined, for there are good indications that the Zionists may have won the ideological and political battle only to lose the long-term war on the social arena.

The Czech-Jewish Affinity for Masaryk

During the last quarter of the nineteenth century the Jewish population of the Czech lands underwent a social, political, and cultural transformation of major proportions. In the process of this change, an organized movement emerged that promoted the political rapprochement of Czechs and Jews, a more thoroughgoing acculturation of Jews to Czech language and sensibilities, and Jewish support for Czech national aspirations. The lawyers, doctors, journalists, shopkeepers, and clerks who made up the ranks of this Czech-Jewish movement allied themselves on the whole with the National Liberal, or Young Czech, Party—the most powerful political force at the time on the regional scene. They supported Young Czech candidates in local, provincial, and imperial elections; promoted the party's cultural and educational programs for Prague and rural Bohemia; and tolerated what many acknowledged to be the rhetorically excessive tones of such newspapers as *Národní listy*.[2]

One could say that the leaders of the Young Czech Party and the Czech-Jewish movement had arrived at an implicit modus vivendi concerning their mutual behavior. Both sides, it was agreed, would place pressure on Bohemian Jewry to move into the Czech national camp and to cease supporting German national interests. Moreover, the National Liberals and their major institutions would remain faithful to the party's formal position of rejecting both antisemitism and clericalism, and would disassociate with the more radical manifestations of Czech nationalism. This unwritten agreement worked until the second half of the 1890s. But it collapsed under pressure from a number of directions: the radicalization of student politics in Prague, the government's disastrous handling of the Badeni language ordinances of 1897, the Hilsner ritual murder trial of 1899, and the irresistible appeal of popular antisemitism. It had already buckled during the outbursts of popular violence that erupted in Prague and elsewhere in 1897 and was probably dead before the Hilsner affair provided the coup de grace two years later.[3]

By the end of the next decade, Czech-nationalist Jews had searched for and found new political allies. They were the "Realists" of Masaryk's Czech People's Party and, to a lesser degree, the Radical Progressives of Antonin Hajn, and the Czech Social Democrats. Together they constituted what could be called the progressive wing of the Czech national movement. Czech Jews on the whole demonstrated the greatest enthusiasm for Masaryk and his small party, seeing in him a staunch opponent of antisemitism, a defender of Jewish aspirations for social and political acceptance, and a promoter of the democratic secular state.

Viktor Vohryzek (1864–1918), a Jewish physician and political figure in Pardubice, laid the foundation for an entirely new approach to Czech national politics in 1900 when he published in *Českožidovské listy* a series of articles entitled "Letters to Czech Jews."[4] Vohryzek's "Letters" set a new tone for Czech-Jewish writing, arguing that the causes of Jewish suffering and persecution in all countries lay not in some misdirected historical evolution, in poorly conceived governmental policies, or in the stubborn refusal of Jews to assimilate. The basic factors lay in human nature itself. Antisemitism was in the end a psychological and moral phenomenon arising from atavistic instincts, and as such was primarily a European—not a Jewish—problem.[5] On the local level it stemmed from a moral defect in the character of the Czech people, one that was being exploited by nationalist politicians for selfish and shortsighted purposes. In the last analysis, however, it was the Czech soul, not the Jewish one, that suffered.

Vohryzek's advice to Czech Jewry was twofold. In the long term, Jews were to wait out the decline of the National Liberal Party; until that happened, they were to prepare an "antidote" to the poison that had infected the Czech nation. "Our antidote," he wrote, "is the strengthening of all progressive influences ... the battle against hyper-nationalism and clericalism. The antidote is the struggle against the dark."[6] Vohryzek called upon Czech Jews to learn how to defend themselves—to strengthen their backs, as he put it—and not to "fall down in the dust before every journalistic bandit." They had to act with dignity and pride in order that basic human consideration dictate the conduct of others toward them.

At the same time, Vohryzek felt that it was just as incumbent upon Jews to examine their faults as to defend their rights. Jews continued to pursue dangerous and unsavory economic occupations such as money lending and the production and distribution of liquor. Jewish life required a thorough, ongoing reform—a renewal based on the spiritual purposefulness, the social ethics, and the progressive outlook of the Old Testament prophets. But the issue of internal reform and redirection, Vohryzek warned, was for Jews to face on their own. Society at large was in no position to pass judgment.[7]

As we saw in chapter 7, a formidable opposition to the mainstream of the Czech-Jewish movement developed around Vohryzek, Eduard Lederer (1859–1941) and Bohdan Klineberger (1859–1928) during the first decade of the twentieth century. Based in the beginning in Vohryzek's home town of Pardubice, the Czech-Jewish "progressives" published a newspaper, *Rozvoj,* and organized a broad range of cultural and educational programs, which sought to deepen the sense of Czech national identity among Jews, effect a social and economic reorientation and modernization of Czech-Jewish life, and promote a new religious sensibility—teaching Jews the difference (as *Rozvoj* put it) between religion and piety.[8]

By 1907 *Rozvoj* succeeded in replacing *Českožidovské listy* as the paper of choice among Czech-nationalist Jews. The latter ceased publication that year; *Rozvoj* changed from a fortnightly to a weekly, expanded its format, and moved its editorial offices to Prague. From there it continued to be the single most influential organ of Czech-Jewish opinion until the Nazi occupation of 1939.[9] Vohryzek also effected an institutional *Putsch* in 1907 when he formed the Association of Progressive Czech Jews (*Svaz českých pokrokových židů*). Designed to serve as an alternative to the Czech-Jewish Political Union—which coordinated Jewish support

for the Young Czech Party—Vohryzek's progressive association consisted primarily of Jewish supporters of Masaryk's Realist party and encouraged Czech Jews to support socially "progressive" political causes.[10]

What was it that the Czech-Jewish movement felt it had found in
Masaryk? To begin with, the movement had discovered a political
leader who appeared to eschew all manifestations of radicalism. The
Realists publicly opposed the intransigence of the nationalist Right,
which based its argument for autonomy on the historic claims of the
ancient Czech kingdom rather than the natural rights of the Czech
people. They were equally opposed to revolutionary Marxism, arguing
that only peaceful and democratic avenues could lead to social
progress. Moreover, in his commitment to the scientific method and
to positivism in social analysis, as well as in his anticlericalism,
Masaryk may have been the most faithful heir on the Czech political
scene to the legacy of the Enlightenment.[11] Yet Masaryk's party undoubtedly made its greatest impact on Czech Jews as a result of its rejection of both economic and political antisemitism. *Naše doba* had
been one of the few Czech periodicals at the turn of the century to be
critical of *Svůj k svému,* the nationally inspired boycott movement directed against Germans and Jews.[12] And at the height of the Hilsner
murder trial, Masaryk rose—at some risk to his personal safety—to denounce the blood libel and to demand that Hilsner be given a new
trial.[13]

The reasons behind Masaryk's popularity among Czech Jews, in
short, are not hard to find. In a highly contentious society—one divided along national, class, and religious lines and in which much political capital could be gained by exploiting natural antagonisms and
prejudices—Masaryk and his party offered the best hope for Jewish integration into a Czech milieu. Moreover, Czech-Jewish thinkers found
in Masaryk the philosopher and sociologist a model and inspiration for
their own creative work. Even his idiosyncratic blend of anticlericalism
and concern for the religious foundations of modern culture had a direct influence on turn-of-the-century Czech-Jewish thought.

The *Rozvoj* circle at the turn of the century was largely made up of secularized Jewish intellectuals—contributors to Vohryzek's newspaper and,
often, leading members of the SČAŽ. Curiously, Viktor Vohryzek and
others among this group issued what amounted to an "anti-secularist"
manifesto of their own in the years following 1900, partly as a tactical
maneuver to cut the wind from the sails of both the new antisemitism

and the growing Zionist movement. At the same time, they may have reasoned that a revitalization of the religious element in national life would underscore the purely religious definition of Jewish distinctiveness and provide a much-needed boost to the involvement of Jews *as Jews* in the Czech national revival. Since the real value of a people was determined by its spirit, its religious character, a demonstration of the spiritual qualities of Judaism—of its universal appeal—would add to the desirability of Jewish cooperation in the eyes of the Czech population.[14]

The *Rozvoj* intellectuals also found an opportunity to correct the abuses of Czech politics in Masaryk's oft-repeated call for an infusion of the spiritual values of the Czech Reformation into national life. Eduard Lederer was paying homage to his mentor when he argued in his 1902 work, *The Jew in Contemporary Society*, that Czech society needed to operate along radically different lines, that the idea of social justice as expressed in the Gospels had to temper that of nationality. The Czech Reformation—as reformulated by its turn-of-the-century interpreters— was said to rest on the foundations of religious and social democracy, the primacy of peaceful means and intentions, and the insistence on political and social justice.[15] True national renewal, moreover, sprang from moral regeneration. In a frequently repeated quote from 1910, Masaryk is heard to urge: "Regenerate, reform the individual; regenerate, reform the whole people."[16]

When *Rozvoj* opened its pages during its early years to a wide-ranging discussion of the moral transformation of Czech society, it did so not only out of devotion to the teachings of Masaryk, but also because it felt that Judaism had a special contribution to make in this regard. Czech Jews were in a position to draw upon the resources of rabbinic and especially biblical Judaism in the creation of a new ethical consensus, a religious and philosophical synthesis that would "unite us in a single cultural whole."[17] Vohryzek in particular envisioned a morally honed Judaism of the future, whose *national* function would consist of an emphasis on the hallowing of God's name through ethical behavior. This "renewed" Judaism would serve both as a vehicle for the improved integration of the Jew into Czech society and as an active ingredient in the transformation of society as a whole, directing the nation along a more moderate course, leading it away from the hypernationalism of the past toward a new humanism. Judaism's task, in the end, amounted to nothing less than the modulation, if not the sublimation, of the national impulse.[18]

Masaryk's Affinity for Zionism

For all of the exuberance shown by the Czech-Jewish movement for its newly found political and cultural allies, the relationship between the two parties was hardly a smooth one. To begin with, a veil of misunderstanding and wishful thinking clouded the judgment of the Czech-nationalist Jews. They may have recognized in Masaryk a man of religious tolerance and Enlightenment thinking but they consistently underestimated the importance he gave to the national revival and, in particular, to the moral definition that he applied to this endeavor. "It is the duty of every thinking person," he wrote in *The Czech Question* (*Ceská otázka,* 1895), "to participate actively in the rebirth of his nation."[19] He elaborated on this theme in his 1905 publication, *National Philosophy of the Modern Era* (*Národnostní filosofie doby novější*), when he argued:

That which is most holy within the nation is its moral character.... The Czech becomes German only out of impure motives; he is without character, and what is remarkable is that the Germans are willing to take him in.
... A person of solid character would under no circumstances be untrue to his nation.[20]

In expressing disapproval of cultural assimilation, Masaryk may have had in mind the behavior of the sizeable Czech population in Vienna. But in a 1909 interview with the Vienna correspondent of *Wschód,* a Lwów weekly, he applied a similar judgment to the Jews. Here he labeled national assimilation "impossible and in fact laughable," adding that it had made no real strides over the past ten years.[21] These remarks, which also appeared in the Prague Zionist weekly, *Selbstwehr,* caused a stir among *Rozvoj*'s readership; its editor, Viktor Teytz, asked the Czech leader to clarify his anti-assimilationist stance. The reply appeared in *Rozvoj* on 9 April 1909. Interestingly, it displayed only a minor retreat from Masaryk's original position. Masaryk claimed to have been misquoted by the Polish paper. He had not intended to promote any specific Jewish party but rather had had in mind only the "general idea" of Zionism. What he was sympathetic to in the movement was the awakening of the self-consciousness of the Jewish masses. The notion of colonizing Palestine he still held to be utopian.[22]

Masaryk cautioned that Zionism ought not to work at cross purposes with Jewish emancipation. On the contrary, it was important for Jews to fight for their rights where they presently lived. Nor did he want to demean the value of the Czech-Jewish movement. His views on assimila-

tion, he explained, were meant to apply to racial assimilation, not to social or cultural integration. But he equivocated on this point, unable to
accommodate the Czech-Jewish movement to the degree it would have
wanted: "The nation is not a single entity; it has a whole array of traits:
language, origins, religion, and traditions. And language is certainly the
most important. Of course the Jews can become culturally Czech, but
there still remains a difference: that of separate origins, of race—which
of course cannot be exactly established—of religion, and of tradition."[23]
Moreover, Masaryk added, one ought not to underestimate the importance that religion has had in preserving the cultural and social isolation
of the Jews in Europe. He concluded his explanation with a remark that
could not have pleased the Jewish assimilationists: "It is certainly no
misfortune if the Jews form a distinct element for a while within the nation."[24]

In retrospect, Masaryk's position in the *Wschód* interview ought not
to have surprised the editors of *Rozvoj*. He had expressed similar opinions on the question of Jewish nationalism as far back as 1883, when he
reviewed Ernest Renan's *Le Judaisme comme race et comme religion* (Judaism as a race and as a religion) for the journal *Sborník historický*. Here
Masaryk took issue with Renan's contention that Judaism was not a national religion and that the Jews were not a pure nationality but rather a
racial mixture.[25] The Jews, Masaryk contended, were in fact less racially
mixed than their European neighbors. "The antagonism between Jews
and Europeans has always been so strong on both sides that one cannot
conceive of the kind of mixing that occurred, for example, between Romans and Gauls, Romans and Germans, or Germans and Slavs." We
must consider the Jews, he argued, "as a nation completely different
than ourselves."[26]

Masaryk went on to suggest that Jewish self-consciousness provided
the best means of insuring peaceful coexistence between Jews and non-
Jews. One could not effectively fight antisemitism by arguing, as Renan
had, that the Jews were not a pure race or nation. "National hatred,"
Masaryk quipped, "does not ask whether the blood of one's adversary is
pure or not." The issue at hand was not one of racial purity but of character. By this he meant to suggest that national antagonisms emerged from
cultural defects, from character shortcomings on both sides of a conflict:
"Under these circumstances, let us both—Semites and non-Semites—
recognize what differentiates us, what character traits repel one another;
let each recognize his own faults and shortcomings; and let us both
work to find that cement which up to now has not been found."[27]

Although Masaryk harbored a deep-seated mistrust of assimilationist movements in general and argued in favor of a Jewish nationality, his attitudes toward Jews were not uniformly positive. Masaryk justly gained notoriety in 1899 and 1900 as a defender of the Jews against the newly revived, medieval blood libel. The conviction of Leopold Hilsner on murder charges in Kutná Hora had stemmed from a trial in which allegations of ritual murder were aired long and loud. In two celebrated pamphlets Masaryk railed against the belief in Jewish ritual murder and demanded a new trial for the luckless defendant.[28] Yet, as Masaryk later admitted on a number of occasions, he had not been drawn to defend either Hilsner or the Jews out of philosemitic motives. Masaryk claimed to have become involved in the Hilsner trial to protect neither the Jews nor Hilsner, but "to defend Christians from superstition." It was only at the behest of a former student that he expressed any opinion at all about the Hilsner trial—this in the form of a letter that was subsequently published in Vienna's *Neue Freie Presse*. And only after the completion of the first trial was he moved first to investigate the matter carefully and then to intervene forcefully against the libel.[29]

In point of fact, Masaryk's pious Catholic mother had taught her children to fear Jews. She herself believed the blood libel and informed her children of the Jewish "need" for Christian blood at Easter time. As a boy Masaryk simply assumed that the libel was true and used to go out of his way to avoid contact with the two or three Jewish families who lived in his village. Later he would find himself involuntarily inspecting the hands of Jews whom he met to see if they contained telltale traces of blood.[30]

Masaryk related on a number of occasions that his attitude toward Jews did not change until he became a gymnasium student in Hustopeče. There, for the first time, he shared a classroom with Jewish students, at least one of whom caused him to appreciate the moral significance of an individual's commitment to Judaism.[31] Yet, as Masaryk admitted to Karel Čapek, he was never able to "overcome ... the antisemitism of the common people" emotionally. Only in his "reason," in his pursuit of rational justice, did he seek to combat it.[32] Reason and instinct, however, coexisted in an uneasy alliance in Masaryk's thought, and throughout his career he managed to combine support for the Jews of Bohemia with naive prejudices and expressions of resentment and mistrust. Thus, when he assessed the long-term political impact of his defense of Leopold Hilsner, he remarked: "During the war I saw how useful the affair had been to me: the press of the world is largely managed or financed by Jews; they knew me from the Hilsner case, and repaid me for what I had done for them then by writing favorably about our cause—or at least not unfavorably."[33] Later, during the early months of the First World War, Masaryk was known to have complained to the governor of Bohemia, Prince Thun, about the "aggressive and excited" behavior of the Germans of Prague, particularly the Jews. He urged the governor to "hold back the Jews and render them less aggressive" lest a "Jewish pogrom" ensue.[34] And as he prepared to go into exile, Masaryk offered the same advice to the Prague Jewish writer and Zionist leader Max Brod.[35]

When Masaryk picked up his pen a second time to write on the Jewish question, in 1898, it was in the course of a long essay on the philosophical and sociological foundations of Marxism.[36] In this piece he criticized Marx for underestimating both the religious and the national sides of the Jewish question and for drawing his generalizations concerning Jews and the nature of Judaism not from empirical observation but from Feuerbach's critical imagination.

Marx refuses to see in the Jewish question a national and racial dimension, which nevertheless is there. The Jews are a distinct nation even though they have long given up their spoken language. But language is not the only, nor the most important, attribute of nationality.

... Marx does not sufficiently analyze the particular character of the Jews and therefore does not differentiate between the good and bad sides of their character. Neither does he investigate the good and bad characteristics of Christians in different nations. Thus his judgment of the Jews does not differ much from that of [Max] Stirner. And yet the Jewish nation is characterized not only by barterers, but also by Jeremiah, Spinoza, and also Christ.[37]

While he accepted Marx's call for a universal, human emancipation, Masaryk was quick to point out that precisely such efforts were being carried out within the Jewish national movement. "I see a bit of this work at revitalization in Zionism," he wrote. "By this I do not mean the emigration of Jews to Palestine. They can calmly stay where they are. But they must understand that their moral condition and their entire outlook on the world is in need of reform."[38]

Today's Jews lack the self-criticism of the prophets.... Out of fear of the majority, the Jews do not dare look into their own conscience. It is true that Christians are partly to blame for this, but only partly. The Jews are all too self-satisfied—that is their current shortcoming. The same holds true, by the way, for the Christian antisemites."[39]

Three main themes emerge from Masaryk's discussion of Marx and the Jewish question. First, the Jews—whatever the arguments to the contrary and despite the fact that they appear to have lost their common spoken language—had to be understood as forming a separate nationality among the European family of nations. Other Czech Realists, such as the journalist Jan Herben and the philosopher František Krejčí, would later echo this point of view. Krejčí would build his case for a distinct Jewish nationality on the argument that the unique religion of the Jews functioned in much the same way that linguistic culture did for other groups.[40] Herben would admit to a more basic, emotional response to the question. He considered the Jews to be a nation for the simple reason that they "looked like one" (*protože je to na nich vidět*), and he was bemused by the fact that statements of this nature caused his Czech-Jewish acquaintances such pain.[41]

In Masaryk's writings, both of these reasons for regarding the Jews as a separate nation exist side by side. Since he bestowed on religion a major role in the formation of national culture in general, he was prone to do the same with regard to the specific case of Judaism and the Jewish people. Yet it was also completely reasonable for him, as well as for most other children of rural and small-town Moravia, to view the Jews as a distinct cultural element, alien from Czech or Slovak Catholic society because, to paraphrase Herben, they obviously were.[42]

Second, the Jewish community as a whole, like most industrial societies in Europe, was in need of ethical reform. Here Masaryk offered little in the way of elaboration, feeling perhaps that the critique was obvious. He made oblique references to the materialism and the moral complacency of the Jews but had few specific complaints to lodge. One suspects that here, too, the combination of inbred cultural attitudes and more formal cultural criticism came into play. Third, Masaryk credited the Zionist movement with pointing the way for modern Jewry to achieve moral regeneration—a regeneration that all of the nations of Europe could use and that Masaryk himself was urging upon the Czech people.

Over the years Masaryk did not move very far from these three basic positions. Contributing to a 1900 publication entitled *Zionisten und Christen*—which incidentally was dedicated to him—Masaryk wrote: "I understand Zionism ... from a primarily moral perspective. The thinking, progressive Jew becomes conscious of the defects in his character and *Weltanschauung*. I see in Zionism, to borrow a well-known phrase, 'a drop of the oil of the prophets.'"[43] The "thinking Jew," Masaryk explained, acknowledges his own responsibility for the deficiencies of cultural work (*Kulturarbeit*) in the past. He wants to be "born anew," and therefore must proceed forward, far beyond the "general shortcomings" of our civilization. "For this, changing the local milieu alone will not help; for this, what is needed is a regeneration from within, one to which, to be sure, Christians must also contribute, as [they are] equally guilty."[44]

Masaryk's fascination with "regeneration from within" led him, with the help of young Zionist intellectuals in Prague, to discover and appreciate the work of the Russian Jewish writer Aḥad Ha'am (Asher Ginsberg, 1856–1927). Reviewing religious and ecclesiastical developments for *Naše doba* in 1905, Masaryk wrote: "I am indebted to several Jews who understood my interest in their religious question and who brought to my attention a thinker from whom one can draw very positive instruction."[45] Masaryk was aware of the fact that Aḥad Ha'am had a reputation as a master of Hebrew prose style and was a major figure in the renaissance of literary Hebrew. But what impressed him the most was Aḥad Ha'am's critical stance toward Western liberalism, his cultural modernism, which nevertheless was infused with spiritual concerns:

Aḥad Ha'am is in the first instance an opponent of liberalism and hence an opponent of Western Judaism [literally, "Jewish Westernness"]. He is not impressed with the freedom of Western Jewry, its liberal blend of chauvinism and cosmopolitanism. 'Should I envy these brothers of ours their rights? No, and again, no! I, it is true, have none, but neither have I had to give up my soul for them....' Aḥad Ha'am is a Jew, simply a Jew; he does not understand at all the question of why he remains a Jew.[46]

Aḥad Ha'am's views appeared to Masaryk to highlight his own. Neither advocated that their people forsake the Enlightenment or remove themselves from European culture; but neither wished for their people to lose their "national nature" in the process of becoming "modern." Masaryk, who felt that one could be anticlerical without becoming antireligious, modern without abandoning traditional culture, showed particular interest in what to some must have appeared an arcane dispute within the Jewish national movement between Aḥad Ha'am and writers such as M. J. Berdyczewski, who were strongly influenced by Nietzsche and his concept of the "transvaluation of all values." To this group, all elements of traditional Judaism had to be left behind in order for a true cultural renaissance to be achieved. To Masaryk's obvious satisfaction, Aḥad Haʿam denounced this anarchistic approach to culture, arguing instead for a renaissance of Hebrew language and literature that used the religious-literary tradition as a necessary base upon which to build.[47]

Most important for Masaryk, Aḥad Haʿam called upon the Jews to effect a "reawakening of the heart," an internal rebirth. In Aḥad Ha'am Masaryk clearly recognized a kindred spirit. But he also found in him a nobility of character that he felt was lacking in the Czech-Jewish assimilationists, even those who had determined to stand up to antisemitism within the Czech national movement. "Thus he approaches antisemitism in an entirely different way than do most Jews: antisemitism must not be the reason and motive for the efforts at national revival; these efforts must emerge from one's own deepest consciousness."[48] "In a word," Masaryk concluded, "Aḥad Haʿam points to the improvement of Jewry through a spiritual and religious awakening."[49] This emphasis Zionism placed on self-improvement provided the movement with unassailable moral strength.

Political Negotiations under the New Order

Whatever differences had separated progressive Czech nationalists from the Czech-Jewish movement in the past, by the close of 1918 the two parties stood united as promoters and defenders of the new political order. With the establishment of an independent Czechoslovakia, a major part of the political, if not the cultural, program of the Czech-Jewish movement was realized. Czech-speaking Jews no longer needed to defend the legitimate aspirations of a national movement in a provincial capital. Their political purpose now appeared to be reduced to insuring Jewish support for the new state, their cultural program to achieving a more effective integration with the Czech national majority.

Yet the very tensions that had led to cleavage during the last decades of the empire continued to frustrate relations between Czech-nationalist Jews and the Realists in the new state. One source of discomfort was popular antisemitism, which erupted intermittently between 1918 and 1920 and which fused demonstrations against the German minority with physical attacks on Jewish property and institutions.[50] Ultimately more troubling for patriotic Czech Jews, however, was the growing number

of political successes registered by the Zionists. Zionist efforts to organize Czechoslovak Jewry along national lines and to promote Jewish national interests in the new state threatened the integrationist program of
the Czech-Jewish movement. Not surprisingly, the Zionists received a
sympathetic hearing from the heads of the Czechoslovak government;
this fact alone was enough to throw the Czech-Jewish camp into alarm.

The Zionists emerged from the First World War better organized
and more politically adroit on the whole than did the assimilationists.
Yet all of their energy and readiness would have mattered little had it
not also been for the fact that during the war Masaryk and Beneš had
acquired for themselves the status of symbolic heads of state in the eyes
of the Western powers. This recognition from the outside world placed
the Realists in a position of authority far above their true electoral
strength. The World Zionist Organization, in turn, exploited the situation perfectly, offering support for Czech national aspirations during
the war while capitalizing on the friendly relations that already existed
between Masaryk and the Czech Zionists.

In September 1918, following verbal assurances from President Wilson that the "Czechoslovak nation" would enjoy independence in the
new European order, the Zionist Organization of America sent a
telegram of congratulations to the Czech leader. Masaryk replied with a
promise that the same rights that were to be granted the German national minority in Czechoslovakia would also apply to the Jews. "As re-
gards Zionism," he added, "I can only express sympathy with it and
with the national movement of the Jewish people in general, since it is
of great moral significance."[51] Masaryk also sent an unsolicited telegram
to Max Brod, recalling a meeting they had had at the start of the war
and guaranteeing that Jewish rights would be respected fully in the future state.[52]

On the eve of the proclamation of the Czechoslovak Republic, the
Jewish nationalists, including a number of non-Zionists, organized
themselves into a Jewish National Council (Národní rada židovská, or
Jüdischer Nationalrat). Six days later, on 28 October, the council approached the Czech National Committee (Národní výbor) and presented it with the demands of the Jewish minority.[53] The memorandum
of the Jewish National Council called for official recognition of the
Jewish nationality and for the right of Jews to declare it in censuses and
elections. No individual was to be compelled to list his nationality as
Jewish, "but by the same token no one desiring to profess it [was to] be
prohibited from doing so officially or unofficially."[54] The memorandum

went on to call for the full civil and legal equality of the Jews. Jewish minority rights, in other words, were not "to be construed as affecting those rights which are their due as Czech citizens." Rather, Jews would enjoy what had been denied them previously under the terms of the emancipation of 1867: full civil equality combined with full national rights.[55]

The Jewish nationalists demanded cultural autonomy in the areas of education, cultivation of the Hebrew language, relations with Palestine, and social welfare. They asked for the right to establish Jewish elementary and high schools—"along modern (not sectarian) lines"—where circumstances permitted. The Jewish religious communities, recognized as corporations in public law, were to be recast along democratic lines and were to choose a "joint representative body" with headquarters in Prague. Finally, to the extent that cultural projects were to be recipients of state funds in the future, Jewish institutions would be entitled to proportionate assistance.[56]

During the first fifteen months of the new republic, the Czech Zionists worked the political fields of Prague and of Paris—where the peace treaties ending the war were being negotiated—with unusual sophistication and self-assurance. They had prepared themselves for this role during the last years of the war and certainly gave the appearance of seasoned political professionals. Yet the secret of their success lay not so much in knowing how and when to apply pressure as in their sympathetic appreciation of the underlying assumptions of liberal Czech nationalism. The Zionists understood that Masaryk and his associates would not readily deny the Jews the cultural self-determination that the Czechs themselves had treasured. In addition, the Czech Zionists relied on the self-interest of the Czechoslovak government to achieve recognition of the Jewish nationality. If the Jews of Bohemia and Moravia were given the opportunity to register their nationality as Jewish, the result might be a significant reduction in the size of the German-national camp. Similarly, the Jews of Slovakia might thereby be induced to abandon the Hungarian cause. Hence to some within the government, accommodating the Zionists made good political sense, if only to weaken the national rivals of the Czechs and Slovaks.[57]

As it turned out, the road to recognition of Jewish nationality in Czechoslovakia was not free of obstacles. Beneš resisted efforts to include specific references to Jewish minority rights in the Treaty of St. Germain because, as he explained in a letter to Ludvík Singer, the new state regarded human rights as a matter of course. "We have fulfilled our obligations thus far and will continue to do so." Beneš acknowledged, moreover, the difficult position that the government was being asked to assume: to render judgment on the relative merits of Jewish nationalism versus assimilationism. "The Czechoslovak delegation is not competent to broach this question," he concluded, "and therefore cannot broach it."[58] Not competent in a formal sense, perhaps, but both Beneš and Masaryk undoubtedly had strong personal sentiments on this matter. A few days later, Beneš tried to reassure Nahum Sokolow, chairman of the *Comité des délégations juives* at the Paris Peace Conference, of his sympathy for Jewish nationalism. He insisted, however, that to sign the so-called Jewish articles of the Polish treaty, for example, would represent a "yellow badge" for Czechoslovakia, a stigma of which only Poland and Romania were deserving because of their long history of antisemitism.[59]

In the end neither Masaryk nor Beneš would agree to the inclusion of so-called Jewish clauses in the Treaty of St. Germain. It was not until the promulgation of the Czechoslovak constitution in February 1920 that the government formally announced its recognition of the Jewish nationality.[60] Now the Jewish National Council received essentially what it had been asking for all along. Jews who regarded themselves as members of a separate nationality had the right to express this choice in censuses and elections, yet they could not be required by the state to do so. The Jews, moreover, were the only national minority not to be defined by a linguistic criterion, nor did they necessarily have to identify with the Jewish religion.[61]

Conclusion

In the context of interwar East Central Europe, Czechoslovakia's concessions to Jewish nationalism were, in fact, unprecedented. This was the first time in European history that an industrialized parliamentary democracy with a fairly long tradition of Jewish emancipation recognized the claim to Jewish national distinctiveness. The state, moreover, made room for Jewish cultural and national self-expression without diminishing the value of emancipation or intending to reduce Jewish social and political integration. Masaryk's government had, as it were, fulfilled the demands once voiced by the historian Simon Dubnov: to realize emancipation for Jews not as individuals, which had been the model of the French Revolution, but as a nation, according to the new model of Eastern Europe.[62]

In legitimizing Jewish national politics in the new state, Masaryk and the Realists remained faithful to long-held, if conflicting, convictions. On the one hand, childhood impressions combined with popular attitudes to produce in the Czech leaders a general stance of distance and suspicion toward the Jews. Moreover, the lessons of intercommunal conflict and coexistence in the Czech-dominated countryside had taught even the most liberal of Czech nationalists that the Jews formed a separate ethnic group. Often Czech leaders simply lumped the Jews together with the more sizeable German minority; on occasion they viewed the Jews as a third player in the national struggle. Rarely, however, did they entertain the conviction that the Jews were, or could become, fully Czech.

On the other hand, the emotional distance that separated Czech society and Jewish society did not prevent Realist intellectuals from sympathizing with the goals of Jewish nationalism in Europe. This too was not without precedent. Among Zionism's more vocal supporters in interwar Poland, for example, were the National Democrats—by no stretch of the imagination friends of the Jews. The approach of the Czech Realists, however, to both Jewish emancipation and Jewish nationalism diverged from that of other East European political parties in two ways. The first was the ability to separate their emotional predisposition toward the Jews from their philosophical commitment to democracy and social equality. The second, more telling, factor was the Czech propensity to see in Jewish nationalism on the European continent a version of their own national renascence, an echo of their own efforts to secure a Czech future through cultural and political autonomy.

On both points credit must be given to Masaryk for having broken the chains of habit. He consciously strove to overcome popular prejudice through a commitment to European rationalism and empirical science (though in his own case the mythical foundation for his cultural attitudes was particularly strong). He then translated this personal stance into a courageous and personally costly public crusade. Moreover, his peculiarly moralistic interpretation of Czech nationalism encouraged a sympathetic encounter with the cultural nationalism of Aḥad Haʿam and the Prague Zionists. Masaryk could not help but approve of what he saw going on in the small camp of Jewish nationalists, but he also lent the weight of his own personal prestige to the Zionist endeavour. Unlike many Polish nationalists, who were happy to endorse Zionism if that meant removing from the scene a large and problematic national minority, Czech nationalists under Masaryk's tutelage could straddle two apparently contradictory rails. In the eyes of East European Zionism, of course, there was no contradiction. National identity and cultural autonomy were seen as vehicles for a truer, deeper, more successful integration in a multinational environment. Masaryk and the Czech Realists agreed.

Leaders of the Czech-Jewish movement, meanwhile, reacted to the Realist-Zionist relationship with disappointment bordering on anger. A front-page editorial that appeared in *Rozvoj* in June 1919 complained bitterly of Zionist policies in the new state. The unsigned article contended that Zionist support for the state and its overt neutrality on the Czech-German issue was a masquerade designed to conceal its basically German makeup. Sardonically it recalled how the Czech Zionists had demonstrated in favor of Masaryk and an independent Czechoslovakia after the national revolution had already taken place, and how everyone was careful to speak only Czech at the meetings of the Prague Zionists though their Czech was really quite hopeless.[63]

Max Lederer (1875–1937), an activist in the Czech-Jewish movement since the early 1900s, in reviewing Karel Čapek's *Conversations with Masaryk* (*Hovory s TGM*) in April 1929, used the occasion to highlight Masaryk's fundamentally ambiguous relationship to the Jews. The title of his essay, "Staronový Masaryk" (The old-new Masaryk), itself contained a double entendre. On the one hand it alluded to the venerable history of the Prague Jewish community and to its symbolic representation, the thirteenth-century Altneu (Staronová) synagogue. The second meaning alluded to Masaryk himself. He was a creative genius, continually surprising his public with seemingly new and unexpected pronouncements. In reality, however, his views demonstrated remarkable stability over time, and his seemingly startling statements about Jews in Čapek's *Conversations* in fact reflected basic attitudes.

"In the end," Lederer writes, "all of us who have had close relations with Masaryk recognize that he was never a philosemite."[64] He was never able completely to overcome childhood fears and prejudices. Lederer concludes that there were two Masaryks: one passionately committed to rationality and justice, and one who had a "fundamentally emotional misunderstanding" of the Jewish question.[65]

Lederer's assessment, though ultimately incorrect, does suggest a useful psychological model for understanding the ambiguity of

Masaryk's relationship to Czech Jewry. Masaryk's attitudes turned on the dichotomy between his affective, or emotional, disposition and his rational, ideological convictions. Emotionally, Masaryk never completely overcame the mistrust and suspicion of Jews he had learned as a child. Similarly, his intuition that the Jews constituted a distinct national element in the larger social body stemmed from a naive reading of his early social-cultural environment. This does not negate the fact, however, that in Masaryk the village boy and the university professor, the Moravian Catholic and the Enlightenment rationalist, were constantly at odds. It was this struggle that produced the creative tension in Masaryk's life and work. It was the reasoning ideologist of political democracy and the enemy of cultural backwardness who defended the right of Jews to enter Czech society as equal members. And it was the critic both of Marxism and of Western liberalism, the theologian of national renewal, who discovered in Aḥad Haʿam and the Zionist movement the spirit of Hus and the "oil of the prophets."

In the end, both the Zionist victory and the Czech-Jewish defeat proved to be more ephemeral than real. The government's recognition of the Jewish nationality did not alter long-term social and cultural developments within Czech Jewry. The Zionists did not achieve a revolution in Jewish consciousness, nor did the pace of Jewish integration slow down. In fact the reverse was true. Most indicators showed a dramatic increase in Jewish integration into Czech society at all levels between 1918 and 1939.[66] Masaryk's religious and cultural inclinations may have favored the Zionists over the assimilationists, but the liberal foundations of the new political order, together with the force of Czech nationalism in general, had the overall effect of encouraging Czech-Jewish self-definition and the progressively stronger movement of Jews into the Czech mainstream. The real loser in the Realist, Czech-Jewish, Zionist confrontation was the older German orientation of the Jewish community. Historical forces that had been well in place since the late nineteenth century had long been eroding the German-Jewish synthesis of the emancipation era. The Czech-nationalist Jews, the Zionists, and the Realists combined to deliver it the final blow.

A Sitting Room in Prague

In June 1964 on the occasion of the opening of a Kafka exhibition in Prague, Max Brod (1884–1968) returned to his native city following an absence of twenty-five years. Brod, Kafka's lifelong friend and literary executor, had been active in Central European Zionism since 1911, was a founding member of the Jewish National Council at the close of the First World War, and enjoyed prominence as a writer and journalist during the interwar years. He managed to leave Prague just at the last minute, as it were, following the German occupation of Bohemia and Moravia in March 1939, emigrating to Palestine and set-tling in Tel Aviv, where he remained until his death in 1968. It was from Palestine and—after 1948—the State of Israel that Brod continued his lifelong project of cultivating and directing Kafka's posterity; the Prague roots of the "Prague Circle," meanwhile, came to occupy in-creasingly the realm of memory and abstraction. The city of Kafka—its culture and, surely, its Jewish inhabitants—had been obliterated. There was little to come home to.[1]

The political thaw of the mid-1960s—a stage-setter for the Prague Spring of 1968—had allowed for greater openness on the part of Czech academics toward Western influences on Czech culture and provided the immediate opportunity for Brod's visit. In a symbolic marking of sorts of the beginnings of Czech liberalization, the Germanists Paul Reimann and Eduard Goldstücker (the former, director of the Institute for the History of the Communist Party of Czechoslovakia; the latter, professor of German literature at Charles University and head of its

Germanics department) convened an international conference devoted to the work of Franz Kafka in the Liblice castle outside of Prague in May 1963, approximately the eightieth anniversary of his birth.[2] Two years later, Goldstücker organized another conference at the same venue, devoted more generally to the theme of Prague German literature.[3] Sandwiched between the two was the Kafka exhibit in Prague, to which Max Brod was officially invited and which he addressed, in Czech, during the opening ceremonies.[4]

Thirty-two years later, in 1996, Goldstücker related an anecdote concerning Brod's visit to the city of his birth, which I shall attempt to retell here.[5] By way of introduction I should make note of the fact that Goldstücker himself had gone into exile following the Soviet-led invasion of 1968 and returned to Prague only after the collapse of Communist rule in 1989. The story opens with an informal gathering that took place at the home of the Czech playwright František Langer (1888–1965), at which were also present Max Brod, Eduard Goldstücker (b. 1913), and the Marxist philosopher and mathematician Arnošt Kolman (1892–?). As the four men sat reminiscing about life in Prague before the war, one of them remarked that here—in Langer's living room—were gathered four types of Jews, each of whom represented one of the cultural options open to Czech Jewry in the twentieth century, and each option, it seemed, had led to a particular fate.

Goldstücker, the professor of Germanics who endeavored to reintroduce the study of German literature to the cultural agenda of the Czechoslovak state, was emblematic of the German-Jewish culture of Prague.[6] Langer, the playwright, novelist, and physician, whose first dramatic effort, *Svatý Václav*, was produced by the National Theater in Prague when he was twenty-three years old, stood for the assimilation of Jews to modern Czech culture.[7] Brod represented the "third way"— Jewish nationalism. And Kolman, who once had translated Martin Buber's *Drei Reden über das Judentum* into Czech and who later made a career for himself as a cyberneticist and mathematician, both in Moscow and in Prague, was perhaps best known as a Communist activist, a committed Bolshevik.[8]

The story continues. One of the four present made the remark that each "option"—and, I suppose, its corresponding fate—had been, as it were, freely chosen. Max Brod then intervened, observing that not all Czech-Jewish options were, in fact, represented at the gathering. Two individuals and the life choices they represented were conspicuous in their absence. They were Jiří (Georg Mordechai) Langer (1894–1943), the youngest brother of František, who on the eve of the First World War had run away to Galicia and become a Hasid, and Alfred Fuchs (1892–1941), a former student activist in the Czech-Jewish movement (also at one time a Zionist), who had converted to Catholicism—apparently for genuinely religious reasons—and later pursued a career in Czech and Catholic journalism. Both individuals had perished during the Second World War, but in very different circumstances: Langer as a refugee in Palestine and Fuchs as an inmate of the Dachau concentration camp.[9]

Goldstücker's story concerning identities and fates, choices and (often unintended) consequences, was offered for reasons that were partly pedagogical, partly nostalgic, and partly polemical. It was meant, first of all, to illustrate the richly diverse cultural universe in which Prague Jews such as Franz Kafka had lived and worked. Kafka had not been, in the first instance, a German writer from Prague; he was a Prague Jew, educated in German high culture, to be sure, but whose father had come from a Czech village. He had used Czech in his day-to-day life, and his very biography connected him in intimate ways with European Zionism, the traditional Jewish culture of Eastern Europe, and the national aspirations of the Czech people. The extent to which Kafka's "German" identity was mitigated by competing claims to self-definition was exemplified in his personal ties to the many "non-Germans" who populated Prague's cityscape: the Max Brods, the Felix Weltsches, the Jiří Langers, the František Langers, and by extension, the Čapeks and Hašeks of the non-Jewish Czech pantheon.

The observation made at the Langer gathering concerning "paths freely chosen" cuts two ways. It argues, first of all, against the notion that identities are inherited more or less automatically from one's parents or the environment. Rather, identities are formed, sought after, invented, or adopted. For the Jews of the Czech lands, in the years both preceding and following the First World War, the path to adult identity was in no way predetermined or inevitable. Social structures and environment, moreover, perform only moderately well as predictors of the choices that individual Jews were to make. Max Brod and Felix Weltsch (1884–1964), sons of long-standing Prague Jewish families, educated in a German milieu, opted during their school days—or shortly thereafter—for a Jewish national identity. Arnošt Kolman and Eduard Goldstücker traveled a path that led from labor Zionism to Marxism to membership in the Communist Party. Alfred Fuchs moved from the Czech wing of Prague Zionism to the markedly anti-Zionist Czech-

Jewish movement to Czech Catholicism. Ludvík Singer (1876–1931), on the other hand, followed to some extent the reverse course, from membership in the Czech-Jewish student movement to a leading position in interwar Czech Zionism.[10]

The complex and often unpredictable ways in which social structures and family background interact with the formation of ethnic identity is aptly illustrated in the case of František Langer and his brother Jiří. The family exhibited most of the cultural traits that I normally would associate with the formation of an integrationist, Czech-Jewish identity: roots in Czech village life, intimacy with Czech language and local culture, migration to a Czech provincial city or to Prague, and a generation or more of secularization within the family.[11] The boys' father attended synagogue in Prague's Královské Vinohrady suburb, belonged to numerous Czech civic associations, including Sokol (the gymnastics society), and sent his sons to Czech schools. František's evolution into a celebrated Czech playwright and writer of fiction who served in both the Czechoslovak Legion in Russia during the First World War and the Czechoslovak army in exile in the Second World War seems appropriate to this context. But how is one to explain his youngest brother's apparent indifference to the same cultural stimuli and social inducements in favor of what, in the context of early-twentieth-century Prague, was a decidedly solitary pursuit of Jewish mysticism?

Jiří Langer embarked on a journey of five hundred kilometers and of centuries when he boarded a train for the Eastern Galician town of Belz in 1913. His first sojourn among the Belz Hasidim proved to be something of a shock even to the young ascetic, although he must have tried to prepare himself psychologically for entry into a world dissonant with the one he had come from. He returned briefly to the city of his birth before the start of the First World War. František's memoir portrays deftly and with irony the web of miscalculations and unlikely expectations that greeted his brother's return. "It might have been expected," he writes, "that his [Jiří's] return to Prague, with its civilization and other advantages, would be an occasion of great rejoicing for him."

With what abandon he would embrace his parents! Perhaps on the very first day he would want to go to gaze on the Vltava and the magnificent panorama of the Hradčany. Perhaps he would travel to the mountains and the forests, fragrant with the scent of resin, so different from the plains of Galicia with their swamps and stench of stagnant water. On Friday evening he would visit the glorious synagogue at Vinohrady, with its thousand lights shining on the ornaments which his own uncle had guilded and its five hundred silken top hats on the heads of worthy, well-to-do believers, with the organ playing in the choir and the solo sung in Hebrew by a Christian from the German theater.[12]

This was not what lay in store for the Langer family. František knew that something was amiss from the tone in his father's voice when he told of Jiří's sudden return home. "He stood before me in a frayed black overcoat clipped like a caftan, reaching from his chin to the ground."

On his head he wore a broad round hat of black velvet, thrust back towards his neck. He stood there in a stooping posture; his whole face and chin were covered with a red beard, and side-whiskers in front of his ears hung in ringlets down to his shoulders. All that remained to be seen of his face was some white, unhealthy skin and eyes which at moments appeared tired and others feverish. My brother had not come back from Belz, to home and civilization; he had brought Belz with him.[13]

It did not take long to realize how difficult it would be to merge Belz with the civic culture of late-imperial Prague. Jiří added to his previous eccentricities by shunning as untrustworthy Prague's kosher restaurants, by refusing to touch women or look directly at them when speaking, and, as František writes, by "[saying] his prayers aloud, in a sing-song voice, running around the room in a sort of trance." He also drew quite a bit of attention on the street. "The appearance of a solitary Polish Jew on the streets of Vinohrady in 1913, belonging to a well-known Vinohrady family, positively cried out to be noticed."[14]

The true crisis in the life of the family came when Jiří was drafted into the Austrian army shortly after war broke out in 1914. Having returned to Belz, Jiří fled with the *rebbe*'s entourage from the Russian occupation of Eastern Galicia into Hungary; it was here that he received his enlistment papers. František, meanwhile, was serving in the medical corps on the Eastern front. When he came back to Prague on leave in 1915, he learned that Jiří had been sent to army prison where he awaited court martial proceedings. Apparently the Austrian military had been willing to tolerate the young Hasid's habit of waking up an hour before reveille each morning in order to say the morning prayers and prepare for himself a meal of bread and onion, but it lost all patience when he refused to carry a rifle or perform any work on Saturdays. Following his arrest Jiří proceeded to confound the court martial by refusing to speak at all in his defense. František, by virtue of his status as a medical officer, intervened in the case, offering both scientific and family testimony concerning Jiří's behavior over the preceding few years. As a result, the younger brother, judged to be insane, was sent home with a medical disability and managed to spend the rest of the war with his *rebbe*. František, on the other hand, returned to the Galician front, where he was an eyewitness to the wrenching sufferings of its remaining Jewish population—mainly Hasidic—now reduced to desperate flight.[15]

I have dwelt at length on the Langer family—and there is a good deal more that could be told—because their story calls into question the rhetorical underpinnings of the original Goldstücker anecdote: the notion that those present (and those absent) in František Langer's sitting-room in 1964 constituted six distinct types, or categories, of Czech Jewish identity. The first question to ask is whether the individuals mentioned matched the categories assigned to them. To what extent did they function as prototypes? Max Brod, for example, might just as easily have stood for the German-Jewish culture of Prague as for the Zionist alternative. German had remained his language of choice for literary expression long after his emigration to Palestine in 1939, during which time he continued to direct most of his professional energies to writing and criticism, as well as to the editing and publishing of the works of Franz Kafka. Beyond the fact that one might have found "better," or less ambiguous, examples of commitment to Jewish nationalism than Brod (names such as Hugo Bergmann, Ludvík Singer, and Leo Herrmann come to mind), the more pertinent question is: What separates a German Jew of Prague from a Zionist or, for that matter, from a Czech Jew?

Arnošt Kolman was said to represent the Communist path to mobility and security; Eduard Goldstücker, a harbinger of the once-prevalent German model of acculturation. But how different was one from the other? Both were Zionists in their youth: Kolman, it will be recalled, as a member of Spolek Theodor Herzl, translated Martin Buber's influential addresses on Judaism—which had been delivered in Prague between 1909 and 1911 at the behest of the Bar Kochba Verein—into Czech.[16] Goldstücker was a member of the Marxist-oriented ha-Shomer ha-Tsa'ir. This, coupled with the fact that he grew up in Slovakia, hardly warrants his association with German-Jewish culture, other than from a purely professional perspective. Goldstücker did not personally take part in Prague's German-Jewish life. It might have made more sense to characterize *both* Kolman and Goldstücker in terms of the political choices open to Jews in the thirties, forties, and fifties—in their case, with the decision to enter the Communist Party. Kolman became a

Bolshevik in 1918 in the wake of his experiences as a Russian prisoner of war, and he fought on a variety of fronts for the Red Army between 1918 and 1920. Goldstücker joined the Party in 1933. Indeed, he would not have been in a position to host international conferences on Franz Kafka and on Prague German literature in the 1960s or to serve as head of the Department of Germanics at Charles University if he had not also enjoyed a relatively high status in the party.[17]

Alfred Fuchs is held up as a radically assimilated Jew whose entry into the Czech nation encompassed religious conversion. Yet in terms of his family background, schooling, and youthful interests, he is virtually indistinguishable from the ultra-orthodox Jiří Langer—except perhaps for the fact that in their gymnasium years Fuchs was a good deal more interested in Judaism than was Langer.[18] The fact of the matter is that as classmates Fuchs and Langer shared a youthful interest in religious mysticism and studied Jewish texts together. Fuchs's interests drew him closer and closer to Catholic spirituality—even as he remained active in the Czech-Jewish movement—while Jiří Langer was drawn to the Talmud, Orthodox Judaism, and eventually Galician Hasidism. The boundary that separates these two life paths is a fragile one. Langer and Fuchs are more or less interchangeable pieces of the social puzzle that constituted Czech Jewry before the 1930s.

Add to the puzzle František Langer, the celebrated playwright and decorated army veteran. Is he a truer representative of the "Czech-Jewish option" than either his brother or Alfred Fuchs? Perhaps. But only because he more closely approximated conventional models: his works were well known and performed in legitimate Czech theater; he was close to the Čapek brothers and was a regular member of Tomáš Masaryk's "Friday Group"; he remained a Jew, though he had long ceased to practice Judaism. What label should he wear? What imaginary border divides him from the others? During Jiří's "post-adolescent crisis," the smell of onions cooking on a portable stove greeted František every day when he entered his home, the flat where the two had lived since childhood. Perhaps, in our mind's eye, we could draw a line across the middle of the kitchen floor that would demarcate Czech-Jewish and neo-Hasidic spaces. Yet one still would have to imagine a transaction in which the works of the Czech poet Otakár Březina were passed from one side to the other. For we know that František Langer directed the fifteen-year-old Jiří to Březina's poetry when asked for the name of a Czech poet interested in mystical themes. And we know that Jiří devoured the works of the Czech mystics before he had read a word of

Talmud. This apartment in the Vinohrady district of Prague thus produced richly differing manifestations of a single living culture: Březina and Hebrew literature, the Masaryks (father and son) and the Belzer Rebbe, Czech rationalism and Jewish mysticism.

The very categories German, Czech, Jew; liberal, Communist, patriot; mystic, rationalist, Orthodox, and assimilationist, which were reported to be present in the Langer apartment (in body or in spirit) on that June day in 1964, existed in a state of perpetual movement—seeming to appear only to collapse, regroup, and melt away. Any attempt to establish hard and fast categories of ethnicity and social status is fraught with danger. This is particularly true when the boundary drawer ventures into pre–Second World War Central Europe. And when the point of reference is Jewish Prague between the wars, one might as well give up. Why, then, did the members of the Langer gathering bring up the question of "type" in the first place? The point may have been to conjure up the very diversity that defied classification. "Look how different we all are, yet we are all Prague Jews." "Though we share a common origin, look at the different places to which fate has taken us."

What does the story mean to tell us about Jewish destinies in the Czech lands? Here, perhaps, one should begin with those who no longer were present in 1964. Jiří Langer had returned to Prague in the autumn of 1918 sporting "modern" dress but maintaining Orthodox Jewish practice. He soon added to his interest in Jewish mysticism a growing fascination with Freudian psychoanalysis. Over the next two decades his creative work took place on three apparently nonintersecting planes: psychoanalytic studies of Jewish ritual and of the Kabbalah, published in German; his famous literary evocation of Hasidism, the *Nine Gates,* published in Czech; and poetry, written in—or anthologized from—Hebrew.[19]

Caught in Prague during the German occupation, Jiří left for Slovakia in the fall of 1939, hoping to travel down the Danube to Istanbul and on to Palestine. The trip was tortuously slow and dangerous; refugees who secured steerage for themselves on the iron barges suffered the ravages of winter weather and lack of food, water, and hygiene. Most ships were prevented by the German authorities from leaving the Danube delta in Romania to reach freedom on the high seas. Once again František came to the aid of his brother (mail somehow had made it from the barge to Paris), employing the good offices of Jan Masaryk to prevail upon the British to send an aid ship. By the time Jiří was rescued from his "prison of ice," however, he had already contracted the kidney disease from which he would eventually die in Tel Aviv in 1943. František made efforts from London to send money from time to time; it was Max Brod who saw to Langer's hospitalization and burial in Palestine, as well as to the disposition of his literary estate; and it was Jan Masaryk who telegraphed František with condolences when he received news of Jiří's death in March 1943.[20]

Langer's childhood friend, Alfred Fuchs, underwent baptism within two years of the publication of a second edition of his *On the Jewish Question* (*O židovské otázce,* 1919). Ultimately, however, his embrace of the Church afforded him little protection. During the occupation he was arrested by the Gestapo and removed from the grounds of a monastery where he had sought shelter. He died in the Dachau concentration camp from tortures inflicted during interrogations. His body now lies in the grounds of the Břevnov monastery in Prague.[21] Thus were the two victims of Nazism: one a Jewish mystic and scholar, the other a pious Catholic. Both saintly figures and innocent martyrs. This characterization of Jewish victimization is meant, I think, to be both touching and ironic. It is also unintentionally disturbing. Those who possessed the most religious faith, the story goes, perished cruelly. The Jewish mystic reenacted the desperate wanderings of his ancestors. The Catholic convert died because the Nazis had designated him both a political and a racial enemy.

The politically active, the *bojovníci,* lived—though in strikingly differing circumstances. Max Brod's Zionists were able to build a future for themselves in Israel, away from Europe. Prague was transformed into a memory or a tourist destination. František Langer, the literary celebrity and Czech patriot, survived the war to return home. Having escaped from Nazi-occupied Prague via Poland to France, he became the head of the Czechoslovak Army Medical Corps. With the fall of France, he followed the Czechoslovak Army in Exile to England; spent the remainder of the war years in London, where he performed medical service during the air raids and continued to write; and eventually achieved the rank of general. Both of his brothers had died during the occupation: Jiří, as we have seen, in Palestine; Josef, by his own hand before his deportation to Terezín.[22]

František was a survivor—not only of the Second World War but also of the Communist regime in Czechoslovakia. Arguably, his involvement in the Czechoslovak Legion in Russia at the end of the First World War, his close ties to the Masaryk family—indeed, his standing in the liberal establishment of the First Republic—rendered him politically suspect in post-1948 Czechoslovakia. Yet he never was arrested or put on trial; though he suffered the effects of literary censorship, he never lost his freedom. It seems to me that he owed this good fortune to two factors: he had no political aspirations (and never made the mistake of joining the Communist Party), and he had the good fortune to retire from the military in 1948, at age sixty. From that date until his death in 1965 he lived in relatively obscure retirement in Prague, unscathed by the turmoil, political infighting, and show trials of the late Stalinist years.[23] Many of his Communist coreligionists were not so lucky.

Fate took party members Arnošt Kolman and Eduard Goldstücker in a different direction. A committed Bolshevik, Kolman had spent much of the twenties, thirties, and forties in Moscow and had acquired Soviet citizenship. In 1945 he returned to Prague to take up a position at the university. Soon, however, his vocal criticisms of segments of the Party leadership in Prague, both in print and at meetings of the Central Committee, got him into considerable trouble. In September 1948, on orders from the USSR, Kolman was arrested and taken to the Soviet Union, where he was imprisoned until 1952. Eventually rehabilitated, Kolman did not wind his way back to Prague until 1959, when he was appointed director of the Philosophical Institute of the Czechoslovak Academy of Sciences. By the early sixties Kolman was again running afoul of the top leadership in the Party; after expressing criticism of President Antonín Novotný in 1963, he sought refuge, ironically, in Moscow.[24]

Among the enemies Kolman had made, interestingly, was Rudolf Slánský (1901–52), the secretary-general of the Party and deputy premier, who was later himself to become the centerpiece of a show trial directed from Moscow, in which fourteen defendants—eleven of whom were Jews—stood accused of espionage and treason. Both anti-Zionism and antisemitism played a significant part in the prosecution of the case; each Jewish defendant was defined as such in the official indictment against him, and the treason and espionage charges laid claim to an international conspiracy linking the United States, the State of Israel, and "bourgeois Jewish nationalists." In the end, eight Jews and three non-Jews were executed; the former group included, in addition to Slánský, Ludvík Frejka, Bedřich Gemeinder, Bedřich Reicin, Rudolf Margolius, Otto Fischl, Otto Sling, and André Simone.[25]

Goldstücker, who had been employed since 1945 by the Foreign Ministry, was one whose name often appeared in documents from the period as someone who *ought* to be purged. He had been posted to the embassy in London from 1947 to 1949, and from 1949 to 1951 he served as Czechoslovakia's first ambassador to Israel. Recalled from Sweden in 1951, he eventually was implicated in the Slánský affair. In 1953 Goldstücker was sentenced to life imprisonment as a "bourgeois Jewish nationalist"; he was released at the end of 1955.[26] It was then that he began his academic career as a professor of German literature at Charles University. When we meet up with him in 1964, it will be recalled, Goldstücker is playing a leading role in a very public campaign not only to rehabilitate the image of Franz Kafka, tarnished by the "official verdict" of bourgeois nihilist, but also to find a place in the collective memory of Czechoslovakia for the once-proud German culture of Prague.[27]

What was not foreseen in the Langer sitting room at the time were the cultural and political liberalizations of 1968—the so-called Prague Spring—and the invasion of the armies of the Warsaw Pact, which took place in August of that year. By 1968 Goldstücker had become the chairman of the Czechoslovak Writers' Union and was deeply implicated in the cultural side of the Dubček reforms. He became a major—one might say reflexive—target of criticism on the part of antiliberal elements in the Party.[28]

In June 1968 Goldstücker received an anonymous and ominously threatening letter, which he printed in full, together with his own response, in *Rudé Právo*. The letter began, "Mr. Goldstücker—Zionist hyena bastard," and deteriorated from there. Expressing regret that its recipient had not been hanged for his "part in the Slánský affair," the letter managed to connect Goldstücker rhetorically to Israeli aggressors, Jewish intellectuals, class and national enemies, Mrs. Slánský, and Adolf Hitler.

Jews used to try to claim to be part of the Germanic race. You and your Jewish followers didn't even want to speak Czech, you preferred German— the language of Hitler the hyena. And our people remember it well. You don't just want to rule in Israel, your Zionist cravings make you want to rule the whole world, wherever possible, so you and Hitler might just as well shake hands on that.[29]

The letter opened by promising to send Goldstücker's "file" to the Soviet Union. It closed with the warning that his time would come, the dirty Jew. In his response, Goldstücker noted that he had come across the language of his accuser many times in the past. "It is the speech of my Růzyně investigators in 1951–1953, of my Pankrác, Leopoldov, and Jáchymov prison guards from 1953 to 1955, of my indictment and the introductory statement by the counsel for the prosecution ... which ended with a demand for the death penalty."[30]

Goldstücker bravely called upon his anonymous correspondent to make public his identity as well as the name of the party organization that gave him the authority to write the letter in the first place.

Come out of the sewers that hide you into the light of day. Hand over the fruits of your criminal investigation to the judgment of the people in whose name you are unjustly operating. Tell them the proofs you have of the "Zionist plot," which is always brought up when an attack on freedom is in the offing because it is felt that this atavistic bogy is enough to make people abandon their ability to reason and give up the fruits of the long and difficult struggle toward a freer life and toward becoming a more worthy human being.[31]

Later that year, Goldstücker left his native country once more and began a new life in England.

Not a particularly uplifting tale. Its various biographical components proffer object lessons in the doomed nature of the European-Jewish relationship in the twentieth century. What begins as a reminiscence, a successful connection of personal and historical memory—of past and of present—leaves us with an overwhelming sense of discontinuity. The historical patterns of Jewish culture and society in the Czech lands (as well as in other parts of Central Europe) are shattered by successive political nightmares: Nazism, German occupation, state-sponsored genocide, Communist rule, and Soviet occupation. A story structured around presences and absences, living prototypes, and fond memories of genuine historical choices is in the end populated exclusively with ghosts. None of the Czech-Jewish "types" could be found in Prague five years hence. The Zionists had been transported across continents, their movement long since declared a criminal conspiracy. The heroes of the Czech-Jewish ideal, relegated to irrelevancy and anachronism, no longer spoke. The German option, which in the interwar years was already but a shadow of its former self, was rendered absurd with the entry of the first German troops in 1939. The Jewish Communists, representing the final chapter in the history of Jewish emancipation in the Czech lands, were consumed by the revolution itself. The last sounds they heard were the echoes of nationalist and racialist antisemitism. It could be argued, I think, that modern Jewish history in the Czech lands began with Joseph II and ended with Rudolf Slánský or perhaps with Eduard Goldstücker.

The tale itself, on the other hand, is rich in historical allusion. The lives of its protagonists are of a piece with the Jewish historical experience in the Czech lands. Jiří Langer's pilgrimage to Belz recalls images of another Galician rabbi, Solomon Judah Rapoport, when he was brought to Prague in 1840 to assume the office of chief rabbi. We are reminded of the close ties that existed between Bohemia and Moravia and the world of the Polish *yeshivah,* extending back in time to the life of Ezekiel Landau and beyond. The Prague Zionists' rediscovery of Jewish culture, their search for individual and collective deliverance in an ancestral promise, evoke memories of earlier Jewish messianists of Bohemia, of David Reuveni's mysterious mission to the Holy Roman Emperor, of the writings of the Maharal and of Isaiah Ha-Levi Horowitz. František Langer's stature in the Czech literary pantheon represents a consummation of sorts of the Kapper-Kuh-Nebeský campaign of the 1840s. And in the Bohemian Jewish radicals of 1848, who sought political equality and social advancement under the humanistic banner of democratic revolution, we can discern the antecedents of Jewish involvement in the Czechoslovak Communist movement of our own century. The story is one of connectedness—to the past. One listens, hopefully, for a heartbeat to the future.

Franz Klutschak's Rendition of the Golem Folktale

Panorama des Universums, *vol. 8 [1841]*

Der Golam des Rabbi Löw

Groß war der Weisheit des hohen Rabbi Löw in Prag. Im Talmud war er bewandert, wie wenige Rabbiner der Welt vor und nach ihm, und Astronomie und die Künste der Kabbala betrieb und verstand er, daß auf weit und breit in der Judenschaft wie unter den Christen sein Name genannt wurde, und selbst der Kaiser Rudolph der Zweite sich herabließ und den gelehrten Rabbi Liwa in seinem schlichten Hause in der Judenstadt besuchte. Des hohen Rabbi Löw Name wird noch jetzt von den Kindern Abrahams mit Ehrfurcht und Bewunderung genannt, und wenn die Rabbiner an seinem Hause in der breiten Gasse, auf welchem noch heute ein Löwe eingemeiselt zu sehen ist, vorübergehen, da wünschen sie sich im Geiste des hohen Liwa Gelehrsamkeit und Ruhm, und erzählen den Bochern von seinen Wundern.

Gar viele Wunder werden von ihm berichtet, und in der Altneuschule, dem düstern ehrwürdigen Gebäude, dessen Wände keines Menschen Hand vom Jahrhunderte alten Staube zu reinigen wagen darf, bewahrt man noch den Golam des hohen Löwen. Der Rabbi hatte mittelst seines kabbalistischen Wissens ein menschenartiges Wesen aus Lehm gebildet, ihm Leben eingehaucht und es zum Golam (Diener) der Altneuschul bestimmt, welche bekanntlich die Engel gleich nach Zerstörung des Tempels in Jerusalem erbaut hatten. Aber selbst die Weiseste hat Stunden der Schwäche und Rabbi Löw hatte, als er dem Golam den belebendem Odem einhauchte, ein Gebet herzusagen vergessen, und dadurch erlangte der Golam eine Macht, die selbst die Zaubergewalt des Rabbi überstieg. Glücklicherweise war sich der Golam seiner magischen Kräfte nicht bewußt und der hohe Löw erhielt dadurch Muße, sein Vergehen zu erkennen,

Mehre andre Sagen von Rabbi Löw findet man in meinem Aufsatze: "Der Judenfriedhof und seine Sagen," in *Panorama des Universums* 1838, p. 292, welcher Aufsatz aus dieser Zeitschrift auch in die *Zeitung des Judentums* übergegangen war.

und auf Mittel zu sinnen, wie es wieder gut zu machen. Er ververtigte für jeden der sieben Tagen der Woche einen Talisman, der die Kräfte des Golam in Schranken, und seinen Sinn blos auf das Gute gerichtet hielt, und wenn der Rabbi am Abend beim Beginne des Tages in die Synagoge kam, nahm er den alten Sem (Talisman) aus dem Munde des Golam und vertauschte ihn mit einem neuen.

Der Rabbi hatte eine Tochter, Esther, die er sehr liebte, und der er jeden Sabbath Abend, wenn er aus der Synagoge kam, die Hände auf's Haupt legte und sie aus vollem Herzen mit dem vorgeschriebenen Spruche segnete: "Gott erfreue Dich, wie Sarah, Rebekka, Rachel und Lea." Esther trat eben in die Jahre, wo sie "Godolah" (volljährig) wurde, da ward sie krank. Rabbi Löw nahm zu seinen geheimen wissenschaften Zuflucht, um Esther zu heilen, aber auch hier fand er keine Hilfe, und Esther gesundete nicht, sondern ward immer kränker und kränker. So verfloß Tag auf Tag und Rabbi Löw nahm sich kaum Zeit, in der Synagoge zu heiligen Gebete zu verrichten. Der Freitag nahte seinem Ende, und Esther war noch kränker als zuvor. Da kam der Chassan (Vorsänger) aus der Synagoge und sprach: "Rabbi, wolltest Du heute den Sabbath nicht früher beginnen, denn es ist ein sehr heißer Tag und die Seelen im Fegefeuer bedürfen der Kühlung."[1] Der Rabbi warf einen traurigen blick auf das Bett seiner Tochter, und erwiederte, die Gemeinde solle nur heute ohne ihn den Sabbath beginnen, und der Chassan ging, und Rabbi Löw ließ die Lichter[2] anzunden, und betete daheim neben dem Bette seiner Tochter das Kabala [sic] Schabbat, und die kranke Esther flüsterte es leise mit. Noch waren sie aber nicht bis zum zehnten Verse gekommen, da stürzte der Chassan athemlos und ganz bleich vor Schrecken wieder herein und vermochte vor Grausen kaum aufzuschreien: "Rabbi! Der Golam!"

Bei diesem Schreckensrufe erinnerte sich der Rabbi, daß er heute vergessen, dem Golam einen neuen Talisman in dem Mund zu thun, und daß dieser vielleicht zum Bewußtsein seiner Kraft gelangt sey. Es war nicht ein Augenblick zu verlieren, denn kannte der Golam wirklich seine Macht, so war das ärgste zu befürchten, und er konnte die ganze Stadt verderben. Der Rabbi trat daher zum Bette der kranken, legte ihr segnend die Hände auf's Haupt, empfal sie dem Schutze des Allerhöchsten, nahm einen neuen Talisman und eilte mit diesem in die Altneusynagoge. Als er in das düstere Innere derselben trat, beteten eben die erschrockenen Juden den ersten Psalm, und riefen die Verse desselben um so eifriger und lauter, je mehr Unheil und Spuk der Golam bald hinter ihrem Rücken, bald vor ihnen trieb. Eben als der Meister eintrat, rüttelte der Golam

---

[1] Dem Rabbinerglauben zufolge feiern auch die Seelen im Fegefeuer den Sabbath, und verlassen, sobald die Sabbath-feier in der Synagoge begonnen, den Ort ihrer Qualen, und fliegen dem nächsten Wasser zu, in welchem sie sich so lange baden und abkühlen, bis der Sabbath zu Ende ist. Darum sollen auch die Juden am Sabbath aus keinem Bache trinken oder schöpfen, damit den Seelen nichts [nicht?] von ihrer Kühlung genommen werde.

[2] Die Lichter beim Beginne des Sabbaths zünden die Weiber an, zur Sühne für die Sünde des ersten Weibes, welches durch den Biß in den verbotenen Apfel der Sonne einen Theil ihres Glanzes geraubt hat.

an den Mauern des uralten Gebäudes, daß die Altneusynagoge in ihrem tiefsten Grundfesten erbebte, und die Lade Aron Hakadosch [*sic*], die an der Mauer gegen Morgen stand, umfiel, und die Leuchter niederstürtzten, und die Lichter erloschen, und die Finsterniß herrschte, als nahe der Tag des Weltendes. Als dies der Rabbi Löw ersah, rief er den Psalmenbetenden mit mächtiger Stimme zu: "Haltet inne!" Und sie hielten inne, und gebrochen war dadurch des Golams Macht, denn so lange der erste Psalm nicht zu Ende gebetet ist, hat der Sabbath eigentlich noch nicht begonnen und der Freitagstalisman des Golam kam wieder in Kraft. Der Golam sah plötzlich seine Macht gehemmt und der Rabbi trat mit dem neuen Talisman auf ihn zu, nahm ihm den alten aus dem Munde und that ihm den neuen hinein, und der Golam war dadurch wieder in den gehorsamsten Diener verwandelt, und vermochte kein Unheil weiter zu üben.

Und als nun die Ruhe wieder hergestellt und die Lichter wieder angezündet waren, da priesen die Juden laut die Weisheit des Rabbi Löw, die sie gerettet hat vor dem Verderben, und beteten inbrünstiger als je den ersten Psalm und die Gebete des Sabbaths, und sandten mit solcher Gluth ein Gebet um Genesung der Tochter des hohen Rabbis zu Jehovah, daß Jehovah gerührt den Malach Hamawod [*sic*] (den Würgengel), den er bereits in das Haus des Rabbis gesandt hatte, zurückrief, und der Rabbi, als er seine Wohnung kam, seine Tochter Esther gesund fand.

Das Andenken an diesen Sabbath wird aber in der Altneusynagoge noch immer gefeiert, und so oft am Beginne des Sabbaths der erste Psalm gesprochen wird, brechen die Betenden plötzlich ab, und beginnen erst nach einer viertelstündigen Pause von neuem den Psalm: "Wohl dem, der nicht wandelt im Rathe der Gottlosen, und nicht tritt auf den Weg der Sünder, noch sitzet, wo die Spötter sitzen."

Und der Golam wird noch heute mit mehren anderen Reliquien berühmter Rabbi's aufbewahrt unter dem Dachstuhle der Altneusynagoge.

Notes

Introduction: Language, Community, and Experience

1. Milan Kundera, "The Tragedy of Central Europe," *New York Review of Books*, 26 April 1984; reprinted in *From Stalinism to Pluralism: A Documentary History of Eastern Europe since 1945*, ed. Gale Stokes (New York, 1991), pp. 217–23.

2. Ibid., p. 220.

3. Ibid., pp. 220–21.

4. On the anthropology of experience, see Edward M. Bruner, "The Opening Up of Anthropology," in *Text, Play, and Story: The Construction and Reconstruction of Self and Society*, ed. Edward M. Bruner (Washington, D.C., 1984), pp. 1–16; idem, "Experience and Its Expressions," in *The Anthropology of Experience*, ed. Victor W. Turner and Edward M. Bruner (Urbana and Chicago, 1986), pp. 3–30; and Roger D. Abrahams, "Ordinary and Extraordinary Experience," in ibid., pp. 45–72.

5. John Dewey, *Experience and Nature* (Chicago, 1929), p. 10; also quoted in Abrahams, "Ordinary and Extraordinary Experience," p. 59.

6. Abrahams, "Ordinary and Extraordinary Experience," p. 49. Edward M. Bruner stresses that those who study experience make a critical distinction between *reality* ("what is really out there, whatever that may be"), *experience* ("how that reality presents itself to consciousness"), and *expressions* ("how individual experience is framed and articulated"). Put another way, "the distinction is between life as lived (reality), life as experienced (experience), and life as told (expression)" (Bruner, "Experience and Its Expressions," p. 6).

7. Abrahams, "Ordinary and Extraordinary Experience," p. 50.

8. Ibid., p. 60.

9. See, inter alia: Livia Rothkirchen, "The Jews of Bohemia and Moravia, 1938–1945, in *The Jews of Czechoslovakia*, vol. 3, ed. Avigdor Dagan et al. (Philadelphia, 1984), pp. 3–74; Erich Kulka, "The Annihilation of Czech

Jewry," in ibid., pp. 262–328; Avigdor Dagan, "The Czechoslovak Government in Exile and the Jews," in ibid., pp. 449–95; H.G. Adler, *Theresienstadt 1941–1945: Das Antlitz einer Zwangsgemeinschaft,* 2d rev. ed. (Tübingen, 1960); Vojtěch Mastný, *The Czechs under Nazi Rule: The Failure of National Resistance, 1939–1942* (New York, 1971); Rudolf M. Wlaschek, *Juden in Böhmen: Beiträge zur Geschichte des europäischen Judentums im. 19. und 20. Jahrhundert* (Munich, 1990); Ladislav Lipscher, *Die Juden im slowakischen Staat, 1939–1945* (Munich, 1979); Ruth Bondy, *"Elder of the Jews": Jakob Edelstein of Theresianstadt* (New York, 1989); and *Židé v Protektoratu: Hlásení židovské náboženské obce v roce 1942. Dokumenty* (Jews in the Protectorate: Reports of the Jewish religious community in 1942. Documents) (Prague, 1997).

10. Rothkirchen, "Jews of Bohemia and Moravia," pp. 29, 54.

Chapter 1. Czech Landscape, Habsburg Crown

1. See chapter 5.

2. Alexandr Putík, "On the Topography and Demography of the Prague Jewish Town Prior to the Pogrom of 1389," *Judaica Bohemiae* 30/31 (1994–95): 7.

3. See V. Ryneš, "L'incendie de la synagogue du faubourg du chateau de Prague en 1142 (Contribution à l'histoire des débuts de la ville juive pragoise)," *Judaica Bohemiae* 1 (1965): 9–25.

4. Putík discusses the divergent views concerning the origins of Jewish settlement in the vicinity of the Altneuschul ("Topography and Demography," p. 9). According to Ryneš, this area was settled in the thirteenth century by Jews who had originally lived beneath the Vyšehrad castle. M. Moutvic traces its emergence to the 1140s, when the Prague marketplace was moved to the Old Town Square. And M. Vilímková dates it to sometime between 1159 and 1172, when the main commercial roads of the city were moved to accommodate the construction of a stone bridge across the Vltava. (See Ryneš, "L'incendie"; M. Moutvic, "Dvorce přemsylovských družiníků a vývoj Prahy románského období," (The courts of the Přemyslid entourage and the development of Prague in the Romanesque period) *Pražský Sborník Historický* 22 (1989): 7–32; and M. Vilímková, *The Prague Ghetto* (Prague, 1990), pp. 14, 16, 105–6.)

5. *Encyclopaedia Judaica* (Jerusalem, 1972), 4:1173–74 and 12:296; István Végházi, "The Role of Jewry in the Economic Life of Hungary," in *Hungarian Jewish Studies,* ed. Randolph L. Braham (New York, 1969), p. 41.

6. B. Bretholz, *Quellen zur Geschichte der Juden in Mähren 1067–1411* (Prague, 1935), pp. 2–10; G. Bondy and F. Dvorsky, *Zur Geschichte der Juden in Böhmen, Mähren und Schlesien 906–1620* (Prague, 1906), 1:17–32; Végházi, "The Role of Jewry," p. 42.

7. See Guido Kisch, "Linguistic Conditions among Czechoslovak Jewry," *Historia Judaica* 8 (1946): 19–20, and the bibliographical references listed there.

8. *Seliḥot mi-kol ha-shanah ke-minhag polin, pein, ungarin, u-mehrin* (Penitential prayers for the entire year according to the Polish, Bohemian, Hungarian, and Moravian rite) (London, 1770).

9. *Encyclopaedia Judaica,* 12:296–99. On the expulsion from the royal cities of Moravia, see Alfred Engel, "Die Ausweisung der Juden aus den königlichen Städten Mährens und ihre Folgen," *Jahrbuch der Gesellschaft für Geschichte der Juden in der Čechoslovakischen Republik* (hereafter *JGGJČR*) 2 (1930): 50–96.

10. Jaroslav Klenovský, *Židovské památky Mikulova* (The Jewish monuments of Mikulov) (Mikulov, 1994), pp. 5–28; also I. Z. Kahane, "Nikolsburg," in *ʿArim ve-ʾimahot be-yisraʾel* (Great Jewish communities) (Jerusalem, 1950), 4: 210–313.

11. See Otto Muneles, ed., *Prague Ghetto in the Renaissance Period* (Prague, 1965), passim, as well as the Heřman articles cited in note 12, this chapter.

12. Jan Heřman, "La communauté juive de Prague et sa structure au commencement des temps modernes (la première moitié du 16-e siècle)," *Judaica Bohemiae* 5 (1969): 31–70; idem, "The Conflict between Jewish and Non-Jewish Population in Bohemia before the 1541 Banishment," *Judaica Bohemiae* 6 (1970): 39–54; and Jonathan Israel, *European Jewry in the Age of Mercantilism, 1550–1750.* 3d ed. (London and Portland, Ore., 1998), pp. 31–32.

13. Quoted in George Alter, *Two Renaissance Astronomers: David Gans, Joseph Delmedigo* (Prague, 1958), pp. 31–32.

14. Otto Dov Kulka, "Ha-reka ha-histori shel mishnato ha-leʾumit vehaḥinuḥit shel ha-Maharal mi-Prag" (The historical background of the national and educational teachings of Rabbi Judah Löw ben Bezalel of Prague), *Zion* (jubilee volume) 50 (1985): 277–320.

15. On the life, career, and educational philosophy of Judah Löw ben Bezalel, see Frederic Thieberger, *The Great Rabbi Loew of Prague: His Life and Work and the Legend of the Golem* (London, 1955); A. F. Kleinberger, *Ha-maḥshava ha-pedagogit shel ha-Maharal mi-Prag* (The pedagogical thought of the Maharal of Prague) (Jerusalem, 1962); Vladimír Sadek, "Rabbi Loew—sa vie, héritage pédagogique et sa légende," *Judaica Bohemiae* 15 (1979), 27–41; and Byron Sherwin, *Mystical Theology and Social Dissent: The Life and Works of Judah Loew of Prague* (Rutherford and London, 1982).

16. See Alexandr Putík, "The Origin of the Symbols of the Prague Jewish Town, the Banner of the Old-New Synagogue, David's Shield, and the 'Swedish' Hat," *Judaica Bohemiae* 29 (1993): 10–11.

17. Israel, *European Jewry,* p. 40; *Encyclopaedia Judaica,* 11:1262–63.

18. Israel, *European Jewry,* pp. 72–74; Anna Drabek, "Die Juden in den böhmischen Ländern zur Zeit des landesfürstlichen Absolutismus," in *Die Juden in den böhmischen Ländern,* ed. Ferdinand Seibt (Munich and Vienna, 1983), pp. 124–25.

19. Drabek, "Die Juden in den böhmischen Ländern," p. 127.

20. See, for example, Käthe Spiegel, "Die Prager Juden zur Zeit des dreissigjährigen Krieges," in *Die Juden in Prag: Bilder aus ihrer tausendjährigen Geschichte,* ed. S. Steinherz (Prague, 1927), pp. 122–24.

21. Putík, "Symbols of the Prague Jewish Town," pp. 4–37.

22. Ibid., p. 13.

23. Drabek, "Die Juden in den böhmischen Ländern," pp. 126–27.

24. See Jaroslav Prokeš, "Der Antisemitismus der Behörden und das Prager Ghetto," *JGGJČR* 1 (1929): passim, but esp. 199–262.

25. Jan Heřman puts the Jewish population of Prague in 1702 at 11,618. This would place Prague third among Jewish communities of the world. (Amsterdam had about 12,000 Jews at the time, and Salonika—certainly the giant among world Jewries—had between 25,000 and 30,000 Jewish inhabitants.) By 1726 the Jewish population of Prague stood at only 10,500, as much of the community had been killed by plague. If 8,541 represented the total number of Jewish families in Bohemia, one might safely conclude that some 32,000 Jews resided in the province outside of Prague. The Jewish population of Moravia at the time probably stood at about 25,500. (On these and other imprecise figures, see Jan Heřman, "The Evolution of the Jewish Population of Bohemia and Moravia, 1754–1953," *Papers in Jewish Demography 1973* [Jerusalem, 1977], pp. 255–65; idem, "The Evolution of the Jewish Population in Prague, 1869–1939," *Papers in Jewish Demography 1977* [Jerusalem, 1980], pp. 53–67; Ruth Kestenberg-Gladstein, *Neuere Geschichte der Juden in den böhmischen Ländern. Erster Teil: Das Zeitalter der Aufklärung, 1780–1830* [Tübingen, 1969], pp. 1–3, 8–12; and Wilfried Brosche, "Das Ghetto von Prag," in *Die Juden in den böhmischen Ländern*, ed. Ferdinand Seibt [Munich and Vienna, 1983], pp. 117–19.)

26. See Ruth Kestenberg-Gladstein, "Mifkad yehudei Beim she-miḥuẓ le-Prag bi-shnat 1724" (The census of Jews outside of Prague in the year 1724), *Zion* 9 (1944): 1–26; Jaroslav Prokeš, "Die Prager Judenkonskription vom Jahre 1729," *JGGJČR* 4 (1932): 297–331; and "Statistische Tabellen über alle israelitische Gemeinden, Synagogen, Schulen und Rabbinate in Böhmen," in *Die Notablenversammlung der Israeliten Böhmens in Prag*, ed. Albert Kohn (Vienna, 1852), pp. 383–414.

27. *Encyclopaedia Judaica* 14:1679; Evyatar Friesel, ed., *Atlas of Modern Jewish History* (New York, 1990), pp. 34–35.

28. On the War of the Austrian Succession and the various occupations of Prague, see Charles Ingrao, *The Habsburg Monarchy, 1618–1815* (Cambridge, 1994), pp. 150–59. On the temporary expulsion, see Josef Bergl, "Das Exil der Prager Judenschaft von 1745–1748," *JGGJČR* 1 (1929): 263–331; Gerson Wolf, *Die Vertreibung der Juden aus Böhmen im Jahre 1744 und deren Rückkehr im Jahre 1748* (Leipzig, 1869); Tomáš Pěkný, *Historie Židů v Čechách a na Moravě* (The history of the Jews in Bohemia and Moravia) (Prague, 1993), pp. 79–85; and Drabek, "Die Juden in den böhmischen Ländern," pp. 131–35.

29. Tobiaš Jakobovits, "Das Prager und Böhmische Landesrabbinat Ende des siebzehnten und Anfang des achtzehnten Jahrhunderts," *JGGJČR* 5 (1933): 79–136.

30. On Jewish autonomy in Moravia and Bohemia, see Salo Baron, *The Jewish Community* (Philadelphia, 1945), 1:338–39; and Drabek, "Die Juden in den böhmischen Ländern," pp. 135–42.

31. The so-called *Takkanot ha-medinah* of Rabbi Moses Lwów (Lemberger, 1754–58). The German translation of the *Takkanot medinat Mehrin* was published by Gerson Wolf in 1880 as *Die ältesten Statuten der jüdischen Gemeinden in Mähren*. In 1952 Israel Halperin published a critical edition of the *Takkanot* in the original Hebrew.

32. On Jewish emancipation as a multifaceted process, see Jacob Katz, *Out of the Ghetto: The Social Background of Jewish Emancipation, 1770–1830* (Cam-

bridge, Mass., 1973); also Pierre Birnbaum and Ira Katznelson, eds., *Paths of Emancipation: Jews, States, and Citizenship* (Princeton, 1995). For discussions of this process within the Habsburg monarchy, see Wolfgang Häusler, "Toleranz, Emanzipation und Antisemitismus: Das österreichische Judentum des bürgerlichen Zeitalters (1782–1918)," in *Das österreichische Judentum: Voraussetzungen und Geschichte,* ed. Nikolaus Vielmetti (Vienna and Munich, 1974); and Wolfdieter Bihl, "Die Juden," in *Die Habsburgermonarchie, 1848–1918,* ed. Adam Wandruszka and Peter Urbanitsch, vol. 3, *Die Völker des Reichs* (Vienna, 1980), pp. 890–96.

33. A. F. Příbram, ed., *Urkunden und Akten zur Geschichte der Juden in Wien,* (Vienna, 1918), 1:476 (my translation). On the various edicts of toleration and their impact, see chapter 2; also Michael Silber, "The Historical Experience of German Jewry and Its Impact on the Haskalah and Reform in Hungary," in *Toward Modernity: The European Jewish Model,* ed. Jacob Katz (New Brunswick, N.J., 1987), pp. 107–57; idem, "The Enlightened Absolutist State and the Transformation of Jewish Society: Tradition in Crisis?" (paper presented at the conference "Tradition and Crisis Revisited," Harvard University, 1988); and Ludvík Singer, "Zur Geschichte der Toleranzpatente in den Sudetenländern," *JGGJČR* 5 (1933): 231–311.

34. Příbram, *Urkunden,* pp. 494–500; Katz, *Out of the Ghetto,* pp. 161–64. The census of 1724 and 1729, dealing with the Jews of Bohemia and of Prague respectively, indicated that over 27 percent of Prague Jews and 19 percent of Bohemian Jews worked as artisans; some 50 percent of Prague Jews and 52 percent of Bohemian Jews were listed as involved in trade (Kestenberg-Gladstein, *Neuere Geschichte,* p. 12).

35. Silber, "The Enlightened Absolutist State and the Transformation of Jewish Society"; and idem, "The Historical Experience of German Jewry," p. 121.

36. On the occasion of *Shabbat ha-gadol* 1782, which fell between the issuance of the *Toleranzpatent* and the opening of the Prague *Normalschule,* Landau delivered a famous sermon. Referring to Wessely's program for educational reform he remarked: "I have seen a world turned upside down.... From our nation has arisen a wicked and arrogant man for whom the Torah is not worth anything, for whom profane subjects are better than the study of Torah.... He who fears the Lord, he truly understands [*'einav be-rosho*]; he is able to hold fast to both matters [sacred and profane]; but Torah is central" (Ezekiel Landau, *Derushei ha-Ẓelaḥ* (Sermons) [Warsaw, 1886; Jerusalem, 1966], fol. 53a.)

37. This theme is developed more fully in chapter 2.

38. *Encyclopaedia Judaica* 15:75–79; Hugo Stransky, "The Religious Life in Slovakia and Subcarpathian Ruthenia," in *The Jews of Czechoslovakia* (Philadelphia, 1971), 2:367–69.

39. See, for example, David Kuh, "Ein Wort an Juden und Slaven," *Allgemeine Zeitung des Judentums,* 1 April, 8 April, and 15 April 1844. On the Czech-Jewish rapprochement in the 1840s see chapter 3; also Michael Riff, "Jüdische Schriftsteller und das Dilemma der Assimilation im böhmischen Vormärz," in *Juden im Vormärz und in der Revolution von 1848,* ed. W. Grab and J. H. Schoep (Stuttgart and Bonn, 1983), pp. 58–82.

40. *Der Orient* 9 July 1844.

41. Adapted from Guido Kisch, *In Search of Freedom: A History of American Jews from Czechoslovakia* (London, 1949), pp. 36–38 and 213–14; and Oskar Donath, *Siegfried Kappers Leben und Wirken* (Berlin, 1909), p. 434.

42. On this and other modern transformations, see Hillel J. Kieval, *The Making of Czech Jewry: National Conflict and Jewish Society in Bohemia, 1870–1918* (New York and Oxford, 1988).

43. Ibid., pp. 198–203.

44. Bureau für Statistik der Juden, *Die Juden in Österreich* (Berlin, 1908), p. 109.

45. Jacob Toury, "Jewish Townships in the German-Speaking Parts of the Austrian Empire—before and after the Revolution of 1848/49," *Leo Baeck Institute Yearbook* 26 (1981): 55–72.

46. In Moravia: 47.84 percent chose the Jewish nationality; 15.71 percent Czechoslovak; and 34.85 percent German. In Bohemia: 14.6 percent chose the Jewish nationality; 49.49 percent Czechoslovak; and 34.63 percent German. That is to say, Jewish nationalism enjoyed the same strength among the Jews of Moravia as Czech nationalism did among the Jews of Bohemia. The Slovak figures are also informative. Here religious traditionalism provided the bridge to a modern national identity: 54.28 percent of the Jews chose the Jewish nationality; 22.27 percent Czechoslovak; 6.68 percent German; and 16.49 percent Hungarian. See Bruno Blau, "Nationality among Czechoslovak Jewry," *Historia Judaica* 10 (1948): 147–54; and František Friedmann, *Einige Zahlen über die tschechoslowakischen Juden* (Prague, 1933), p. 23.

47. On the Jewish context of Kafka's life, see Kieval, *Making of Czech Jewry*, pp. 99–203 passim; Ernst Pawel, *The Nightmare of Reason: A Life of Franz Kafka* (New York, 1984); and Ritchie Robertson, *Kafka: Judaism, Politics, and Literature* (Oxford, 1985).

Chapter 2. Caution's Progress

1. Robin Okey, *Eastern Europe, 1740–1980: Feudalism to Communism* (Minneapolis, 1982), pp. 9–11.

2. For a general discussion of the problems of modernization in East Central Europe see N. T. Gross, "The Habsburg Monarchy, 1750–1914," in *Fontana Economic History of Europe*, ed. Carlo M. Cipolla, vol. 4, *The Emergence of Industrial Societies* (New York, 1976), pt. 1, pp. 228–78; and Okey, *Eastern Europe*, passim.

3. Naphtali Herz Wessely, *Divrei shalom ve-'emet* (Words of peace and truth) (Berlin, 1782). For the reaction of traditionalists to the pamphlet, see Alexander Altmann, *Moses Mendelssohn: A Biographical Study* (Philadelphia and Tuscaloosa, 1973), pp. 474–89. Among the rabbis who openly condemned the dangers of the *haskalah* following the appearance of Wessely's work were Ezekiel Landau of Prague (see below in chapter), David Tevele of Lissa, Joseph Hazaddik of Posen, and Pinhas Halevi Horowitz of Frankfurt am Main.

4. *Encyclopaedia Judaica*, 4:1177; Kestenberg-Gladstein, *Neuere Geschichte*, pp. 1–4. On the demographic configuration of German Jewry in the eighteenth century, see Azriel Shoḥet, *'Im ḥilufei tekufot* (Beginnings of the *haskalah* among German Jewry) (Jerusalem, 1960), pp. 20–21. For Hungary, see Péter Hanák, "Jews and the Modernization of Commerce in Hungary, 1760–1918," in *Jews in the Hungarian Economy 1760–1945*, ed. Michael K. Silber (Jerusalem, 1992), pp. 23–39; and László Katus, "The Occupational Structure of Hungarian Jewry in the Eighteenth and Twentieth Centuries," in ibid., pp. 92–105.

In contrast to the approximately eight hundred localities in Bohemia in which Jews lived in the early eighteenth century, Moravian Jewry was distributed among fifty-two communities of "medium" size (Kestenberg-Gladstein, "Mifkad yehudei Beim."

5. J. Prokeš, "Antisemitismus der Behörden," pp. 42–43; Kestenberg-Gladstein, *Neuere Geschichte*, pp. 29–30.

6. *Encyclopaedia Judaica*, 4:1177; Kestenberg-Gladstein, "Mifkad yehudei Beim."

7. See *Encyclopaedia Judaica*, 4:1177; and Kestenberg-Gladstein, *Neuere Geschichte*, pp. 1–3, 8–12. Kestenberg-Gladstein feels that the Jewish population of Bohemia in 1754 stood closer to 40,000.

8. "Statistische Tabellen über alle israelitischen Gemeinden, Synagogen, Schulen und Rabbinate in Böhmen."

9. A. Klíma, "Industrial Development in Bohemia, 1648–1781," *Past and Present* 11 (April 1957): 87–97; H. Freudenberger, "Industrialization in Bohemia and Moravia in the Eighteenth Century," *Journal of Central European Affairs* 19 (1960): 347–56.

10. Klíma, "Industrial Development," pp. 89–91.

11. A. Klíma, "Mercantilism in the Habsburg Monarchy—with special reference to the Bohemian Lands," *Historica* 11 (1965): 95–119; Freudenberger, "Industrialization"; and Gross, "Habsburg Monarchy."

12. Klíma, "Mercantilism"; Gross, "Habsburg Monarchy," pp. 237–61.

13. Gross, "Habsburg Monarchy"; see also Knut Borchardt, "Germany 1700-1914," in *The Fontana Economic History of Europe*, ed. Carlo M. Cipolla, vol. 4, *The Emergence of Industrial Societies* (New York, 1976), pt. 1, pp. 76–160.

14. Joseph von Wertheimer, *Die Juden in Österreich* (Leipzig, 1842), 1:137; "Ein Despot wie der Frühling, der des Winters Eis zerbricht."

15. P. Bernard, "Joseph II and the Jews: The Making of the Toleration Patent of 1782," *Austrian History Yearbook* 4/5 (1970); Katz, *Out of the Ghetto*, pp. 161–67. See also R. J. Kerner, *Bohemia in the Eighteenth Century* (New York, 1969), passim.

16. In a Resolution distributed by the emperor on 1 October 1781, he assured the Staatsrat: "Meine Absicht gehet keineswegs dahin, die Jüdische Nation in den Erblanden mehr auszubreiten oder da, wo sie nicht toleriert ist, neu einzuführen, sondern nur, da wo sie ist und in der Maass, wie sie als tolerirt bestehet, dem Staate nützlich zu machen" (Příbram, *Urkunden* 1:137).

17. Letter of Joseph II to Count Blümegen, 13 May 1781 (Příbram, *Urkunden*, p. 440). Concerning both Joseph's original intentions and the ultimate

effects of the law, see Singer, "Toleranzpatent"; Bernard, "Joseph II and the Jews"; and Katz, *Out of the Ghetto*, pp. 161–67. A text of the Edict for the Austrian hereditary lands is found in Příbram, *Urkunden*, 1:494–500.

18. Kestenberg-Gladstein, *Neuere Geschichte*, pp. 96–105; Příbram, *Urkunden*, pp. 494–97; Singer, "Toleranzpatent," pp. 258–61.

19. Kestenberg-Gladstein, *Neuere Geschichte*, pp. 66–85; Ludvík Singer, "Zur Geschichte der Juden in Böhmen in den letzten Jahren Josefs II und unter Leopold II," *JGGJČR* 6 (1934): 197–99.

20. Kestenberg-Gladstein's magisterial work *Neuere Geschichte der Juden* stands as the only study to date of the Prague *haskalah*. Outside of this there are the primary sources themselves: the works of such figures as Baruch Jeitteles, Juda Jeitteles, Israel Landau, M. I. Landau, Solomon Löwisohn, Peter Beer, Herz Homberg, and Solomon Judah Rapoport, as well as the sermonic writings of Ezekiel Landau and Eleazar Fleckeles.

21. See Kestenberg-Gladstein, *Neuere Geschichte*, pp. 115–331. The four phases divide chronologically as follows: (1) 1780s; (2) 1790s; (3) 1800–1820; and (4) 1820s.

22. The major Bohemian contributor to *Ha-me'asef* during this period was Baruch Jeitteles (1762–1813), son of the physician and proto-*maskil* Jonas Jeitteles (1735–1806). Subscribers to the *Bi'ur* from Austria and Bohemia following the publication of Mendelssohn's 1778 *Prospectus* numbered fifty-seven (Altmann, *Mendelssohn*, p. 377).

23. The specific incident over which the two groups split is discussed later.

24. The clearest sign of Prague's original course arose in 1802 with the establishment of the Gesellschaft der jungen Hebräer and the publication of the *Jüdisch-deutsche Monatschrift*. Chief among the contributors to the third and fourth stages of the Prague *haskalah* were Ignaz and Juda Jeitteles, M. I. Landau, and S. Löwisohn.

25. Kestenberg-Gladstein, *Neuere Geschichte*, pp. 146–69, 191–236. See also Kestenberg-Gladstein, "Ofiyah ha-le'umi shel haskalat Prag" (The national character of the Prague *haskalah*), *Molad* 23 (1965): 221–33.

26. This, for example, is Kestenberg-Gladstein's view. She stresses throughout the national and conservative character of the Prague *haskalah* and at one point states bluntly, "Die Eigentümlichkeit des Prager Weges ist also der *rationale* Aspekt" (*Neuere Geschichte*, p. 200; emphasis in the original).

27. Landau, *Derushei ha-Zelaḥ*, fols. 53a–54a.

28. Ibid., fol. 53a.

29. Ibid.

30. Ibid., fol. 53b.

31. From the Haskama to Sussmann Glogau's Pentateuch translation, reproduced in *Hame'asef* (1786), pp. 142–44; and in English translation in Altmann, *Mendelssohn*, pp. 382–83. A number of Prague *maskilim*, including Avigdor Levi and Juda Jeitteles, testified that Landau resisted clamorings for legal action against Mendelssohn and for the issuance of a ban against the *Bi'ur*. He did, nevertheless, rule that Mendelssohn's Pentateuch could not be introduced into the curriculum of the Prague Jewish School (Altmann, *Mendelssohn*, pp. 396–98).

32. Baruch Jeitteles, who had been educated at Landau's *yeshivah,* apparently ran away to Berlin at some point in his young adult life, only to return and achieve a reconciliation with both father and teacher. (This point is alluded to in Juda Jeitteles' biography of his father Jonas, *B'nei ha-ne'urim* [The sons of youth] [Prague, 1821], pp. 1–86). Similarly, Ezekiel Landau may have been inclined not to issue a formal ban on Mendelssohn's work because at least one of Landau's sons, Samuel, was a subscriber to the *Bi'ur* as well as, later, to *Ha-me'asef.*

33. Jeitteles' retort to *Ha-me'asef* appeared in the work *Ha'orev* (The one who lies in wait) (Salonika, 1795), published under the pseudonym Pinhas Hananya Argosi de Silva. His attack on the Prague Frankists appeared in the satirical work *Siḥa bein shenat 5560 u-vein 5561* (Dialogue between the years 5560 and 5561) (Prague, 1800). Apparently the autumn of 1800 had seen a number of open conflicts between Frankists and their adversaries in Prague, culminating in the brief imprisonment of Eleazar Fleckeles and Samuel Landau. See Kestenberg-Gladstein, *Neuere Geschichte,* pp. 133–46, 173–91.

34. In 1793 Israel Landau issued a critical edition, with commentary, of Abraham Farissol (ca. 1451–1525), *Iggeret 'orḥot 'olam* (Epistle on the ways of the world). Landau attempted to further the cause of popular education in the fundamentals of Judaism with his own 1798 work, *Ḥok le-Yisrael* (A law unto Israel), a compilation of the positive and negative commandments of the Hebrew Bible translated into the German-Jewish dialect of Bohemia.

35. *Encyclopaedia Judaica,* 10:1389–90.

36. Kestenberg-Gladstein, *Neuere Geschichte,* p. 126.

37. *Encyclopaedia Judaica* 10:1391 (on Eliezer Landau [1778–1831]). On M. I. Landau (1788–1852) see Kestenberg-Gladstein, *Neuere Geschichte,* pp. 249–53, 315–16.

38. On the Landau family in Opatów, see Gershon David Hundert, *The Jews in a Polish Private Town: The Case of Opatów in the Eighteenth Century* (Baltimore, 1992), pp. 116–33.

39. On the appointment of Solomon Judah Rapoport, see David Kaufmann, ed., *Das Centenarium S.J.L. Rapoport's: Festgabe der "Österreichischen Wochenschrift"* (Vienna, 1890).

40. The *Jüdisch-deutsche Monatschrift* published six issues during the winter, spring, and summer of 1802 (Adar through Tamuz), totaling less than two hundred pages.

41. *Sulamith: Eine Zeitschrift zur Beförderung der Kultur und Humanität unter der jüdischen Nation,* ed. D. Fraenkel and J. Wolf (Leipzig, 1806; Dessau, 1807; etc.).

42. *Sulamith* (1806), p. 164; quoted in M. Meyer, *The Origins of the Modern Jew: Jewish Identity and European Culture in Germany, 1749–1824* (Detroit, 1967), p. 120.

43. See note 34, this chapter.

44. Kestenberg-Gladstein, *Neuere Geschichte,* pp. 195–209, 222–34.

45. Both Jewish and non-Jewish sources from medieval times down to the end of the eighteenth century employ terminology that today rings with nationalist overtones. For example, the universities of medieval Europe were divided into many "nations," and rabbinic literature continually distinguished be-

tween the "nation of Israel" and the "nations of the world." Moreover, most government authorities, whatever their relationship to the Enlightenment, quite simply held the Jews to be a nation and referred to them as such down to the end of the century.

46. "Shalmei todah" (Offerings of thanks), the second foreword to the Landau edition of Farissol's work, printed in Kestenberg-Gladstein, *Neuere Geschichte*, p. 151.

47. The historical entries of the *Jüdisch-deutsche Monatschrift* were included under the general heading "Biographien grosser Männer unserer Nation," but this turns out to be a direct borrowing of phraseology found in 1784 in *Hame'asef* (Kestenberg-Gladstein, *Neuere Geschichte*, p. 208). In these essays the *gedolei 'am Yisrael* were invoked simply to demonstrate that models of "virtue" could be found in the Jewish past. Contributions like Ignaz Jeitteles' "Die Macht der Tugend," *Sulamith* (1806), and the biography of Josephus Flavius, which appeared in the second number of the *Monatschrift*, served essentially the same purpose: to demonstrate that both the sources of Judaism and the history of the Jews could produce examples of virtue, beauty, and truth worthy of any classical or enlightened standard.

48. Quoted in Kestenberg-Gladstein, *Neuere Geschichte*, p. 196, emphasis in the original.

49. Naphtali Herz Wesseley is an often-cited example of this phenomenon. His pamphlet *Divrei shalom ve-'emet* appeared shortly after the issuance of the *Toleranzpatent* and included a plea for the Jewish communities of the monarchy to put the provisions of Joseph's educational reforms into place. See Katz, *Out of the Ghetto*, pp. 66–69.

50. Wenzel Hammer, *Geschichte der Volksschule Böhmens von der ältesten Zeit bis zum Jahre 1870* (Warnsdorf, 1904), pp. 79–81.

51. Hammer, *Geschichste*, p. 82, also Eduard Winter, *Ferdinand Kindermann Ritter von Schulstein* (Augsburg, 1926), pp. 43–44. On general educational reform during the period of enlightened absolutism see idem, *Barock, Absolutismus und Aufklärung in der Donaumonarchie* (Vienna, 1971), pp. 171–77, 202–10.

52. Singer, "Toleranzpatent," pp. 264–65; see also Moses Wiener, *Nachricht von dem Ursprunge und Fortgange der deutschen jüdischen Hauptschule zu Prag* (Prague, 1785).

53. Altmann, *Mendelssohn*, p. 475; Winter, *Kindermann*, passim; and idem, *Barock*, pp. 202–10.

54. Singer, "Toleranzpatent," pp. 267–68.

55. Winter, *Kindermann*, p. 132; Singer, "Toleranzpatent," pp. 264–66, 269–70.

56. Singer, "Toleranzpatent," p. 267; Wiener, *Nachricht*.

57. Singer, "Toleranzpatent," p. 267; Kestenberg-Gladstein, *Neuere Geschichte*, pp. 46–52.

58. Altmann, *Mendelssohn*, pp. 474–76; Singer, "Toleranzpatent," p. 267.

59. Ferdinand Kindermann to Moses Mendelssohn, 5 January 1783 (Depositum Robert von Mendelssohn, C II, nQ 34), translated and published in Altmann, *Mendelssohn*, pp. 475–76.

60. Altmann, *Mendelssohn,* p. 488; Kestenberg-Gladstein, *Neuere Geschichte,* pp. 54–56.

Some communities within the Habsburg monarchy proved to be not as willing as Prague to enact the educational provisions of Joseph II's edict. Vienna and Pressburg (Bratislava/Pozsony) provide interesting contrasts, the former as an example of a progressive but structurally weak community, the latter representing steadfast traditionalism. Leaders of the Pressburg community apparently informed the emperor in 1784 that they found it difficult to reconcile themselves to the new school system. Joseph II is reported to have replied to the Jewish leaders of Pressburg, "Gehts nur nach Prag; dort bin ich recht wohl mit der Schule zufrieden." (Winter, *Kindermann,* p. 167.)

In Vienna Jews reacted with resentment, not because of their ties to traditional religious values, but rather as an expression of their political impatience. Since the seventeenth-century expulsion, Viennese Jews had been denied the right to establish a legal community or even to erect a synagogue, and now they were being asked to establish schools at their own expense. Hence they responded coolly and ultimately refused.

A statement from community leaders cited a number of interesting reasons for their refusal. One of these was that well-to-do Jews already employed private tutors for their children (apparently for secular as well as traditional subjects). Another was that the children of less wealthy Jews were simply attending German *Normalschulen* and had already been provided with the Prague reader for the primary schools. By refusing to establish their own schools the Viennese Jews may have hoped to exert leverage for the attainment of a legal corporate status. They may also have felt that separate Jewish schools would only act as an impediment to their ultimate aim of full integration into Viennese culture and society.

Trieste, on the other hand—the Habsburg monarchy's port city on the Adriatic—reflected the broad cultural outlook of Italian Jewry. Its Jewish community demonstrated just as much enthusiasm as that of Prague, with none of the latter's conservatism. Trieste's Jewish leaders, with the blessing of the chief rabbi, Isacco Formiggini, informed the governor of the province, Count Zinzendorf, of the Jewish community's readiness to establish a primary school and asked his advice on the procurement of textbooks "for religious and moral instruction." Later the Jews of Trieste, as well as a number of Italian rabbis, proved to be important supporters of Naphtali Herz Wessely and his educational manifesto. (On Vienna, see Altmann, *Mendelssohn,* pp. 476–77; on Pressburg, see Kindermann to Oberamtsverwalter J. Braum in Schurz, undated, August/September 1784 or 85 [repr. in Winter, *Kindermann,* pp, 166–68]; and on Trieste, Lois C. Dubin, "Trieste and Berlin: The Italian Role in the Cultural Politics of the Haskalah," in *Toward Modernity: The European Jewish Model,* ed. Jacob Katz [New Brunswick, N.J., 1987], pp. 189–224.)

61. Singer, "Toleranzpatent," p. 264.

62. Kestenberg-Gladstein, *Neuere Geschichte,* pp. 34–65, passim.

63. Ibid., pp. 62–65. From 1814 to 1838 two men, both Christians, occupied the position of headmaster: Anton Raaz and Johann Wanniczek.

64. Singer, "Toleranzpatent," p. 267; Winter, *Barock,* pp. 204–5. The *maskil* Peter Beer (ca. 1758–1838), who had attended the Prague and Pressburg *yeshivot,*

was one of the first Jews to be trained as a teacher under the new program. He taught at his native Nový Bydžov from 1785 until his call to Prague in 1811.

65. I. Böhm, *Historische Nachricht von der Enstehungsart und der Verbreitung des Normalinstituts in Böhmen* (Prague, 1784); J. A. Riegger, *Materialien zur alten und neuen Statistik von Böhmen*, vol. 7, *Zustand der Normal- Bürger- und Landschulen in Böhmen* (Prague, 1787), pp. 43 ff., cited in Singer, "Toleranzpatent," pp. 269–70.

66. Johann Wanniczek, *Geschichte der Prager Haupt- Trivial- und Mädchenschule der Israeliten* (Prague, 1832).

67. Herz Klaber, *Beschreibung der am 30. mai gehaltenenen fünfzigjährigen Jubelfeyer der israel. deutschen Hauptschule in Prag, nebst einer Geschichte dieser Schule* (Prague, 1833).

68. Singer, "Toleranzpatent," p. 269.

69. Ibid., p. 270.

70. Kestenberg-Gladstein, *Neuere Geschichte*, pp. 47–49.

71. Klaber, *Beschreibung*, pp. 63 ff.

72. Ibid., p. 64.

73. Ibid., pp. 68–72.

74. Herz Homberg, *Bnei Zion: Ein religiös-moralisches Lehrburch für die Jugend israelitischer Nation* (Vienna, 1812). See Kestenberg-Gladstein, *Neuere Geschichte*, pp. 47–48; and Klaber, *Beschreibung*, pp. 65–67.

75. Klaber, *Beschreibung*, pp. 69–75.

76. Kestenberg-Gladstein, *Neuere Geschichte*, p. 48; cf. tables in Wanniczek, *Geschichte*.

77. Figures provided by ibid., p. 49.

78. If one assumes that the 10,000 Jews in the city were divided roughly among 2,000 families and that each family had school-age children for approximately ten years, then in any given year only one quarter of the families (i.e., 500) contributed to the pool of potential students (Wanniczek's tables extend over a period of forty years). Moreover, in any given year each family would have had no more than two children of school age. Thus the total pool could not have been much higher than 1,000 per year. (My thanks to Michael Silber for reviewing these figures with me.)

79. See Kestenberg-Gladstein, *Neuere Geschichte*, pp. 49–50; Altmann, *Mendelssohn*, p. 477.

80. Klaber, *Beschreibung*, p. 64.

81. Peter Beer, *Sefer toledot Yisrael, kolel sippur kol hakorot 'asher kar'u ... 'im rimzei midot tovot u-musar haskel ... le-to'elet ḥinukh Benei Yisrael* (History of Israel, including the story of all that happened ... with allusions to virtue and morality ... for the education of Jewish children) (Vienna, 1810).

82. Klaber, *Beschreibung*, p. 68.

83. See, for example, Ezekiel Landau's sermon for the Ten Days of Repentance in 1782 or 1783, in *Derushei ha-Ẓelaḥ*, fol. 42a–42b. On Jewish education in turn-of-the-century Prague, see Shmuel Hugo Bergman [Hugo Bergmann] "Petaḥ Davar" (Foreword) in *Yahadut Tshekhoslovakia* (Czechoslovak Jewry) (Jerusalem, 1969), pp. 7–10.

84. The legal validity of the ghetto was formally abolished in 1848, and Jews were permitted to reside in all areas of the Crown lands. Franz Josef's Constitutional Edict of 1849 granted Jews equal status with Christians under law. After 1859, the last barriers to free economic activity and association were torn down, and the government also confirmed the right of Jews to own land. Full political emancipation was proclaimed only in 1867. See Bihl, "Die Juden," pp. 890–96.

85. On the Jewish role in German ethnic politics and social life in Prague, see Gary B. Cohen, *The Politics of Ethnic Survival: Germans in Prague, 1861–1914* (Princeton, 1981).

Chapter 3. The Social Vision of Bohemian Jews

1. Other stepping stones toward legal emancipation included the lifting of the prohibition on Jewish ownership of landed property (1841), and Franz Josef's Constitutional Edict of 1849, which granted Jews equality with Christians under law. For a brief survey, see chapter 1.

2. On the politics of nationalism in the Habsburg monarchy, see generally Adam Wandruszka and Peter Urbanitsch, eds., *Die Habsburgermonarchie, 1848–1918*, vol 3, *Die Völker des Reichs* (Vienna, 1980); Robert A. Kann, *The Multinational Empire, 1848–1918*, 2 vols. (New York, 1950); and *Austrian History Yearbook* 3 (1967).

3. See Paul Mendes-Flohr, "The Study of the Jewish Intellectual: Some Methodological Proposals," in *Essays in Modern Jewish History*, ed. Frances Malino and Phyllis Cohen Albert (Rutherford, N.J., 1982), pp. 142–72; repr. in Mendes-Flohr, *Divided Passions: Jewish Intellectuals and the Experience of Modernity* (Detroit, 1991), pp. 23–53; also Georg Simmel, "The Stranger," in *The Sociology of Georg Simmel*, trans. and ed. Kurt H. Wolff (New York, 1950), pp. 403–8; and J. P. Nettl, "Ideas, Intellectuals, and Structures of Dissent," in *On Intellectuals: Theoretical Studies, Case Studies*, ed. Philip Rieff (Garden City, N.Y., 1969).

4. On the system of German-Jewish primary schools after 1815, see Wanniczek, *Geschichte;* also Kestenberg-Gladstein, *Neuere Geschichte;* and chapter 2.

5. The main biographical sources consulted were the following:

For Hartmann: Constant von Wurzbach, *Biographisches Lexikon des Kaiserthums Österreich* (Vienna, 1856–91), 8:4–11; Heribert Sturm, ed., *Biographisches Lexikon zur Geschichte der böhmischen Länder* (Vienna, 1975–84), 1:544; S. Wininger, *Grosse jüdische Nationalbiographie* (Czernowitz, 1925–36), 3:8–10; and Otto Wittner, *Moritz Hartmanns Jugend* (Vienna, 1903).

For Heller: Wurzbach, *Lexikon Österreich*, 8:272–75; Sturm, *Lexikon der böhmischen Länder,* 1:589.

For Hock: David Kaufmann, introduction to *Die Familien Prags nach den Epitaphien des alten jüdischen Friedhofs in Prag*, by Simon Hock (Pressburg, 1892), pp. 1–36; and Kisch, *In Search of Freedom*, pp. 43, 270–71, 272–73.

For Kapper: Donath, *Siegfried Kappers Leben und Wirken;* idem, "Siegfried Kapper," *JGGJČR* 6 (1934): 323–442; Wurzbach, *Lexikon Österreich*, 10:451–52; and Sturm, *Lexikon der böhmischen Länder,* 2:102.

For Kompert: Stefan Hock, "Komperts Leben und Schaffen," in *Sämtliche Werke,* by Leopold Kompert (Leipzig, 1906), 1:v–lviii; Wilma Iggers, "Leopold Kompert, Romancier of the Bohemian Ghetto," *Modern Austrian Literature* 6 (1973): 117–38; Wurzbach, *Lexikon Österreich,* 12:404–10; Wininger, *National-biographie,* 3:506–7; and Sturm, *Lexikon der böhmischen Länder,* 2:238.

For Kuh: Wurzbach, *Lexikon Österreich,* 13:340; *Allgemeine Zeitung des Judentums,* 11 February 1879; and Christoph Stölzl, "Zur Geschichte der böhmischen Juden in der Epoche des modernen Nationalismus," parts 1 and 2, *Bohemia* 14 (1973): 200–203; 15 (1974): 138–42.

6. Johann Wanniczek, who served as director of the *Normalschule* in Prague from 1827 to 1838, railed in writing against the practice of many Jewish families of circumventing the state school in favor of private tutoring. The government sought to curb the practice after 1815 by clamping down on the many private tutors (*Bocherim*) who plied their trade in Prague with measures that included the expulsion of many them. An ordinance of 1819, moreover, required all *Hauslehrer* to receive instruction in the teaching methods of *B'nei Zion*—since 1812 the required textbook of Jewish morality—from the author himself, Herz Homberg. Previous ordinances had made an examination in this text obligatory for all prospective Jewish brides and grooms as well as for all Jewish students who chose not to attend the community school.

7. For Kuh, see Wurzbach, *Lexicon Österreich,* 13:340; for Kompert, ibid., 12:404–10; Wininger, *Nationalbiographie,* 3:506–7; and Hock, "Komperts Leben und Schaffen."

8. Wurzbach, *Lexikon Österreich,* 8:272–75.

9. Wittner, *Moritz Hartmanns Jugend,* pp. 9–11; Wurzbach, *Lexikon Österreich,* 8:5. In 1832 the young Hartmann presented himself at the *Hauptschule* in Neukollin, where an aunt of his lived, and took an examination that apparently was required of students who sought to circumvent the primary schools. He passed the examination and the following year, chaperoned by his father, moved to Prague, where he attended the first class of the Altstädter gymnasium. For reasons that are unclear—perhaps because the business required the father to return home—this arrangement did not work out. It was at this point that Hartmann set out for his grandfather's home in Mladá Boleslav.

10. Donath, "Siegfried Kapper," pp. 325–26; and Siegfried Kapper, "Autobiographie I," in "Siegfried Kapper," by Oskar Donath, *JGGJČR,* 6 (1934), p. 396.

11. Donath, "Siegfried Kapper," p. 326; Donath, *Siegfried Kappers Leben und Wirken,* pp. 404–5; and Kapper, "Autobiographie II," in "Siegfried Kapper," by Uskar Donath, *JGGJČR* 6 (1934), p. 398.

12. Kaufmann, introduction to *Die Familien Prags,* pp. 5–8. Hock once recounted to the writer Salomon Kohn that the same man who warmed *cholent* for the sabbath afternoon meals for Prague Jews also ran a lending library of secular works consisting largely of German fiction. For a nominal fee, he lent books out on Friday afternoon, when servants or other household members would bring pots of food for warming over the sabbath. Hock shocked his mother when, as a nine- or ten-year-old boy, he asked her for the few kreuzer that it cost to borrow books from this make-shift library. In panic, she offered to pay him ten times the amount he was seeking if he agreed to refrain from reading such works.

13. Kaufmann, introduction to *Die Familien Prags,* pp. 9–12.

14. Wittner describes Isaac Spitz as "pious, without clinging to dogma, himself a poet with a clear knowledge of the world and of man" (*Mortiz Hartmanns Jugend,* p. 11).

15. Ibid., pp. 20–21.

16. The elder Kapper, though a native of Smíchov, had apparently spent the years 1801 to 1816 abroad in activities that ranged from fighting for the French to teaching for the Swiss. According to Siegfried Kapper, his father learned the craft of glassmaking upon his return to Bohemia in order to be exempted from the provisions of the *Familiantengesetze* and thus be allowed to marry ("Autobiographie I," p. 396).

17. Donath, "Siegfried Kapper," pp. 327–28; Donath, *Siegfried Kappers Leben und Wirken,* pp. 405–8.

On the Dvůr Králové and Zelená Hora manuscripts, see Hanus Jélinek, *Histoire de la littérature tchèque: Des origines à 1850.* 2d ed. (Paris, 1930), pp. 275–84. Jélinek explains the cultural significance of the forgeries as follows: "La nation tchèque, qui réclamait sa place parmi ses soeurs, et qui, elle aussi, avait une histoire si glorieuse, serait-elle seule condamnée à ne point posseder de chants digne de ce passé? Prouver par des vestiges littéraires l'existence d'une antique civilisation slave indépendente de l'Occident latin et germanique, tel était le rêve des patriotes" (p. 278).

18. Moritz Hartmann complained in retrospect of his "wasted" *Gymnasium* years to Alfred Meissner.

Wie wurden wir im Vormärz um unsere Jugen betrogen! Sechs Jahre sassen wir auf den Banken des Gymnasiums, um nichts zu tun, als die schönste, früchtsbarste Zeit des Lebens zu verlieren, also um die Jahre vorübergehen zu lassen, welche in anderen Ländern die Saemonate des Lebens sind, und brach liegen zu bleiben. Sechs Jahre lernten wir wörtlich lateinische Regeln auswendig, ohne je einen ordentlichen lateinischen Autor lesen zu dürfen; vier Jahre lernten wir Griechisch, um an Ende nicht zwei Verse Homers übersetzen zu können, und noch lernten wir Lateinisch und Griechisch besser als unsere Muttersprache. (Quoted in Wittner, *Moritz Hartmanns Jugend,* p. 10.)

19. Ibid., p. 11.

20. Leopold Kompert, *Aus dem Ghetto: Geschicten.* 3d. ed. (Berlin, 1882), pp. 125–28.

21. Donath relates that Kapper "schon am Gymnasium als 'Poet' fühlte." When he arrived in Prague in the autumn of 1837, he quickly gravitated toward the circle of aspiring poets known as "Young Bohemia": "Die Dichter des 'Jungen Böhmen' standen unter dem Einfluss Byrons, Lenaus und des 'Jungen Deutschland.' Sie waren Freiheitssänger und Dichter des Weltschmerzes" (Donath, "Siegfried Kapper," p. 329).

22. Donath, "Siegfried Kapper," p. 329; Wittner, *Moritz Hartmanns Jugend,* p. 14, 17–20; Wurzbach, *Lexikon Österreich,* 12:405–6.

23. Ibid., 8:273; 13:340.

24. Donath, "Siegfried Kapper," pp. 328–29; Wittner, *Moritz Hartmanns Jugend,* pp. 17–20.

25. Wittner, *Moritz Hartmanns Jugend,* p. 23.

26. See ibid., pp. 23–24. Glaser sketched out his ambition for the journal in its June 1837 announcement:

The interests of the cultured nations are becoming more and more similar; more and more the spatial and spiritual distance between them is disappearing; and everything that furthers this goal will be taken up with great favor. May this new literary undertaking also serve in part ... as a literary mediation between the Slavic East and Germany and thereby contribute to the world literature, which is still taking shape. What country would be more appropriate [to this endeavor] than Bohemia, with its half-Slavic, half-German population; Bohemia, the border between the European East and West; a country rich in writers who are familiar with all of the Slavic dialects." (Reproduced in Alois Hoffman, *Die Prager Zeitschrift "Ost und West": Ein Beitrag zur Geschichte der deutsch-slawischen Verständigung im Vormärz* [Berlin, 1957], table 1, and p. 27.)

27. Ibid., pp. 316 ff.

28. Ibid.; W. Wessely, "Zur Anthologie der Rabbinen," *Ost und West*, 7 February 1845. Wessely introduced his brief anthology with the remark: "Der Sagenschatz und Mythenkreis der alten Hebräer, so wie ihr grosser Gnomenreichthum ist trotz des vielen Schönen, das Herder in seiner Blumenlese zur Kenntniss brachte, und trotz der merhrfachen Bearbeitung, die sie, namentlich die Gnomeologie in neuerer Zeit gefunden hat, noch immer viel zu wenig bekannt und gewürdigt worden."

29. See, for example, Kapper's "Autobiographie I," p. 397: "So blieb mir nur die Nacht zum Studieren und der Weg vom Hause zum Clementinum und zurück zum Versemachen. An Sonn- und Ferialtagen schrieb ich Dramen."

30. Wittner, *Moritz Hartmanns Jugend*, pp. 23–24, 38; Wurzbach, *Lexikon Österreich*, 8:6.

31. Wurzbach, *Lexikon Österreich*, 8:273.

32. Donath, "Siegfried Kapper," p. 331–32.

33. Ibid., pp. 352–63.

34. Wurzbach, *Lexikon Österreich*, 12:406–7.

35. Kaufmann, introduction to *Die Familien Prags*, pp. 9–10.

36. In Kaufmann's words,

Wohl ging die Wirksamkeit Zunzens in Prag wie ein schneller Traum vorüber, aber schon 1836 trat die glänzende Erscheinung Michael Sachsens an seine Stelle, durch die macht seines Wortes, durch den Zauber seiner Rede wie durch ein hoheitsvolles Wesen mit sich fortreissend und emportragend. In solcher Sprache waren die Lehren und Gedanken des Judenthums noch nicht verkündet worden; es war dies die Erfüllung einer ungestillten Sehnsucht, die Verwirklichung eines Ideals, der Bund jüdischen Geistes und deutscher Cultur, die goldenen Früchte des Judenthums in den silbernen Schalen der klassischen Bildung. (Introduction to *Die Familien Prags*, p. 11.)

On the careers of Sachs and Rapoport in Prague, see David Rosin, "Erinnerungen an S. L. Rapoport," in *Das Centenarium S. J. L. Rapoport's. Festgabe des "Österreichischen Wochenschrift"* (Vienna, 1890), pp. 400–3.

37. Kaufmann, introduction to *Die Familien Prags*, pp. 11–12.

38. Kapper first began to study Serbian language, literature, and folk culture in Prague under the influence of the writings of Jakob Grimm. Later, while in

Vienna, he befriended the writer Vuk Stefanovic Karadzic and continued his studies in South Slavic culture. (Donath, "Siegfried Kapper," p. 333.)

39. For a biographical sketch of Nebeský, see Wurzbach, *Lexikon Österreich,* 20:109–12, and Sturm, *Lexikon der böhmischen Länder,* 3:13.

40. See Wurzbach, *Lexikon Österreich,* 20:110.

41. Donath, "Siegfried Kapper," p. 333–34; and Donath, *Siegfried Kappers Leben und Wirken,* p. 427.

42. Quoted in Donath, "Siegfried Kapper," p. 334, and Donath, *Siegfried Kappers Leben und Wirken,* p. 427. Donath does not indicate who the recipient of the letter was.

43. Articles in *Der Orient,* particularly those that originated from the Habsburg monarchy, were often published anonymously or with the author's initials only. This may have been done to bypass Austrian censorship laws and to evade the scrutiny of the secret police (though the newspaper in question was published in Leipzig). The censorship laws were not lifted until March 1848, during the early phase of the revolution, and the *Österreichisches Central-Organ*—the voice of liberal, Austrian-Jewish opinion in 1848—stands out for the prominent by-lines that it attached to its articles. Nevertheless, Kuh's series in the *Allgemeine Zeitung des Judentums* ("Ein Wort an Juden und Slaven," 1 April, 8 April, and 15 April 1844) did appear under his full name. The report from Prague in *Der Orient* of 1 February 1844, which inaugurated the Nebeský-Kuh-Kapper newspaper campaign, resembles the series in the *Allgemeine Zeitung des Judentums* in tone, style, and language.

44. *Der Orient,* 13 May 1844.

45. Ibid.

46. Ibid.

47. Ibid.

48. *Der Orient,* 14 May 1844; see also the follow-up report of David Kuh to the *Allgemeine Zeitung des Judentums,* "Aus Böhmen," 6 May 1844.

49. *Der Orient,* 14 May 1844.

50. Kuh, "Juden und Slaven," 1 April 1844.

51. Ibid.

52. Ibid.

53. Kuh, "Juden und Slaven," 8 April 1844.

54. Ibid.

55. Ibid.

56. Ibid.

57. Kuh, "Juden und Slaven," 15 April 1844.

58. Ibid.

59. See, for example, Stölzl, "Zur Geschichte," pt. 1, pp. 200–21; Kisch, *In Search of Freedom,* pp. 33–44; and Donath, *Siegfried Kappers Leben und Wirken,* pp. 426–35. In contrast, Michael Riff argues that Hartmann's *Kelch und Schwert* was never intended to be a pro-Czech statement and, moreover, that Hartmann accepted the notion of German-Jewish acculturation "without any question." My own view is that this conclusion applies only after 1844. Cf. Riff, "Jüdische Schriftsteller," pp. 58–82.

60. Kuh, "Juden und Slaven," 15 April 1844.

61. Nebeský, "Opět něco o poměru Slovanů a židů," *Květy* (July 1844), quoted in Donath, *Siegfried Kappers Leben und Wirken,* p. 431.

62. Ibid, pp. 431–32. Kuh followed up his series in the *Allgemeine Zeitung des Judentums* with a progress report in the 6 May issue. He remarked that the rapprochement of Jews and Slavs had taken a small, though not unimportant, step forward. A number of Jewish notables, including Leopold Edler von Lämel and Forchheimer, had donated money to the Matice česká (Foundation for Czech National Culture). Kuh reported on Nebeský's piece in *Květy,* adding that he was the first Slav writing for a Slavic newspaper who presented the Jews in an appreciative and unprejudiced light. Finally, Kuh remarked that many among Prague's Jews expressed the desire to see the establishment of a chair in Czech language at the German-Jewish *Normalschule.* ("Aus Böhmen," *Allgemeine Zeitung des Judentums,* 6 May 1844.)

63. Stölzl, "Zur Geschichte," pt. 1, p. 188; William O. McCagg, *A History of Habsburg Jews, 1670–1918* (Bloomington, 1989), pp. 75–76.

64. Stölzl, "Zur Geschichte," pt. 1, p. 204; McCagg, *Habsburg Jews,* 77–78.

65. Riff, "Jüdische Schriftsteller," p. 69; see also the reports of Prague correspondents to *Der Orient* in the 9, 23, and 30 July 1844 issues.

66. Stölzl, "Zur Geschichte," pt. 1, p. 205; also the report in *Der Orient,* 22 October 1844, pp. 333–34.

67. The dispatches of 23 and 24 June appeared in *Der Orient* on 9 July 1844; the report dated 10 July appeared on 23 July 1844; and the 22 July report appeared in the 30 July 1844 issue of the paper. The dispatch dated 26 June and signed "24" was published in *Der Orient* on 23 July 1844.

68. *Der Orient,* 9 July 1844.

69. See note 24, this chapter.

70. *Der Orient,* 23 July 1844 (dispatch dated 10 July); also *Der Orient,* 9 July 1844.

71. *Der Orient,* 30 July 1844.

72. Ibid.

73. *Der Orient,* 23 July 1844, report of 26 June.

74. For example: "[Die Behörden] die in der Stunde de Gefahr, uns mit väterlicher Sorgfalt bedacht, mit bewunderungswürdiger Gewandheit Strenge und Milde zu paaren, und die gehörigen Mittel zu ergreifen gewusst, um den Aufruhr im Keime zu ersticken, und das Schiff der Ordnung durch die gefährlichen Klippen, sicher in den hafen des Friedens zu steuern" (*Der Orient,* 23 July 1844).

75. Ibid.

76. Ibid.

77. See Schulhof's contributions to *Der Orient* of 3 September, 15 October, and 22 October 1844, and 3 September, 10 September, and 12 November 1845. I have not been able to obtain any biographical information on him, but cannot help but wonder whether he was perhaps the father or uncle of the early-twentieth-century Czech-Jewish writer and activist, Stanislav Schulhof.

78. For Kapper's *České listy* see Donath, "Siegfried Kapper," pp. 338–41; and Kisch, *In Search of Freedom,* pp. 34–36, 202–12.

79. Partial texts of Havlíček's review are printed in Kisch, *In Search of Freedom*, 213–14 (in Czech, with an English translation on pp. 36–38), and in Donath, *Siegfried Kappers Leben und Wirken*, p. 434 (in German). My translation is based upon both sources.

80. Karel Havlíček Borovský, "Emancipace židů," in *Politické Spisy*, ed. Z. Tobolka (Prague, 1902), 3:402–8.

81. Kisch, *In Search of Freedom*, p. 37.

82. Siegfried Kapper, "Na devátý ab" (The ninth of Ab), in *České listy* (Czech leaves) (Prague, 1946); repr. and trans. in Kisch, *In Search of Freedom*, pp. 210–12.

83. Siegfried Kapper, "Ben-Oni" (Son of Sorrow), in *České listy* (Czech leaves) (Prague, 1946); repr. and trans. in Kisch, *In Search of Freedom*, p. 208.

84. Kompert, *Aus dem Ghetto*, p. 91.

85. Ibid., pp. 141–42.

86. "If the Jews want to know our personal opinion, we would advise them, if they insist on throwing overboard their language and literature, to attach themselves to the Germans and German literature, since the German language has become the second mother tongue of the Jews" (Kisch, *In Search of Freedom*, p. 38).

87. See, again, the entries on Nebeský in Wurzbach, *Lexikon Österreich*, 20:109–12; and Sturm, *Lexikon der böhmischen Länder*, 3:13.

88. Hartmann to Meissner, in Otto Wittner, ed., *Briefe aus dem Vormärz: Eine Sammlung aus dem Nachlass Moritz Hartmanns* (Prague, 1911), pp. 255–56.
Kelch und Schwert did eventually appear (Leipzig, 1845), not reduced by half, but complete.

89. Hartmann to Meissner.

90. The works by Kapper in question are "Die Kohlen," which appeared in *Libussa* in 1849; *Herzel und seine Freunde: Federzeichnungen aus dem böhmischen Schulleben* (Leipzig, 1853); and *Falk: Eine Erzählung* (Dessau, 1853). On Kapper's later years, see Donath, "Siegfried Kapper," pp. 345–87; Wurzbach, *Lexikon Österreich*, 10:451–52; and Riff, "Jüdische Schriftsteller," pp. 71–79.

91. Wurzbach, *Lexikon Österreich*, 8:6; Sturm, *Lexikon der böhmischen Länder*, 1:544; and Wininger, *Nationalbiographie*, 3:8–10.

92. Wurzbach, *Lexikon Österreich*, 8:272–75.

93. Kaufmann, introduction, to *Die Familien Prags*, pp. 19–27; Hock published regular reports from Prague in the *Österreichisches Central-Organ* as well as other articles, among them: "Études aux deux crayons: über jüdische Zustände in Prag"; "Die Prager Judengemeinde im Jahre 48"; and "Im Namen der verfolgten Juden in Böhmen, an ihre verfolgten Brüder in Ungarn."

94. Wurzbach, *Lexikon Österreich*, 13:340; *Allgemeine Zeitung des Judentums*, 11 February 1879 (obituary reprinted from the *Neue Freie Presse* of Vienna).

95. Sturm, *Lexikon der böhmischen Länder*, 2:340.

96. On David Kuh and the Dvůr Králové manuscript, see Stölzl, "Zur Geschichte," pt. 2, pp. 138–42; also Wurzbach, *Lexikon Österreich*, 13:340; and *Allgemeine Zeitung des Judentums*, 11 February 1879.

97. Stölzl, "Zur Geschichte," pt. 2, p. 139.

98. On these and parallel developments in Czech Jewish society, see Kieval, *The Making of Czech Jewry.*

Chapter 4. Pursuing the Golem of Prague

1. Leopold Weisel, "Der Golem," in *Sippurim: Eine Sammlung jüdischer Volkssagen, Erzählungen, Mythen, Chroniken, Denkwürdigkeiten und Biographien berühmter Juden,* edited by Wolf Pascheles, Erste Sammlung, 4th ed. (Prague: Pascheles, 1870), pp. 51–52 (all subsequent citations are to this edition).

2. On the theme of the Golem in the history of Judaism, see Gershom Scholem, "The Idea of the Golem," in *On the Kabbalah and Its Symbolism* (New York, 1965), pp. 158–204; Moshe Idel, *Golem: Jewish Magical and Mystical Traditions on the Artificial Anthropoid* (Albany, 1990); idem, "The Golem in Jewish Magic and Mysticism," in *Golem! Danger, Deliverance, and Art,* ed. Emily Bilski, (New York, 1988), pp. 15–35; and Byron L. Sherwin, *The Golem Legend: Origins and Implications* (Lanham, Md., 1985).

3. On the importation of the Golem motif to general European culture, see Sigrid Mayer, *Golem: Die literarische Rezeption eines Stoffes* (Bern and Frankfurt a.M., 1975); Arnold L. Goldsmith, *The Golem Remembered, 1909–1980: Variations of a Jewish Legend* (Detroit, 1981); Beate Rosenfeld, *Die Golemsage und ihre Verwertung in der deutschen Literatur* (Breslau, 1934); and Emily Bilski, "The Art of the Golem," in *Golem! Danger, Deliverance, and Art,* ed. Emily Bilski (New York, 1988), pp. 44–III.

4. On the *Sefer Yezirah,* see Scholem, "The Idea of the Golem," passim, and esp. pp. 167–73.

5. See Idel, *Golem,* pp. 9–21.

6. Scholem, "The Idea of the Golem," pp. 171–93; Idel, "The Golem in Jewish Magic and Mysticism," pp. 20–30; and idem, *Golem,* pp. 56–61, 81–86, 96–104.

7. Christoph Arnold to J. Christoph Wagenseil, 1674. Letter appended to Arnold's *Sota hoc est Liber Mischnicus de uxore adulterii suspecta,* pp. 198–99. Translated in Scholem, "The Idea of the Golem," pp. 200–201; reproduced here with minor revisions.

8. Moshe Idel has found what appears to be an earlier reference to the creation of a Golem by R. Elijah of Chelm in the manuscript testimony of a Polish kabbalist contained in Ms. Oxford 1309. The Polish kabbalist, writing perhaps between the 1630s and 1650s, relates the following:

I have heard, in a certain and explicit way, from several respectable persons that one man, [living] close to our time, in the holy community of Chelm, whose name is R. Eliyahu, the master of the name, who made a creature of matter [*Golem*] and form [*zurah*], and it performed hard work for him, for a long period, and the name of *emet* was hanging upon his neck, until he finally removed, for a certain reason, the name from his neck and it turned to dust. (Quoted in Idel, *Golem,* p. 208.)

9. Jacob Emden, *Megillath sefer* (The scroll of the book) (Warsaw, 1896), p. 4; his *Responsa,* 2, no. 82; and his *Mitpahat sefarim* (Altona, 1769), p. 45a. See

also Scholem, "The Idea of the Golem," pp. 199–201; and Mayer, *Golem*, pp. 25–30.

10. A survey of Bohemian Jewish history during this period and a description of the career and writings of the Maharal can be found in chapter 1. See also the following works: Muneles *Prague Ghetto;* and Drabek, "Die Juden in den böhmischen Ländern," pp. 123–43; Thieberger, *The Great Rabbi Loew;* Kleinberger, *Ha-Maharal mi-Prag;* Sadek, "Rabbi Loew," pp. 27–41; and Sherwin, *Mystical Theology.*

11. Cf. Thieberger, *The Great Rabbi Loew,* pp. 8–44; and Sherwin, *Mystical Theology,* passim.

12. On the life and policies of Rudolph II, see R. J. W. Evans, *Rudolf II and His World: A Study in Intellectual History, 1576–1612* (Oxford, 1973); idem, *The Making of the Habsburg Monarchy* (Oxford, 1979); and Frances Yates, *The Rosicrucian Enlightenment* (London and Boston, 1972).

13. Yates, *The Rosicrucian Enlightenment,* p. 17.

14. A second, purportedly contemporaneous account—said to have been written by Judah Löw's son-in-law Rabbi Isaac ben Samson Ha-Kohen, discovered in the latter's "Venetian Bible" and published in 1872 in the Hebrew periodical *Ha-Maggid*—is, I am convinced, a modern forgery. I hope to publish a historical note on the subject in the future.

15. On Gans's scientific interests, see Alter, *Two Renaissance Astronomers.* On Gans's activity as a historian, see Mordechai Breuer, "Mavo" (Introduction) to *Sefer Zemah David* (The offspring of David), by David Gans (Jerusalem, 1983), pp. i–xxxiii.

16. Gans, *Sefer Zemah David,* p. 145.

17. Meir Perles, *Megilat yuhasin* (The scroll of relations) (Warsaw, 1864); German trans. by S. H. Lieben, "Megillath Juchassin Mehral miprag," in *Jahrbuch der Jüdisch-Literarischen Gesellschaft* 20 (1929): 315–36.

18. *Encyclopaedia Judaica,* 7:755; also Scholem, "The Idea of the Golem," pp. 202–3. Here he dates the transferral of the legend from Poland to Bohemia "toward the middle of the eighteenth century."

19. Vladimír Sadek, "Stories of the Golem and Their Relation to the Work of Rabbi Löw of Prague," *Judaica Bohemiae* 23, no. 2 (1987): 86; also idem, "Rabbi Loew," p. 36, where he likens the popular pilgrimages to the gravesite of the Maharal to those undertaken by Hasidim to the graves of their Zaddikim.

20. Ze'ev Gries, *Sefer, sofer, ve-sippur be-reshit ha-hasidut* (The book, the writer, and the story in the beginnings of Hasidism) (Tel Aviv, 1992), p. 56.

21. On the presence of Galician refugees in Prague, see Kieval, *The Making of Czech Jewry,* pp. 174–78.

22. Idel, "The Golem in Jewish Magic and Mysticism," p. 35.

23. On the possible significance of these two events, see Mayer, *Golem,* pp. 33–34; and Goldsmith, *The Golem Remembered,* pp. 30–31.

24. Sadek, "Rabbi Loew," p. 36.

25. Drabek, "Die Juden in den böhmischen Ländern," pp. 127–28.

26. Thieberger, *The Great Rabbi Loew,* pp. 77–79; see also the entry by Gershom Scholem on Eibeschütz in *Encyclopaedia Judaica* 6:1074–76.

27. "Es ist auch recht was merckwürdiges, und wohl sonst nirgends in der Welt anzutreffen, daß die Juden zu Prag in der Alt-Neuen Synagog, wie sie dieselbige nennen, eine Orgel haben, die sie aber zum Gottes-Dienst weiter nicht brauchen, als nur, wann sie Freytags Abends das Bewillkommungs-Lied des *Schabbes* singen, und darbey ein Jud diese Orgel schalget..." (Johann Jacob Schudt, *Jüdische Merckwürdigkeiten* [Frankfurt and Leipzig, 1714–18], 1:218).

See also ibid., 2:284–85: "Jedoch gar viele glaubhaftige Juden, die lang in Böhmen gewesen, haben mich für gewiß versichert, daß zu Prag in der Alt-Neuen *Synagoge* eine Orgel seye, die man aber weiter nicht brauche, als zu dem Gesang dieses Liedes (zu Bewillkommung des instehenden *Sabbaths*) in der Neuen *Synagoge* aber, wie auch an Theils andern Orten habe man zu denen Stimmen der Sänger auch allerhand *musicalische Instrumenten.*"

Schudt explains that "Kabbóles Schabbes" means "die Empfangung oder Bewillkommung des Sabbaths" (p. 284). It is unclear from this description, however, whether the "Bewillkommungslied" refers to the Kabbalat Shabbat service in general or specifically to the liturgical poem "Lekha dodi."

28. I have never seen this explanation offered for the Altneuschul practice. It has, however, been suggested to me by Alexandr Putík that if the Altneuschul did possess an organ, it was not used on the Sabbath, and that the instrument itself was probably removed from the synagogue during the tenure of Ezekiel Landau. David Ellenson, in a recent article, notes that the precedent of the "Prague organ" occupied a prominent position in the controversy between Orthodoxy and Reform in Hamburg in 1819. (David Ellenson, "A Disputed Precedent: The Prague Organ in Nineteenth-Century Central-European Legal Literature and Polemics," *Leo Baeck Institute Yearbook* 40 [1995]: 251–64.)

29. Jakob Grimm, in *Zeitung für Einsiedler* (1808); repr. in his *Kleinere Schriften,* vol. 4 (Berlin, 1869) as well as in Beate Rosenfeld, *Die Golemsage,* p. 41.

30. The full title of the journal was *Das Panorama des Universums zur erheitenden Belehrung für Jedermann und alle Länder* (Prague, 1834–48). Klutschak was later to become editor-in-chief and then publisher of the Prague German newspaper *Bohemia.* (See Sturm, *Lexikon der böhmischen Länder,* p. 186; and Österreichische Akademie der Wissenschaften, ed., *Österreichisches biographisches Lexikon 1815–1950* [Graz, 1965], 3:426.)

31. *Das Panorama des Universums* 5 (1838): 292–95.

32. *Das Panorama des Universums* 8 (1841): 75 ff. Of this collection of four tales, "Der Golam [*sic*] des Rabbi Löw" is the only one to deal with a specifically Jewish theme.

33. See Jana Doležalová, "Questions of Folklore in the Legends of the Old Jewish Town Compiled by Leopold Weisel (1804–1870) [*sic*]," *Judaica Bohemiae* 12 (1976): 37–50; also Wininger, *Nationalbiographie* 4:610.

34. Leopold Weisel, "Die Pinchasgasse: Eine jüdische Volkssage," *Das Panorama des Universums* 5 (Prague, 1838): 328–32.

35. The original title of the 1847 collection was *Gallerie der Sipurim* [sic], *eine Sammlung jüdischer Sagen, Märchen und Geschichten als ein Beitrag für Völkerkunde.* It incorporated legends, tales, and biographical sketches from biblical,

rabbinic, and popular sources, and drew on the literary efforts of a number of writers other than Weisel, including Siegfried Kapper (1821–79) and Salomon Kohn (1825–1904). The collection was reissued unchanged following the 1848 Revolution, in 1851, and then in numerous editions until the end of the nineteenth century—three between 1853 and 1864 alone. A German edition in Hebrew type appeared in 1860. A popular version was published by Jakob B. Brandeis, Pascheles' son-in-law and successor, in 1887, which itself ran through three editions in twenty years (1909). (See Peter Demetz, "Nachwort" to *Geschichten aus dem alten Prag: Sippurim* [Frankfurt a.M. and Leipzig, 1994], pp. 361–76; and Otto Muneles, *Bibliographical Survey of Jewish Prague* [Prague, 1952], passim.)

A word of caution regarding the widely distributed 1921 edition (*Sippurim: Prager Sammlung jüdischer Legenden,* In neuer Auswahl und Bearbeitung [Vienna and Leipzig: R. Löwit, 1921]): Wholesale changes were made to the nineteenth-century editions: titles were altered, stories rearranged and abridged, new wording substituted, and, in some instances, incorrect authorship attributed.

36. See appendix for the complete German text.

37. Parenthetic remarks inform the reader that the Hebrew *shem* is to be understood as "talisman," *golam* as "servant," *godolah* as "adult," and so forth. A footnote explains to the reader the practice in which Jewish women light candles on the eve of the Sabbath. Characteristically, the explanation is neither *halakhic* nor textual but folkloristic, based on a popular *midrash* concerning the consumption of the forbidden fruit in the Garden of Eden.

38. Klutschak, "Der Golam [*sic*] des Rabbi Löw," *Panorama des Universums* 8 (1841): 77.

39. Klutschak explains this point with a footnote:

According to the beliefs of the Rabbis, the souls in purgatory also observe the Sabbath; as soon as the celebration of the Sabbath begins in the synagogue, they leave the place of their suffering and flee to the nearest water in which they bathe and cool off until the Sabbath ends. For this reason the Jews are not allowed to drink or draw from brooks and streams on the Sabbath, so as not to disturb the souls during their refreshment. (Ibid.)

40. Ibid., p. 78. As to the misidentification of the Psalm, I can only surmise a reason. It is possible that on this occasion Klutschak's informants failed him. It is also possible, though less likely, that the practice in the Altneuschul was to *begin* the Friday evening prayers with Psalm 92, omitting the preceding six.

41. Weisel, "Der Golem," in Pascheles, *Sippurim,* pp. 50–51.

42. "Diese Volkssage ist oft schon von verschiedenen Schriftstellern benützt worden—und es scheint überflüssig, eine so bekannte Sage nochmals zu bearbeiten; damit man aber nicht glaube, ich hätte sie gar nicht gekannt, will ich sie hier nur in der Kürze anführen" (ibid., p. 51).

43. "Pověsti židovské," *Květy,* 6 August 1844.

44. See chapter 3.

45. Josef Svátek, *Pražské pověsti a legendy* (Prague tales and legends) (Prague, 1875); Alois Jirásek, *Staré pověsti české* (Old Czech tales) (Prague, 1893).

46. The Maharal was either eighty-nine or ninety-seven at the time of his death, depending upon which one accepts as his date of birth: 1512 or 1520.

47. On Yudel Rosenberg's authorship of the works in question, see Ira Robinson, "Literary Forgery and Hasidic Judaism: The Case of Rabbi Yudel Rosenberg," *Judaism* 40, no. 1 (Winter 1991): 61–78; Eli Yassif, introduction to *Hagolem mi-Prag u-maʿasim niflaʾim aḥerim* (The Golem of Prague and other wondrous deeds) by Yehuda Yudel Rosenberg (Jerusalem, 1991), pp. 7–72; and Abraham Benedict, "Haggadat Maharal o Aggadat Maharal?" (The Haggadah of the Maharal, or the *aggadah* [legend] of the Maharal?), *Moriah* 14, no. 3–4 (1985): 102–13.

48. Rosenberg was able to attach approbations from two leading Warsaw rabbis, Petaḥia Hornblum and Isaac ha-Kohen Feigenbaum, to his edition of the Haggadah commentary. For the most part, he succeeded in passing the work off as genuine. It was published in many editions, both by Rosenberg and by others, and has also been accepted by a number of rabbis as an *halakhic* authority "relative to the laws and customs of the Passover Seder." (See Robinson, "Literary Forgery," p. 68.)

49. Thus, for example, Rosenberg identifies the cardinal in Prague at the time of the Maharal as "Jan Sylvester." No such bishop existed in the city. (Jan Sylvester was the name of a sixteenth-century Christian Hebraist.) I also doubt if there was in fact a "priest-sorcerer" in Prague named Thaddeus (Polish: Tadeusz?) who spread the accusation of Jewish ritual murder.

50. Chayim Bloch, *The Golem: Legends of the Ghetto of Prague*, trans. from the German by Harry Schneiderman (Vienna, 1925).

51. Gershon Winkler, *The Golem of Prague* (New York, 1980).

52. The inscription is more elaborate on the inside title page of the edition published in Piotrków: "This is the book of miracles of the Maharal ... in which he miraculously performed great deeds and wonders through the Golem, which he created through the wisdom of the Kabbalah to fight against the blood libel, which was widespread in his day, and to make clear to the eyes of all the truth that the Jews are innocent of this charge" (Y. Rosenberg, *Sefer niflaʾot Maharal* [The book of wonders of the Maharal] [Piotrków, 1909]).

53. Rosenberg explains in his introduction to *Niflaʾot Maharal* that while many knew and spoke of the ability of the Maharal to fashion a creature out of mud and clay (*tit ve-ḥomer*), this knowledge had weakened with the passage of time. Some "*maskilim*" even wished "to deny and uproot everything," to say that it was only a legend (*ki ʾakh mashal hi zot*). For a while, Rabbi Ezekiel Landau had set the record straight by venturing, himself, to the attic of the Altneushul, where the remains of the Golem were said to rest (and thereafter forbidding anyone else to enter this space). But "many people have begun to doubt the matter again." And, Rosenberg adds, "all because this whole episode had not been inscribed in writing in Jewish chronicles" (*vekhol zeh baʿavur shelo neḥkak ba-sefer kol ha-ʿinyan bein korot ha-yehudim*).

Now, the definitive truth has been revealed. "Now all of Israel will know that it was all recorded in writing by the son-in-law of the Maharal, the great Gaon R. Y. Katz, *z"z"l*" (Introduction to *Sefer niflaʾot Maharal*, Piotrków, 1909).

Chapter 5. On Myth, History, and National Belonging in the Nineteenth Century

1. See, for example, Lucien Lévy-Bruhl, *Primitive Mythology: The Mythic World of the Australian and Papuan Natives* (St. Lucia, Queensland, 1983; trans. of 1935 French original); and Bronislaw Malinowski, *Myth in Primitive Psychology* (London, 1926; repr. in *Magic, Science, and Religion* [Garden City, N.Y., 1954]).

A good introduction to the comparative study of myth is to be found in Alan Dundes, ed., *Sacred Narrative: Readings in the Theory of Myth* (Berkeley: University of California Press, 1984).

2. The work of Mircea Eliade, in particular *Myth and Reality* (New York, 1963), is instructive in this regard:

Myths describe the various and sometimes dramatic breakthroughs of the sacred (or the 'supernatural') into the World. It is this sudden breakthrough of the sacred that really *establishes* the World and makes it what it is today.... Because myth relates the *gesta* of Supernatural Beings and the manifestation of their sacred powers, it becomes the exemplary model for all significant human activities (p. 6).

3. On Leenhardt, see Stanley J. Tambiah, *Magic, Science, Religion, and the Scope of Rationality* (Cambridge, Eng., 1990), pp. 106–7. See also Maurice Leenhardt, *Do Kamo: Person and Myth in the Melanesian World* (Chicago, 1979), pp. 170–95.

4. Anthony D. Smith, *The Ethnic Origins of Nations* (Oxford, 1986), pp. 25, 24.

5. Anthony D. Smith, *The Ethnic Revival* (Cambridge, 1981), p. 65.

6. Benedict Anderson also stresses the importance of the organization, production, and dissemination of knowledge in the creation of new, "imagined communities" of mutual interest and fate. The key development in his recovery of the origins of nationalism is "print capitalism," the mass production of books and newspapers as commodities. (*Imagined Communities: Reflections on the Origin and Spread of Nationalism,* rev. ed. [London and New York, 1991], pp. 37–46.)

7. Paul Veyne, *Did the Greeks Believe in Their Myths?* (Chicago, 1988), pp. 24, 28.

8. "Westerners, at least those among us who are not bacteriologists, believe in germs and increase the sanitary precautions we take for the same reason that the Azande believe in witches and multiply their magical precautions against them: their belief is based on trust" (ibid., p. 28).

9. Smith, *Ethnic Revival,* pp. 89–90.

10. Andrew Lass, "The Manuscript Debates," *Cross Currents* 6 (1987): 445.

11. See Eric Hobsbawm, "Inventing Traditions," in *The Invention of Tradition,* ed. E. Hobsbawm and T. S. Ranger (Cambridge, 1983), pp. 1–5.

12. Ernest Gellner, *Nations and Nationalism* (Ithaca, 1983), pp. 124–25.

13. William H. McNeill, "Mythistory, or Truth, Myth, History, and Historians," in *Mythistory and Other Essays* (Chicago, 1986), p. 12.

14. See Robert A. Kann, *A History of the Habsburg Empire 1526–1918* (Berkeley, 1974), pp. 170–99; and C. A. Macartney, *The Habsburg Empire 1790–1918* (New York, 1969), pp. 110–46. On the importance of political centralization

and reform in the formation of modern nationalism, see Smith, *Ethnic Revival,* pp. 87–133; Gellner, *Nations and Nationalism,* pp. 19–52; and Anderson, *Imagined Communities,* pp. 37–82.

15. On Jungmann, see Sturm, *Lexikon der böhmischen Länder* 2:72; *Čeští spisovatelé 19. a počátku 20. století* (Czech writers of the nineteenth century and beginning of the twentieth century) (Prague, 1973), pp. 127–30; and Jan V. Novák and Arne Novák, *Přehledné dějiny literatury české* (Historical survey of Czech literature), 4th rev. and exp. ed. (Olomouc, 1936), pp. 277–85.

16. Antonín Měšťan, *Česká literatura 1785–1985* (Toronto, 1986), pp. 26–27 (German ed.: *Geschichte der tschechischen Literatur im 19. und 20. Jahrhundert* [Cologne and Vienna, 1984]); Hugh LeCaine Agnew, *Origins of the Czech National Renascence* (Pittsburgh, 1993), pp. 65–70; also *Čeští spisovatelé,* pp. 127–28, from which the quote is taken.

17. Měšťan, *Česká literatura,* p. 27.

18. On Dobrovský, Šafařík, and Palacký, see Josef Mühlberger, *Tschechische Literaturgeschichte* (Munich, 1970), pp. 65–67.

19. Novák and Novák, *Přehledné dějiny,* p. 294; Mühlberger, *Tschechische Literaturgeschichte,* p. 75.

20. On the Královédvorský and Zelenohorský manuscripts, see Milan Otáhal, "The Manuscript Controversy in the Czech National Revival," *Cross Currents* 5 (1986): 247–77; Lass, "The Manuscript Debates," pp. 445–60; idem, "Romantic Documents and Political Monuments: The Meaning-Fulfillment of History in Nineteenth-Century Czech Nationalism," *American Ethnologist* 15 (1988): 456–71; Novák and Novák, *Přehledné dějiny,* pp. 291–303; Měšťan, *Česká literatura,* pp. 25–32; J. Hanuš, *Rukopisové Zelenohorský a Královédvorský* (The Zelenohorský and Královédvorský manuscipts) (Prague, 1911); and Josef Polák, *Česká literatura 19. století* (Czech literature in the nineteenth century) (Prague, 1990), pp. 49–55.

The Královédvorský manuscript comprised two parts. The first, consisting of fragments of eight epic poems, was said to date from the thirteenth century but included reworkings of material from as far back as the eleventh century. The second section was made up of six lyrical love poems. The epic poems all dealt with events from the "heroic" and, in some instances, pre-Christian, past: the expulsion of the Poles from Bohemia in 1004; the battle of Beneš Heřmanův against the Silesians, ca. 1203; the victory of the Christian Moravians, under the leadership of Jaroslav, over the Tatars, ca. 1241, etc. Both Jungmann and Hanka subjected the Zelenohorský manuscript to "scientific" analysis and concluded that it contained literary relics from the ninth century—including an epic account of the "judgment of Libuša," which attested to the rich legal traditions of the Czech people during pagan times. (Novák and Novák, *Přehledné dějiny,* pp. 295–97; Polák, *Česká literatura,* p. 50.)

21. Jan and Arne Novák assign credit for the lyrical sections of the Královédvorský manuscript to Hanka; the epic sections of the Královédvorský manuscript as well as all of the Zelenohorský manuscript they credit to Linda. Hanka is said to have taken care to transcribe the entire project into Old Czech. (Novák and Novák, *Přehledné dějiny,* p. 297.) Antonín Měšťan, on the other hand, feels that Hanka had no poetic ability and that the lyrical sections of both

manuscripts had to have been written by Linda. Hanka was almost certainly the philological cosmetician who effected the scholarly trompe-l'oeil. (Měšťan, *Česká literatura*, p. 30.)

22. William E. Harkins, "The Periodization of Czech Literary History, 1774–1879," in *The Czech Renascence of the Nineteenth Century*, ed. Peter Brock and H. Gordon Skilling (Toronto, 1970), p. 11.

23. H. Jélinek, *La littérature tchèque contemporaine: Cours professé à la Sorbonne en 1910* (Paris, 1912), p. 56.

24. Otáhal, "Manuscript Controversy," p. 252.

25. Ibid.

26. A formidable scholarly literature has grown around James Macpherson and the Ossian controversy. Two bibliograhic sources are George F. Black, "Macpherson's Ossian and the Ossianic Controversy," *Bulletin of the New York Public Library* 30 (1926): 1:424–39, 2:508–24; and John J. Dunn, "Macpherson's Ossian and the Ossianic Controversy: A Supplementary Bibliography," *Bulletin of the New York Public Library* 75 (1971): 465–73. Recent monographs include Paul J. deGategno, *James Macpherson* (Boston: Twayne, 1989); Ian Haywood, *The Making of History: A Study of the Literary Forgeries of James Macpherson* (Rutherford, 1986); and Fiona Stafford, *The Sublime Savage: A Study of James Macpherson and the Poems of Ossian* (Edinburgh, 1988).

27. A. V. Svoboda, *Hornmeyer Archive* (1824); cited in Otáhal, *Manuscript Controversy*, p. 253.

28. Ibid.

29. From a diary entry of 1819, quoted in ibid., p. 254.

30. On Palacký's historical writings, see Mühlberger, *Tschechische Literaturgeschichte*, pp. 66–67; Polák, *Česká literatura*, pp. 37–38; and Otáhal, *Manuscript Controversy*, pp. 254–59.

31. Otáhal, *Manuscript Controversy*, p. 253. For the circumstances surrounding the conflict over the manuscripts in the 1850s, see below.

32. The academic and political struggles over the Czech manuscripts are summarized in Novák and Novák, pp. 300–301.

33. On the history of the Jews in the Czech lands, see Hillel J. Kieval, "The Lands Between: The Jews of Bohemia, Moravia, and Slovakia to 1918," in *Where Cultures Meet: The Story of the Jews of Czechoslovakia*, ed. Natalia Berger (Tel Aviv, 1990), pp. 23–51; Pěkný, *Historie Židů;* and Ferdinand Seibt, ed., *Die Juden in den böhmischen Ländern* (Munich and Vienna, 1983).

34. Kisch, "Linguistic Conditions among Czechoslovak Jewry," pp. 19–32; Kestenberg-Gladstein, *Neuere Geschichte*, pp. 27–28, 39.

35. On the "German-Jewish" *Normalschulen*, please refer to chapter 2. See also Wannizcek, *Geschichte;* and Klaber, *Beschreibung.*

36. On Bohemian Jewish intellectuals during this period, see chapter 3.

37. Novák and Novák, *Přehledné dějiny*, p. 298.

38. In addition to the narrative in chapter 3, see also McCagg, *History of Habsburg Jews*, pp. 76–82, 223–26; and Riff, "Jüdische Schriftsteller."

39. Stölzl, "Zur Geschichte," pt. 2, p. 139; Otáhal, *Manuscript Controversy*, p. 258.

40. This conclusion seems to be indisputable and was originally put forward in a 1930 article by F. Roubík, "Účast policie v útoku na Rukopisy roku 1858" (The participation of the police in the attack on the manuscripts in 1858), in *Od pravěku k dnešku* (From prehistoric times to the present), vol. 2 (Prague, 1930). Stölzl, in repeating the story, refers to the once-secret files of the Prague Police Praesidium (PPT) now housed in the Státní Ústřední Archiv.

41. Stölzl, "Zur Geschichte," pt. 2, p. 139.

42. On the reforms of 1860–61, see Macartney, *History of the Habsburg Empire,* pp. 495–516; and, particularly with a view to the ways in which political contest expressed itself in stridently ethnic terms, Cohen, *The Politics of Ethnic Survival,* pp. 45–72.

43. See Gary B. Cohen, "Jews in German Liberal Politics: Prague, 1860–1914," *Jewish History* 1(1986): 55–74; and Stölzl, "Zur Geschichte," pt. 2, pp. 146–48.

44. Stölzl, "Zur Geschichte," pt. 2, pp. 147–48.

45. Markus Teller, *Die Juden in Böhmen und ihre Stellung in der Gegenwart* (Prague, 1863). Stölzl, Kestenberg-Gladstein, and Kisch all attribute authorship to Teller, as does Otto Muneles's *Bibliographical Survey of Jewish Prague,* p. 221. According to Muneles, Teller also wrote a number of articles for the Jewish democratic newspaper of the 1848 Revolution, *Österreichisches Central-Organ für Glaubensfreiheit, Cultur, Geschichte und Literatur der Juden* (p. 182).

46. "In the dim, distant past, shortly after the entry of the boyars into [Bohemia], many of the sons of Israel were to be found [there]. They themselves had looked for a resting place there, and this new homeland would from that time until the present be the Fatherland to millions [*sic!*] of Jews. It is unfortunate that so little from the history of the first entry of Jews to Bohemia has been preserved; otherwise one might be able to trace their striving for what is better and higher back to Bohemia's prehistory [*Urzeit*]" (Teller, "Aus dem königgrätzer Kreise," *Der Orient,* 9 July 1842. Stölzl makes reference to this article in "Zur Geschichte," pt. 1, p. 200).

47. "Doch findet man, daß die Juden in den alten Zeiten die Träger der Intelligenz bei verschiedenen Völkern gewesen, daß sie ihnen bei verschiedenen Staatsactionen wichtige Dienste geleistet, und daß sie bestrebt waren, das Epitheton eines auserwählten Volkes in mannigfacher Beziehung augeszeichnet findet" (Teller, *Die Juden in Böhmen,* p. 1).

48. Ibid., pp. 1–2.

49. Ibid., p. 2.

50. Ibid., p. 87.

51. Ibid., pp. 87–88.

52. Ibid., p. 90.

53. *Die Juden und die Nationalen: Ein Gegenstück zur Broschüre: "Die Juden in Böhmen."* Von einem Juden. (Prague, 1863).

54. "Long ago, before the Germans had migrated to Bohemia and forced their language and culture upon the residents of this land, there were—as Virbig, the wife of Count Conrad wrote [in 1090]—Jews here 'with much gold and silver.' They must have been here much earlier as well, and as late as the

fourteenth century still could possess landed property and even enjoyed a certain autonomy" (*Die Juden und die Nationalen,* p. 10).

55. Ibid., pp. 11–12.

56. Ibid., p. 12.

57. Ibid., p. 13; this entire paragraph is emphasized in the original.

58. On the social and cultural origins of the Czech-Jewish movement, see Kieval, *The Making of Czech Jewry,* pp. 10–63.

59. I do not know of anyone else who has questioned the authorship of this pamphlet or who has arrived at a similar conclusion.

60. *Die Juden und die Nationalen,* pp. 8–9.

61. Ibid., p. 9.

62. Ibid., p. 15.

63. These themes are all treated more fully in Kieval, *The Making of Czech Jewry,* passim.

64. McNeill, "Mythistory," p. 14.

Chapter 6. Education and National Conflict

1. For recent literature on the theory of modern nationalism, see Smith, *The Ethnic Origins of Nations;* idem, *The Ethnic Revival;* Gellner, *Nations and Nationalism;* Anderson, *Imagined Communities;* and Liah Greenfeld, *Nationalism: Five Roads to Modernity* (Cambridge, Mass. 1992).

2. See the discussion in Smith, *The Ethnic Revival,* pp. 87–133.

3. See Friedrich Prinz, "Das kulturelle Leben," in *Handbuch der Geschichte der böhmischen Länder,* ed. K. Bosl (Stuttgart, 1970), 4:153–88.

4. Karel Adámek, *Z naší doby* (Of our times), (Velké Meziříčí, 1887), 2:60.

5. Franz Perko, "Die Tätigkeit des deutschen Schulvereines in Böhmen," *Deutsche Arbeit* 3 (1903–4): 391.

6. Ibid.

7. Jan Šafránek, *Školy české: Obraz jejich vývoje a osudů* (Czech schools: Portrait of their development and fortunes) (Prague, 1918), 2:226–32; Jaroslav Kopač, *Dějiny české školy a pedagogiky v letech 1867–1914* (History of the Czech school and pedagogy, 1867–1914) (Brno, 1968), pp. 16–19; and, most recently, Gary B. Cohen, *Education and Middle-Class Society in Imperial Austria, 1848–1918* (West Lafayette, 1996), pp. 36–54.

8. See, inter alia: Cohen, *Education and Middle-Class Society,* pp. 55–75; Perko, "Tätigkeit"; Adámek, *Z naší doby,* vol. 2; Prinz, "Das kulturelle Leben," p. 160; and Jiří Kořalka and R. J. Crampton, "Die Tschechen," in *Die Habsburgermonarchie 1848–1918,* ed. Adam Wandruszka and Peter Urbanitsch, vol. 3 (Vienna, 1980), 3:489–521.

9. Heinrich Rauchberg, *Der Nationale Besitzstand in Böhmen* (Leipzig, 1905), 1:8–11; František Friedmann, "Židé v Čechách" (Jews in Bohemia), in *Židé a židovské obce v Čechách v minulosti a v přítomnosti* (The Jews and Jewish communities of Bohemia in the past and in the present), ed. Hugo Gold (Brno, 1934), p. 733.

10. See the discussion in Rauchberg, *Der Nationale Bestizstand,* 1:10–14; also Emil Brix, *Die Umgangssprachen in Altösterreich zwischen Agitation und Assimilation* (Vienna, 1982), passim.

11. Dr. Inama-Sternegg, in 1900; quoted in Rauchberg, *Der Nationale Besitzstand,* 1:13–14.

12. Friedmann, "Židé v Čechách," p. 733; also Ezra Mendelsohn, "Jewish Assimilation in L'viv: The Case of Wilhelm Feldman," in *Nationbuilding and the Politics of Nationalism: Essays on Austrian Galicia,* ed. Andrei S. Markovits and Frank E. Sysyn (Cambridge, Mass., 1982), p. 94.

13. Ludmila Karníková, *Vývoj obyvatelstva v českých zemich 1754–1914* (Evolution of the population in the Czech lands) (Prague, 1965), pp. 348–51; cited in Bruce M. Garver, *The Young Czech Party,* p. 326.

14. Cohen, *The Politics of Ethnic Survival,* pp. 92–93. By "Prague" is meant the eight districts of the city proper plus the four "inner suburbs" of Karlín, Smíchov, Vinohrady, and Žižkov.

15. Gary B. Cohen, "Ethnicity and Urban Population Growth: The Decline of the Prague Germans, 1880–1920," in *Studies in East European Social History,* ed. Keith Hutchins (Leiden, 1981), 2:11.

16. The figures come from Adámek, *Z naší doby,* 2:10–11, which in turn were based on official census reports.

17. Figures derived from *Österreichische Statistik,* vol. 63, pt. 3 (Vienna, 1902); cited in Kořalka and Crampton, "Die Tschechen," p. 511.

18. Cohen, *Education and Middle-Class Society,* p. 55.

19. Adámek, *Z naší doby,* 2:77.

20. *Statistisches Handbuchlein des Kaisertums Österreich für das Jahr 1865* (Vienna, 1867), p. 52; *Österreichisches Statistisches Handbuch* 34 (1915), p. 316; cited in Kořalka and Crampton, "Die Tschechen," p. 510.

21. Adámek, *Z naší doby,* 2:12, 77.

22. Ibid., 2:11–12.

23. Ibid., 2:12.

24. Ibid., 2:83.

25. *Österreichisches Statistisches Handbuch* 10 (1891): 40–43. On the eve of the partition of the University of Prague (winter and summer semesters, 1880–81), Czechs comprised 66.2 percent and 67.3 percent of the total student body. Ibid., 1 [1882]: 46–49.)

26. Ibid., pp. 56–59.

27. Ibid., 10 (1891): 48–51.

28. Adámek, *Z naší doby,* 2:81.

29. Austrian law stipulated that in order for the state to set up a minority language school in any district, first, the parents of minority children had to request one, and second, there had to be a minimum of forty children divided among five grades. (Perko, "Tätigkeit," p. 391.)

30. See Prinz, "Das kulturelle Leben," p. 160; Perko, "Tätigkeit"; and Adámek, *Z naší doby,* vol. 2, passim.

31. Perko, "Tätigkeit," pp. 388, 408–9.

32. Garver, *Young Czech Party,* pp. 112–13.

33. *Österreichische Statistik,* vol. 64, pt. 3 (Vienna, 1902); Bureau für Statistik der Juden, *Die Juden in Österreich* (Berlin, 1908), p. 109. See also Gustav Otruba, "Statistische Materialien zur Geschichte der Juden in den böhmischen Ländern seit dem Ausgang des 18. Jahrhunderts," in *Die Juden in den böhmischen Ländern,* ed. Ferdinand Seibt (Munich and Vienna, 1983), pp. 323–51.

34. *Österreichische Statistik,* vol. 63 (1902), pp. 78–79; Heřman, "The Evolution of the Jewish Population in Prague, 1869–1939," in *Papers in Jewish Demography 1977,* edited by U. O. Schmelz, P. Glikson, and S. Della Pergola (Jerusalem, 1980), p. 54.

35. On the role of the *Normalschule* in the transformation of Jewish life after 1780, see chapter 2.

36. Adámek, *Z naší doby,* 2:14. The figure of 4,470 may have included non-Jewish students who for one reason or another attended German-Jewish schools. Adámek lists them as Jews, but Kořán, writing in the *Kalendář česko-židovský* (1886–87), claims that 192 Catholics and 17 Protestants were enrolled in Jewish communal schools in the Czech countryside in 1885–86 (p. 101). The total number of Jewish students enrolled in *Volks-* and *Bürgerschulen* (*Obecné* and *Měšťánské školy*), both public and private, in Bohemia in 1880 was 13,574—about 1.6 percent of the total primary school enrollment. (See *Österreichisches Statistisches Handbuch* 1 [1882], pp. 82–83.) *Die Juden in Österreich* (Berlin, 1908) gives the percentage of Jewish boys at public elementary schools in all of Austria as 2 percent in 1880, 2.35 percent in 1890, and 2.6 percent in 1900. The percentage of girls was 3.18 percent in 1880, 3.81 percent in 1890, and 4.31 percent in 1900. (Bureau für Statistik der Juden, *Die Jüden in Österreich,* p. 87.)

37. Adámek, *Z naší doby,* 2:14.

38. See Ruth Kestenberg-Gladstein, "The Jews between Czechs and Germans in the Historic Lands, 1848–1918," in *The Jews of Czechoslovakia* (Philadelphia, 1968), 1: 49–50.

39. Šafránek, *Školy české,* 2: 201.

40. Josef Kořán, "Židovské školy v Čechách" (Jewish schools in the Czech lands, *Kalendář česko-židovský* (hereafter *KČŽ*) 6 (1886–87): 97–102; and idem, "Žid)ovské školy v Čechách roku 1894–95" (Jewish schools in the Czech lands in 1894–95), *KČŽ* 16 (1896–97): 152–57.

41. Cohen, "Ethnicity and Urban Population Growth," pp. 25–26; idem, *The Politics of Ethnic Survival,* pp. 224–25; and idem, "Jews in German Society: Prague, 1860–1914," *Central European History* 10 (1977), p. 38.

42. Bureau für Statistik der Juden, *Die Juden in Österreich,* p. 92. *Österreichisohes Statistisches Handbuch* 1 (1882) gives slightly different figures. For the academic year 1880–81: number of Jewish students at *Gymnasien* and *Realgymnasien* in Bohemia—1,761 (11.1% of the total); at *Realschulen/Reálky*—544 (10.8%). (*Österreichisches Statistisches Handbuch* 1 (1882): 70–71.)

By comparison, only 8.2 percent of all gymnasium students in Galicia in 1869 were Jews (Filip Friedman, *Die galizischen Juden im Kampfe um ihre Gleichberechtigung* [*1848–1868*] [Frankfurt a.M., 1929]; cited in Mendelsohn, "Jewish Assimilation in L'viv," p. 99).

43. Bureau für Statistik der Juden, *Die Juden in Österreich,* p. 94. The tables compiled by Gustav Otruba in *Die Juden in den böhmischen Ländern*—which are derived from *Österreichische Statistik,* vol. 9, pt. 1—are largely in agreement. One exception concerns Jewish attendance at Czech *Reálky (Realschulen),* which is given as 48 by *Juden in Österreich* but as 495 by Otruba! The latter is obviously in error. A perusal of figures for the two decades beginning in 1882 reveals that the number of Jewish students at Czech *Reálky* never exceeded 315. As late as 1890, the number was only 76.

The city of Lwów (Lemberg) in Eastern Galicia offers an instructive contrast to the situation in Prague and Bohemia. By the end of the nineteenth century, German culture had lost much of its hold on the Jews in the Galician cities and towns. Most assimilating Jews chose to affiliate with the more prominent—and politically the more attractive—Polish culture. Jews comprised 18.3 percent of all gymnasium students in Lwów in 1896, and over 64 percent of the Jewish students attended Polish institutions; the remainder frequented the German school. See Mendelsohn, "Jewish Assimilation in L'viv," p. 99.

44. For the "Austrian" half of the monarchy generally, see Cohen, *Education and Middle-Class Society,* pp. 140-69. Jewish attendance at Austrian universities (determined by religious declaration) grew from 1.38 per one thousand Jews in 1869-70 to 3.67 per thousand in 1909-10. During this same period, the Catholic rate of enrollment grew from 0.44 to 0.98 per thousand, the Protestant rate from 0.92 to 1.58 per thousand, and the Eastern Orthodox from 0.36 to 1.27 per thousand. One might also compare Jews (as an ethnic group) to Germans and Czechs, recognizing that the latter two categories included Jews as well as non-Jews. During the period 1879-80 to 1909-10, German attendance at Austrian universities grew from 0.57 per one thousand Germans to 1.12 per thousand. Czech attendance rose from 0.30 to 0.70 per thousand. (See table 4/3 in Cohen, p. 148.)

45. G. Otruba, "Die Universitäten in der Hochschulorganisation der Donau-Monarchie," in *Student und Hochschule im 19. Jahrhundert,* ed. M. Rassem (Göttingen, 1975), pp. 75-155; *Österreichisches Statistisches Handbuch* 1 (1882): 46-49 and 56-59. I do not have at my disposal the precise number of Bohemian Jews who chose to attend the University of Vienna rather than the University of Prague. Marsha Rozenblit's *The Jews of Vienna, 1867-1914: Assimilation and Identity* (Albany, 1983) offers data on the place of birth of Jewish gymnasium students in Vienna but nothing concerning Jewish university students.

46. Bureau für Statistik der Juden, *Juden in Österreich,* p. 102. To resume the comparison with Lwów, Mendelsohn points out that in 1901-02, 21.9 percent of all the students at the University of Lwów—which was to all extents a Polish institution—were Jews. Jews also comprised 14.3 percent of the Lwów Technical College (Mendelsohn, "Assimilation in L'viv," p. 99).

47. Adámek, *Z naší doby,* 2:20.

48. On Havlíček's rejection of Kapper's pro-Czech writings, see chapter 3.

49. Adámek, *Z naší doby,* 2:32-33.

50. For the exact location of these towns and villages, see Jiří Fiedler, *Jewish Sights of Bohemia and Moravia* (Prague: Sefer, 1991).

51. Adámek, *Z naší doby,* 2:33. In the fourth and final volume of the work, published in 1890, Adámek indicated that the *Schulverein* subsidized 14 percent of the private Jewish elementary schools in Bohemia, certainly a low figure given the ardor of the Czech national grievance against the Jews. (4:80.)

52. Josef Kořán, "Židovské školy v Čechách," *KČŽ* 6 (1886–87): 97–102.

53. Ibid., p. 101.

54. J. S. Kraus, "Německo-židovské školy v Čechách" (The German-Jewish schools of Bohemia), *KČŽ* 2 (1882–83): 117–25.

55. On the impact of Czech culture and politics on Jewish society in Bohemia, see Kieval, *The Making of Czech Jewry.*

56. Bondy won a seat in the Bohemian Diet in 1883 as a representative of Prague's Staré Město. Zalud and Julius Reitler were sent to the Diet the same year from Josefov—the old Jewish quarter of Prague, long considered to be a stronghold of German power—and Zucker was elected to the Imperial Diet in Vienna in 1885. On Bondy, see *Ottův slovník naučný* (Otta's Encyclopedia) (1891), 4:337, and *KČŽ* 4 (1884–85): 57–59. For Zucker, *KČŽ* 6 (1886–87): 58–63. And for Žalud, *KČŽ* 8 (1888–89): 55–58.

57. The National Liberals broke away from Rieger's National Party in 1874 over the issue of "passive resistance," i.e., nonparticipation in the Diet and the Reichsrat, a policy that had been practiced by the National Party since 1867. On the split between Old and Young Czechs, see Garver, *The Young Czech Party,* pp. 1–87.

58. The largest and most powerful of the national unions were the Národní jednota pošumavská (founded in 1884) and the Národní jednota severočeská (1885). In addition to providing peripheral support to the Central School Foundation, the national unions offered legal aid to Czechs in predominantly German districts who were involved in litigation with local or imperial authorities, and conducted private censuses in such districts, encouraging Czech residents to take the opportunity to declare their Czech allegiance. See Garver, *The Young Czech Party,* pp. 112–15.

59. Svaz Čzechů-židů v Československé republice, *Dějiny českožidovského hnutí* (History of the Czech-Jewish movement) (Prague, 1932), p. 8.

60. "Naš úkol" (Our mission), *Českožidovské listy,* 15 September 1894. *Českožidovské listy* (1894–1907) began as a fortnightly publication but eventually appeared every week. Issued from Prague, it reflected the official views of both the SČAŽ and the Czech-Jewish National Union. It was also closely allied to the Young Czech Party on national issues.

61. *Českožidovské listy,* 15 October 1894, pp. 1–2.

62. *Českožidovské listy,* 1 November 1894, p. 1.

63. Kořán, "Židosvké školy v Čechách roku 1894–95."

64. Kořán, "Židovské školy v Čechách roku 1894–95," pp. 155–56. Many of these Catholic and Protestant children actually attended Jewish-supported schools (180 Catholics and 17 Protestants in 1885; 163 and 13, respectively, in 1894).

65. Kořán, "Židovské školy v Čechách roku 1894–95," pp. 155–57. Kořán continued to demonstrate dissatisfaction with the overall educational situation

of the Jews. In 1890 there were more children between the ages of six and fourteen in Jewish schools than the total number of registered Germans in those localities (a measurement that ordinarily would indicate the need for a minority school). In Nový Bydžov, for example, only 28 people in the entire town registered as Germans, yet there were 53 children in the German school; in Hořice the figures were 14 (Germans) and 28 (children); in Mělník, 18 and 40; in Kolín, 98 and 131. There were even instances of German-Jewish schools in areas where not a single person had registered as a German. These statistics indicate a sociocultural phenomenon unique to Bohemian Jewry. Normally bilingual and sensitive to the political climate, they readily indicated their national standing as Czech, yet demonstrated unwavering loyalty to the ideal of a German education.

66. *Českožidovské listy,* 1 February 1898.

67. See *Českožidovské listy,* 1 January 1898, p. 7.

68. *Českožidovské listy,* 15 March 1898, p. 3.

69. Ibid., pp. 3–4.

70. "Národní jednota Českožidovská," *KČŽ* 26 (1906–7): 181–82.

71. Compare the figures in the two articles by Kořán: "Židovské školy v Čechách" and "Židovksé školy v Čechách roku 1894–95." Even the attendance figure of 4,240 for 1885 represented a drop of over 600 from that of 1880 (Bureau für Statistik der Juden, *Die Juden in Österreich,* p. 82).

72. The population of the school dropped by about 23 percent (from 190 to 147) between 1885 and 1898. The 1885 figure is given in Kořán, "Židovské školy v Čechách," *KČŽ* 6 (1886–87).

73. *Statistická příručka království českého* (Statistical handbook of the Kingdom of Bohemia) (Prague, 1913), p. 131; and Bureau für Statistik der Juden, *Die Juden in österreich,* p. 87.

74. Bureau für Statistik der Juden, *Die Juden in Österreich,* pp. 82–84.

75. Ferdinand Seibt, ed., *Die Juden in den böhmischen Ländern* (Munich, 1983). Appendix 5: "Der Anteil der Juden am höheren Schulwesen Böhmens, Mährens, und Schlesiens," pp. 348–49. The figures in this table accord in nearly all instances with the data provided by Bureau für Statistik der Juden, *Die Juden in Österreich* for the school years 1881–82 through 1903–4.

76. Seibt, *Die Juden in den böhmischen Ländern,* pp. 348–49.

77. The total number of Jewish students registered at Bohemian middle schools rose in absolute terms only slightly between 1882 and 1912, from 3,129 to 3,441. As a percentage of the student body, the second figure represented a decline from 12.1 percent to 8.4 percent. According to the Bureau für Statistik der Juden, *Die Juden in Österreich,* the Jewish population in Bohemian *Gymnasien* and *Realschulen* may have reached its peak in absoute terms in 1903–4, when it reached 2,744. However, the relative weight of Jewish attendance was never greater than in 1888–89, when 2,528 Jewish students in *Gymnasien* and *Realschulen* stood for 12 percent of the student body (pp. 94–95, 97).

78. Figures derived from Seibt, *Die Juden in den böhmischen Ländern,* pp. 348–49.

In the technical high schools (*Reálky* or *Realschulen*) Jewish attendance patterns took a different course. In 1882, the 495 Jews who went to Czech *Reálky* represented a healthy 11.3 percent of the student body. Thereafter the number dropped off precipitously (250, or 2.3 percent, by 1912), but the reasons for this are not apparent. On the German side, meanwhile, the number of Jews attending *Realschulen* nearly doubled between 1882 and 1912 (from 448 to 804), while their relative weight as a percentage of the whole declined slightly from 18.6 to 15.8 percent.

79. Seibt, *Die Juden in den böhmischen Ländern,* p. 350; *Österreichisches Statistisches Handbuch* 1 (1882): 46–47. In contrast, Jews comprised more than 25 percent of the student body at the University of Vienna in 1880–81, 11.7 percent at the University of Lemberg, 8.9 percent at Cracow, and 27.7 percent at Czernowitz.

80. *Österreichisches Statistisches Handbuch* 10 (1891): 40–43.

81. *Österreichisches Statistisches Handbuch* 20 (1901): 78–81; Seibt, *Die Juden in den böhmischen Ländern,* p. 350. During the same winter semester, 1899–1900, Jews comprised 24.7 percent of the student body at the University of Vienna, 19.8 percent at the University of Lemberg, 15.8 percent at Cracow, and 44.4 percent at Czernowitz.

82. Figures derived from Bureau für Statistik der Juden, *Die Juden in Österreich,* p. 102.

83. Ibid., pp. 103–4.

84. Ratios derived from ibid., p. 103.

Chapter 7. Jan Hus and the Prophets

1. On Jewish life in preemancipatory Prague, see chapters 1 and 2. On the ethnic balance in Prague in the 1840s, see Cohen, *The Politics of Ethnic Survival,* pp. 20–26.

2. We read in the reminiscence of David Rosin of Breslau: "Allein modern war an ihm nur sein wissenschaflichter Geist, sein Forscherdrang, sein geistlicher Sinn, sein Fühlen und Streben, mit einem Worte, sein Inneres; äußerlich erschien er in der etwas ermäßigten Tracht der Glaubensgenossen seines Heimatlandes, seine Sprache war deutsch, trug jedoch Klang und Farbe des Jargons, aus dem sie künstlich umgebildet worden war, noch ungewollt zur Schau" ("Erinnerungen an S. L. Rapoport," in Kaufmann, *Das Centenarium S.J.L. Rapoport's,* p. 401).

3. On the scholarly career of Solomon Judah Rapoport, see David Kaufmann, "Zu S.J.L Rapoport's hundertstem Geburtstag," in *Das Centenarium S.J.L. Rapoport's,* pp. 389–94; Simon Bernfeld, *Toledot Shir* (History of S[olomon] J[udah] R[apoport]) (Warsaw, 1899); and Isaac Barzilay, *Shlomoh Yehudah Rapoport (Shir), 1790–1867, and His Contemporaries: Some Aspects of Jewish Scholarship of the Nineteenth Century* (Israel, 1969).

4. The memoirs of such individuals as Fritz Mauthner (*Prager Jugendjahre* [Frankfurt a.M., 1969]); Bergmann ("Prag," pp. 83–91; also his general introduction, "Petaḥ davar," to the same volume); and Franz Kafka (*Diaries, 1910–1923* [New York, 1948], and *Letter to His Father* [New York, 1953]) are informative in this regard. Mauthner's family moved to Prague from the Bo-

hemian village of Hořice. Kafka's father, Hermann, grew up in Osek in southern Bohemia. And Bergmann, although born in Prague, spent long periods of time as a child in the village of Chrastice.

5. Vladimír Sadek, "La Synagogue réformée de Prague (La 'Vieille Ecole') et les études juives au cours du 19è siècle," *Judaica Bohemiae* 16 (1980): 119–23.

6. To date there is no systematic study of Jewish life in the Czech countryside. Inferences can be drawn from both Czech-Jewish and German-Jewish memoirs. The following works are also worthy of mention: Kestenberg-Gladstein, "The Jews between Czechs and Germans"; Salomon Ehrmann, "Böhmische Dorfjuden: Erinnerungen aus früher Jugend," *B'nai B'rith: Monatsblätter der Grossloge für den Čechoslovakischen Staat* 4 (1925), 217–23, 235–44, and 261–68; and Albert Kohn, ed., *Die Notablenversammlung der Israeliten Böhmens in Prag: Ihre Berathungen und Beschlüße* (Vienna, 1852).

7. Kestenberg-Gladstein, *Neuere Geschichte*, passim.

8. Vojtěch Rakous, "Drobné vzpomínky" (Minor reminiscences), *KČŽ* 38 (1918–19), 21–23.

9. Ibid.

10. *Českožidovské listy*, 15 December 1898, p. 2.

11. On the early history of the Czech-Jewish movement, see Vlastimila Hamáčková, "Débuts du mouvement assimilateur tchécho-juif," *Judaica Bohemiae* 14 (1978): 15–23; Josef Vyskočil, "Die Tschechisch-Jüdische Bewegung," *Judaica Bohemiae* 3 (1967): 36–55; and *Dějiny českožidovské hnutí*.

12. "The need has long been felt, but up to now not fulfilled, that the prayers of the Jews—professors of the Mosaic faith, living in the Czech lands and having command of the Czech language—should for once appear in the national tongue" (from the introduction to Kraus's 1847 *Siddur*; quoted in August Stein, Předmluva [Foreword] to *Maarche-Lew: Modlitby Israelitův* [Prague, 1884]). See also Viktor Teytz, "Trochu retrospektivy a vzpomínek" (A little retrospect and some memories), *KČŽ* 28 (1908–9): 155–59—on Hynek Kraus and Siegfried Kapper.

13. Stein, "Předmluva" (Foreword) to *Maarche-Lew: Modlitby Israelitův*.

14. Vojtěch Rakous, "Hrst vzpomínek" (A fistful of memories), *KČŽ* 25 (1905–6); also in idem, *Vojkovičtí a přespolní* (The folks of Vojkovičtí and from out of town) (Prague, 1910), pp. 127–28.

15. J. S. Kraus, "Or-Tomid," *KČŽ* 4 (1884–85): p. 112.

16. Josef Žalud, "Z minulosti a přítomnosti …" (From the past and the present), *KČŽ* 12 (1892–93): p. 67.

17. Hynek Kraus, *Modlitby pro dcery israelské* (Prayers for Jewish daughters) (Prague, 1881).

18. Mořic Kraus, *Haggadah pro první dva večery pasahu* (Prague, 1889).

19. By Mořic Kraus: *Žalmy a modlitby v den narozenin Jeho Veličenstva* (1886); *Pátero modliteb pro sabat a svátky* (1886); *Pohřební modlitba* (1887); and *České modlitby při veřejné bohoslužbě v synagoze "Or-Tomid"* (1888).

20. Stein, *Maarche-Lew: Modlitby Israelitův*.

21. Stein, "Předmluva" to *Maarche-Lew: Modlitby Israelitův*, pp. i–iii.

22. On the radicalization of political life in the 1890s, see: Kieval, *The Making of Czech Jewry*, pp. 64–77; and Michael Riff, "Czech Antisemitism and the

Jewish Response before 1914," *Wiener Library Bulletin* 29 (1976): 8–20. Concerning the Czech economic boycott, *Svůj k svému* (Each to his own), see J. Svozil, "Několik slov o hesle 'Svůj k svému'" (A few words concerning the slogan "Each to his own"), *Naše doba* 8 (1900–1): 641–46, for a moderate Czech view on the use of economic boycott as a weapon in the national controversy; and *Českožidovské listy,* 1 March 1898, pp. 1–2 for a Czech-Jewish view.

23. Both incidents reported in Riff, "Czech Antisemitism," p. 10. On the interplay of nationalism, antisemitism, and ritual murder discourse, see chapter 8.

24. The franchise for the 1897 elections was expanded to include all males over age twenty-four in a new fifth curia (Garver, *The Young Czech Party,* pp. 231–237). On Březnovský, see Christoph Stölzl, *Kafkas böses Böhmen: Zur Sozialgeschichte eines Prager Juden* (Munich, 1975), pp. 61–62.

25. Berthold Sutter, *Die Badenischen Sprachverordnungen von 1897: Ihre Genesis und ihre Auswirkungen vornehmlich auf die innerösterreichischen Alpenländer,* vol. 1 (Graz and Cologne, 1960); Stanley B. Winters, "Kramář, Kaizl, and Hegemony of the Young Czech Party, 1891–1901," in *The Czech Renascence of the Nineteenth Century,* ed. Peter Brock and H. Gordon Skilling (Toronto, 1970), p. 304.

26. See the discussions in Kieval, *The Making of Czech Jewry,* pp. 71–77; Sutter, *Die Badenischen Sprachverordnungen,* 2:231–32; and Riff, "Czech Antisemitism," pp. 11–12.

27. Riff, "Czech Antisemitism," p. 12; Sutter, *Die Badenischen Sprachverordnungen,* 2:31.

28. "Bouřlivý den v Praze" (Stormy day in Prague), *Národní listy,* 30 November 1897; and "Druhý den po německé provokáci" (The second day after the German provocations), *Národní listy,* 1 December 1897. Cited in Riff, "Czech Antisemitism," pp. 11–12.

29. Quoted in František Červinka, "The Hilsner Affair," *Leo Baeck Institute Yearbook* 13 (1968): 145.

30. Two general treatments of the Polná ritual murder trial have appeared recently in Czech: Bohumil Černý, *Justičný omyl: Hilsneriáda* (A judicial error: The Hilsner affair) (Prague, 1990); and Jiří Kovtun, *Tajuplná vražda; Případ Leopolda Hilsnera* (A mysterious murder: The case of Leopold Hilsner) (Prague, 1994). See also Hillel J. Kieval, "Representation and Knowledge in Medieval and Modern Accounts of Jewish Ritual Murder," *Jewish Social Studies: History, Culture, Society,* n.s., 1 (1994–95): 52–72.

31. Numerous articles appeared on this theme in the Czech-Jewish press between 1897 and 1900. In particular I would point to the lead article ("Svůj k svému") in *Českožidovské listy* for 1 March 1898. It appeared under the by-line "L."

32. Eduard Lederer, "Lueger triumfans," *Českožidovské listy,* 15 April 1897, in which he reported on a recent meeting held in Prague among the supporters of the antisemitic mayor of Vienna, Karl Lueger. Lederer listed the names of several Czech political leaders who were in attendance, among them Březnovský, Father Simon of the Christian Social Party, and Karel Baxa.

Also Lederer, "Politické strany české a hnutí českožidovské" (The Czech political parties and the Czech-Jewish movement) *Českožidovské listy,* 15 September 1897.

33. Lederer, "Politické strany české a hnutí českožidovské." *Samostátnost* (Independence) was a "radical progressive" journal founded by Antonín Hajn in 1897. *Rozhledy* (Perspectives) was edited by progressive reformist intellectuals from 1892 to 1901.

34. Eduard Lederer, "Pražská tragedie židovská" (The Prague Jewish tragedy), *Českožidovské listy*, 15 December 1897.

35. Maxim Reiner, "O nynějších poměrech hnutí českožidovského" (On the current relations of the Czech-Jewish movement) (speech delivered to the general meeting of the Czech-Jewish Political Union on 10 June 1899), published in *Českožidovské listy*, 15 June 1899.

36. Ibid., p. 4.

37. Eduard Lederer, "Židé a sociální demokracie" (The Jews and social democracy) *Českožidovské listy*, 15 June 1898. The paper's editors, aware of the volatile nature of the piece, placed the word *uvažuje* (contemplates) in front of the author's name rather than the usual *napsal* (written by).

38. Ibid., p. 2.

39. Viktor Vohryzek, "Epištoly k českým židům" (Letters to Czech Jews), *Českožidovské listy*, 15 March 1900; repr. in *K židovské otázce: Vybrané úvahy a články* (On the Jewish question: Selected essays and articles) (Prague, 1923), pp. 15–16.

40. Ibid., pp. 26–31, 35.

41. Ibid., pp. 33–34.

42. Ibid., p. 34.

43. Ibid.

44. "Zpráva o činnosti spolku 'Rozvoj'" (Report on the activities of the "Rozvoj" association), *KČŽ* 25 (1905–6): 178–79. The organization set for itself three main goals: the transformation of Czech national identity among the Jews from mere overcoating to real consciousness, firmly implanted in the heart of each individual; the social and economic reorientation and modernization of Bohemian Jewry; and lastly, the transformation of Judaism itself—to teach the Jews the difference, as the group put it, between religion and piety.

45. Cf. Vohryzek's inaugural article in *Rozvoj*, "Několik slov úvodem" (A few words of introduction), repr. in *K židovské otázce*, pp. 41–47. Vohryzek's overriding fear was that with the loss of purpose and direction, the Czech-Jewish movement would eventually lose whatever influence it once had on Bohemian Jewry. "Our intellectual fund has not sufficed," he complained, "has not equalled the difficulties of our tasks. If our defense is to be successful, it will be necessary to advance further toward the revision of our program" (p. 42).

46. Ibid., p. 43.

47. Vohryzek wrote in "K myšlenkové krisi naších dnů" (On the intellectual crisis of our times): "What we long for is not the philosophical transformation of religion, but the religious transformation of philosophy; we do not want religion to become popular philosophy, but rather philosophy [i.e., moral philosophy] to be our faith" (*K židovské otázce*, p. 106).

48. Vohryzek, "Několik slov úvodem," p. 43. In an apologetic tone Lederer argued that the modern Jew, on the strength of Judaism's ethical teachings, could grow to the same moral and humanistic heights as his Christian neigh-

bor. Moreover, the values of Judaism as manifested in the ideals of the prophets were worthy of serving as ethical models for all people the world over (*Žid v dnešní společnosti* [The Jew in contemporary society] [Prague, 1902], pp. 73–74).

49. Perhaps the clearest statement of Masaryk's views on Hus, the Czech Reformation, and contemporary Czech nationalism can be found in a speech that he delivered several years later, in 1910. Entitled "Master Jan Hus and the Czech Reformation," it has been reprinted as "Jan Hus and the Czech Reformation" in T. G. Masaryk, *The Meaning of Czech History* (Chapel Hill, 1974), pp. 3–14.

50. Lederer, *Žid v dnešní společnosti*, p. 152; T. G. Masaryk, *Česká otázka: snahy a tužby národního obrození* (The Czedu question: effects and aspirations of the national rebirth) (Prague, 1895); and idem, *Naše nynější krise: Pád strany staročeské a počátkové směru nových* (Our current crisis: The fall of the old Czech Party and the beginnings of new directions) (Prague, 1905).

51. Masaryk, "Jan Hus and the Czech Reformation," p. 14.

52. Viktor Vohryzek, "Národohospodářské úvahy" (Reflections on the national economy), *Rozvoj*, 1904; repr. in *K židovské otázce*, p. 127.

53. Vohryzek, "Několik slov úvodem," p. 46.

54. Lederer, "Žid v dnešní společnosti," p. 111.

55. Viktor Vohryzek, "Jakými cestami by se mělo bráti naše hnutí!" (What roads ought our movement to have taken!), *Rozvoj*, 1904; repr. in *K židovské otázce*, p. 78.

56. Lederer's views on the subject can be seen most plainly in *Žid v dnešní společnosti* (pp. 47–84). In his exposition on rabbinic Judaism, Lederer was able to quote from a wide variety of sources, including *Tanchuma Lech Lecha, Pesikta Rabbati, Exodus Rabba,* and *Sifra* (all *midrashic* compilations), as well as from various tractates of the Talmud. It is not clear, however, whether he used the Hebrew and Aramaic originals or German translations.

57. Viktor Vohryzek, "Úvodem k třetímu ročníku *Rozvoje*" (Introduction to the third volume of *Rozvoj*), *Rozvoj*, 1906; repr. in *K židovské otázce*, pp. 197–98.

58. Viktor Vohryzek, "Pryč od Haliče" (Away from Galicia), *Rozvoj*, 1904; repr. in *K židovské otázce*, pp. 134, 135.

59. Vohryzek, "K myšlenkové krisi," pp. 105–6.

60. When Masaryk urged his listeners at a gathering in 1910 to "break [their] ties with Rome," he meant that they must loosen their ties to the Catholic Habsburg dynasty and at the same time overcome the "Rome" within themselves in order to bring about a moral rebirth of the nation. (Masaryk, "Jan Hus and the Czech Reformation," pp. 13–14.)

61. Moritz Lazarus, *The Ethics of Judaism,* trans. Henrietta Szold (Philadelphia, 1900–1901), 1:113–14. On pp. 112–13, Lazarus writes: "The fundamental law, 'you shall be holy,' which sums up all morality in one comprehensive expression, does not continue with 'for I so will it,' nor with 'for I so command'; it reads, 'you shall be holy, for I am Holy,' and other moral laws close simply with the declaration, 'I am God.'"

62. Viktor Vohryzek, "Zápas o reformy" (Struggle for reform), *Rozvoj*, 1906; repr. in *K židovské otázce*, pp. 207–8.

63. Ibid., p. 208.

64. Vohryzek, "K myšlenkové krisi," p. 111. In a similar tone, Bohdan Klineberger proclaimed in a small work in 1911 that the password of the renewed Judaism would be "integrity toward everyone." By this he meant openness and honesty on the part of Jews toward all members of society. (Klineberger, *Naše budoucnost* [Our future] [Prague, 1911], p. 40.)

65. Klineberger, *Naše budoucnost*, p. 41.

66. Otakár Kraus, "Počátky berlínské reformy" (The beginnings of the Berlin reform), *KČŽ* 25 (1905–6), pp. 119–25, in which he gives his full support to the Berlin reform movement led by Samuel Holdheim. The basis of religion, Kraus argues, is not ritual practice but good behavior and thought. See also his contribution of the following year: "O vývoji židovského náboženství" (On the evolution of the Jewish religion), *KČŽ* 26 (1906–7).

Bohdan Klineberger, *Náboženský cit: Rozbor hodnoty náboženství* (Religious feeling: An analysis of the value of religion) (Prague, 1906). A lengthy philosophical-psychological study of the nature of religious sensibility.

Chapter 8. Death and the Nation

1. Convenient sources for the Xanten affair are *The Jewish Chronicle* (London) and *Neue Freie Presse* (Vienna) for 1892; see also *Der Fall Buschhof: Aktenmässige Darstellung des Xantener Knabenmord-Prozesses* (Frankfurt a.M., 1892); and *Der Xantener Knabenmord vor dem Schwurgericht zu Cleve 4.–14. Juli 1892: Vollständiger stenographischer Bericht* (Berlin, 1893).

For the Hilsner trial, see Artur Nussbaum, *Der Polnaer Ritualmordprozess: Eine Kriminalpsychologische Untersuchung auf aktenmässiger Grundlage* (Berlin, 1906); Georg R. Schroubek, "Der 'Ritualmord' von Polná: Traditioneller und moderner Wahnglaube," in *Antisemitismus und jüdische Geschichte*, ed. Rainer Erb and Michael Schmidt, pp. 149–71 (Berlin, 1987); and Červinka, "The Hilsner Affair."

Recent treatments of the Polná trial in Czech are Černý, *Justičný omyl: Hilsneriáda;* and Kovtun, *Tajuplná vražda.*

2. See, in this regard, Hillel J. Kieval, "Antisémitisme ou savoir social? Sur la genèse du procès moderne pour meurtre rituel," *Annales: Histoire, Sciences Sociales* 49, no. 5 (1994): 1091–1105; and idem, "The Importance of Place: Comparative Aspects of the Ritual Murder Trial in Modern Central Europe," in *Comparing Jewish Societies*, ed. Todd M. Endelman, pp. 135–65 (Ann Arbor, 1997).

3. A good selection of such reports can be found in the Central State Archive in Prague (hereafter SÚA), PM 8/1/9/1, for the years 1881 to 1900.

4. SÚA, PM (1881–1890), 8/1/9/1 (105).

5. SÚA, PM (1881–1890), 8/1/9/1 (3169, 4036, 4391, and 4511).

The last file contains several reports from the *Bezirkshauptmannschaft* in Příbram concerning Rohling's brochure, its content, and its local impact. It includes a copy of the newspaper *Horymír: Tydenník zábavný a poučný* from Příbram, dated 28 April 1883. There is an ad for the Czech edition of the book on the back page (above a much larger advertisement for Dr. Rosa's "balsam of life," which promised "a quick and sure aid against all diseases of the stomach and their consequences." (SÚA, 8/1/9/1, 1883, [4511].)

6. SÚA, PM (1881–1890) 8/1/9/1 (3785).

7. SÚA, PM (1881–1890) 8/1/9/1 (4761, 4925).

8. On Czech politics in the 1890s, see Winters, "Kramář, Kaizl, and the Hegemony of the Young Czech Party"; Garver, *The Young Czech Party;* and Tomáš Vojtěch, *Mladočeší a boj o politickou moc v Čechách* (The Young Czechs and the struggle for political power in Bohemia) (Prague, 1980).

9. On the relationship between economic boycott and antisemitism, see Kieval, *The Making of Czech Jewry,* pp. 64–83. On the campaign to close the German-language Jewish normal schools, see chapter 6.

10. On the accusation in Corfu see Hermann L. Strack, *The Jew and Human Sacrifice: Human Blood and Jewish Ritual. An Historical and Sociological Inquiry* (London, 1909), pp. 213–15; Ludwig Corel, *Das Blutmärchen: Seine Entstehung und Folgen bis zu den jüngsten Vorgängen auf Korfu* (Berlin, 1891), pp. 38–42; also Pearl L. Preschel, "The Jews of Corfu" (Ph.D. diss., New York University, 1984).

11. State Regional Archive, Prague (hereafter SOA), Prague Criminal Court (ZST Praha) C 613/1891.

Naše zájmy, a monthly paper, carried the subtitle "Czech Political Journal" (*Český časopis politický*) followed by the slogans "Each to his own!" (*Svojí k svému!*) and "Buy only from Christians!" *České zájmy,* also published by Hušek, had the subtitle "Journal for National-Economic and Social Repair" (*Časopis pro opravy národohospodářské a společenské*). Both papers could be characterized as radical, state right (*státní právo*), nationalist, and populist. In addition to being pointedly antisemitic, Hušek's papers also voiced strongly Pan-Slavic sentiments. Each issue of *Naše zájmy* carried two dates: the Julian and the Gregorian; both papers carried articles in Russian.

12. SOA, ZST Praha, C 729/1892.

13. Josef Deckert, *Ein Ritualmord: Aktenmäßig nachgewiesen* (Dresden, 1893). Deckert remarks in his introduction: "Es giebt aber gleichwohl solche Blutthaten, die gerichtlich und geschichtlich nachgewiesen wurden und die kein wahrheitsliebender Geschichtsforscher ableugnen kann" (p. 3).

14. For more recent literature on the case of Simon of Trent, see R. Po-Chia Hsia, *The Myth of Ritual Murder: Jews and Magic in Reformation Germany* (New Haven, 1988), pp. 42–65; and idem, *Trent 1475: Stories of a Ritual Murder* (New Haven, 1992).

15. The testimony in question came from a Jew named Engel:

Gefragt wie das komme, gestehe er, er habe gehört, daß man in dieser Weise bei der Ermordung von Christenkindern vorzugehen pflege. Er behauptet ferner, daß die Juden Christenkinderblut eintrocknen lassen und im pulverisierten zustande bei der Beschneidung ihrer Kinder gebrauchen, indem sie von diesem Pulver etwas auf die Beschneidungswunde streuen; das diene zur Schliessung der Wunde und zur Stillung des Blutes; Rabbi Joseph de Riva, der seine Kinder beschnitten habe, hätte solches Christenblut besessen und dabei gebraucht. (Deckert, *Ein Ritualmord,* p. 28.)

16. Ibid., p. 35.

17. Ibid., pp. 36-37.

18. Ibid., p. 37.

19. Ibid., pp. 37-38.

20. The State's Attorney ordered the booklet confiscated on 23 March 1893 on the usual grounds of incitement against a religious community. (ZST Praha, C 287/1893.)

21. *Jewish Chronicle*, 1 July 1892.

22. SÚA, PM (1891–1900), 8/1/9/1 (3786).

23. SÚA, PM (1891–1900), 8/1/9/1 (3786). That *Polaban* was the source of the "news" that Havlínová had died not by drowning but by a violent death is confirmed by *Naše zájmy*, a newspaper edited by Jaromír Hušek and sympathetic to *Polaban*.

24. SÚA, PM (1891–1900), 8/1/9/1 (3786).

25. SÚA, PM (1891–1900), 8/1/9/1 (3739).

26. Corel, *Das Blutmärchen*, p. 39.

27. *Naše zájmy*, 23 April 1893, p. 26; on the confiscation by the Prague Criminal Court, see ZST Praha, C 360/1893.

News of what had transpired in Kolín soon spread to other parts of the Bohemian countryside. Police informers in Kutná Hora, for example, reported an increase in anti-Jewish agitation; in Kladno, northwest of Prague, the Jews were threatened with revenge for an alleged ritual murder in that locality. (Riff, "Czech Antisemitism," p. 9; cf. SÚA, PM [1891–1900], 8/1/9/1 [3965].)

28. This development prompted an investigation by the Kutná Hora regional court, which resulted in no criminal indictments. (SOA, KS Kutná Hora, B 1892/147.)

29. Expressions of Czech economic nationalism tinged with antisemitism can be found in the following works: Adámek, *Z naší doby*, vol. 4; idem, *Slovo o židech* (A word about the Jews) (Chrudim, 1899); and Jaroslava Procházková, *Český lid a český žid* (The Czech people and the Czech Jew) (Žižkov, 1897).

30. "Svůj k svému" (Each to his own), *Polaban*, 23 August 1893; for the criminal case see SOA, KS Kutná Hora, C 1893/518.

31. "Svůj k svému" (Each to his own), *Polaban*, 30 August 1893.

32. My thanks to Kathryn Brown for suggesting to me this line of interpretation.

33. Cf. SOA, KS Kutná Hora, C 1885/151, 190, 199, 201, 261, 272.

34. SOA, KS Kutná Hora, C 1886/279.

35. SOA, KS Kutná Hora, C 1886/457; C 1891/230; C 1892/271, 530, 274.

36. SÚA, PM (1891–1900), 8/1/9/1 (13537/892).

37. *Píseň o židech*

[1)] A když je holce šestnác let každý žid ji chytá a když je jiz letita žádný žid ji nechytá[.]

2) Křesťanskou krev musí mít a kdyby ji nemněli tak by hodné smrděli.

3) Josefa Urbanová byla divka poctivá, nic zlého netvořila[?]

4) Tu hned židi přibjehli a Josefu svazali, košerák hned tady stál Josefu košeroval.

5) A když mněli krve dost židi přinesli strůžok[?], hned ji do něj zasili a v noci pryč odvezli. (Ibid.)

38. "Němčina v Čechách," *Naše doba* (1895), pp. 572–73; cf. Riff, "Czech Antisemitism," p. 10.

39. *Krakonoš: Politický a národohospodářský list,* 30 April 1893.

40. "Protižidovské hnutí v Čáslavsku," *Naše zájmy,* 23 April 1893.

41. Břetislav Reyrich, "Židé a Polná" (The Jews and Polná) (typescript, n.d.), Muzeum Vysočiny, pobočka Polná.

42. Ibid., p. 37.

43. Břetislav Reyrich [but spelled Rérych] *Polná: Průvodce po městě a okolí* (Polná: Guide through the city and surroundings) (Polná, 1927), p. 49.

44. According to the census returns of 1890, 198 Jews in Polná declared themselves to be Czech, 140 German. (See Černý, *Justičný omyl,* p. 10.)

45. Reyrich, "Židé a Polná," p. 43.

46. Ibid.

47. Ibid., esp. p. 47.

48. *Naše zájmy,* 23 April 1893, pp. 1–2.

49. *Vražda v Polné: Otisk článků "Radikálních listů" z 20. dubna, 3., 6., a 15. června 1899* (Murder in Polná: Reprint of articles from *Radikální listy* of 20 April, 3, 6, and 15 June 1899) (Prague, 1899), pp. 8–9.

Chapter 9. Masaryk and Czech Jewry

1. On Masaryk's role in combating antisemitism, see Ernst Rychnovsky, "Im Kampf gegen den Ritualmordaberglauben," in *Masaryk und das Judentum,* ed. Ernst Rychnovsky, pp. 166–273 (Prague, 1931); Jaroslav Rokycana, "Freunde in der Not," in ibid., pp. 300–315; and Jan Herben, "T.G. Masaryk über Juden und Antisemitismus," in ibid., pp. 274–99. Radical antisemites were just as prone as Masaryk's Jewish admirers to equate him with pro-Jewish policies. See Jan Rýs, *Hilsneriáda a TGM: K ctyřicatému výroči vražd polenských* (The Hilsner affair and T.G. Masaryk: On the fortieth anniversary of the Polná murders) (Prague, 1939).

2. See Kieval, *The Making of Czech Jewry,* pp. 10–63.

3. Leopold Hilsner, a Jewish vagabond, was accused of murdering a nineteen-year-old dressmaker, Anežka Hrůzová, in the town of Polná. The former Young Czech politician Karel Baxa participated in the trial as counsel for the victim's family and did much to promote "ritual murder" as the motive behind the killing. See bibliographical references in chapter 8.

4. Vohryzek, "Epištoly."

5. Ibid., pp. 15–16.

6. Ibid., p. 34.

7. Ibid.

8. "Zpráva o činnosti spolku 'Rozvoj.'" See also Kieval, *The Making of Czech Jewry,* pp. 77–92.

9. Oskar Donath, *Židé a židovství v české literatuře 19. a 20. století* (Jews and Judaism in nineteenth- and twentieth-century Czech literature) (Brno, 1930), 2:186–94.

10. *Dějiny českožidovského hnutí,* pp. 10–11.

11. On Masaryk's national and religious thought, see Roman Szporluk, *The Political Thought of Thomas G. Masaryk* (Boulder, 1981), pp. 55-125; Hanuš J. Hajek, *T. G. Masaryk Revisited: A Critical Assessment* (Boulder, 1983); and Masaryk's own works: *Česká otázka; Naše nynější krise;* and *Otázka sociální: Základy marxismu filosofické a sociologické* (The social question: Philosophical and social foundations of Marxism), 2 vols. (Prague, 1946).

On Czech-Jewish receptivity, see Evžen Štern, *Názory T. G. Masaryka* (The opinions of T. G. Masaryk) (Prague, 1910); Rychnovsky, "Im Kampf gegen den Ritualmordaberglauben"; and Rokycana, "Freunde in der Not."

12. See, for example, the piece by J. Svozil, "Několik slov o hesle 'Svůj k svému.'" Though the author argues in favor of limiting the influx of "foreign capital" and building up the "productive forces" of the Czech nation, he sets limits on the legitimate use of economic boycott as a weapon in the national struggle.

13. T. G. Masaryk, *Nutnost revidovat proces polenský* (The need to revise the Polná trial) (Prague, 1899); and idem, *Die Bedeutung des Polnaer Verbrechens für den Ritualaberglauben* (Berlin, 1900). On Masaryk's role in the defense of Hilsner, see Rychnovsky, "Im Kampf gegen den Ritualmordaberglauben," and Červinka, "The Hilsner Affair."

14. Vohryzek, "Několik slov úvodem." Also idem, "K myšlenkové krisi našich dnů."

For a more complete discussion of this theme, see chapter 7.

15. Lederer, *Žid v dnešní společnosti,* p. 152. Cf. Masaryk, "Jan Hus and the Czech Reformation."

16. Masaryk, "Jan Hus and the Czech Reformation," p. 14.

17. Vohryzek, "Národohospodářské úvahy," p. 127.

18. See chapter 7.

19. Quoted in Felix Weltsch, "Masaryk und der Zionismus," in *Masaryk und das Judentum,* ed. Ernst Rychnovsky (Prague, 1931), p. 104.

20. T. G. Masaryk, *Národnostní filosofie doby novější* (Contemporary national philosophy) (Jičín, 1905), p. 14; quoted in Weltsch, "Masaryk und der Zionismus," p. 102.

21. The *Wschód* interview quoted Masaryk as saying: "I confess that assimilation as a popular movement is downright impossible and laughable. The last decade, after all, has demonstrated this: despite all of its efforts assimilation has not achieved real results" (quoted in "Rozmluva s prof. Masarykem" [Conversation with Professor Masaryk], *Rozvoj,* 9 April 1909. See also Weltsch, "Masaryk und der Zionismus," pp. 72-74).

22. "Rozmluva s prof. Masarykem," *Rozvoj,* 9 April 1909.

23. Ibid.

24. Ibid.

25. T. G. Masaryk, "Ernest Renan o židovství jako plemenu a náboženství (*Le Judaisme comme race et comme religion,* 1883)" (Ernest Renan on Judaism as a race and a religion), *Sborník historický,* 1 (1883); repr. in *Masarykův sborník,* ed. V. K. Skvech (Prague, 1924-30), 1:61-68.

26. Ibid., pp. 67-68.

27. Ibid.

28. See note 14, this chapter.

29. From Masaryk's comments to the Austrian Reichsrat of 5 December 1907, quoted in Ernst Rychnovsky, *Masaryk* (Prague, 1930), pp. 92–95. He later repeats much the same story to Karel Čapek, who records it in his *Hovory s TGM* (Conversations with T. G. Masaryk), published originally between 1928 and 1935. See Čapek, *Hovory s TGM* (Prague, 1969), pp. 101–2.

30. Rychnovsky, *Masaryk*, pp. 93–94; Čapek, *Hovory s TGM*, p. 17.

31. This lesson came upon him one day during a class outing. After dinner, while his classmates ran about and amused themselves, a Jewish student slipped away. Masaryk followed him out of curiosity and discovered that he had gone behind a gate in order to say his prayers. The action of the Jewish student elicited in Masaryk a naive, emotional response: "I was ashamed somehow that a Jew should be praying while we were playing about. I could not get it out of my head that he had been praying as devoutly as we did, and that he had not forgotten his prayers, even for games" (Čapek, *Hovory s TGM*, p. 17; English trans. in Čapek, *President Masaryk Tells His Story* [New York, 1971], p. 29).

32. Čapek, *Hovory s TGM*, p. 17; idem, *President Masaryk*, p. 29.

33. Čapek, *Hovory s TGM*, p. 102; idem, *President Masaryk*, p. 189. Masaryk makes a less extreme claim in his memoirs of the war years, *Svetová revoluce: Za války a ve válce, 1914–1918* (The world revolution: During the war and in the war, 1914–1918) (Prague, 1925); published in English as *The Making of a State: Memoirs and Observations, 1914–1918* (New York, 1927):

I had many personal meetings with representatives of Orthodox Jewry as well as with Zionists. Among the latter I must mention Mr. Brandeis, a Judge of the Supreme Court, who came originally from Bohemia and enjoyed President Wilson's confidence. In New York Mr. Mack was a leading Zionist and I met Nahum Sokoloff, the influential Zionist leader. In America, as in Europe, Jewish influence is strong in the press, and it was good that it was not against us. Even those who did not agree with my policy were reserved and impartial. (*The Making of a State*, pp. 236–37.)

34. R. W. Seton-Watson, "Memorandum on Conversations with Masaryk (October 1914)," in *Masaryk in England* (Cambridge and New York, 1943), pp. 40–41.

35. Max Brod, *Streitbares Leben* (Munich, 1969), pp. 95–98.

36. Masaryk, *Otázka sociální*.

37. Ibid., 2:180–81. See also Jaroslav Dresler, ed., *Masarykova abeceda: Výbor z myšlenek Tomaše Garrigua Masaryka* (The Masaryk ABC: Selections from the thoughts of T. G. Masaryk) (Zurich, 1976), p. 110.

38. Masaryk, *Otázka sociální*, 2:182; cited (incompletely) in Weltsch, "Masaryk und der Zionismus," p. 70.

39. Masaryk, *Otázka sociální*, cited in Weltsch, "Masaryk und der Zionismus," p. 70.

40. Krejčí's remarks were published in *Selbstwehr* (Prague), 11 June 1909, under the title "Assimilation und Zionismus vom ethischen Standpunkt."

41. Jan Herben recalls the incident in "Julius Taussig," *KČŽ* 32 (1912–13), pp. 15–16. See also Vohryzek's remarks in "Náboženská společnost, či národnost?" (A religious society or a nationality?) *Rozvoj*, 1906; repr. in *K židovské otázce*, pp. 218–28.

42. See the chapter in Čapek's *Hovory s TGM* entitled "Dítě a jeho svět." Also the autobiographical fragment "Naš pan Fixl" (Our Mr. Fixl), published originally in *Besedy Času*, 24 February 1911 and reprinted in Jaromír Doležal, *Masarykova cesta životem* (Masaryk's way of life) (Brno, 1920–21), 2:37–39.

43. Kronberger, *Zionisten und Christen* (Leipzig, 1900); quoted in Weltsch, "Masaryk und der Zionismus," p. 71.

44. Ibid.

45. T. G. Masaryk, "Život církevní a náboženský roku 1904" (Church and religious life in 1904), *Naše doba* 12 (1905): 522. In this article Masaryk reviewed the first German translation of Aḥad Ha'am's collected essays, *'Al parashat derakhim* (published as *Am Scheidewege: Ausgewählte Essays,* authorized trans. by Israel Friedlaender [Berlin, 1904]).

46. Ibid., pp. 522–23.

47. "Aḥad Ha'am fights against Nietzschean individualism; he demonstrates that the Old Testament in the end is social, demanding loyalty to the collectivity" (ibid., p. 523).

48. Ibid.

49. Ibid.

50. In early December 1918 recently demobilized troops and other civilians together marauded the streets of Prague, physically attacking Jews and Jewish property. Demonstrations in May 1919 against profiteering and high prices led to the looting of shops and businesses in Prague and the suburbs. Many, but not all, of the establishments affected were owned by Jews. The most disturbing acts of violence occurred in November 1920, when mobs broke into the ancient Jewish Town Hall, tore apart paintings and furnishings, rifled through desk drawers, and destroyed priceless documents relating to the history of the Jews in the city. See Antony Polonsky and Michael Riff, "Poles, Czechoslovaks, and the 'Jewish Question', 1914–1921," in *Germany in the Age of Total War,* ed. Volker Berghahn and Martin Kitchen (London, 1981), pp. 88–93, 99; and Christoph Stölzl, "Die 'Burg' und die Juden: T. G. Masaryk und sein Kreis im Spannungsfeld der jüdischen Frage," in *Die "Burg"; Einflussreiche politische Kräfte um Masaryk und Beneš,* ed. Karl Bosl (Munich and Vienna, 1974), 2: 79–110, esp. pp. 94–98.

51. Quoted in Aharon Moshe Rabinowitz, "The Jewish Minority," in *The Jews of Czechoslovakia* (Philadelphia, 1968), 1:165.

52. Brod, *Streitbares Leben,* p. 104.

53. "Der jüdische Nationalrat beim Národní výbor," *Selbstwehr,* 1 November 1918. See also Max Brod, "Prag—Wien—Erinnerungen," in *The Jews of Austria,* ed. Josef Frankel (London, 1967), pp. 241–42; Oskar K. Rabinowicz, "Czechoslovak Zionism: Analecta to a History," in *The Jews of Czechoslovakia* (Philadelphia, 1971) 2:31; and Weltsch, "Masaryk und der Zionismus," pp. 79–86.

54. *Selbstwehr,* 8 November 1918, p. 2; Weltsch, "Masaryk und der Zionismus," pp. 79–86; Rabinowicz, "The Jewish Minority," pp. 159–61. Rabinowicz produces an English translation of the memorandum, ibid., pp. 218–21.

55. *Selbstwehr,* 8 November 1918, p. 2; Rabinowicz, "The Jewish Minority," pp. 218–19.

56. *Selbstwehr,* 8 November 1918, p. 2; Rabinowicz, "The Jewish Minority," pp. 219–20.

57. See the discussion in Ezra Mendelsohn, *The Jews of East Central Europe between the World Wars* (Bloomington, 1983), pp. 148–49.

58. Eduard Beneš to Ludvík Singer, 25 August 1919 (Central Zionist Archives, Jerusalem, Z4/583). Full text of the letter quoted (in English translation) in Rabinowicz, "The Jewish Minority," pp. 172–73.

59. Report of N. Sokolow (Central Zionist Archives, Z4/583); reproduced in Rabinowicz, "The Jewish Minority," pp. 174–77.

60. The constitution itself did not indicate expressly who the legally recognized national minorities were. Instead, this was spelled out in documents that accompanied and clarified the constitution.

61. Weltsch, "Masaryk und der Zionismus," pp. 88–89; Rabinowicz, "The Jewish Minority," pp. 186–87, 199.

62. See Simon Dubnov, *Nationalism and History: Essays on Old and New Judaism* (New York: 1970), esp. pp. 100–115.

63. "Falešná hra sionistů" (The false game of the Zionists), *Rozvoj,* 28 June 1919.

64. Max Lederer, "Staro-nový Masaryk" (Old-new Masaryk), *Rozvoj,* 26 April 1929.

65. Ibid.

66. Jan Heřman, "The Development of Bohemian and Moravian Jewry, 1918–1938," in *Papers in Jewish Demography 1969,* ed. U. O. Schmelz, P. Glikson, and S. Della Pergola (Jerusalem, 1973), pp. 191–206; idem, "The Evolution of the Jewish Population of Prague 1869–1939"; and Friedmann, "Židé v Čechách," pp. 733–34.

One extreme measure of Jewish integration—mixed marriages—indicates a dramatic shift after 1918. For the city of Prague, the percentage of mixed couples out of all marriages involving at least one Jewish spouse was 9.8 between 1911 and 1914, 16.4 in 1921–1922, 40.1 in 1925, and 43.6 from 1926 to 1930. See Heřman, "Jewish Population of Prague," pp. 60–61.

Epilogue: A Sitting Room in Prague

1. Max Brod's autobiography *Streitbares Leben* (Munich, 1960) was published before his return to Prague. Brod refers to the visit himself in *Der Prager Kreis* (Stuttgart, 1966; Frankfurt a.M., 1979), pp. 112–15. See also "Max Brod v Praze po 25 letech" (Max Brod in Prague after twenty-five years), *Literární noviny* 13, no. 28 (11 July 1964).

2. The conference bore the title "Franz Kafka from the Perspective of Prague 1963" (Franz Kafka aus Prager Sicht 1963), and its proceedings took place within the limits of Marxist discourse. See Paul Reimann, ed., *Franz Kafka aus Prager Sicht 1963* (Prague, 1965).

3. The 1965 Liblice conference published its proceedings under the title *Weltfreunde,* a clear allusion to Franz Werfel's first volume of poetry published

in Berlin in 1911 (*Der Weltfreund*). See Eduard Goldstücker, ed., *Weltfreunde: Konferenz über die Prager deutsche Literatur* (Prague, 1967).

4. Brod, *Prager Kreis*, p. 113: "I spoke in Czech. Later I translated the speech into German." The original version, retrieved from the verbatim transcript that had been published in *Literární noviny*, is preserved in the recent Czech edition of Brod's memoir, *Pražský kruh* (The Prague circle) (Prague, 1993), pp. 94-95.

5. Meeting between Goldstücker and University of Washington students and faculty, Prague, April 1996.

6. See *Encyclopaedia Judaica*, 7:750; and Jiři Pelikán, ed., *The Czechoslovak Political Trials, 1950-1954* (Stanford, 1971), p. 332 and passim.

7. On František Langer, see his "Curriculum Vitae," in *Byli a bylo* (There were and there was) (Prague, 1991), pp. 5-7 (dated 13.3.64); Jiří Holý, "Svět Františka Langra" (The world of František Langer), in ibid., pp. 301-6; and *Encyclopaedia Judaica*, 10:1419-20.

8. Buber's lectures were serialized in 1912 in the Czech Zionist paper *Židovský lidový list* and also published as a separate book (*Tři řeči o židovství* [Prague, 1912]). On Kolman, see S. Goshen, "Zionist Student's Organizations," *The Jews of Czechoslovakia* (Philadelphia, 1971), 2:178; Pelikán, *The Czechoslovak Political Trials*, p. 339 and passim; and *Encyclopaedia Judaica*, 10:1164-65.

9. On Jiří Langer, see especially František Langer, "My Brother Jiří," foreword to *Nine Gates to the Chassidic Mysteries*, by Jiří Langer, trans. Stephen Jolly (New York, 1976), pp. vii–xxxi.

On Alfred Fuchs, see C.M., "Kdo Byl Alfred Fuchs? K 40. výročí tragické smrti" (Who was Alfred Fuchs? On the fortieth anniversary of his tragic death), *Nový život* 33, nos. 1-2 (January-February 1981): 8-10; Jaroslav Kunc, *Slovník soudobých českých spisovatelů* (Dictionary of contemporary Czech writers) (Prague, 1945), 1:174-75; and Antonín Dolenský, *Kulturní adresář ČSR: Biografický slovník žijících kulturních pracovníků a procovnic* (Cultural directory of the Czechoslovak Republic: Biographical dictionary of living men and women active in culture), (Prague, 1936), p. 126; and *Encyclopaedia Judaica*, 7:212.

10. On Felix Weltsch, see *Encyclopaedia Judaica*, 16:445-46; Brod, *Der Prager Kreis*, pp. 154-65; and Brod, *Streitbares Leben*, passim.

Eduard Goldstücker had been a member of the ha-Shomer ha-Tsa'ir youth movement in Slovakia. He joined the Communist Party in 1933, fled to England following the Nazi occupation of Bohemia and Moravia, and pursued German studies at Oxford from 1940-43. (See *Encyclopaedia Judaica*, 7:750; and Pelikán, *The Czechoslovak Political Trials*, p. 332 and passim.)

On Ludvík Singer, see Kieval, *The Making of Czech Jewry*, pp. 98, 170, 187-88.

11. Langer, "My Brother Jiří," pp. viii–xi.

12. Ibid., pp. xiv–xv.

13. Ibid., p. xv.

14. Ibid., pp. xv–xvi.

15. Ibid., pp. xviii–xix.

16. On Martin Buber and the Prague Zionists, see Kieval, *Making of Czech Jewry*, pp. 124-53.

17. On Kolman, see Pelikán, *The Czechoslovak Political Trials*, p. 339, and *Encyclopaedia Judaica*, 10:1164–65. On Goldstücker, see Pelikán, *The Czechoslovak Political Trials*, p. 332, and *Encyclopaedia Judaica*, 7:750.

18. See Langer, "My Brother Jiří," pp. xii–xiii.

19. Langer's main works, in chronological order, are *Die Erotik der Kabbalah* (Prague, 1923); "Zur Funktion der jüdischen Türpfenrolle" (On the function of the Mezuzah), *Imago* 14 (1928); *Piyutim ve-shirei yedidut* (Poems and songs of friendship) (Prague, 1929); "Die jüdischen Gebetriemen-Phylakterien" (Jewish phylacteries), *Imago* 16 (1931); *Devět bran: Chasidů tajemství* (Nine Gates to the Chassidic Mysteries) (Prague, 1937); *Talmud: Ukázky a dějiny* (Talmud: Extracts and history) (Prague, 1938); *Zpěvy zavřených* (Songs of the rejected [anthology of Hebrew poetry in Czech]) (Prague, 1939); and *Meʿat Zori* (A little balsam) (Tel Aviv, 1942). The order of publication is significant, because it demonstrates that Langer did not move from one "phase" to another. Rather, he wrote in three modes simultaneously.

20. See the relevant correspondence from 1939 to 1943 in Jiří Langer, *Studie, recenze, články, dopisy* (Studies, reviews, articles, and letters) (Prague, 1995), pp. 193–224.

21. C. M., "Kdo Byl Alfred Fuchs?" p. 8; Langer, "My Brother Jiří," pp. xii–xiii.

22. Langer, "Curriculum Vitae"; *Encyclopaedia Judaica*, 10:1419–20; and Holý, "Svět Františka Langra."

23. Langer, "Curriculum vitae."

24. Pelikán, *The Czechoslovak Political Trials*, pp. 64–66, 339. See also H. Gordon Skilling, *Czechoslovakia's Interrupted Revolution* (Princeton, 1976), p. 557.

25. On the Slánský trial, see, inter alia, Pelikán, *The Czechoslovak Political Trials*; Karel Kaplan, *K politickým procesu v Československu 1948–1954* (On the Czechoslovak political trials 1948–1954) (Prague, 1994); Evžen Loebl, *Die Revolution rehabilitiert ihre Kinder* (Vienna, 1968); idem, *Sentenced and Tried: The Stalinist Purges in Czechoslovakia* (London, 1969); Josefa Slánská, *Report on My Husband* (London, 1969); and Heda Kovály, *Under a Cruel Star: A Life in Prague, 1941–1968* (New York, 1997).

26. Pelikán, *The Czechoslovak Political Trials*, p. 332; also "Documents: Anatomy of a Show Trial," *Studies in Comparative Communism* 2, no. 2 (1969): 95–117.

27. See the description of the political significance of this activity in Skilling, *Czechoslovakia's Interrupted Revolution*, pp. 94–98.

28. Ibid., passim.

29. Both the letter and Goldstücker's response are quoted in full in Robin Alison Remington, ed., *Winter in Prague: Documents on Czechoslovak Communism in Crisis* (Cambridge, Mass., 1969), pp. 189–94.

30. Ibid., p. 192.

31. Ibid., p. 193.

Bibliography

Archival Collections

Central Zionist Archives, Jerusalem: Jewish National Council for the Czechoslovak Republic (Z4/583).

Státní Oblastní Archiv (State Regional Archive), Prague: Proceedings of the Prague Criminal Court (ZST Praha), 1891–93; Proceedings of the Kutná Hora regional court (KS Kutná Hora), 1883–1905.

Státní Ústřední Archiv (Central State Archive), Prague: Presidium českého místodřitelství (Signature files PM 8/1/9/1), 1881 to 1900.

Newspapers and Periodicals

Allgemeine Zeitung des Judentums (1844, 1879)
České zájmy (1891–93)
Českožidovské listy (1894–1907)
Das Panorama des Universums zur erheitenden Belehrung für Jedermann und alle Länder (1834–48)
Der Orient (1840–51)
Ha-Maggid (1872)
The Jewish Chronicle (1892, 1899–1900)
Jüdisch-deutsche Monatschrift (1802)
Kalendář česko-židovský (1881–1939)
Krakonoš: Politický a národohospodářský list (1893)
Květy (1844–45)
Národní listy (1897, 1899)
Naše doba (1895–1901)
Naše zájmy (1891–93)
Neue Freie Presse (1892, 1899–1900)

Ost und West (1837–48)

Österreichische Wochenschrift [also known as *Dr. Bloch's Österreichische Wochenschrift*] (1884–1920)

Österreichisches Central-Organ für Glaubensfreiheit, Cultur, Geschichte und Literatur der Juden (1848)

Rozvoj (1904–39)

Selbstwehr (1907–38)

Sulamith: Eine Zeitschrift zur Beförderung der Kultur und Humanität unter der jüdischen Nation (1806–12)

The Jewish Chronicle (1892, 1899–1900)

Židovský lidový list (1910–12)

Books and Articles

Abrahams, Roger D. "Ordinary and Extraordinary Experience." In *The Anthropology of Experience,* edited by Victor W. Turner and Edward M. Bruner, pp. 45–72. Urbana and Chicago: University of Illinois Press, 1986.

Adámek, Karel. *Slovo o židech* (A word about the Jews). Chrudim, 1899.

———. *Z naší doby* (Of our times), 4 vols. Velké Meziříčí: J. F. Šašek, 1887–90.

Adler, H. G. *Theresienstadt 1941–1945: Das Antlitz einer Zwangsgemeinschaft.* 2d rev. ed. Tübingen: Mohr, 1960.

Agnew, Hugh LeCaine. *Origins of the Czech National Renascence.* Pittsburgh: University of Pittsburgh Press, 1993.

Aḥad Ha'am [Asher Ginsberg]. *Am Scheidewege: Ausgewählte Essays.* Authorized translation of *'Al parashat derakhim.* Translated by Israel Friedlaender. Berlin: Jüdischer Verlag, 1904.

Alter, George. *Two Renaissance Astronomers: David Gans, Joseph Delmedigo.* Prague: Československá Akademie Věd, 1958.

Altmann, Alexander. *Moses Mendelssohn: A Biographical Study.* Philadelphia: Jewish Publication Society of America; Tuscaloosa: University of Alabama Press, 1973.

Anderson, Benedict. *Imagined Communities: Reflections on the Origin and Spread of Nationalism.* Rev. ed. London and New York: Verso, 1991.

"Der Anteil der Juden am höheren Schulwesen Böhmens, Mährens, und Schlesiens." In *Die Juden in den böhmischen Ländern,* edited by Ferdinand Seibt. Appendix V, pp. 348–49. Munich and Vienna: Oldenbourg, 1983.

Baron, Salo Wittmayer. *The Jewish Community.* 3 vols. Philadelphia: Jewish Publication Society of America, 1945.

Barzilay, Isaac. *Shlomoh Yehudah Rapoport (Shir), 1790–1867, and His Contemporaries: Some Aspects of Jewish Scholarship of the Nineteenth Century.* Israel: Massada Press, 1969.

Beer, Peter. *Lebensgeschichte.* Prague: M. I. Landau, 1839.

———. *Sefer toledot Yisrael, kolel sippur kol hakorot asher karu ... 'im rimzei midot tovot umusar haskel ... leto'elet ḥinukh Benei Yisrael* (History of Israel, including the story of all that happened ... with allusions to virtue and morality ... for the education of Jewish children). Vienna, 1810.

Benedict, Abraham. "Haggadat Maharal o Aggadat Maharal?" (The Haggadah of the Maharal, or the *aggadah* [legend] of the Maharal?). *Moriah* 14, no. 3–4 (1985): 102–13.

Bergl, Josef. "Das Exil der Prager Judenschaft von 1745–1748." *Jahrbuch der Gesellschaft für Geschichte der Juden in der Čechoslovakischen Republik* 1 (1929): 263–331.

Bergman, Shmuel Hugo [Hugo Bergmann]. "Petaḥ davar" (Foreword) and "Prag." In *Yahadut Tshekhoslovakia* (Czechoslovak Jewry), pp. 7–10, 83–91. Jerusalem: Ministry of Education, 1969.

Bernard, Paul P. "Joseph II and the Jews: The Making of the Toleration Patent of 1782." *Austrian History Yearbook* 4/5 (1970).

Bernfeld, Simon. *Toledot Shir* (History of S[olomon] J[udah] R[apoport]). Warsaw, 1899.

Bihl, Wolfdieter. "Die Juden." In *Die Habsburgermonarchie, 1848–1918*, edited by Adam Wandruszka and Peter Urbanitsch. Vol. 3, *Die Völker des Reichs*. Vienna: Österreichische Akademie der Wissenschaften, 1980).

Bilski, Emily. "The Art of the Golem." In *Golem! Danger, Deliverance, and Art*, edited by Emily Bilski, pp. 44–111. New York: The Jewish Museum, 1988.

Birnbaum, Pierre and Ira Katznelson, eds. *Paths of Emancipation: Jews, States, and Citizenship*. Princeton: Princeton University Press, 1995.

Black, George F. "Macpherson's Ossian and the Ossianic Controversy." *Bulletin of the New York Public Library* 30 (1926): 1:424–39, 2:508–24.

Blanický, O.G. *O antisemitismu v českém národě* (Concerning antisemitism in the Czech nation). Prague: "Obrození," 1919.

Blau, Bruno. "Nationality among Czechoslovak Jewry." *Historia Judaica* 10 (1948): 147–54.

Bloch, Chayim. *The Golem: Legends of the Ghetto of Prague*. Translated from the German by Harry Schneiderman. Vienna: The Golem, 1925.

Böhm, I. *Historische Nachricht von der Enstehungsart und der Verbreitung des Normalinstituts in Böhmen*. Prague, 1784.

Boldt, Frank. *Kultur versus Staatlichkeit: Zur Genesis der modernen politischen Kultur in den böhmischen Ländern im Widerspiel von kulturellem und politischem Bewußtsein bei den böhmischen Tschechen und Deutschen bis zum Jahre 1898*. Prague: Karolinum, 1996.

Bondy, G. and F. Dvorsky, *Zur Geschichte der Juden in Böhmen, Mähren und Schlesien 906–1620*. Prague: G. Bondy, 1906.

Bondy, Ruth. *"Elder of the Jews": Jakob Edelstein of Theresienstadt*. New York: Grove Press, 1989.

Borchardt, Knut. "Germany 1700–1914." In *Fontana Economic History of Europe*, edited by Carlo M. Cipolla. Vol. 4, *The Emergence of Industrial Societies*, pt. 1, pp. 76–160. New York: Fontana, 1976.

Bretholz, B. *Quellen zur Geschichte der Juden in Mähren 1067–1411*. Prague: Taussig u. Taussig, 1935.

Brix, Emil. *Die Umgangssprachen in Altösterreich zwischen Agitation und Assimilation*. Vienna: Böhlau, 1982.

Brock, Peter and H. Gordon Skilling, eds., *The Czech Renascence of the Nineteenth Century*. Toronto: University of Toronto Press, 1970.

Brod, Max. "Prag—Wien—Erinnerungen." In *The Jews of Austria,* edited by Josef Frankel, pp. 241–42. London: Valentine, Mitchell, 1967.

——. *Der Prager Kreis.* Stuttgart: Kohlhammer, 1966; Frankfurt a.M.: Suhrkamp, 1979. Czech edition: *Pražský kruh* (The Prague circle). Prague: Akropolis, 1993.

——. *Streitbares Leben.* Munich: F. A. Herbig, 1969.

Brosche, Wilfried. "Das Ghetto von Prag." In *Die Juden in den böhmischen Ländern,* edited by Ferdinand Seibt, pp. 87–122. Munich and Vienna: Oldenbourg, 1983.

Bruner, Edward M. "Experience and Its Expressions." In *The Anthropology of Experience,* edited by Victor W. Turner and Edward M. Bruner, pp. 3–30. Urbana and Chicago: University of Illinois Press, 1986.

——. "The Opening Up of Anthropology." In *Text, Play, and Story: The Construction and Reconstruction of Self and Society,* edited by Edward M. Bruner, pp. 1–16. Washington, D.C.: The American Ethnological Society, 1984.

Buber, Martin. *Drei Reden über das Judentum.* Frankfurt a.M.: Ritten & Loening, 1911. Czech edition: *Tři řeči o židovství.* Prague, 1912.

Bureau für Statistik der Juden. *Die Juden in Österreich.* Berlin: Louis Lamm, 1908.

C. M. "Kdo byl Alfred Fuchs? K 40. výročí tragické smrti" (Who was Alfred Fuchs? On the fortieth anniversary of his tragic death). *Nový život* 33, nos. 1–2 (January–February 1981): 8–10.

Čapek, Karel. *Hovory s TGM* (Conversations with T. G. Masaryk). Prague: Československý spisovatel, 1969. English edition: *President Masaryk Tells His Story.* New York: Arno Press and the New York Times, 1971.

Černý, Bohumil. *Justičný omyl: Hilsneriáda* (A judicial error: The Hilsner affair). Prague: Magnet-Press, 1990.

Červinka, František. "The Hilsner Affair." *Leo Baeck Institute Year Book* 13 (1968): 142–57. Reprinted in *The Blood Libel Legend: A Casebook in Anti-Semitic Folklore,* edited by Alan Dundes, pp. 135–61. Madison: University of Wisconsin Press, 1991.

České modlitby při veřejné bohoslužbě v synagoze "Or-Tomid" (Czech prayers for public worship at the "Or Tomid" synagogue). Prague, 1888.

Čeští spisovatelé 19. a počátku 20. století (Czech writers of the nineteenth century and beginning of the twentieth century). Prague: Československý spisovatel, 1973.

Cohen, Gary B. "Deutsche, Juden und Tschechen in Prag: das Sozialleben des Alltags, 1890–1914." In *Allemands, Juifs et Tchèques à Prague/Deutsche, Juden und Tschechen in Prag/1890–1924,* edited by Maurice Godé, Jacques Le Rider, and Françoise Mayer, pp. 55–69. Montpellier: Bibliothèque d'Études Germaniques et Centre-Européennes, Université Paul-Valéry, 1996.

——. *Education and Middle-Class Society in Imperial Austria, 1848–1918.* West Lafayette: Purdue University Press, 1996.

——. "Ethnicity and Urban Population Growth: The Decline of the Prague Germans, 1800–1920." In *Studies in East European Social History,* edited by Keith Hutchins, 2:3–26. Leiden, 1981.

——. "Jews in German Liberal Politics: Prague, 1860–1914." *Jewish History* 1 (1986): 55–74.

——. "Jews in German Society: Prague, 1860–1914." *Central European History* 10 (1977): 28–54.

——. *The Politics of Ethnic Survival: Germans in Prague, 1861–1914*. Princeton: Princeton University Press, 1981.

Corel, Ludwig. *Das Blutmärchen: Seine Entstehung und Folgen bis zu den jüngsten Vorgängen auf Korfu*. Berlin: J. Gnadenfeld, 1891.

Dagan, Avigdor. "The Czechoslovak Government in Exile and the Jews." In *The Jews of Czechoslovakia: Historical Studies and Surveys*, by the Society for the History of Czechoslovak Jews, vol. 3, edited by Avigdor Dagan et al., pp. 449–95. Philadelphia. Jewish Publication Society of America, 1984.

Deckert, Josef. *Ein Ritualmord: Aktenmäßig nachgewiesen*. Dresden: Glöß, 1893.

deGategno, Paul J. *James Macpherson*. Boston: Twayne, 1989.

Dějiny českožidovského hnutí (History of the Czech-Jewish movement). Prague: Svaz Čechů-židů v Československé republice, 1932.

Demetz, Peter. *Prague in Black and Gold: Scenes from the Life of a European City*. New York: Hill and Wang, 1997.

——. "Tschechen und Juden: Der Fall Siegfried Kapper (1821–1879)." In *Allemands, Juifs et Tchèques à Prague/Deutsche, Juden und Tschechen in Prag/ 1890–1924*, edited by Maurice Godé, Jacques Le Rider, and Françoise Mayer, pp. 19–27. Montepellier: Bibliothèque d'Études Germaniques et Centre-Européennes, Université Paul-Valéry, 1996.

——, ed. *Geschichten aus dem alten Prag: Sippurim*. Frankfurt a.M and Leipzig: Insel, 1994.

Dewey, John. *Experience and Nature*. Chicago: Open Court, 1929.

"Documents: Anatomy of a Show Trial." *Studies in Comparative Communism* 2, no. 2 (1969): 95–117.

Dolenský, Antonín. *Kulturní adresář ČSR: Biografický slovník žijících kulturních pracovníků a procovnic* (Cultural directory of the Czechoslovak Republic: Biographical dictionary of living men and women active in culture). Prague, 1936.

Doleželová, Jana. "Questions of Folklore in the Legends of the Old Jewish Town Compiled by Leopold Weisel (1804–1870 [sic])." *Judaica Bohemiae* 12 (1976): 37–50.

Donath, Oskar. "Siegfried Kapper." *Jahrbuch der Gesellschaft für Geschichte der Juden in der Čechoslovakischen Republik* 6 (1934): 323–442.

——. *Siegfried Kappers Leben und Wirken*. Berlin, 1909 (Special offprint from *Archiv für slavische Philologie* 30).

——. *Židé a židovství v české literatuře 19. a 20. století* (Jews and Judaism in nineteenth- and twentieth-century Czech literature). 2 vols. Brno: O. Donath, 1923–1930.

Drabek, Anna. "Die Juden in den böhmischen Ländern zur Zeit des landesfürstlichen Absolutismus." In *Die Juden in den böhmischen Ländern*, edited by Ferdinand Seibt, pp. 123–43. Munich and Vienna: Oldenbourg, 1983.

Dresler, Jaroslav, ed. *Masarykova abeceda: Výbor z myšlenek Tomáše Garrigua Masaryka* (The Masaryk ABC: Selections from the thoughts of T. G. Masaryk). Zurich: Konfrontace, 1976.

Dubin, Lois C. *The Port Jews of Habsburg Trieste: Absolutist Politics and Enlightenment Culture*. Stanford: Stanford University Press, 1999.

———. "Trieste and Berlin: The Italian Role in the Cultural Politics of the Haskalah." In *Toward Modernity: The European Jewish Model,* edited by Jacob Katz, pp. 189–224. New Brunswick, N.J.: Transaction Books, 1987.

Dubnov, Simon. *Nationalism and History: Essays on Old and New Judaism.* New York: Atheneum, 1970.

Dundes, Alan, ed., *Sacred Narrative: Readings in the Theory of Myth.* Berkeley: University of California Press, 1984.

Dunn, John J. "Macpherson's Ossian and the Ossianic Controversy: A Supplementary Bibliography." *Bulletin of the New York Public Library* 75 (1971): 465–73.

Ehrmann, Salomon. "Böhmische Dorfjuden: Erinnerungen aus früher Jugend." *B'nai B'rith: Monatsblätter der Grossloge für den Čechoslovakischen Staat* 4 (1925): 217–23, 235–44, and 261–68.

Eliade, Mircea. *Myth and Reality.* New York: Harper and Row, 1963.

Ellenson, David. "A Disputed Precedent: The Prague Organ in Nineteenth-Century Central-European Legal Literature and Polemics." *Leo Baeck Institute Yearbook* 40 (1995): 251–64.

Emden, Jacob. *Megillath sefer* (The Scroll of the Book). Warsaw: Schuldberg, 1896; New York: Gelbman et al., 1926.

Encyclopaedia Judaica. Jerusalem: Keter Publishing House, 1972.

Engel, Alfred. "Die Ausweisung der Juden aus den königlichen Städten Mährens und ihre Folgen." *Jahrbuch der Gesellschaft für Geschichte der Juden in der Čechoslovakischen Republik* 2 (1930): 50–96.

Evans, R. J. W. *The Making of the Habsburg Monarchy.* Oxford: Clarendon, 1979.

———. *Rudolf II and His World: A Study in Intellectual History, 1576–1612.* Oxford: Clarendon, 1973.

"Falešná hra sionistů" (The false game of the Zionists). *Rozvoj,* 28 June 1919.

Der Fall Buschhof: Aktenmässige Darstellung des Xantener Knabenmord-Prozesses. Frankfurt a.M.: Koenitzer, 1892.

Farissol, Abraham. *Iggeret 'orhot 'olam* (Epistle on the ways of the world). Edited by Israel Landau. Prague, 1793.

Fiedler, Jiří. *Jewish Sights of Bohemia and Moravia.* Prague: Sefer, 1991.

Frankl, Ludwig August. *Erinnerungen.* Prague: J. G. Calvische k. u. k. Hof- und Universitäts-Buchhandlung, 1910.

Freudenberger, H. "Industrialization in Bohemia and Moravia in the Eighteenth Century." *Journal of Central European Affairs* 19 (1960): 347–56.

Friedländer, M. H. *Tiferet Jisrael: Schilderungen aus dem inneren Leben der Juden in Mähren in vormärzlichen Zeiten.* Brno: M. H. Friedländer, 1878.

Friedman, Filip. *Die galizischen Juden im Kampfe um ihre Gleichberechtigung (1848–1868).* Frankfurt a.M., 1929.

Friedmann, František. *Einige Zahlen über die tschechoslowakischen Juden.* Prague, 1933.

———. "Židé v Čechách" (Jews in Bohemia). In *Židé a židovské obce v Čechách v minulosti a v přítomnosti* (Jews and Jewish communities in Bohemia in the past and the present), edited by Hugo Gold, pp. 729–35. Brno and Prague: Židovské nakladatelství, 1934.

Friesel, Evyatar. *Atlas of Modern Jewish History.* New York: Oxford University Press, 1990.

Gans, David. *Sefer Zemaḥ David* (The offspring of David), edited by Mordechai Breuer. Jerusalem: Magnes Press, 1983.

Garver, Bruce M. *The Young Czech Party 1874–1901 and the Emergence of a Multi-Party System.* New Haven: Yale University Press, 1978.

Gellner, Ernest. *Nations and Nationalism.* Ithaca: Cornell University Press, 1983.

Godé, Maurice, Jacques Le Rider, and Françoise Mayer, eds. *Allemands, Juifs et Tchèques à Prague/Deutsche, Juden und Tschechen in Prag/1890–1924.* Montpellier: Bibliothèque d'Études Germaniques et Centre-Européennes, Université Paul-Valéry, 1996.

Goldberg, Sylvie-Anne. *Crossing the Jabbok: Illness and Death in Ashkenazi Judaism in Sixteenth- through Nineteenth-Century Prague.* Berkeley and Los Angeles: University of California Press, 1996.

Goldsmith, Arnold L. *The Golem Remembered, 1909–1980: Variations of a Jewish Legend.* Detroit: Wayne State University Press, 1981.

Goldstücker, Eduard, ed. *Weltfreunde: Konferenz über die Prager deutsche Literatur.* Prague: Academia, 1967.

Goshen, S. "Zionist Student Organizations." In *The Jews of Czechoslovakia: Historical Studies and Surveys,* by the Society for the History of Czechoslovak Jews, 2:173–84. Philadelphia: Jewish Publication Society of America, 1971.

Greenfeld, Liah. *Nationalism: Five Roads to Modernity.* Cambridge, Mass.: Harvard University Press, 1992.

Gries, Ze'ev. *Sefer, sofer, ve-sippur be-reshit ha-ḥasidut* (The book, the writer, and the story in the beginnings of Hasidism). Tel Aviv: Hakibbutz Hameuchad, 1992.

Grimm, Jakob. *Kleinere Schriften.* Vol. 4. Berlin: Millenhoff, 1869.

Gross, N. T. "The Habsburg Monarchy, 1750–1914." In *Fontana Economic History of Europe,* edited by Carlo M. Cipolla. Vol. 4, *The Emergence of Industrial Societies,* pt. 1, pp. 228–78. New York: Fontana, 1976.

Hajek, Hanuš J. *T. G. Masaryk Revisited: A Critical Assessment.* Boulder: East European Monographs, 1983.

Halpern, Israel, ed. *Takkanot medinat Mehrin* (The regulations of the Jewish community of Moravia). Jerusalem: Mekize Nirdamim, 1952.

Hamáčková, Vlastimila. "Débuts du mouvement assimilateur tchécho-juif." *Judaica Bohemiae* 14 (1978): 15–23.

Hammer, Wenzel. *Geschichte der Volksschule Böhmens von der ältesten Zeit bis zum Jahre 1870.* Warnsdorf: Commissions-Verlag von A. Opitz, 1904.

Hanák, Péter. "Jews and the Modernization of Commerce in Hungary, 1760–1918." In *Jews in the Hungarian Economy 1760–1945,* edited by Michael K. Silber, pp. 23–39. Jerusalem: Magnes Press, 1992.

Hanuš, J. *Rukopisové Zelenohorský a Královédvorský* (The Zelenohorský and Královédvorský manuscripts). Prague, 1911.

Harkins, William E. "The Periodization of Czech Literary History, 1774–1879." In *The Czech Renascence of the Nineteenth Century,* edited by Peter Brock and H. Gordon Skilling, pp. 3–13. Toronto: University of Toronto Press, 1970.

Hartmann, Moritz. "Bruchstücke revolutionärer Erinnerungen." In *Gesammelte Werke,* vol. 10. Stuttgart: J. G. Cotta, 1874.

———. *Kelch und Schwert.* Leipzig, 1845.

Häusler, Wolfgang. "Toleranz, Emanzipation und Antisemitismus: Das öster-reichische Judentum des bürgerlichen Zeitalters (1782–1918)." In *Das öster-reichische Judentum: Voraussetzungen und Geschichte,* edited by Nikolaus Viel-metti. Vienna and Munich: Jugend und Volk, 1974.

Havlíček Borovský, Karel. "Emancipace židů." *Slovan,* 12 October 1850; reprinted in *Politické Spisy,* edited by Z. Tobolka, 3:402–8. Prague, 1902.

Haywood, Ian. *The Making of History: A Study of the Literary Forgeries of James Macpherson.* Rutherford, N.J.: Fairleigh Dickinson University Press, 1986.

Herben, Jan. "Julius Taussig." *Kalendář česko-židovský* 32 (1912–13): 15–16.

———. "T.G. Masaryk über Juden und Antisemitismus." In *Masaryk und das Ju-dentum,* edited by Ernst Rychnovsky, pp. 274–99. Prague: Marsverlagsge-sellschaft, 1931.

Heřman, Jan. "La communauté juive de Prague et sa structure au commence-ment des temps modernes (la première moitié du 16-e siècle)." *Judaica Bo-hemiae* 5 (1969): 31–71.

———. "The Conflict between Jewish and Non-Jewish Population in Bohemia before the 1541 Banishment." *Judaica Bohemiae* 6 (1970): 39–54.

———. "The Development of Bohemian and Moravian Jewry, 1918–1938." In *Papers in Jewish Demography 1969,* edited by U.O. Schmelz, P. Glikson, and S. Della Pergola, pp. 191–206. Jerusalem: Institute of Contemporary Jewry, 1973.

———. "The Evolution of the Jewish Population in Prague, 1869–1939." In *Pa-pers in Jewish Demography 1977,* edited by U.O. Schmelz, P. Glikson, and S. Della Pergola, pp. 53–67. Jerusalem: Institute of Contemporary Jewry, 1980.

———. "The Evolution of the Jewish Population of Bohemia and Moravia, 1754–1953." In *Papers in Jewish Demography 1973,* edited by U.O. Schmelz, P. Glikson, and S. Della Pergola, pp. 255–65. Jerusalem: Institute of Contem-porary Jewry, 1977.

Hobsbawm, Eric. "Inventing Traditions." In *The Invention of Tradition,* edited by E. Hobsbawm and T.O. Ranger. Cambridge: Cambridge University Press, 1983.

Hock, Simon. *Die Familien Prags nach den Epitaphien des alten jüdischen Fried-hofs in Prag.* Pressburg, 1892.

Hock, Stefan. "Komperts Leben und Schaffen." In *Sämtliche Werke,* by Leopold Kompert, 1: v–viii. Leipzig, 1906.

Hoffman, Alois. *Die Prager Zeitschrift "Ost und West": Ein Beitrag zur Geschichte der deutsch-slawischen Verständigung im Vormärz.* Berlin: Akademie-Verlag, 1957.

Holý, Jiří. "Svět Františka Langra" (The world of František Langer). In *Byli a bylo,* by František Langer, pp. 301–6. Prague: Státní pedagogické nakl., 1991.

Homberg, Herz. *Bnei Zion: Ein religiös-moralisches Lehrbuch für die Jugend is-raelitischer Nation.* Vienna: K.K. Schulbücher Verschleiß, 1812.

Hsia, R. Po-Chia. *The Myth of Ritual Murder: Jews and Magic in Reformation Germany.* New Haven: Yale University Press, 1988.

———. *Trent 1475: Stories of a Ritual Murder.* New Haven: Yale University Press, 1992.

Hundert, Gershon David. *The Jews in a Polish Private Town: The Case of Opatów in the Eighteenth Century.* Baltimore: Johns Hopkins University Press, 1992.

Idel, Moshe. "The Golem in Jewish Magic and Mysticism." In *Golem! Danger, Deliverance, and Art,* edited by Emily Bilski, pp. 15–35. New York: The Jewish Museum, 1988.

———. *Golem: Jewish Magical and Mystical Traditions on the Artificial Anthropoid.* Albany: State University of New York Press, 1990.

Iggers, Wilma. "Leopold Kompert, Romancier of the Bohemian Ghetto." *Modern Austrian Literature* 6 (1973): 117–38.

———, ed. *The Jews of Bohemia and Moravia: A Historical Reader.* Detroit: Wayne State University Press, 1992.

Ingrao, Charles. *The Habsburg Monarchy, 1618–1815.* Cambridge: Cambridge University Press, 1994.

Israel, Jonathan. *European Jewry in the Age of Mercantilism, 1550–1750.* 3d ed. London and Portland, Ore. Littman Library of Jewish Civilization, 1998.

Jakobovits, Tobiaš. "Das Prager und Böhmische Landesrabbinat Ende des siebzehnten und Anfang des achtzehnten Jahrhunderts." *Jahrbuch der Gesellschaft für Geschichte der Juden in der Čechoslovkischen Republik* 5 (1933): 79–136.

Jeitteles, Baruch. *Siḥa bein shenat 5560 u-vein 5561* (Dialogue between the years 5560 and 5561). Prague, 1800.

Jeitteles, Juda. *B'nei hane'urim* (The sons of youth). Prague, 1821.

Jélinek, Hanus. *Histoire de la littérature tchèque: Des origines à 1850.* 2d ed. Paris, 1930.

———. *La littérature tchèque contemporaine: Cours professé à la Sorbonne en 1910.* Paris, 1912.

Jirásek, Alois. *Staré pověsti české* (Old Czech tales). Prague, 1893.

Die Juden und die Nationalen: Ein Gegenstück zur Broschüre: "Die Juden in Böhmen." Von einem Juden. Prague: Anton Renn, 1863.

"Der jüdische Nationalrat beim Národní výbor." *Selbstwehr,* 1 November 1918.

Kafka, Franz. *Diaries, 1910–1923.* 2 vols. New York: Schocken, 1948.

———. *Letter to His Father.* New York: Schocken, 1953.

Kahane, I. Z. "Nikolsburg." In *'Arim ve-'imahot be-yisra'el* (Great Jewish communities), 4: 210–313. Jerusalem: Mosad Ha-Rav Kook, 1950.

Kann, Robert A. *A History of the Habsburg Empire 1526–1918.* Berkeley: University of California Press, 1974.

———. *The Multinational Empire, 1848–1918.* 2 vols. New York: Columbia University Press, 1950.

Kaplan, Karel. *K politickým procesům v Československu 1948–1954* (On the Czechoslovak political trials 1948–1954). Prague: Ustav pro soudobé dějiny AVČR, 1994.

Kapper, Siegfried. "Autobiographie I" and "Autobiographie II." In Oskar Donath, "Siegfried Kapper," *Jahrbuch der Gesellschaft für Geschichte der Juden in der Čechoslovakischen Republik* 6 (1934), pp. 396–98.

———. *České listy* (Czech leaves). Prague: Calve, 1846.

———. *Falk: Eine Erzählung.* Dessau, 1853.

———. *Herzel und seine Freunde: Federzeichnungen aus dem böhmischen Schulleben.* Leipzig, 1853.

———. "Die Kohlen." *Libussa* (1849).

Karníková, Ludmila. *Vývoj obyvatelstva v českých zemich 1754–1914* (Evolution of the population in the Czech lands). Prague, 1965.

Katus, László. "The Occupational Structure of Hungarian Jewry in the Eighteenth and Twentieth Centuries." In *Jews in the Hungarian Economy 1760–1945,* edited by Michael K. Silber, pp. 92–105. Jerusalem: Magnes Press, 1992.

Katz, Jacob. *Out of the Ghetto: The Social Background of Jewish Emancipation, 1770–1830.* Cambridge, Mass.: Harvard University Press, 1973.

——, ed. *Toward Modernity: The European Jewish Model.* New Brunswick, N.J.: Transaction Books, 1987.

Kaufmann, David. Introduction to *Die Familien Prags nach den Epitaphien des alten jüdischen Friedhofs in Prag,* by Simon Hock, pp. 1–36. Pressburg, 1892.

——. "Zu S. J. L Rapoport's hundertstem Geburtstag." In *Das Centenarium S. J. L. Rapoport's: Festgabe der "Österreichischen Wochenschrift,"* edited by D. Kaufmann, pp. 389–94. Vienna: Österreichische Wochenschrift, 1890.

——, ed. *Das Centenarium S. J. L. Rapoport's: Festgabe der "Österreichischen Wochenschrift."* Vienna: Österreichische Wochenschrift, 1890.

Kerner, R. J. *Bohemia in the Eighteenth Century.* New York: A. M. S. Press, 1932, 1969.

Kestenberg-Gladstein, Ruth. "The Jews between Czechs and Germans in the Historic Lands, 1848–1918." In *The Jews of Czechoslovakia: Historical Studies and Surveys,* by the Society for the History of Czechoslovak Jews, 1:21–71. Philadelphia: Jewish Publication Society of America, 1968.

——. "Mifkad yehudei Beim she-miḥuẓ le-Prag bi-shnat 1724" (The census of Jews outside of Prague in the year 1724). *Zion* 9 (1944): 1–26.

——. *Neuere Geschichte der Juden in den böhmischen Ländern. Erster Teil: Das Zeitalter der Aufklärung, 1780–1830.* Tübingen: Mohr, 1969.

——. "Ofiyah ha-le'umi shel haskalat Prag" (The national character of the Prague *haskalah*). *Molad* 23 (1965): 221–33.

Kieval, Hillel J. "Antisémitisme ou savoir social? Sur la genèse du procès moderne pour meurtre rituel." *Annales: Histoire, Sciences Sociales* 49, no. 5 (1994): 1091–1105.

——. "The Importance of Place: Comparative Aspects of the Ritual Murder Trial in Modern Central Europe." In *Comparing Jewish Societies,* edited by Todd M. Endelman, pp. 135–65. Ann Arbor: University of Michigan Press, 1997.

——. "The Lands Between: The Jews of Bohemia, Moravia, and Slovakia to 1918." In *Where Cultures Meet: The Story of the Jews of Czechoslovakia,* edited by Natalia Berger, pp. 23–51. Tel Aviv: Beth Hatefutsoth; Ministry of Defence, 1990.

——. *The Making of Czech Jewry: National Conflict and Jewish Society in Bohemia, 1870–1918.* New York and Oxford: Oxford University Press, 1988.

——. "Representation and Knowledge in Medieval and Modern Accounts of Jewish Ritual Murder." *Jewish Social Studies: History, Culture, Society,* n.s., 1 (1994–95): 52–72.

Kisch, Guido. *In Search of Freedom: A History of American Jews from Czechoslovakia.* London: Goldston & Son, 1949.

——. "Linguistic Conditions among Czechoslovak Jewry." *Historia Judaica* 8 (1946): 19–32.

Klaber, Herz. *Beschreibung der am 30. mai gehaltenenen fünfzigjährigen Jubelfeyer der israel. deutschen Hauptschule in Prag, nebst einer Geschichte dieser Schule.* Prague: M. I. Landau, 1833.

Kleinberger, A. F. *Ha-maḥshava ha-pedagogit shel ha-Maharal mi-Prag* (The pedagogical thought of the Maharal of Prague). Jerusalem: [n.p.], 1962.

Klenovský, Jaroslav. *Židovské památky Mikulova* (The Jewish monuments of Mikulov). Mikulov: Regonální muzeum v Mikulově, 1994.

Klíma, A. "Industrial Development in Bohemia, 1648–1781." *Past and Present* 11 (April 1957): 87–97.

———. "Mercantilism in the Habsburg Monarchy—with special reference to the Bohemian lands." *Historica* 11 (1965): 95–119.

Klineberger, Bohdan. *Náboženský cit: Rozbor hodnoty náboženství* (Religious feeling: An analysis of the value of religion). Prague, 1906.

———. *Naše budoucnost* (Our future). Prague, 1911.

Klutschak, Franz. "Der Golam des Rabbi Löw." *Panorama des Universums* 8 (1841): 77–78.

Kohn, Albert, ed. *Die Notablenversammlung der Israeliten Böhmens in Prag: Ihre Berathungen und Beschlüße.* Vienna: Sommer, 1852.

Kompert, Leopold. *Aus dem Ghetto: Geschichten.* 3rd ed. Berlin: L. Gerschel, 1882.

Kopač, Jaroslav. *Dějiny české školy a pedagogiky v letech 1867–1914* (History of the Czech school and pedagogy, 1867–1914). Brno: Universita J. E. Purkyne, 1968.

Kořalka, Jiří and R. J. Crampton. "Die Tschechen." In *Die Habsburgermonarchie 1848–1918,* edited by Adam Wandruszka and Peter Urbanitsch, vol. 3, pp. 489–521. Vienna: Akademie der Wissenschaften, 1980.

Kořán, Josef. "Židovské školy v Čechách" (Jewish schools in the Czech lands). *Kalendář česko-židovský* 6 (1886–87): 97–102.

———. "Židosvké školy v Čechách roku 1894–95" (Jewish schools in the Czech lands in 1894–95). *Kalendář česko-židovský* 16 (1896–97): 152–57.

Kovály, Heda. *Under a Cruel Star: A Life in Prague, 1941–1968.* New York: Holmes & Meier, 1997.

Kovtun, Jiří. *Tajuplná vražda: Případ Leopolda Hilsnera* (A mysterious murder: The case of Leopold Hilsner). Prague: Sefer, 1994.

Kraus, J. S. "Německo-židovské školy v Čechách" (The German-Jewish schools of Bohemia). *Kalendář česko-židovský* 2 (1882–83): 117–25.

———. "Or-Tomid." *Kalendář česko-židovský* 4 (1884–85).

Kraus, Otakar. "O vývoji židovského náboženství" (On the evolution of the Jewish religion). *Kalendář česko-židovský* 26 (1906–7): 120–28.

———. "Počátky berlínské reformy" (The beginnings of the Berlin reform). *Kalendář česko-židovský* 25 (1905–06): 119–25.

Křen, Jan. *Konfliktní společenství: Češi a Němci, 1780–1918* (The conflictual community: Czechs and Germans, 1780–1918). Prague: Academia, 1990.

Kuh, David. "Ein Wort an Juden und Slaven." *Allgemeine Zeitung des Judentums,* 1 April, 8 April, and 15 April 1844.

Kulka, Erich. "The Annihilation of Czechoslovak Jewry." In *The Jews of Czechoslovakia: Historical Studies and Surveys,* by the Society for the History of

Czechoslovak Jews, vol. 3, edited by Avigdor Dagan et al., pp. 262–328. Philadelphia and New York: Jewish Publication Society of America, 1984.

Kulka, Otto Dov. "Ha-reka ha-histori shel mishnato ha-leumit veha-ḥinuḥit shel ha-Maharal mi-Prag" (The historical background of the national and educational teachings of Rabbi Judah Löw ben Bezalel of Prague). *Zion* (jubilee volume) 50 (1985): 277–320.

Kunc, Jaroslav. *Slovník soudobých českých spisovatelů* (Dictionary of contemporary Czech writers). 2 vols. Prague: Orbis, 1945–46.

Kundera, Milan. "The Tragedy of Central Europe." *New York Review of Books,* 26 April 1984. Reprinted in *From Stalinism to Pluralism: A Documentary History of Eastern Europe since 1945,* edited by Gale Stokes, pp. 217–23. New York: Oxford University Press, 1991.

Landau, Ezekiel. *Derushei ha-Zelaḥ* (Sermons). Warsaw, 1886; Jerusalem: Beferush uve-remez, 1966.

Landau, Israel. *Ḥok le-Yisrael* (A law unto Israel). Prague, 1798.

Langer, František. "Curriculum Vitae." In *Byli a bylo* (There were and there was), pp. 5–7. Prague: Státní pedagogické nakl., 1991.

———. "My Brother Jiří." Foreword to *Nine Gates to the Chassidic Mysteries,* by Jiří Langer, translated by Stephen Jolly, pp. vii–xxxi. New York: Behrman House, 1976.

Langer, Jiří [Georg Mordechai]. *Devět bran: Chasidů tajemství* (Nine Gates to the Chassidic Mysteries). Prague, 1937; Prague: Československý spisovatel, 1965.

———. *Die Erotik der Kabbalah.* Prague: Josef Flesch, 1923.

———. "Die jüdischen Gebetriemen-Phylakterien" (Jewish phylacteries). *Imago* 16 (1931).

———. *Me'at Zori* (A little balsam). Tel Aviv: Davar, 1942.

———. *Piyutim ve-shirei yedidut* (Poems and songs of friendship). Prague, 1929.

———. *Studie, recenze, články, dopisy* (Studies, reviews, articles, and letters). Prague: Sefer, 1995.

———. *Talmud: Ukázky a dějiny* (Talmud: Extracts and history). Prague: Svaz Čechů Židů v ČSR, 1938.

———. *Zpěvy zavřených* (Songs of the rejected [anthology of Hebrew poetry in Czech]). Prague, 1939; Prague: Prah/Martin Vopenka, 1993.

———. "Zur Funktion der jüdischen Türpfenrolle" (On the Function of the Mezuzah). *Imago* 14 (1928).

Lass, Andrew. "The Manuscript Debates." *Cross Currents* 6 (1987): 445–60.

———. "Romantic Documents and Political Monuments: The Meaning-Fulfillment of History in Nineteenth-Century Czech Nationalism." *American Ethnologist* 15 (1988): 456–71.

Lazarus, Moritz. *The Ethics of Judaism,* 2 vols. Translated by Henrietta Szold. Philadelphia: Jewish Publication Society of America, 1900–1.

Lederer, Eduard. "Lueger triumfans." *Českožidovské listy,* 15 April 1897.

———. "Politické strany české a hnutí českožidovské" (The Czech political parties and the Czech-Jewish movement). *Českožidovské listy,* 15 September 1897.

———. "Pražská tragedie židovská" (The Prague Jewish tragedy). *Českožidovské listy,* 15 December 1897.

——. *Žid v dnešní společnosti* (The Jew in contemporary society). Prague: E. Lederer, 1902.

——. "Židé a sociální demokracie" (The Jews and social democracy). *Českožidovské listy*, 15 June 1898.

Lederer, Max. "Staro-nový Masaryk" (Old-new Masaryk). *Rozvoj*, 26 April 1929.

Leenhardt, Maurice. *Do Kamo: Person and Myth in the Melanesian World*. Chicago: University of Chicago Press, 1979.

Lévy-Bruhl, Lucien. *Primitive Mythology: The Mythic World of the Australian and Papuan Natives*. St. Lucia: University of Queensland Press, 1983.

Lipscher, Ladislav. *Die Juden im slowakischen Staat, 1939–1945*. Munich: Oldenbourg, 1979.

Loebl, Evžen [Eugen]. *Die Revolution rehabilitiert ihre Kinder*. Vienna: Europa Verlag, 1968. English edition: *Sentenced and Tried: The Stalinist Purges in Czechoslovakia*. London: Elek, 1969.

Maarche-Lew: Modlitby Izraelitův pro dný všední, pro sabaty i svátky (Dispositions of the heart: Jewish prayers for weekday, Sabbath, and festivals). Prague, 1884.

Macartney, C. A. *The Habsburg Empire 1790–1918*. New York: Macmillan, 1969.

Malinowski, Bronislaw. *Myth in Primitive Psychology*. London, 1926. Reprinted in *Magic, Science, and Religion*. Garden City, N.Y.: Doubleday, 1954.

Masaryk, T. G. *Die Bedeutung des Polnaer Verbrechens für den Ritualaberglauben*. Berlin: H. S. Hermann, 1900.

——. *Česká otázka: snahy a tužby národního obrození* (The Czech question: Efforts and aspirations of the national rebirth). Prague, 1895.

——. "Ernest Renan o židovství jako plemenu a náboženství (*Le Judaisme comme race et comme religion*, 1883)" (Ernest Renan on Judaism as a race and a religion). *Sborník historický* 1 (1883). Reprinted in *Masarykův sborník*, edited by V. K. Skvech, 1: 61–68. Prague: Čin, 1924–30.

——. "Jan Hus and the Czech Reformation." In *The Meaning of Czech History*, edited and with an introduction by René Wellek, translated by Peter Kussi, pp. 3–14. Chapel Hill: University of North Carolina Press, 1974.

——. *The Meaning of Czech History*. Edited and introduction by René Wellek, translated by Peter Kussi. Chapel Hill: University of North Carolina Press, 1974.

——. *Národnostní filosofie doby novější* (Contemporary national philosophy). Jičín: Fr. Holvek, 1905.

——. "Naš pan Fixl" (Our Mr. Fixl). *Besedy času*, 24 February 1911. Reprinted in *Masarykova cesta Životem* (Masaryk's way of life), edited by Jaromír Doležal, 2:37–39. Brno: Polygrafia, 1920–21.

——. *Naše nyněší krise: pád strany staročeské a počátkové směru nových* (Our current crisis: The fall of the Old Czech Party and the beginnings of new directions). Prague, 1905.

——. *Nutnost revidovat proces polenský* (The need to revise the Polná trial). Prague: Čas, 1899.

——. *Otázka sociální: Základy marxismu filosofické a sociologické* (The social question: The philosophical and sociological foundations of Marxism). Prague: Jan Laichter, 1898; Čin, 1946. German edition: *Die philosophischen und sociologischen Grundlagen des Marxismus*. Vienna: C. Konegen, 1899.

——. *Světová revoluce: Za války a ve válce, 1914–1918* (The world revolution: During the war and in the war, 1914–1918). Prague: Čin a Orbis, 1925. English edition, *The Making of a State: Memoirs and Observations, 1914–1918.* New York: Stokes, 1927.

——. "Život církevní a náboženský roku 1904" (Church and religious life in 1904). In six parts. *Naše doba* 12 (1905).

Mastný, Vojtěch. *The Czechs under Nazi Rule: The Failure of National Resistance, 1939–1942.* New York: Columbia University Press, 1971.

Mauthner, Fritz. *Prager Jugendjahre.* Frankfurt a.M.: S. Fischer, 1969.

"Max Brod v Praze po 25 letech" (Max Brod in Prague after twenty-five years). *Literární noviny* 13, no. 28 (11 July 1964).

Mayer, Françoise. "Être Tchèque en restant juif: La combinatoire identitaire tchéco-juive de la revue progressiste Rozvoj, 1904–1914." In *Allemands, Juifs et Tchèques à Prague/Deutsche, Juden und Tschechen in Prag/1890–1924,* edited by Maurice Godé, Jacques Le Rider, and Françoise Mayer, pp. 353–63. Montpellier: Bibliothèque d'Études Germaniques et Centre-Européennes, Université Paul-Valéry, 1996.

Mayer, Sigrid. *Golem: Die literarische Rezeption eines Stoffes.* Bern and Frankfurt a.M.: Lang, 1975.

McCagg, William O. *A History of Habsburg Jews, 1670–1918.* Bloomington: Indiana University Press, 1989.

McNeill, William H. *Mythistory and Other Essays* (Chicago: University of Chicago Press, 1986.

Mendelsohn, Ezra. "Jewish Assimilation in L'viv: The Case of Wilhelm Feldman." In *Nationbuilding and the Politics of Nationalism: Essays on Austrian Galicia,* edited by Andrei S. Markovits and Frank E. Sysyn, pp. 94–110. Cambridge, Mass.: Harvard Ukrainian Research Institute, 1982.

——. *The Jews of East Central Europe between the World Wars.* Bloomington: Indiana University Press, 1983.

Mendes-Flohr, Paul. "The Study of the Jewish Intellectual: Some Methodological Proposals." In *Essays in Modern Jewish History,* edited by Frances Malino and Phyllis Cohen Albert, pp. 142–72. Rutherford, N.J.: Fairleigh Dickinson University Press, 1982. Reprinted in Paul Mendes-Flohr, *Divided Passions: Jewish Intellectuals and the Experience of Modernity,* pp. 23–53. Detroit: Wayne State University Press, 1991.

Měšťan, Antonín. *Česká literatura 1785–1985* (Czech literature 1785–1985). Toronto: Sixty-Eight Publishers, 1986. German edition: *Geschichte der tschechischen Literatur im 19. und 20. Jahrhundert.* Cologne and Vienna, 1984.

Meyer, Michael A. *The Origins of the Modern Jew: Jewish Identity and European Culture in Germany, 1749–1824.* Detroit: Wayne State University Press, 1967.

Moutvic, M. "Dvorce přemyslovských družiníků a vývoj Prahy románského období" (The courts of the Přemyslid entourage and the development of Prague in the Romanesque period). *Pražský Sborník Historický* 22 (1989): 7–32.

Mühlberger, Josef. *Tschechische Literaturgeschichte.* Munich: 1970.

Muneles, Otto. *Bibliographical Survey of Jewish Prague.* Prague: Jewish State Museum of Prague, 1952.

——, ed. *Ketuvot mi-bet ha-ʿolmin ha-yehudi ha-ʿatik be-prag* (Epitaphs from the ancient Jewish cemetery of Prague). Jerusalem: Israel Academy of Sciences and Humanities, 1998.

——. *Prague Ghetto in the Renaissance Period.* Prague: State Jewish Museum, 1965.

Nebeský, Václav Bolemír. "Něco o poměru Slovanů a židů" (Concerning the relations between Slavs and Jews). *Květy,* 22 February 1844.

——. "Pověsti židovské" (Jewish tales). *Květy,* 6 August 1844.

Neruda, Jan. *Pro strach židovský: Politická studie* (For the fear of Jews: A political study). Prague: Grégr a Dattel, 1870.

Nettl, J.P. "Ideas, Intellectuals, and Structures of Dissent." In *On Intellectuals: Theoretical Studies, Case Studies,* edited by Philip Rieff. Garden City, N.Y.: Doubleday, 1969.

Novák, Jan V. and Arne Novák. *Přehledné dějiny literatury české* (Historical survey of Czech literature). 4th rev. and exp. ed. Olomouc, 1936.

Nussbaum, Artur. *Der Polnaer Ritualmordprozess: Eine Kriminalpsychologische Untersuchung auf aktenmässiger Grundlage.* Berlin: Hayn, 1906.

Okey, Robin. *Eastern Europe, 1740–1980: Feudalism to Communism.* Minneapolis: University of Minnesota Press, 1982.

Österreichische Akademie der Wissenschaften. *Österreichisches biographisches Lexikon.* Graz: Bohlaus, 1954–1999.

Österreichische Statistik. Vols. 63–64. Vienna, 1902.

Österreichisches Statistiches Handbuch 1 (1882); 10 (1891); 20 (1901); 34 (1915).

Otáhal, Milan. "The Manuscript Controversy in the Czech National Revival." *Cross Currents* 5 (1986): 247–77.

Otruba, Gustav. "Statistische Materialien zur Geschichte der Juden in den böhmischen Ländern seit dem Ausgang des 18. Jahrhunderts." In *Die Juden in den böhmischen Ländern,* edited by Ferdinand Seibt, pp. 323–51. Munich: Oldenbourg, 1983.

——. "Die Universitäten in der Hochschulorganisation der Donau-Monarchie." In *Student und Hochschule im 19. Jahrhundert,* edited by M. Rassem, pp. 75–155. Göttingen, 1975.

Pascheles, Wolf, ed. *Sippurim: Eine Sammlung jüdischer Volkssagen, Erzählungen, Mythen, Chroniken, Denkwürdigkeiten und Biographien berühmter Juden.* Erste Sammlung. 4th edition. Prague: W. Pascheles, 1870.

Pawel, Ernst. *The Nightmare of Reason: A Life of Franz Kafka.* New York: Farrar, Straus, Giroux, 1984.

Pěkný, Tomáš. *Historie Židů v Čechách a na Moravě* (The history of the Jews in Bohemia and Moravia). Prague: Sefer, 1993.

Pelikán, Jiří, ed. *The Czechoslovak Political Trials, 1950–1954.* Stanford: Stanford University Press, 1971.

Perko, Franz. "Die Tätigkeit des deutschen Schulvereines in Böhmen." *Deutsche Arbeit* 3 (1903–04): 386–410.

Perles, Meir. *Megilat yuhasin* (The scroll of relations). Warsaw, 1864. German translation: "Megillath Juchassin Mehral miprag," translated by S.H. Lieben, in *Jahrbuch der Jüdisch-Literarischen Gesellschaft* 20 (1929): 315–36.

Polák, Josef. *Česká literatura 19. století* (Czech literature in the nineteenth century). Prague: Státní pedagogické nakladatelství, 1990.

Polonsky, Antony and Michael Riff. "Poles, Czechoslovaks, and the 'Jewish Question', 1914–1921." In *Germany in the Age of Total War,* edited by Volker Berghahn and Martin Kitchen, pp. 63–101. London: Croom Helm, 1981.

Preschel, Pearl L. "The Jews of Corfu." Ph.D. diss., New York University, 1984.

Příbram, A. F., ed. *Urkunden und Akten zur Geschichte der Juden in Wien.* 2 vols. Vienna: Braumüller, 1918.

Prinz, Friedrich. "Das kulturelle Leben." In *Handbuch der Geschichte der böhmischen Länder,* edited by K. Bosl, 4:153–88. Stuttgart: A. Hiersemann, 1970.

Procházková, Jaroslava. *Český lid a český žid* (The Czech people and the Czech Jew). Žižkov, 1897.

Prokeš, Jaroslav. "Der Antisemitismus der Behörden und das Prager Ghetto." *Jahrbuch der Gesellschaft für Geschichte der Juden in der Čechoslovakischen Republik* 1 (1929): 41–262.

———. "Die Prager Judenkonskription vom Jahre 1729." *Jahrbuch der Gesellschaft für Geschichte der Juden in der Čechoslovakischen Republik* 4 (1932): 297–331.

Putík, Alexandr. "The Hebrew Inscription on the Crucifix at Charles Bridge in Prague: The Case of Elias Blackoffen and Berl Tabor in the Appellation Court." *Judaica Bohemiae* 32 (1996): 26–103.

———. "On the Topography and Demography of the Prague Jewish Town Prior to the Pogrom of 1389." *Judaica Bohemiae* 30/31 (1994–95): 7–46.

———. "The Origin of the Symbols of the Prague Jewish Town, the Banner of the Old-New Synagogue, David's Shield, and the 'Swedish' Hat." *Judaica Bohemiae* 29 (1993): 4–37.

Rabinowicz, Oskar K. "Czechoslovak Zionism: Analecta to a History." In *The Jews of Czechoslovakia: Historical Studies and Surveys,* by the Society for the History of Czechoslovak Jews, 2: 19–136. Philadelphia: Jewish Publication Society of America, 1971.

Rabinowitz, Aharon Moshe. "The Jewish Minority." In *The Jews of Czechoslovakia: Historical Studies and Surveys,* by the Society for the History of Czechoslovak Jews, 1:155–265. Philadelphia: Jewish Publication Society of America, 1968.

Rakous, Vojtěch. "Drobné vzpomínky" (Minor reminiscences). *Kalendář českožidovský* 38 (1918–19): 21–23.

———. "Hrst vzpomínek" (A fistful of memories). *Kalendář česko-židovský* 25 (1905–6).

———. *Vojkovičtí a přespolní* (The folks of Vojkovice and from out of town). Prague: Spolek Českých Akademiků Židů, 1910.

Rauchberg, Heinrich. *Der Nationale Besitzstand in Böhmen.* 3 vols. Leipzig: Duncker & Humblot, 1905.

Reimann, Paul, ed. *Franz Kafka aus Prager Sicht 1963.* Prague: Verlag der Tschechoslowakischen Akademie der Wissenschaften, 1965.

Reiner, Maxim, "O nynějších poměrech hnutí českožidovského" (On the current relations of the Czech-Jewish movement). *Českožidovské listy,* 15 June 1899.

Remington, Robin Alison, ed. *Winter in Prague: Documents on Czechoslovak Communism in Crisis.* Cambridge, Mass.: M. I. T. Press, 1969.

Reyrich [Rérych], Břetislav. *Polná: Průvodce po městě a okolí* (Polná: Guide through the city and surroundings). Polná: Klub Čs. Turistů, 1927.

——. "Židé a Polná" (The Jews and Polná) (typescript, n.d.). Muzeum Vysočiny, pobočka Polná.

Riegger, J. A. *Materialien zur alten und neuen Statistik von Böhmen.* Vol. 7, *Zustand der Normal- Bürger- und Landschulen in Böhmen.* Prague: Widtmann, 1787.

Riff, Michael. "Czech Antisemitism and the Jewish Response before 1914." *Wiener Library Bulletin* 29 (1976): 8–20.

——. "Jüdische Schriftsteller und das Dilemma der Assimilation im böhmischen Vormärz." In *Juden im Vormärz und in der Revolution von 1848,* edited by Walter Grab and Julius H. Schoeps, pp. 58–82. Stuttgart and Bonn: Burg, 1983.

Robertson, Ritchie. *Kafka: Judaism, Politics, and Literature.* Oxford: Clarendon Press, 1985.

Robinson, Ira. "Literary Forgery and Hasidic Judaism: The Case of Rabbi Yudel Rosenberg." *Judaism* 40, no. 1 (Winter 1991): 61–78.

Rokycana, Jaroslav. "Freunde in der Not." In *Masaryk und das Judentum,* edited by Ernst Rychnovsky, pp. 300–315. Prague: Marsverlagsgesellschaft, 1931.

Rosenberg, Yudel. *Sefer nifla'ot Maharal* (The book of wonders of the Maharal). Piotrków, 1909; Lemberg: Steinmetz, 1910.

Rosenfeld, Beate. *Die Golemsage und ihre Verwertung in der deutschen Literatur.* Breslau: Priebatsch, 1934.

Rosin, David. "Erinnerungen an S. L. Rapoport." In *Das Centenarium S.J.L Rapoport's: Festgabe des "Österreichischen Wochenschrift,"* pp. 400–3. Vienna: Österreichische Wochenschrift, 1890.

Rothkirchen, Livia. "The Jews of Bohemia and Moravia, 1938–1945." In *The Jews of Czechoslovakia: Historical Studies and Surveys,* by the Society for the History of Czechoslovak Jews, vol. 3, edited by Avignor Dagan et al., pp. 3–74. Philadelphia and New York: Jewish Publication Society of America, 1984.

Roubík, František. "Účast policie v útoku na Rukopisy roku 1858" (The participation of the police in the attack on the manuscripts in 1858). In *Od pravěku k dnešku* (From prehistoric times to the present). Vol. 2. Prague, 1930.

Rozenblit, Marsha L. *The Jews of Vienna, 1867–1914: Assimilation and Identity.* Albany: State University of New York Press, 1983.

"Rozmluva s prof. Masarykem" (Conversation with Professor Masaryk). *Rozvoj,* 9 April 1909.

Rychnovsky, Ernst. "Im Kampf gegen den Ritualmordaberglauben." In *Masaryk und das Judentum,* edited by Ernst Rychnovsky, pp. 166–273. Prague: Marsverlagsgesellschaft, 1931.

——. *Masaryk.* Prague: Staatlice Verlagsanstalt, 1930.

——, ed. *Masaryk und das Judentum.* Prague: Marsverlagsgesellschaft, 1931.

Ryneš, V. "L'incendie de la synagogue du faubourg du chateau de Prague en 1142 (Contribution à l'histoire des débuts de la ville juive pragoise)." *Judaica Bohemiae* 1 (1965): 9–25.

Rýs, Jan. *Hilsneriáda a TGM: K ctyřicatému výroči vražd polenských* (The Hilsner affair and T. G. Masaryk: On the fortieth anniversary of the Polná murders). Prague: Alois Wiesner, 1939.

Sadek, Vladimír. "Rabbi Loew—sa vie, héritage pédagogique et sa légende." *Judaica Bohemiae* 15 (1979): 27–41.

——. "Stories of the Golem and their Relation to the Work of Rabbi Löw of Prague." *Judaica Bohemiae* 23, no. 2 (1987): 85–91.

——. "La Synagogue réformée de Prague (La 'Vieille Ecole') et les études juives au cours du 19è siècle." *Judaica Bohemiae* 16 (1980): 119–23.

Šafránek, Jan. *Školy české: Obraz jejich vývoje a osudů* (Czech schools: Portrait of their development and fortunes). 2 vols. Prague: Nakl. Matice česká, 1913, 1918.

Schimmer, G. A. *Statistik des Judenthums.* Vienna: Staatsdruckerei, 1873.

Scholem, Gershom. "The Idea of the Golem." In *On the Kabbalah and Its Symbolism,* pp. 158–204. New York: Schocken Books, 1965.

Schroubek, Georg R. "Der 'Ritualmord' von Polná: Traditioneller und moderner Wahnglaube." In *Antisemitismus und jüdische Geschichte,* edited by Rainer Erb and Michael Schmidt, pp. 149–71. Berlin: Wissenschaftlicher Autorenverlag, 1987.

Schudt, Johann Jacob. *Jüdische Merckwürdigkeiten.* 2 vols. Frankfurt and Leipzig: S. T. Hocker, 1714–18.

Seibt, Ferdinand, ed. *Die Juden in den böhmischen Ländern.* Munich and Vienna: Oldenbourg, 1983.

Selihot mi-kol ha-shanah ke-minhag polin, pein, ungarin, u-mehrin (Penitential prayers for the entire year according to the Polish, Bohemian, Hungarian, and Moravian rite). London, 1770.

Servant, Catherine. "Aux commencements du *Calendrier tchéchojuif* (années 1880–1890)." In *Allemands, Juifs et Tchèques à Prague/Deutsche, Juden und Tschechen in Prag/1890–1924,* edited by Mauriee Godé, Jacques Le Rider, and Françoise Mayer, pp. 339–52. Montpellier: Bibliothèque d'Études Germaniques et Centre-Européennes, Université Paul-Valéry, 1996.

Seton-Watson, R. W. *Masaryk in England.* Cambridge and New York: Cambridge University Press, 1943.

Sherwin, Byron L. *The Golem Legend: Origins and Implications.* Lanham, Md.: University Press of America, 1985.

——. *Mystical Theology and Social Dissent: The Life and Works of Judah Loew of Prague.* Rutherford, N. J. and London: Fairleigh Dickinson University Press, 1982.

Shohet, Azriel. *'Im Hilufei Tekufot* (Beginnings of the *haskalah* among German Jewry). Jerusalem: Bialik Institute, 1960.

Silber, Michael. "The Enlightened Absolutist State and the Transformation of Jewish Society: Tradition in Crisis?" Paper presented at the conference "Tradition and Crisis Revisited," Harvard University, 1988.

——. "The Historical Experience of German Jewry and Its Impact on the Haskalah and Reform in Hungary." In *Toward Modernity: The European Jewish Model,* edited by Jacob Katz, pp. 107–57. New Brunswick, N.J.: Transaction Books, 1987.

Simmel, Georg. "The Stranger." In *The Sociology of Georg Simmel,* translated and edited by Kurt H. Wolff, pp. 403–8. New York: Free Press, 1950.

Singer, Ludvík. "Zur Geschichte der Juden in Böhmen in den letzten Jahren Josefs II und unter Leopold II." *Jahrbuch der Gesellschaft für Geschichte der Juden in der Čechoslovakischen Republik* 6 (1934): 193–284.

———. "Zur Geschichte der Toleranzpatente in den Sudetenländern." *Jahrbuch der Gesellschaft für Geschichte der Juden in der Čechoslovakischen Republik* 5 (1933): 231–311.

Skilling, H. Gordon. *Czechoslovakia's Interrupted Revolution.* Princeton: Princeton University Press, 1976.

Slánská, Josefa. *Report on My Husband.* London: Hutchinson, 1969.

Smith, Anthony D. *The Ethnic Origins of Nations.* Oxford: Blackwell, 1986.

———. *The Ethnic Revival.* Cambridge: Cambridge University Press, 1981.

Society for the History of Czechoslovak Jews. *The Jews of Czechoslovakia: Historical Studies and Surveys.* 3 vols. Philadelphia: Jewish Publication Society of America, 1968–1984.

Spiegel, Käthe. "Die Prager Juden zur Zeit des dreissigjährigen Krieges." In *Die Juden in Prag: Bilder aus ihrer tausendjährigen Geschichte,* edited by S. Steinherz, pp. 107–86. Prague: B'nai B'rith, 1927.

Stafford, Fiona. *The Sublime Savage: A Study of James Macpherson and the Poems of Ossian.* Edinburgh: Edinburgh University Press, 1988.

Statistická příručka království českého (Statistical handbook of the Kingdom of Bohemia). Prague, 1913.

"Statistische Tabellen über alle israelitische Gemeinden, Synagogen, Schulen und Rabbinate in Böhmen." In *Die Notablenversammlung der Israeliten Böhmens in Prag,* edited by Albert Kohn, pp. 383–414. Vienna: Sommer, 1852.

Statistisches Handbuchlein des Kaisertums Österreich für das Jahr 1865. Vienna, 1867.

Stein, August. "Předmluva" (Foreword) to *Maarche-Lew: Modlitby Israelitův pro dny všední, pro sabaty i svátky.* Prague, 1884, pp. i–iii.

Štern, Evžen. *Názory T. G. Masaryka* (The opinions of T. G. Masaryk). Prague: Grossman a Svoboda, 1910.

Stokes, Gale, ed., *From Stalinism to Pluralism: A Documentary History of Eastern Europe Since 1945.* New York: Oxford University Press, 1991.

Stölzl, Christoph. "Die 'Burg' und die Juden: T. G. Masaryk und sein Kreis im Spannungsfeld der jüdischen Frage." In *Die "Burg": Einflussreiche politische Kräfte um Masaryk und Beneš,* edited by Karl Bosl, 2:79–110. Munich and Vienna: Oldenbourg, 1974.

———. *Kafkas böses Böhmen: Zur Sozialgeschichte eines Prager Juden.* Munich: Edition Text & Kritik, 1975.

———. "Zur Geschichte der böhmischen Juden in der Epoche des modernen Nationalismus." Parts 1 and 2. *Bohemia* 14 (1973): 200–3; 15 (1974): 138–42.

Strack, Hermann L. *The Jew and Human Sacrifice: Human Blood and Jewish Ritual. An Historical and Sociological Inquiry.* London: Cope & Fenwick, 1909.

Stransky, Hugo. "The Religious Life in Slovakia and Subcarpathian Ruthenia." In *The Jews of Czechoslovakia: Historical Studies and Surveys,* by the Society for the History of Czechoslovak Jews, 2:347–92. Philadelphia: Jewish Publication Society of America, 1971.

Sturm, Heribert, ed. *Biographisches Lexikon zur Geshichte der böhmischen Länder.* 3 vols. Munich: Oldenbourg, 1975–84.

Sutter, Berthold. *Die Badenischen Sprachverordnungen von 1897: Ihre Genesis und ihre Auswirkungen vornehmlich auf die innerösterreichischen Alpenländer,* 2 vols. Graz and Cologne: Böhlaus, 1960–65.

Svátek, Josef. *Pražské pověsti a legendy* (Prague tales and legends). Prague, 1875.

Svozil, J. "Několik slov o hesle 'Svůj k svému'" (A few words concerning the slogan "Each to his own"). *Naše doba* 8 (1900–1): 641–46.

"Svůj k svému" (Each to his own). Parts 1 and 2. *Polaban,* 23 and 30 August 1893.

Szporluk, Roman. *The Political Thought of Thomas G. Masaryk.* Boulder: East European Monographs, 1981.

Tambiah, Stanley J. *Magic, Science, Religion, and the Scope of Rationality.* Cambridge: Cambridge University Press, 1990.

Teller, Markus. *Die Juden in Böhmen und ihre Stellung in der Gegenwart.* Prague: Silber und Schenk, 1863.

Teytz, Viktor. "Trochu retrospektivy a vzpomínek" (A little retrospect and some memories). *Kalendář česko-židovský* 28 (1908–9): 155–59.

Thieberger, Frederic. *The Great Rabbi Loew of Prague: His Life and Work and the Legend of the Golem.* London: East and West Library, 1955.

Toury, Jacob. "Jewish Townships in the German-Speaking Parts of the Austrian Empire—before and after the Revolution of 1848/49." *Leo Baeck Institute Yearbook* 26 (1981): 55–72.

Turner, Victor W. and Edward M. Bruner, eds., *The Anthropology of Experience.* Urbana and Chicago: University of Illinois Press, 1986.

Veber, Václav, ed. *Židé v novodobých dějinách* (The Jews in modern history). Prague: Ústav Světových Dějin FF UK, 1997.

Véghàzi, István. "The Role of Jewry in the Economic Life of Hungary." In *Hungarian Jewish Studies,* edited by Randolph L. Braham. New York: World Federation of Hungarian Jews, 1969.

Veyne, Paul. *Did the Greeks Believe in Their Myths?* Chicago: University of Chicago Press, 1988.

Vilímková, M. *The Prague Ghetto.* Prague: Aventinum, 1990.

Vohryzek, Viktor. "Epištoly k českým židům" (Letters to Czech Jews). *Českožidovské listy,* 15 March 1900. Reprinted in *K židovské otázce: Vybrané uvahy a články* (On the Jewish question: Selected essays and articles), pp. 15–40. Prague: Akademický spolek "Kapper," 1923.

———. "Jakými cestami by se mělo bráti naše hnutí!" (What roads ought our movement to have taken!). *Rozvoj,* 1904. Reprinted in *K židovské otázce: Vybrané uvahy a články* (On the Jewish question: Selected essays and articles), pp. 77–84. Prague: Akademický spolek "Kapper," 1923.

———. "K myšlenkové krisi našich dnů" (On the intellectual crisis of our times). *Rozvoj,* 1904. Reprinted in *K židovské otázce: Vybrané uvahy a články* (On the Jewish question: Selected essays and articles), pp. 103–18. Prague: Akademický spolek "Kapper," 1923.

———. *K židovské otázce: Vybrané uvahy a články* (On the Jewish question: Selected essays and articles). Prague: Akademický spolek "Kapper," 1923.

———. "Náboženská společnost, či národnost?" (A religious society or a nationality?) *Rozvoj,* 1906. Reprinted in *K židovské otázce: Vybrané uvahy a články* (On the Jewish question: Selected essays and articles), pp. 218–28. Prague: Akademický spolek "Kapper," 1923.

———. "Národohospodářské úvahy" (Reflections on the national economy). *Rozvoj,* 1904. Reprinted in Vohryzek, *K židovské otázce: Vybrané uvahy a články* (On the Jewish question: Selected essays and articles), pp. 123–29. Prague: Akademický spolek "Kapper," 1923.

———. "Několik slov úvodem" (A few words of introduction). *Rozvoj,* 1904. Reprinted in Vohryzek, *K židovské otázce: Vybrané uvahy a články* (On the Jewish question: Selected essays and articles), pp. 41–47. Prague: Akademický spolek "Kapper," 1923.

———. "Pryč od haliče" (Away from Galicia). *Rozvoj,* 1904. Reprinted in Vohryzek, *K židovské otázce: Vybrané uvahy a články* (On the Jewish question: Selected essays and articles), pp. 130–35. Prague: Akademický spolek "Kapper," 1923.

———. "Zápas o reformy" (Struggle for reform). Reprinted in Vohryzek, *K židovské otázce: Vybrané uvahy a články* (On the Jewish question: Selected essays and articles), pp. 204–8. Prague: Akademický spolek "Kapper," 1923.

Vojtěch, Tomáš. *Mladočeší a boj o politickou moc v Čechách* (The Young Czechs and the struggle for political power in Bohemia), Prague: Academia, 1980.

Vražda v Polné: Otisk článků "Radikálních listů" z 20. dubna, 3., 6., a 15. června 1899 (Murder in Polná: Reprint of articles from *Radikální listy* of 20 April; 3, 6, and 15 June 1899). Prague: Radikální listy, 1899.

Vyskočil, Josef. "Die Tschechisch-Jüdische Bewegung." *Judaica Bohemiae* 3 (1967): 36–55.

Waber, Leopold. "Die Zahlenmässige Entwicklung der Völker Österreichs 1846–1910." *Statistische Monatschrift,* n.s., 20 (1915): 593–721.

Wandruszka, Adam and Peter Urbanitsch, eds. *Die Habsburgermonarchie, 1848–1918.* Vol. 3, *Die Völker des Reichs.* Vienna: Akademie der Wissenschaften, 1980.

Wanniczek, Johann. *Geschichte der Prager Haupt- Trivial- und Mädchenschule der Israeliten.* Prague: M. I. Landau, 1832.

Weisel, Leopold. "Die Pinchasgasse: Eine jüdische Volkssage." *Das Panorama des Universums* 5 (1838): 328–32.

Weltsch, Felix. "Masaryk und der Zionismus." In *Masaryk und das Judentum,* edited by Ernst Rychnovsky, pp. 67–116. Prague: Marsverlagsgesellschaft, 1931.

Wertheimer, Joseph von. *Die Juden in Österreich.* Leipzig: Mayer und Wigand, 1842.

Wessely, Naphtali Herz. *Divrei shalom ve-'emet* (Words of peace and truth). Berlin, 1782.

Wessely, Wolfgang. "Zur Anthologie der Rabbinen." *Ost und West,* 7 February 1845.

Wiener, Moses. *Nachricht von dem Ursprunge und Fortgange der deutschen jüdischen Hauptschule zu Prag.* Prague, 1785.

Wininger, S. *Grosse jüdische Nationalbiographie.* 7 vols. Czernowitz, 1925–36.

Winkler, Gershon. *The Golem of Prague.* New York: Judaica Press, 1980.

Winter, Eduard. *Barock, Absolutismus und Aufklärung in der Donaumonarchie.* Vienna: Europa Verlag, 1971.

——. *Ferdinand Kindermann Ritter von Schulstein.* Augsburg: Stauda, 1926.

Winters, Stanley B. "Kramář, Kaizl, and Hegemony of the Young Czech Party, 1891–1901." In *The Czech Renascence of the Nineteenth Century,* edited by Peter Brock and H. Gordon Skilling, pp. 282–314. Toronto: University of Toronto Press, 1970.

Wittner, Otto, ed. *Briefe aus dem Vormärz: Eine Sammlung aus dem Nachlass Moritz Hartmanns.* Prague: J. G. Calve, 1911.

——. *Moritz Hartmanns Jugend.* Vienna: O. Wittner, 1903.

Wlaschek, Rudolf M. *Juden in Böhmen: Beiträge zur Geschichte des europäischen Judentums im 19. und 20. Jahrhundert.* Munich: Oldenbourg, 1990.

Wolf, Gerson. *Die Vertreibung der Juden aus Böhmen im Jahre 1744 und deren Rückkehr im Jahre 1748.* Leipzig, 1869.

Wurzbach, Constant von. *Biographisches Lexikon des Kaiserthums Österreich.* 60 vols. Vienna, 1856–91.

Der Xantener Knabenmord vor dem Schwurgericht zu Cleve 4–14. Juli 1892. Vollständiger stenographischer Bericht. Berlin: Cronbach, 1893.

Yahadut Tshekhoslovakia (Czechoslovak Jewry). Jerusalem: Ministry of Education, 1969. (Also published in *Gesher* 15, nos. 2–3 [1969].)

Yassif, Eli. Introduction to *Ha-golem mi-Prag u-ma'asim nifla'im aherim* (The Golem of Prague and other wondrous deeds), by [Yehuda] Yudel Rosenberg, pp. 7–72. Jerusalem: Mosad Bialik, 1991.

Yates, Frances. *The Rosicrucian Enlightenment.* London and Boston: Routledge and Kegan Paul, 1972.

Žalud, Josef. "Z minulosti a přítomnosti …" (From the past and the present). *Kalendář česko-židovský* 12 (1892–93).

Židé v Protektoratu: hlásení židovské náboženské obce v roce 1942. Dokumenty. (Jews in the Protectorate: Reports of the Jewish religious community in 1942. Documents). Prague: Ústav pro soudobé dějiny, 1997.

"Zpráva o činnosti spolku 'Rozvoj'" (Report on the activities of the "Rozvoj" association). *Kalendář česko-židovský* 25 (1905–6): 178–79.

Index

Abrahams, Roger D., 3–4
Adámek, Karel, 136, 146–47
Aḥad Haʿam, 209–10
Allgemeine Zeitung des Judentums, 79–81, 84
Altneuschul, 95, 104, 108, 256n28
Antisemitic Congress, 183
antisemitism: Aḥad Haʿam on, 210; Reyrich on, 194; Vohryzek on, 170–71, 200. *See also* ritual murder
Arnold, Christoph, 97–98
Association of Czech Academic Jews. *See* Spolek českých akademiků-židů
Association of Progressive Czech Jews, 201–2
Austria, 6, 266n44

Badeni, Casimir, 166
Bar Kochba, 33
Beer, Peter, 59, 62
Beneš, Eduard, 199, 212–13
Bloch, Chaim, 111
Bohemia: foreign capital in, 42; identity in, 5, 6; industrial riots in (1844), 30, 82–86. *See also* Jews, Bohemian; Prague
Böhmische Landesjudenschaft, 24
Bondy, Rabbi Filip, 163, 164
Březina, Otakár, 223
Březnovský, Václav, 166
Brod, Max, 217, 218, 222
Bruner, Edward M., 235n6

Central Europe: definition of, 1–2; Jewish community in medieval, 12; weakening of Jewish communities in, 38–39
Central School Foundation (Ústřední matice školská), 141, 150
Česká včela, 87, 89
Českožidovské listy (Czech-Jewish press), 150, 152–53, 200, 201
Charles VI, 21
Chatterton, Thomas, 123
Communist Party, 8–9; Jews in, 219, 222–23
Corfu, 184
Cosmas of Prague, 11
Court Jew, 17–18
Czech-Jewish Almanac (Kalendář česko-židovský), 134, 147, 148
Czech-Jewish movement, 36, 94; attacks upon Orthodox Judaism by, 176–79; push to close German-language schools by, 150, 152–53; reaction to riots by (1897), 167–70; redefinition by younger generation of, 170–80; response to Czech nationalism by, 148–51; substitution of Czech for German in worship services by, 162–65
Czech-Jewish National Union (Národní jednota českožidovská), 149, 150, 152, 153
Czech-Jewish Political Union, 169
Czech language: as definer of Czech nation, 119–20; publication in, 121; use by

Designer:	Nola Burger
Indexer:	Andrew L. Christenson
Compositor:	Impressions Book and Journal Services, Inc.
Text:	10/13 Galliard
Display:	Galliard
Printer:	Edwards Brothers, Inc.
Binder:	Edwards Brothers, Inc.